P9-DVF-733

The Psychiatrist in the Courtroom

Bernard L. Diamond, M.D.

The Psychiatrist in the Courtroom

Selected Papers of Bernard L. Diamond, M.D.

edited by
Jacques M. Quen, M.D.

 THE ANALYTIC PRESS

1994   Hillsdale, NJ   London

Published by
The Analytic Press, Inc.
365 Broadway
Hillsdale, New Jersey 07642

Earlier versions of the chapters in this volume were published previously and appear here, in revised form, by permission of their copyright owners. Full publication information for each chapter appears in Dr. Diamond's Bibliography, beginning on p. xi.

Typeset in Goudy by Sally Ann Zegarelli, Long Branch, NJ

Library of Congress Cataloging-in-Publication Data

Diamond, Bernard L. (Bernard Lee), 1912-1990
    The psychiatrist in the courtroom : selected papers of
    Bernard L. Diamond / edited by Jacques M. Quen.
            p.   cm.
    Includes bibliographical references and index.
    ISBN 0-88163-160-4
    1. Forensic psychiatry.   I. Quen, Jacques M., 1928-
II. Title.
    [DNLM: 1. Diamond, Bernard L. (Bernard Lee), 1912-1990.
    2. Forensic Psychiatry—collected works. W 740 D537p 1994]
RA1151.D53   1994
614\.1—dc20
DNLM/DLC
for Library of Congress   94-33422
                                                                CIP

Printed in the United States of America
10 9 8 7 6 5 4 3 2 1

Dedicated to the Memory of
Bernard Lee Diamond

For the last decade of his life, Bernard L. Diamond bestowed on me a warm friendship and was a mentor who tolerated with good humor and respect our numerous discussions and our several differences on professional issues. Like Isaac Ray, he was a giant who, through his writings, his example, and his students, gave far more than his colleagues appreciated and who continues to give to his profession.

Acknowledgments

I'm not sure about earlier times, but today no book is written without the input and help of many others. I am particularly indebted to several people. Without the invitation and the generosity of Ann Landy Diamond, this book would never have appeared. I also owe a great deal to the late Eric T. Carlson, founding director of the New York Hospital-Cornell Medical Center Section on the History of Psychiatry. Anthony Platt provided suggestions and a general plan for the book early in its conception and gestation and allowed the inclusion of the two papers he and Bernard Diamond had collaborated on. I would also like to thank Robert Weinstock for permission to quote from his correspondence with Dr. Diamond. The various journals that have granted permission to include the selected papers also deserve sincere thanks.

John Kerr and Eleanor Starke Kobrin (Lenni) of The Analytic Press deserve special benediction for their guidance, encouragement, and understanding during the many times when the demands of my practice and other professional obligations required "revision" of our schedule.

Contents

Bibliography of Bernard L. Diamond

Films/Videotapes

1965 · "Legal Psychiatry" (1/2 hour, 16 mm. color-sound film), *Science in Action* (San Francisco, California Academy of Sciences, 1965).

1970 (with T. Szasz & A. Brooks) · *Concepts and Controversies in Modern Medicine: Psychiatry and Law, How Are They Related?* (Parts 1 & II, 1/2 hour each, available as 16 mm. sound film or videotape), Atlanta, GA National Audiovisual Center, National Library of Medicine, National Institutes of Health.

1979 (with C. Niesson & E. Saltzman et al.) · "California v. Gorshen" (16 mm. film) in *Harvard Evidence Film Project*, Cambridge, MA, Harvard Law School.

Publications

1938 · Are clinical clerkships abused? *J. Assn. Med. Students*, 2:206–208, 217.

1938 · The psychological abdomen: Its surgical importance. *West. J. Surg., Obstet., Gynecol.*, 46:416–425. (Division I, First Prize Essay, Third Year Medical Class, Surgical Division at the University of California Medical School, 1936–1937.)

1938 · The psychological abdomen: Its surgical importance. *West. J. Surg., Obstet., Gynecol.*, 46:498–502. (Division II, First Prize Essay, Third Year Medical Class, Surgical Division at the University of California Medical School, 1936–1937.)

1944 (with H. T. Schmale) · The Mosaic test: I. An evaluation of its clinical applications. *Amer. J. Orthopsychiat.*, 14:237–250.

1945 (with A. Ross) · Emotional adjustment of newly blinded soldiers. *Amer. J. Psychiat.*, 102:367–371.

1953 (with H. Weihofen) · Privileged communication and the clinical psychologist. *J. Clin. Psychol.*, 9:388–390.

1954 · Correspondence (Spelling of "M'Naghten"). *Amer. J. Psychiat.*, 110:705.

1954 · Current conflicts in legal definitions of insanity. *J. Correctional Psychol.*, 1:39–44.

1955 · Review of *The Annual Survey of Psychoanalysis. Arch. Crim. Psychodynam.*, 1:445–450.

1956 · Isaac Ray and the trial of Daniel M'Naghten. *Amer. J. Psychiat.*, 112:651–656.

1956 · The simulation of sanity. *J. Soc. Ther.*, 2:158–165.*

1957 · On aging. *Proceedings of the Conference on the Aging Process.* San Francisco: San Francisco State College, pp. 1–12.

1957 · With malice aforethought. *Arch. Crim. Psychodynam.*, 2:1–45.*

1959 · The fallacy of the impartial expert. *Arch. Crim. Psychodynam.*, 3:221–236.*

1960 · The psychodynamics of the offender. In: *The Mentally Ill Offender, A Symposium.* Atascadero State Hospital, pp. 35–39.

1961 (with B. Karpman et al.) · Symposium: What is insanity? Its relation to psychosis, neurosis, sociopathy, mental deficiency: The problem of responsibility, partial insanity, temporary insanity. *Arch. Crim. Psychodynam.*, 4:285–316.

1961 · Identification and the sociopathic personality. Symposium on psychopathy. *Arch. Crim. Psychodynam.*, 4:456–465.

---

*Entries designated with an asterisk are reprinted in this volume.

1961 - The criminal responsibility of the mentally ill. *Stanford L. Rev.*, 4:59–86.*

1961 - Ten great books in the history of psychiatry. *Mental Hospitals*, 12:32–33.

1961 - Psychiatric testimony from the psychiatrist's standpoint. In: *Criminal Law Seminar*, ed. N. Cohen. Brooklyn: Central Book, pp. 247–253.

1962 (member) - Special Commissions on Insanity and Criminal Offenders: 1st report July 7, 2nd report November 15. Sacramento, CA: State of California.

1962 - From *M'Naghten* to *Currens* and beyond, *Cal. L. Rev.*, 5:189–205.*

1962 - Some observations about the genesis of the Gorshen case. In: *Criminal Law: Problems for Decision in the Promulgation, Invocation and Administration of a Law of Crimes*, ed. R. C. Donnelly, J. Goldstein & R. D. Schwartz. New York: Free Press, pp. 688–691.

1963 - On the spelling of Daniel M'Naghten's name. *Ohio State L. J.*, 25:84–88.

1963 - Law and psychiatry. In: *Encyclopedia of Mental Health*, Vol. 3, ed. A. Deutsch. New York: Franklin Watts, pp. 908–929.

1964 - Preparing psychiatric testimony. In: *California Criminal Law Practice*, I. Regents of University of California, pp. 611–627 (§15.0–§15.20).

1964 - Psychiatry and the criminal: Part I. Rules of criminal responsibility of the mentally ill. *Postgrad. Med.*, 36:A46–A54.

1964 - Review of *Law, Liberty and Psychiatry* by T. Szasz. *Cal. L. Rev.*, 52:899.

1965 - The psychiatrist as a medical witness. *Proceedings, National Medicolegal Symposium*, American Medical Association & American Bar Association, pp. 135–141.

1965 (with D. W. Louisell) · Law and Psychiatry: Detente, entente, or concomitance? *Cornell L. Quart.*, 50:217–234.

1965 (with D. W. Louisell) · The psychiatrist as an expert witness: Some ruminations and speculations. *Mich. L. Rev.,*, 63:1335–1354.

1965 · Clues to spotting mental illness in misdemeanants. *Munic. Court Rev.*, 5:50–57.

1965 (with A. Platt) · The origins and development of the "wild beast" concept of mental illness and its relation to the theories of criminal responsibility. *J. Hist. Behav. Sci.*, 1:355–367.*

1965 · Introduction. *Issues in Criminol.*, 1:v–viii.

1966 · The children of Leviathan: Psychoanalytic speculations concerning welfare law and punitive sanctions. *Cal. L. Rev.*, 54:357–369. (Also published in *The Law of the Poor*, ed. J. ten Broeck et al. San Francisco: Chandler, 1966, pp. 33–45.)

1966 (with A. Platt) · The origins of the "right and wrong" test of criminal responsibility and its subsequent development in the United States: An historical survey. *Cal. L. Rev.*, 54:1227–1260.*

1967 · The invasion of privacy. Alumnae lecture for the inauguration of Robert J. Wert as President of Mills College, October 18, (unpublished: BLD Archives).

1967 · The scientific method and the law. *Hastings L. J.*, 19:179–199.

1968 · Testimony before the New York State Joint Legislative Committee on Crime, Its Causes, Control and Effect on Society. New York City, September 17.

1969 · (transcribed interview) Psychiatrist Bernard L. Diamond tells of the bizarre paranoia he found in Sirhan B. Sirhan. A conversation with T. George Harris. *Psychol. Today*, September, pp. 48–56.

1971 (with M. Rotenberg) · The biblical conception of psychopathy: The law of the stubborn and rebellious son. *J. Hist. Behav. Sci.*, 8:29–38.

1971 - Failures of identification and sociopathic behavior. In: *Sanctions for Evil*, ed. N. Sanford & C. Comstock. San Francisco: Jossey-Bass, pp. 125–135.

1973 - The psychiatrist as advocate. *J. Psychiat. & Law*, 1:5–21.

1973 - From *Durham* to *Brawner:* A futile journey. *Wash. Univ. L. Quart.*, 109–125.

1974 - The psychiatric prediction of dangerousness. *Univ. Pa. L. Rev.*, 123:439–452.*

1975 - Violence! *Mills Quart.*, 57.15–18.

1975 - Murder and the death penalty: A case report. *Amer. J. Orthopsychiat.*, 15:712–722.

1976 - Criminology, criminalistics and violence. *Proceedings of Conference on Application of Blood Identification Techniques to Law Enforcement.* Berkeley: White Mountain Research Station, University of California, pp. 11–20.

1976 - Review of *Forensic Psychiatry, A Practical Guide for Lawyers and Psychiatrists* by R. L. Sadoff (Springfield, IL: Charles C Thomas, 1975). *J. Psychiat. & Law*, fall: 441–442.

1976 - Review of *Psychiatry and Law* by R. Slovenko (Boston: Little, Brown, 1973). *J. Amer. Acad. Child Psychiat.*, 15:772–773.

1977 - Psychological problems of law students. In: *Looking at Law School*, ed. S. Gillers & Amer. Soc. of Law Teachers, New York: Taplinger, pp. 11–20. (Also published, in part, as "Psychic pressure: What happens to your head?" *Juris Doctor*, 1976, 6:40–43.)

1977 - The causes of crime. In: *The Joy of Knowledge Encyclopedia.* London: Mitchell Beazley. (Also published in *The Random House Encyclopedia.* New York, 1977, pp. 914-915.)

1978 - Psychoanalysis in the courtroom. *Dialogue [J. San Francisco Psychoanalytic Society]*, spring: 2–15.*

1978 - Social and cultural factors as a diminished capacity defense in criminal law. *Bull. Amer. Acad. Psychiat. & Law*, 6:195–208.

1988 - Inherent problems in the use of pretrial hypnosis on a prospective witness. *Cal. L. Rev.*, 68:319–349.*

1980 - Resolving doctor-patient conflicts (review of *Taking Care of Strangers: The Rule of Law in Doctor-Patient Relations* by R. A. Burt. New York: Free Press, 1979). *Mich. L. Rev.*, 78:743–749.

1980 - Review of *Restraining the Wicked: The Incapacitation of the Dangerous Criminal* by S. Van Dine, J. P. Conrad & S. Dinitz (Lexington, MA: Heath, 1979). *Crime & Delinq.*, 26:402–405.

1980 - Testimony before the California Assembly Criminal Justice Committee (relative to SB 2033 and 1314). (Representing the California Psychiatric Association and speaking on behalf of the California Attorneys for Criminal Justice.) June 23. Unpublished.

1980 - Review of *The Psychology of Eyewitness Testimony* by A. Daniel Yarney (New York: Free Press, 1979). *J. Psychiat. & Law*, fall: 341–345.

1981 - The mentally ill offender: Problems of a unified approach (review of *Mental Disabilities and Criminal Responsibility* by H. Fingarette & A. Fingarette Hasse. Berkeley: University of California Press, 1979). *Stanford L. Rev.*, 33:567–573.

1981 - The relevance of voice in forensic psychiatric evaluations. In: *Speech Evaluation in Psychiatry*, ed. J. K. Darby. New York: Grune & Stratton, pp. 243–250.

1983 - The psychiatrist as expert witness. *Psychiat. Clin. N. Amer.*, 6:597–609.*

1984 - Forensic psychiatry. In: *Review of General Psychiatry*, ed. H. H. Goldman. Los Altos, CA: Lange, pp. 649–659.

1985 - Reasonable medical certainty, diagnostic thresholds, and definitions of mental illness in the legal context. *Bull. Amer. Acad. Psychiat. & Law*, 13:121–128.*

1985 · (Member, Council on Scientific Affairs [AMA]) Council Report: Scientific status of refreshing recollection by the use of hypnosis. *J. Amer. Med. Assn.*, 253:1918–1923.

1986 · Benefic autonomy: A formulative study. *Dynam. Psychother.*, 4:77.

1986 · The contamination of evidence by hypnotic enhancement of memory of witnesses. In: *Evidence: Cases, Materials, and Problems*, ed. P. F. Rothstein. New York: Matthew Bender.

1986 · Answer · Ask the experts. Question · Agency. *Newsletter Amer. Acad. Psychiat. & Law*, 11:24.

1986 · Addendum to Quen, J. M., "The simulation of sanity: Thomas Erskine, Bernard L. Diamond, and the Marcus kidnapping case." *Newsletter Amer. Acad. Psychiat. & Law*, 11:27–28.

1990 · The psychiatric expert witness: Honest advocate or "hired gun"? In: *Ethical Practice in Psychiatry and the Law*, ed. R. Rosner & R. Weinstock. New York: Plenum Press, pp. 75–84.

1992 · The forensic psychiatrist: Consultant vs. activist in legal doctrine. *Bull. Amer. Acad. Psychiat. & Law*, 20:119–132.

Editor's Introduction

BERNARD LEE DIAMOND
December 8, 1912 – November 18, 1990

Early Career

Bernard Lee Diamond was born on December 8, 1912, the third of the four children of Leon Isaac and Rose (Cohen) Diamond of Fresno, California.

When Bernard was 12, the notorious Leopold and Loeb Case filled the headlines of the newspapers throughout the country. He was intrigued by the case and by the idea of psychoanalysts who studied the workings of the mind and then testified in courtroom trials (see "Psychoanalysis in the Courtroom," this volume).

Bernard Diamond graduated from a vocational high school and entered the University of California (Berkeley) where, in 1934, he received his bachelor's degree with honors in medical sciences. He entered the University of California Medical School (San Francisco) and received his MD in 1939, after serving a year of internship at the Neuropsychiatric Institute at the University of Michigan. He was a psychiatric resident at the Institute during the years 1939–1940 and 1941–1942.

Dr. Diamond's first publication, written while he was a medical student, revealed some of his enduring personality traits. "Are Clinical Clerkships Abused?"[1] was introduced with a note from the editors. *"The contribution below is presented in no muckraking spirit. It is a clear, thoughtful analysis that* THE JOURNAL *highly recommends to all students concerned about the plan of the medical curriculum."* The title suggested an affirmative answer, which it delivered. Diamond protested the exploitation of medical students (clinical clerks) by faculty for obtaining data for their personal research and for pointlessly "treating the chart." Diamond maintained that requiring medical students to do routine laboratory tests, or to obtain clinically unnecessary, extended medical histories for purposes of faculty research, had little educational value and was actively destructive of the learning process. He protested that the very limited time of medical students was far too important to be exploited by others. His thinking was so far ahead of its time that 15 years later, during my own clinical clerkship, we heard, with envy, that there were some medical schools contemplating hiring laboratory technicians to do the routine laboratory work for patients. It was only some years later that this became a standard practice, and medical clerkships increased their emphasis on learning medicine as had been proposed by the student Bernard Diamond.

He won the surgical service's award for an essay by a medical student during the third year ("On the Surgical Importance of the Psychological Abdomen"). It was published as a two-part paper.[2]

In 1940, anticipating America's entry into World War II, he enlisted in the Army Medical Corps as a first lieutenant. He served on active duty in the New York City area for one year and then returned to complete his psychiatric residency. In 1988, in a letter discussing ethics, Bernard Diamond referred to this period in his life, saying, "Many years ago I did serve as an official New York State witness for the execution of two hired gangster killers by electrocution at Sing Sing Prison. Was I a participant? I think so, and I would not do it again."[3] The executions he witnessed, on June 12, 1941, were those of Harry ("Pittsburgh Phil") Strauss, 31 years old, and Martin ("Buggsy") Goldstein, 36, members of the Brownsville murder syndicate of Brooklyn. They died in the electric chair for the murder of Irving ("Puggy") Feinstein, another member of the gang, on September 4, 1939.

He reenlisted in 1942 and remained on active duty through 1945, when he was discharged with the rank of lieutenant colonel. During his Army service, Diamond treated newly blinded soldiers returned to the United States. This deeply affecting experience gave rise to his first clinical publication, in which he wrote:

> In all too many instances, soldiers blinded beyond all hope of recovery had been told by doctors and nurses and other medical personnel during their initial hospitalization overseas or during their evacuation to the United States, that there was a possibility of their eyesight being at least partially restored. Upon being informed subsequently that the prognosis was hopeless, they consistently responded by becoming bitter, resentful and depressed. Evidently the purpose in so misinforming these soldiers was to maintain their spirits and morale until they got home. It cannot be over-emphasized that giving such false hope and casual reassurance is crassly foolish and cruel. . . .

The soldier wants the truth and he wants it immediately. A postponement of the explanation of his disability and its outcome until he "feels better" only perpetuates his doubt, his insecurity, and his anxiety, and may crystallize his thoughts, feelings and actions in such a way as to interfere with his social and economic rehabilitation.[4]

Here one sees not only the passion earlier implied in his paper on clinical clerkships, but also the unyielding commitment to honesty and candor. He is reminiscent, here, of the founder of American forensic psychiatry, Isaac Ray, who wrote, in his 1842 annual report as Superintendent of the Maine Insane Hospital:

Above all things, in order to obtain the confidence of our patients, we find it necessary to abstain from every form of deception in our dealings with them. . . . The case, I think, could seldom happen, in which it would not be far better to encounter a little more resistance, or use a little more force, than to practice a deliberate, systematic deception. The former irritates, but it is soon over; the latter, remains and rankles. It is a cardinal principle in our moral treatment to deal with our patients fairly, honestly and candidly; for we believe that no temporary advantage can counterbalance the mischief that inevitably arises from deceit. . . . The moment a patient discovers we have been deceiving him, his respect for us is gone.[5]

The New Year's Eve following his discharge, Bernard L. Diamond met Ann Landy, a Hungarian-born lawyer friend of his sister. They married soon after and had six children. Bernard had already set up practice in San Francisco, at 291 Geary Street. He spent the rest of his life practicing and teaching in Northern California.

In 1953, Diamond collaborated with Henry Weihofen, Professor of Law at the University of New Mexico, on a paper on privileged communication and the clinical psychologist.[6] In it, the two authors counsel the clinical psychologist to abstain from keeping notes so that a court cannot subpoena them, in order to protect their client's confidentiality. Today, however, following such advice would put one in direct conflict with the law in many jurisdictions, where informative notes are required to be kept. New York State requires that patients' records be made available to them on demand, and such requests can be denied only with the concurrence of a state-appointed committee of physicians.

Bernard Diamond's next publication was a historical review of the trial of Daniel M'Naghten (1843). He wanted to call the attention of his colleagues to the remarkable role played in that trial by American Psychiatric Association founder Isaac Ray. Diamond observed, "It is safe to say that never since, in an English or an American courtroom, has a scientific work by a psychiatrist been treated with such respect as was *A Treatise on the Medical Jurisprudence of Insanity.*" This paper also marks an early expression of his lifelong appreciation of the importance of history in understanding current professional concepts. At the time of his death, Bernard Diamond possessed what was probably the most extensive private collection in America of rare books on the history of psychiatry.

That same year, Diamond published an article on "The Simulation of Sanity" (see this volume), in which he counseled against psychiatrists' excessive focus on unmasking malingerers who were trying to act insane and to focus instead on the much more common, but neglected, phenomenon of defendants' trying to hide their mental illness from the public and even from their own lawyers. This theme is one that was a significant concern during his career.

Later Career

In 1964, he left the private practice of psychiatry and psychoanalysis and became a Professor of Law and Psychiatry at Boalt Hall, the law school of the University of California (Berkeley). That same year, he received the Royer Award of the Regents of the University of California for the advancement of psychiatry. In 1968 he received the Isaac Ray Award of the American Psychiatric Association for the advancement of psychiatry and the law. In 1972 he received the Gold Medal Award of the Mt. Airy Foundation for distinction in psychiatry (see "The Psychiatrist as Advocate," this volume). In 1975 he received the "Golden Apple [AAPL] Award" of the American Academy of Psychiatry and the Law, and in 1980 he was the Yochelson Memorial Lecturer (in Criminology) at the Yale University School of Medicine.

During the course of his career, Diamond served as a consultant in forensic psychiatry to the Veterans Administration Hospital in San Francisco, the U. S. Army Medical Department at Letterman and Tripler Medical Centers, the U. S. Navy Medical Center at Oakland and the California State Department of Mental Health. He was a member of the Advisory Committee of the American Bar Association's Criminal Justice Mental Health Standards Project, the American Medical Association's Diagnostic and Therapeutic Technology Assessment Panel as well as its Committee on the Scientific Status of Refreshing Recollection by the Use of Hypnosis. He was a founding member of the Board of Directors of the American Board of Forensic Psychiatry and the author of more than 50 articles and book chapters on forensic psychiatry, criminal behavior, evidence, and related issues of psychiatry and the law.

In a case heard before the California Supreme Court, in which Bernard Diamond had no role, the quality of his psychiatric testimony in the courts was referred to, in a footnote, as representing the judicially desired standard of testimony by forensic psychiatrists. It was a professional endorsement that ranked high among the ones he treasured.[7]

Perhaps the professional experience that troubled Bernard Diamond the most was the position statement of the American Psychiatric Association on the Insanity Defense of 1983. In a letter to a non-psychiatrist faculty colleague, Diamond wrote:

> I am not as enthusiastic as you seem to be about the American Psychiatric Association position paper. It by no means represents a consensus of psychiatric opinion. . . . Organized psychiatry has never been happy with the role of psychiatrists in the legal system and this position paper represents simply one more effort to eliminate, as much as possible, the role of psychiatry in law. It is an elitist position reflecting the views of a group who are more worried about their public relations than they are about either their patients or their justice system. The APA statement does not reflect a "change of the climate of opinion". . . . Rather, it is the attempt of an organization to climb on the media bandwagon of the Hinckley case, and secure a profit for its own public relations.[8]

While I have spoken at some length about what he has done, I have said relatively little about the nature of the person, the private individual that Bernard L. Diamond was. He was a man of great dedication and concentration, concerned that the reliability of his facts and his reasoning be the best he could produce. During a chance meeting in an airport, we had a half-hour lively discussion about whether or not a comma was intentionally absent in a passage by sixteenth century jurist William Lambard in his book *Eirenarcha*, or was it a terribly important typographic error? The passage was visible in his mind's eye, as we talked and tried to solve the important question he'd raised.[9]

He had a warmth that played a role in his developing a rich personal network of colleagues, acquaintances, and students. Few knew that he maintained a correspondence for over 30 years with Nathan Leopold (of the Leopold-Loeb case). In fact, a little more than a year after Leopold's release, Ann and Bernard Diamond had dinner with him and his wife.

Diamond was a personal friend of Judge David Bazelon, who formulated the well-intentioned but doomed *Durham* rule. Their mutual friend was Albert Deutsch, the journalist/social reformer who in the 1940s and 50s was one of the leaders of the psychiatric hospital reform movement and for whom Diamond had a remarkable admiration. In fact, Bernard Diamond believed that it was Deutsch who had suggested to Bazelon that he attempt to broaden the insanity test beyond M'Naghten via the Durham rule.[10]

From One Generation to the Next

Perhaps a better way to appreciate Diamond's personal style is through his closing words in an address he delivered when he was honored by American Academy of Psychiatry and the Law at its annual meeting in October 1989.

The title of his talk was "The Forensic Psychiatrist: Consultant versus Activist in Legal Doctrine."[11] Diamond spoke about his experiences in the world of law and forensic psychiatry. The following words were addressed to his younger colleagues:

> I particularly urge that psychiatrists publish articles in law reviews and law journals for that greatly increases the likelihood that your ideas will be considered by legal authorities.
>
> Sometimes there is a substantial delay before the appellate courts pick up on one's recommendations, so one must have patience. In a 1962 law review article [see "From *M'Naghten* to *Currens* and Beyond," this volume], I criticized the restrictive clause of the American Law Institute (ALI) Model Penal Code rule of criminal responsibility, which prohibits a condition manifested only by criminal or antisocial behavior from being considered a mental disease or defect for purposes of the insanity defense. I asserted that this clause was discriminatory against poor defendants in that wealthy defendants could hire experts who by spending a great deal of time on examinations in depth could always legitimately find evidence of psychopathology that would be more than criminal or antisocial behavior. But poor defendants, subject to cursory, superficial psychiatric examinations would be dismissed as not mentally ill. No one paid any attention to this until eight years later when the Ninth Circuit Court of Appeals adopted the ALI rule of insanity. It specifically rejected the restrictive clause because of its discriminatory nature and cited my article as authority for that.[12] So you have to be really patient, indeed!
>
> I am convinced that it is possible to practice good psychiatry in relation to the law, and to be a significant influence on the development of the law in line with the humanitarian and ethical values of traditional medicine. The legal system can be influenced by expert testimony, by scholarly writings on research and policy, by teaching in the classroom, and most importantly by example.
>
> Psychiatry has had less control over its own practice than any other medical specialty. Of psychiatric subspecialties, forensic psychiatry has permitted itself to be misused, abused, and perverted to a disgraceful degree, and its low public image is well deserved. I am suggesting how that image might be improved within the humanitarian tradition of medical responsibility. It just may turn out to be good for the law as well.

In closing, one must ask does all this make economic sense for the forensic psychiatrist? Probably not. It probably means that forensic work should not be the sole source of income for a psychiatrist. To refuse to be manipulated by the attorneys who are paying your bill, and to reject cases because their potential does not meet one's ethical standards is not conducive to a successful forensic practice. It is only too easy to slip into the "hired gun" role when your family's economic welfare is at stake. The honest and responsible forensic psychiatrist requires some type of subsidy, so that he is always able to pick and choose his cases independently of his financial needs. In the current American world of law and psychiatry I do not believe it is possible to be incorruptible and also earn a decent living from forensic psychiatry. A combination of a more general psychiatric practice with part-time forensic work seems to work out if one can manage the difficult problems of scheduling. Employment in a clinic, mental health facility, or government agency may be satisfactory if one is not restricted by bureaucratic policies. Academia, preferably with tenure, provides the ideal subsidy. But if feeding your children is contingent upon the goodwill of trial lawyers, you are in deep trouble.

☼ ☼ ☼

Bernard Lee Diamond died on November 18, 1990. In a brief memorial note, Justice Stanley Mosk of the California Supreme Court wrote, "I do not believe I ever met Dr. Bernard Diamond. Nevertheless, over the past fifteen or more years, I have learned to respect his expertise in a remarkable number of areas. . . . I regret that Dr. Diamond's voice has been stilled, his pen silenced. For he was a giant in the field of psychiatry and will be sorely missed."[13]

Forensic Psychiatry

The involvement of physicians in the civil and criminal courts has a long tradition in medicine. When Bernard Diamond learned of it, American psychiatry was in a period of enthusiastic optimism about the potential for treatment and prevention of mental illness. Psychoanalysis and the unconscious (that newly discovered dark continent of the mind) fascinated Americans. And the role of the psychiatrists in the Leopold-Loeb presentencing hearing captured the imagination of the American public and its newspaper moguls.

In the course of American medical history, the role of the forensic psychiatrist has attracted praise and opprobrium. Early in that history, there was a professional confidence that one of the areas, above and beyond patient care where a physician could make substantial and desirable contributions to the community was in the courtroom, where he could help to resolve disputes that had crucial effects on the individual and the community. In the first recorded medical school lecture on medical jurisprudence in the United States, Benjamin Rush propounded that

> [t]hey entertain very limited views of medicine, who suppose its objects and duties are confined exclusively to the knowledge and cure of diseases. Our science was intended to render other services to society. It was designed to extend its benefits to the protection of property and life, and to detect fraud and guilt in many of their forms. This honor has been conferred upon it by the bench and the bar, in all civilized countries both in ancient and modern times.[14]

In his lecture, Rush focused first and foremost on psychiatric issues: "The subjects of medical jurisprudence are, first, all those different diseases of the mind which incapacitate persons from exercising certain civil rights, such as disposing of property and bearing witness in courts, and which exempt them from punishment for the commission of crimes." He went on to enumerate six other areas of general medical jurisprudence: criminal trauma and wounds; toxicology; causes of death, for example, poisons, hanging, drowning, starving, etc.; presence or absence of virginity, impotence, sterility, false pregnancy, natural and induced abortions, stage of gestation, and infanticide; determining medical exemption from civil and military duties, including simulated or feigned diseases; and public health issues such as potability of water, putrid food, unhealthy air, and epidemic diseases.[15]

Rush was one of the earliest physicians to consider chronic drunkenness as a disease beyond the control of the drunkard. Long before abulia was a common psychiatric term, he recognized that men could be controlled not by reason, but by diseased volition. He referred to these conditions under the label "moral derangement," which he saw primarily as a disease of affect and volition. Along with his interest in forensic medical and psychiatric issues, Rush was also greatly interested in criminal justice and in the treatment and rehabilitation of convicts and prisoners. He was a founder of the Philadelphia Prison Society, an organization dedicated to improving conditions in the prisons. A relationship between criminality and the mental states of the mentally ill prisoners was apparent to the members of the Society. This relationship, however, was seen in wider psychiatric circles as one that threatened the public support of the proper medical care of the insane. The recurrent concern about a connection between insanity and criminality troubled even our earliest psychiatrists.

Forensic medicine, as it related to the mentally ill, was significant in American life and courts in the early nineteenth century, as a quick reading of McDade's *Annals of Murder* will show.[16] For example, in a two-year period (1829–1830), Daniel Drake, a prominent physician/educator in the history of American medicine, published three separate articles on a single murder case involving chronic alcoholism and the insanity defense.[17] The first textbook on forensic medicine written by an American was published by Theodric Romeyn Beck in 1823. This two-volume work went through 10 editions. Then, in 1838, a 31-year-old general practitioner with no formal education or experience with the law or the insane, wrote *A Treatise on the Medical Jurisprudence of Insanity*.[18] It was organized so that, in most instances, a chapter describing a clinical condition was followed by a chapter describing that condition's legal significance and consequences. It was both a textbook of psychiatry and a textbook of forensic psychiatry. It is remembered as the outstanding classic of forensic psychiatry and its author, Isaac Ray, is generally considered to be the founder of American forensic psychiatry as a separate discipline with its own body of knowledge, goals, and principles.

In his book, Ray considers so many court cases of a civil nature that the modern reader can readily draw the inference that we were a litigious society even then. Certainly from the beginning, forensic psychiatrists were called into civil cases, especially involving wills, as often as they were asked to participate in criminal cases. Isaac Ray never became interested in the psychiatric aspects of convicted prisoners, although he protested that many insane people who should have been recognized as such were being found guilty and sentenced to prison. Ray's seeming indifference appears to have been related to the same factors that led to the antipathy between organized psychiatry and the Philadelphia Prison Society. On the other hand, Ray was intensely concerned with improving the quality of medical testimony in the courts.

Amariah Brigham, one of the "original 13" founders of the American Psychiatric Association and the first Superintendent of the State Lunatic Hospital in Utica, NY, was also the founding editor of the *American Journal of Insanity* in 1844. It was the first medical specialty journal, as well as the first psychiatric one, in this country. In the following year, the Philadelphia Prison Society published the first issue of *The Pennsylvania Journal of Prison Discipline and Philanthropy*. A significant portion of it was devoted to insane asylums and to insane convicts.

In a brief review in his journal, Brigham attacked the new prison journal, as well as the annual reports of the Boston Prison Discipline Society, for the space and prominence they gave to insanity. The linking of the insane with the criminal was considered invidious. There was a restrained but strong response in the next issue of the prison journal and an editorial of some length in a later issue of the *American Journal of Insanity* (AJI). Brigham overlooked the fact that two of the committees formed at the first meeting of the Association of Medical Superintendents of American Institutions for the Insane (AMSAII) were devoted to prisons and insane prisoners. Tension persisted between the two groups, although they clearly had overlapping interests. In fact, Dorothea L. Dix and Samuel Gridley Howe, both prominent in the asylum movement, were also prominent in prison reform.

Today, forensic psychiatrists as a group are viewed with suspicion and cynicism, not only by many of their psychiatric colleagues but by the lay public as well. How have we come from a position where the physician in the courtroom could take pride in the humanitarian value of his work, to one in which both the populace and our own colleagues look on us with mistrust? Part of the complicated answer to this question lies in the actions of some few psychiatrists of questionable ethics. Another part of the answer lies in the bizarre situation in which psychiatry's leaders and teachers have so many misconceptions about the realities of forensic psychiatry that they shun it in their residency education programs, thus initiating a self-perpetuating ignorance and creating generations of psychiatrists whose only knowledge of the functions and goals of forensic psychiatry come from supermarket tabloids. Beyond this, the complexities of the blend of law and psychiatry are such that they necessarily leave much room for misunderstanding. With educational neglect the problems for psychiatry, society, and the law are compounded.

It may be helpful here to remind ourselves how the psychiatrist becomes involved in court cases, both criminal and civil. The psychiatrist enters into legal proceedings as an expert witness; in this respect, she or he does not differ from pathologists, ballistics experts, and similar specialists. Expert witnesses are called by the court, or by either party to the dispute, to assist the jurors or, in some cases, the judge, in evaluating evidence that is beyond the average person's education or experience. Expert witnesses are, in a sense, the representatives of their particular science or skill, called upon to teach basic and advanced scientific knowledge, to help the "trier of fact" (i.e., jury or judge) to evaluate the evidence.

In America, expert witnesses are distinguished from the usual witnesses of fact in that their opinion not only is allowed to be entered into the record, but is particularly solicited. In contrast to the factual knowledge possessed by an ordinary fact witness (to which the witness *can* be required to testify), the opinions of any individual, whether expert or inexpert, on any given matter are his or her private property and cannot be required by the court. For this reason, unlike witnesses of fact, expert witnesses are paid for their time, knowledge, opinions, and their reasoning.

The basic underpinning of our Anglo-American legal system is a belief in the superiority of the adversarial method for determining truth. Consequently, the first necessary condition for the courts to determine is that the adversaries are competent to play the roles required by our system. They must be able to participate in the trial physically and mentally. For competence to participate mentally, we evaluate whether the parties in question, be the dispute civil or criminal, are adequately able to understand the meaning and significance of the elements of their case, to comprehend the role of the various participants in the trial, and to assist their attorneys in the conduct of that case. If they are not able to do these things, then the legal process must wait. Although this is, in the final analysis, a judicial decision, there is little controversy about the role of the psychiatrist, and the weight given to her or his opinion, in that particular determination.

Accordingly, the psychiatrist expert witness in a competency hearing is called upon, generally, to present to the court her or his evaluation of some aspect of mental or psychiatric adequacy or competence, whether it be competence to make a contract, a will, to exercise various rights (for example, the right to refuse treatment, the right to informed consent, the right to manage property and finances, the right to be at liberty, the right to confidentiality, etc.), as well as to assess the relative desirability of particular persons to serve as parent or guardian in custody cases involving children or disabled adults. The emphasis on the term "competency" is derived from the legal Latin "non compos mentis," or not mentally competent (i.e., to exercise a particular legal right or privilege). The term should be used in conjunction with specific acts or functions, since one may be competent for some actions, and at the same moment be incompetent for others.

In criminal cases, however, the role of the forensic psychiatrist often goes beyond the issue of competency to stand trial, and the expert is asked to address questions of a defendant's legal responsibility for his or her behavior at the time of the alleged crime. In the past several decades, to a remarkable extent because of the work of Bernard L. Diamond, this role in criminal cases has expanded. Diamond based much of his position on the early history of English criminal law, specifically on the two basic requirements for a crime to have occurred: there must be (1) a guilty mind (mens rea) coupled with (2) a guilty act (actus reus). The guilty mind refers to a criminal or wrongful intent on the part of the actor. The antiquity of this principle in British law can be traced back at least to the thirteenth century, when Henri de Bracton wrote:

We must consider with what mind or with what intent a thing is done
. . . in order that it may be determined accordingly what action should
follow and what punishment. For take away the will and every act will
be indifferent because your state of mind gives meaning to your act, and
a crime is not committed unless the intent to injure intervene, nor is a
theft committed except with the intent to steal. . . . And this is in
accordance with what might be said of the infant or madman, since the
innocence of design protects the one and the lack of reason in
committing the act excuses the other.[19]

For Bernard Diamond, the historical-developmental importance of the
concept of the *mens rea* in the law was paramount. Indeed, the basic
concept that the nature of the intention was intrinsic to the nature and
meaning of the act, and thus set a limit to culpability and punishment,
could be traced back to the premises underlying ancient Mosaic law. In an
early paper, he wrote,

I am astonished that this early concept of *mens rea* has been overlooked
by most writers on the subject. Particularly, it is of great significance, for
it establishes as clearly as could possibly be that the Mosaic *Lex Talionis*—
an eye for an eye, a tooth for a tooth—was a maximum, not a mandatory
punishment. The *Lex Talionis*, in its historical context, was a most
humane concept which restricted the maximum punishment that could
be inflicted, under any circumstances of evilness of a crime, to an amount
proportional to the injury done [see "Criminal Responsibility of the
Mentally Ill," this volume].

He was pointing out that, historically, the *Lex Talionis* did not countenance a punishment of *two* eyes for *one* eye, but *only* one eye for one eye.

To return to the courtroom roles of the forensic psychiatrist, in
criminal proceedings one determines whether mental illness was present at
the time of the alleged crime, and if it was, whether it was of such nature
as to prevent the defendant from having the necessary criminal intent. Too
many people assume that this is the only psychological element in a crime.
In law, an act is not the act of the actor unless it is a *voluntary* act. That
is, the mere mechanical movement does not constitute the legal act of the
individual. It must be an act that the person wanted to do. This fine
distinction grew out of the concern for justice, in early English history,
when the Norsemen overran England and forced the captured villagers to
work against the British, and thus appear to be traitors. The captives were
not held responsible for acts they were forced to do. There are some
qualifiers here, as there almost always are in the law, but this is a general
principle, and one that, to the great credit of the English of that time,
provided a defense even against the crimes of murder and treason. The

principle also extends to infants and children who may do things, not volitionally, nor as a matter of choice, but because they are obeying an adult. In such a case, the child may be the instrument of another, rather than the true actor in law. Similarly, a testator making bequests in a will in response to undue influences, threats, or coercion is not performing a valid legal act, nor do those bequests express the will of the testator but, rather, the will or wills of others.

Both elements, the *mens rea* and the *actus reus*, are necessary for a common-law crime to have occurred. The mechanical act, without the volition of the person, is not, in law, *her or his* act and therefore cannot be her or his *actus reus*. Neither is the act, without the necessary defined intent, a crime. It was this principle in the law on which Diamond based much of his reasoning and many of his interpretations.

Sir Matthew Hale, the seventeenth-century jurist, was one of England's outstanding juridical minds. It was Hale who said:

> Man is naturally endowed with these two great faculties, understanding and liberty of will, and therefore is a subject properly capable of a law.
> . . . The consent of the will is that which renders human actions either commendable or culpable; as where there is no law there is no transgression, so regularly, where there is no will to commit an offense, there can be no transgression, or just reason to incur the penalty or sanction of that law . . . . And because the liberty of the will presupposeth an act of the understanding to know the thing or action chosen . . . it follows that where there is a total defect of the understanding, there is no free act of the will in the choice of things or actions.[20]

Underscoring the difficulty of weighing the role of psychiatric factors in determining guilt, Hale said:

> It is very difficult to divide the indivisible line that divides perfect and partial insanity, but it must rest upon circumstances duly to be weighed and considered both by the judge and the jury, lest there be a kind of inhumanity towards the defects of human nature, or on the other side too great an indulgence given to great crimes.[21]

Diminished Capacity and Diamond's Role in the *Wells-Gorshen* Rule

One of the outstanding contributions of Bernard L. Diamond was his crucial role in the development of the diminished capacity defense in California. At the time Diamond proposed his revision of criminal procedure, California had a two-part trial system for defendants who pleaded an insanity defense. The first part, often referred to as the guilt phase, determined whether or not the defendant had performed the criminal act alleged. This part of the trial excluded any psychiatric testimony. Once the defendant had been found guilty, the second phase of the trial was restricted to the issue of legal insanity, which was a total defense to the crime; that is, depending on the finding of sanity or insanity, the person was either guilty or innocent, with no intermediate options. In Diamond's view, this yes-or-no, black-or-white reasoning employed in the courtroom forced too many injustices. His first opportunity to influence this occurred with his late entry into the *Wells* case.

Wesley Robert Wells was a convict who had received an indeterminate sentence and awaited the California Adult Authority's recommendation as to its maximum length.[22] On a technicality, this delay in setting such a maximum made Wells a prisoner with a life sentence. Prisoners serving life sentences were mandated to be executed if found guilty of aggravated assault while in prison.

Wells was a political activist and charismatic leader among the prisoners. He would often leak information to the public media about problems within the corrections system. He had been in solitary confinement and was taken to the prison doctor who determined that Wells was in a "tension state" and should have a tranquilizer and some relief from the psychological stress of solitary confinement. Wells received neither. A prison guard provoked Wells, who threw a cuspidor at him, fracturing one of the guard's facial bones. Wells was tried on aggravated assault charges (which was, for him, a technical life-sentence prisoner, a capital offense). The judge did not allow medical testimony as to Wells's "tension state" because he assumed that *all* psychiatric testimony was prohibited in the first, or guilt, phase of California's bifurcated trial.

The judge's disallowance posed a life-or-death problem for the defense as they had wanted to introduce psychiatric testimony to show that Wells did not possess the requisite *mens rea* for aggravated assault. The appellate court agreed that the judge should have allowed the testimony; but it felt that this was so minor a factor that it would not have affected the conviction, and the court let it stand.

Wells's situation aroused public sympathy, and funds were raised to hire the law firm of Garry, Dreyfus, and McTernan. They retained Bernard L. Diamond as an expert witness and consultant. They asked him to find forensic psychiatry articles they could cite to show that, because of psychopathology, one might not have the mental ability to form the specific intent required for some crimes. Diamond found nothing suitable in the literature and decided to write such a paper himself. He turned to early English law for the principles that would apply to the *Wells* case.

Although Bernard Diamond was not sympathetic to Matthew Hale or to Hale's general legal philosophy as he saw it, it was in Hale's writing that he found what was needed: a clear statement of the concept of partial insanity.[23] Where Diamond wished to go beyond Hale was in linking partial insanity to partial responsibility. For justification of this idea, he went to the law of Scotland, which, in 1867, originated the concept of diminished responsibility. In this way he found an avenue to correct the binary thinking, black or white, sane or insane, of the law, which was well illustrated in his account of the M'Naghten trial.[24]

In 1843, Daniel M'Naghten, in response to a psychotic idea of reference, fatally shot Edward Drummond, private secretary to the Prime Minister, Sir Robert Peel. M'Naghten was acquitted on the ground of insanity, which resulted in a public and political furor. The House of Lords summoned the fifteen judges of the Queen's Bench (equivalent to our Supreme Court justices) and asked them to clarify the relevant law of England by answering five questions. Fourteen of the fifteen judges combined two questions (the second and third) and their answer to that is called the *M'Naghten* rule. It states that the

> jurors ought to be told that . . . to establish a defense on the ground of insanity, it must be clearly proved that at the time of the committing of the act, the party accused was labouring under such a defect of reason, from disease of the mind, as not to know the nature and quality of the act he was doing; or if he did know it, that he did not know he was doing what was wrong.[25]

The judges worried that, between their aggregate judicial weight and the absence of a particular case with its own specific details taken into account, their response would stifle the flexibility necessary to allow the common law to evolve and develop gradually, as it should. And that is what happened. Frequently, the rule was interpreted by the judiciary, American and British, to prevent the kind of fuller clinical inquiry that Diamond and others felt was necessary for the court to understand genuinely a defendant's state of mind. Indeed, it was partly in order to find precedential material older than the *M'Naghten* rule that Diamond went to Matthew Hale's writings.

Arguably, one might see Hale as more liberal than Diamond gave him credit for being, when one considers Hale's suggested standard for the distinction between partial and total insanity: "such a person as labouring under melancholy distempers hath yet ordinarily as great understanding, as ordinarily a child of fourteen years hath, is such a person as may be guilty of treason or felony."[26]

The significance of this standard has to be understood historically, for, at the time Hale wrote, the common-law standard for an absolute defense by virtue of youth and normal developmental limitations of understanding was seven years of age. Children between 7 and 14 might be found guilty of a felony if one could demonstrate that they knew they were doing wrong. Hale proposed that a person older than 14 whose understanding, because of mental illness, was less than that of a 14-year-old, *could not be guilty of a felony*, even if that person had the understanding of a 10-year-old or a 12-year-old, who, insanity not intervening, *could* be tried for and convicted of a felony.

To return to more modern law, despite the dedication of the people involved, the *Wells* case did not turn out as had been hoped. Later, because of chance and political factors, Wells did have his sentence commuted to life imprisonment and was eventually given parole. In 1959, a new case, which seemed tailor-made for the kind of legal reform that Bernard Diamond wanted to achieve, came along in the trial of Nicholas "Sleepy" Gorshen, a longshoreman who, with a policeman at each elbow, nevertheless, pulled out a concealed gun and killed his foreman, Joseph (Red) O'Leary.

The details of the case are included in this volume in Diamond's paper, "The Criminal Responsibility of the Mentally Ill." The kind of historical-developmental analysis that Diamond undertook in his paper "On Malice Aforethought" (see this volume) was only part of the work that was necessary to achieve his goal of moving the law from its binary or digital thinking (yes-or-no, 0-or-1) to one where the recognition of individual factors would provide a spectrum of options for the jury and for the judge. Diamond also had to do exceptional diagnostic probing in each case and had to provide the court with a remarkably high quality of forensic testimony and reasoning. Such was the situation in the *Gorshen* case, where Diamond's clinical acumen and dedication proved pivotal to the entire defense strategy. Diamond was its sole witness and when his testimony was ruled inadmissible in the first or guilt phase of the trial, the basis for an appeal was laid. Without Diamond's persuasive brilliance as a clinician, as well as his scholarship, there would have been no such remarkable achievement as the *Wells-Gorshen* rule.

Diamond discovered that Gorshen was prone to dissociated, or trance, states in which he experienced himself as the sexual plaything of the devil. Gorshen feared that if these states became known, his transportation to that evil world would become permanent. "Only through killing [O'Leary],"

Diamond said, "could he retain his sanity and avoid eternal incarceration in the hell of his trance states. It was this conviction that compelled him to kill his foreman" (see "Criminal Responsibility of the Mentally Ill," this volume). On appeal, the California Supreme Court ruled that Diamond's testimony should have been admitted during the guilt phase of the bifurcated trial:

> While the insanity of the defendant is not in issue under the general plea, yet this does not preclude evidence tending to establish his mental condition . . . at the time the offense was committed for the purpose of showing lack of criminal intent, malice or premeditation.

Unfortunately, like Wells, Gorshen did not benefit from this decision. The Supreme Court did not reduce his conviction for second-degree murder to manslaughter. But the principle as stated by the Supreme Court was now California's law.

What the "diminished capacity" defense, or the *Wells-Gorshen* rule, did was to effect a two-fold improvement in the trial law of California. It was an effective reminder that the burden of proof of *all* elements of the alleged crime rested with the prosecution. This meant that the *mens rea* had to be proved, and the defendant had to be given the opportunity to disprove it.

This was a new legal standard. While defenses had been admissible previously, involving extreme emotional stress, they all required proof that the stress or provocation suffered by the defendant was sufficient to affect the mental state of the "reasonable man." As Diamond observed later:

> The law has always recognized mental and emotional states as relevant to intent. There were laws dealing with intoxication, with crimes of passion, and with provocation and coercion, which could reduce murder to manslaughter; but these laws . . . had an important limitation, and that was the concept or the legal fiction of the reasonable man. In order to establish that a killing was manslaughter due to provocation or due to passion, the defense had to establish that, under the circumstances of the crime, a reasonable man would have been provoked to this same act of killing or that a reasonable man under that emotional state would have killed. Any evidence that had to do with the individual defendant's own psychology, to show that he could not conform to the concept of the reasonable man, or that he was unusually vulnerable to provocations to commit a particular crime or that his emotional states were more intense than average or that he was subject to greater jealousy or paranoid ideation, was irrelevant. Judges normally resisted the introduction of any evidence to that effect because the standard was that of a reasonable man and any differences between the reasonable man and the defendant were

not relevant. . . . In the Wells decision, the court had indirectly
overturned the restriction of the reasonable man.[27]

In order to prevail, these earlier defenses required proof that any *reasonable* person would be driven to act as the defendant had in the circumstances alleged. The *Wells-Gorshen* rule required the court to consider an
individual defendant's specific psychopathology and his particular state of
mind, including his individual fears, phobias, terrors, and so on. The *Wells-
Gorshen* rule required proof that the *actual* state of mind of the defendant
was consistent with the required *mens rea* for the crime alleged. This was
a major advance for criminal jurisprudence and for the mentally ill.

To a significant extent, Diamond's achievement was undercut by a
sensational murder case. On November 27, 1978, Dan White killed San
Francisco Mayor George Moscone and Supervisor Harvey Milk, a popular
member of the city's gay community. Milk's homicide was a particularly
inflammatory act to that community. White pleaded a diminished-capacity
defense based on hypoglycemia, a metabolic condition made infamous, in
this case, as the "Twinkie defense," and he was found guilty of two charges
of manslaughter, instead of murder. The public reaction to the outcome was
particularly intense, with an overwhelming demand for greater punishment
and vengeance.

Bernard Diamond refused to participate in the case because the defense
attorney would not allow Dan White to testify, and it was a principle of
Diamond's not to participate in a trial unless the defendant appeared on
the witness stand. Later, in commenting on the trial, he observed that the
prosecutor probably was ambivalent about this politically charged case, and
did not present as effective a prosecution as he could have.[28] Although the
prosecutor was given advance information about the psychiatric defense, he
offered no psychiatric expert witnesses or rebuttal of the defense expert
testimony.

As a consequence of the public furor about the trial verdict, Proposition 8 and the California legislature (SB 1314 and 2033), in separate pieces
of legislation, formally limited the diminished capacity defense.[29] However,
this still left the *Wells* case as authority, that is, the prosecution in
California still must prove *mens rea*, and the defendant still has the right
to introduce evidence to disprove it. Nonetheless, the new laws, Diamond
felt, did limit the scope of expert witness testimony since the defense
attorney could not connect the psychiatrist's evaluation directly to the issue
of *mens rea*. Without this, he felt that juries, historically disposed to
discounting psychiatric mitigating factors, would not adequately understand
or use the psychiatric evidence in evaluating the degree of criminality of the
defendant's actions.

What the new California statutes and propositions did was to forbid testimony that the defendant was *incapable* of having the requisite psychological state to commit the specific crime. The basic jurisprudential principle, however, remained, that the prosecution must prove *all* elements of the crime, including the psychological. Therefore, the defense still had the right to introduce evidence to disprove the *actual* presence of the intent at the time of the alleged criminal act, or to force the prosecution to prove that the defendant did have the actual and specific intent at the time of the alleged crime.

Testifying before the California Assembly Criminal Justice Committee, in 1980, Diamond commented about the new legislation:

> It is clear that these bills are a response to the trial of Dan White. I have no opinion about the merits of the verdict in that trial. Even if one assumes there was a gross miscarriage of justice and that the diminished capacity defense was inappropriate in this case, it does not follow that such a singular occurrence should justify the destruction of thirty years of legal progress. It does not make sense to discard a law because it may have been improperly applied in one case, however sensational.[30]

With the passage of Proposition 8 and of these bills, the impact of much of Diamond's work in this area was lost to California. He recognized, nevertheless, that it survived in other jurisdictions.

If this were Diamond's only contribution to American forensic psychiatry, it would be enough to warrant recognition that he was the first forensic psychiatrist since Isaac Ray, more than a century earlier, to make such a substantial contribution to the overlapping areas of criminal law and psychiatry.

The Incompetence of Previously Hypnotized Witnesses to Testify

Since 1778, when Franz Anton Mesmer appeared on the Parisian scene, the phenomenon known variously as mesmerism, animal magnetism, and hypnotism has fascinated scientists and laypersons alike. In the 1830s in England, Dr. John Elliotson was convinced that mesmerism was a phenomenon based on a fluid ether and was capable of being a force for remarkable medical good, as well as endowing its subject with superhuman powers, including clairvoyance. By the 1840s, mesmerism was used for surgical anesthesia, only to be subsequently abandoned in favor of the more culturally acceptable chemical anesthesias. Elliotson gradually lost his credibility, and the general medical interest in mesmerism went into a decline despite James Braid's more anatomically oriented studies. Some years later, however, Hippolyte Bernheim discovered the country practitioner Ambroise-Auguste Liébeault, who had been using hypnotism to treat many of his patients quite successfully. By the end of the century mesmerism was again being widely used in France by Bernheim's and Charcot's students. The phenomenon fascinated the medical world once more.

The use of hypnosis to explore the human mind and its potential has been almost continuously present on the western scene during the twentieth century. It was used for age regression, to recover lost memories, for psychoanalysis in its early forms, and to explore "past lives." Eventually, it was used to determine whether or not somebody was telling the truth and to enable eyewitnesses to reconstruct what they had witnessed. In the midtwentieth century it began to assume a nearly infallible credibility in the courts. Hypnotic enhancement of eye-witness memories became the rage, and judges and juries began to base legal decisions and verdicts on the reliability of such recovered memories. By 1980, the use of police hypnotists had become a widespread practice in criminal investigations and to enhance witness recall.

In 1980, Bernard Diamond published a paper advocating the exclusion of the testimony of witnesses who had been subjected to hypnosis to enhance their memory of the events at issue in the trial (see "Inherent Problems in the Use of Pretrial Hypnosis on a Prospective Witness," this volume). He pointed out that there was no reliable way to determine the reality or validity of the recalled or reconstructed memories even though the subjects might be so thoroughly convinced of the genuineness of these memories that they would stake their lives on it. He demonstrated that the subtle communication and interaction between hypnotized subject and hypnotist was so pervasive and powerful, that it was impossible for the hypnotist, the hypnotized subject, or any observer, to know what was an actual recovered memory and what was a memory created to serve the psychological needs of the subject or the hypnotist. Diamond's concern was that the hypnotized subject, now convinced of what may not have occurred, would provide such persuasive testimony that no person and no method could distinguish between the true and the false in the witness's sincere belief. Since it was impossible for attorneys, psychiatrists, or hypnotists to distinguish the true from the false, the use of such testimony demanded that the court's trier of fact do the impossible. Therefore, Diamond argued, the only way to handle it was to consider as incompetent to testify regarding the events at issue everyone who had been hypnotized.

Diamond's article was quoted and relied on as scientific authority in the Arizona Supreme Court in its 1981 decision to exclude such testimony.[31] In 1982, in the California case of People v. Shirley, the court decided that the testimony of a witness who had undergone hypnosis for the purpose of restoring her memory of the relevant events was inadmissible regarding all matters relating to those events, "from the time of the hypnotic session forward."[32] In his California Supreme Court opinion Justice Stanley Mosk noted that Dr. Diamond "is well known to the legal profession. He is the author of numerous articles in the area of psychiatry and the law, and we have often relied on his views. . . . On the present issue . . . the majority [of the experts] are in full agreement with the essential findings and conclusions."[33] And in general, courts across the nation have agreed with this.

In this battle, Diamond was clearly not alone, but his work was sufficiently influential to constitute a substantial contribution to the law of the nation. Here, too, one must consider how few forensic psychiatrists can lay claim to a contribution of such pervasive influence and widespread significance.

Unfortunately, the meaning of Diamond's work on the unacceptability of the results of hypnotically enhanced memory for determining important issues in the real world is too little recognized or appreciated by his own professional colleagues. The American Psychiatric Association remains unwilling to speak out against accepting as valid or real the products of hypnotically "recovered memories" such as physical and sexual abuse during one's own childhood.[34] That such "recovered memories" are undoubtedly real in some instances does not remove the objection that, as Diamond said, there is no way to tell the true from the false. Anyone interested in the "false memory" syndrome debate should read Diamond's paper. Conscientious psychiatrists should stop using hypnosis to "recover" memories for any use outside the psychiatric treatment environment. Likewise, they should desist from presenting such memories as having any other validity than that of "psychological reality" unless, with due diligence and effort, they themselves provide substantial and independent verification.

In addition to being the author of the paper "Inherent Problems in the Use of Pretrial Hypnosis on a Prospective Witness," Diamond was a member of the Committee of the American Medical Association Council on Scientific Affairs, whose report on the scientific status of refreshing recollection by the use of hypnosis concurred with Diamond's earlier paper.[35]

Fallacy of the Impartial Expert

Prior to the entry of Bernard Diamond on the scene, it was generally accepted within the psychiatric profession as well as the legal profession and the judiciary that the role of the expert witness was that of an impartial dispenser of the scientific information accepted by the profession or discipline in question. Within the field of psychiatry, the impartiality of the expert witness was held up as an ethical ideal.

In 1959, Diamond published an editorial article in the *Archives of Criminal Psychodynamics*, at that time a relatively new journal edited by the forensic psychiatrist and psychoanalyst Benjamin Karpman, in which Diamond proposed the then heresy that the much vaunted impartiality of the scientific expert witness was an impossibility and that the law and psychiatry would be better off if they openly acknowledged that the expert witness was, in actuality, an advocate for the side that retained him.

Customarily, an attorney will call a psychiatrist and describe the general outline of a case, asking the psychiatrist if she or he would be interested in exploring the possibility of serving as an expert witness. The psychiatrist, if interested, will then agree to examine the documents available and evaluate the patient. It is at that time such issues as fees and the possibility that the psychiatrist may not wish to go further, are discussed. After the evaluation, depending on whether the psychiatrist's findings are compatible or incompatible with the attorney's view and contemplated legal strategy, the psychiatrist may withdraw or may accept the case. Up to this point, it is rare that there will be a question about impartiality, unless, like Thomas Szasz, one subscribes to a disbelief in mental illness.

Diamond maintained that while it might be possible for an expert witness to start out as impartial, under the adversary system, with cross-examination and efforts to impeach the credibility of the witness, the expert "must necessarily identify himself with his own opinion, and subjectively desire that 'his side' win" (see "The Fallacy of the Impartial Expert," this volume). He also pointed out that when hospital observation is involved, the court often does not hear of the procedures that led to the final diagnostic decision. For example, it may have been arrived at by a split vote of the staff; or the decision may have been strongly influenced by a senior administrator who may unilaterally have had the final diagnostic say or who, because of the hierarchal structure of public service, may have had a very strong influence on the staff opinion because of their personal ambitions.

An unrecognized but also important part of this paper is its closing, in which Diamond gives his substantive criticisms of the state of forensic psychiatry, forensic psychiatrists, and of our society and its criminal justice system. One need not agree with all of Diamond's criticisms to recognize that they came from a psychiatrist who felt and thought deeply and who tried to serve his profession, the law, and society by alerting them to the unfortunate significance of what he saw.

He said later that he did not get much feedback from colleagues about this particular paper, as if they did not want to embarrass or confront him with his errors. It was largely, however, because of Bernard Diamond's position that the current code of ethics of the American Academy of Psychiatry and the Law speaks of "striving for objectivity" rather than "impartiality."

Moreover, the paper arguably had judicial impact. The 1985 decision of the Supreme Court, in *Ake v. Oklahoma*, written by Justice Thurgood Marshall, established the right of the defendant to "a competent psychiatrist who will conduct an appropriate examination and assist in evaluation, preparation, and presentation of the defense."[36] As a logical matter, if the psychiatrist is going to assist in the planning of the defense, he enters as a committed advocate and adversary rather than as an impartial scientist. Thus, the expert witness's function cannot be construed as being merely that of an impartial vessel containing the relevant scientific information necessary for the trier of fact to evaluate the meaning of the evidence. It was precisely this new construction of the psychiatrist's role to which then Justice Rehnquist objected in his lone dissent against the majority opinion.[37] The *Ake* decision was a vindication of the position that Diamond had taken for almost a quarter of a century, that it was appropriate for psychiatric expert witnesses to acknowledge partiality and bias.

Long before *Ake*, Diamond's paper on the fallacy of the impartial expert was considered a classic, even by those who disagreed with him. Many of those who opposed him on this issue also disapproved of his refusal to appear as an expert witness for the prosecution. If impartiality was the desideratum for the expert witness, then to have psychiatrists who designated themselves as "defense psychiatrists," just as attorneys are either prosecution or defense attorneys, was perceived by some psychiatrists as an embarrassment. Moreover, there are still forensic psychiatrists who differ with the *Ake* decision on the issue of frank advocacy and who believe that the psychiatrist should be an impartial representative and teacher of the science, edifying the court but uninvested in the outcome of the specific trial.

The focal point of the controversy encompasses what Diamond referred to as "personal ethics." In my view, his position, as with many other stands he took, grew out of three elements of Diamond's personal philosophy. First was his insistence on scrupulous personal and professional honesty. Second was his conviction that a psychiatrist, as a physician, should not be involved in anything that entailed punishment. Third, he believed that the prosecution should not have access to expert witnesses to prove the elements of *mens rea*. These points did not, however, appear explicitly in this paper. In his writings and lectures, he made it clear that his position derived from his own deeply felt commitment to the role of the healing physician. He was equally clear that his view of the matter was not likely to prevail in his lifetime. In 1973, he wrote:

> I have suggested the principle (which I know to be legally unsound, but which I believe to be medically correct) that psychiatric expert testimony should be reserved exclusively for the defense in criminal trials. Let the prosecutor prove sanity or other elements of the requisite mental state required by the definition of the crime by use of non-expert witnesses or by the circumstances of the crime. Such a procedure would eliminate the troublesome battle of the experts as well as being more compatible with the psychiatrist's role as healer. I have no expectation that this suggestion will be adopted by any court.[38]

Diamond also appreciated that his personal ethics could not be imposed on his colleagues with any justification. About 15 years later, discussing the issue of categories of professional ethics, Diamond wrote that professionals must distinguish between those ethical principles which *all* members of a profession must observe and another group of personally or religiously determined principles of ethics or morality, which

> may be very strongly held and serve as powerful guides to clinical practice for the persons who subscribe to them, but they cannot be forced upon all practitioners . . . . I, as a criminal defense psychiatrist, may think that it is unethical to work for prosecutors, and that all my colleagues should share my scruples.[39]

The organizational ethics of law and of psychiatry are different and, many times, they conflict. For Bernard Diamond, the ethics of the physician prevailed.[40] It was the rare instance when he would defer to the law.[41] It seemed to me, in the brief time that we knew each other, that the unfailing compass that determined his personal and professional course was his personal ethics and honesty, his passionate dedication to justice for the unfavored, and his respect for honest differences responsibly arrived at. On the other hand, he was remarkably intolerant of dishonesty or lack of integrity, and when pushed far enough, he could respond with unequivocal and passionate condemnation.[42]

In general, though the body of forensic psychiatrists has not been willing to follow Diamond's difficult example, it is generally conceded that by his having lived that example and through his teaching, the profession has been brought to recognize important legal and ethical dimensions that had been overlooked.

Psychiatric Prediction of Dangerousness

In 1974, Bernard L. Diamond published a paper on "The Psychiatric Prediction of Dangerousness" (see this volume). The paper is divided into four parts or discussions.

In the first he presents his view that there is no acceptably reliable clinical basis for predicting dangerousness in individual cases. Violent individuals often displayed certain histories, symptoms, or signs with meaningful frequency, but these features were totally absent in some violent persons and present in some nonviolent persons.

In the second section, he points out that the statistical studies of the prediction of dangerousness support his clinical view. Here he relies on the group of papers by Steadman and his colleagues studying a cohort of 967 so-called *Baxstrom* patients.

Diamond then discusses the risk to the psychiatrist who "predicts" nondangerousness, but who is wrong, and the safety of the psychiatrist who overpredicts. "Inevitably, this will result in all concerned doing the 'safe' thing: predicting dangerousness, if there are even the most minimal reasons to justify it."

In the third part, he faced the recurring question about the relationship between mental illness and dangerousness or criminality and found grounds for rejecting any connection. There is no clear cut link between mental illness (or a specific type of mental illness) and dangerousness. Finally, he refers to the failure to provide a universally successful definition of violence, concluding "it is no wonder that . . . psychiatric predictions are devoid of validity and reliability."

Diamond opens his concluding section by decrying the unfortunate tendency in the psychiatric literature to imply that the scientific answers to pressing social problems that are not now known are likely to be available in the very near future. In a footnote here he calls the reader's attention to his having "been equally guilty of making such optimistic predictions as to the ability of psychiatric science to discover new information of great value to the law," referring the reader to his paper "From *M'Naghten* to *Currens* and Beyond" (see this volume). He then goes on to draw the conclusion to his argument: that psychiatrists should not be called in to the legal process until after the individual has been adjudicated, on grounds of actual behavior, suitable for confinement for the protection of the public. Then let the psychiatrist make the appropriate treatment recommendations.

> Dr. Diamond's views were also considered by our court in the celebrated *Tarasoff v. Regents of the University of California.*[43] Once again the psychiatrist's inability to predict future violence was the principle issue. In my concurring opinion, I relied on Dr. Diamond's articles, though he was not cited, and I reiterated my *Burnick* concept: "In the light of recent studies it is no longer heresy to question the reliability of psychiatric predictions. Psychiatrists themselves would be the first to admit that however desirable an infallible crystal ball might be, it is not among the tools of their profession."[44]

Nineteen seventy-four was a year in which several publications appeared, almost synchronously, challenging the belief that psychiatrists could predict dangerousness. It was the year that Ennis and Litwak published their paper on the psychiatric prediction of dangerousness.[45] That same year Steadman and Cocozza published their study of the so-called *Baxstrom* patients,[46] and the Task Force of the American Psychiatric Association published its report on *Clinical Aspects of the Violent Individual.*[47]

In 1966, the U.S. Supreme Court heard the case of *Baxstrom v. Herold.*[48] Johnnie K. Baxstrom, an epileptic alcoholic, convicted for a remarkably violent stabbing, had been committed shortly before the expiration of his sentence and was, under the authority of a New York State statute (Article 15, §384, NY Penal Law), kept in a Department of Corrections psychiatric hospital after his sentence expired. The statute did not include a right to appeal a commitment by recourse to a jury trial. Since civilly committed patients in New York State had that right, this was unequal protection of the law and unconstitutional.

The Supreme Court ordered Baxstrom to be released or civilly committed. The Department of Mental Hygiene lawyers decided that all other patients held under §384 in the correctional hospital system were subject to this same order. They determined that there were 652 such patients. For administrative and other reasons, 315 other prisoner/patients, whose confinements were independent of §384 or questions of dangerousness, were civilly committed and transferred to civil hospitals at the same time. It is important to remember that §384 did not mention and was not restricted in its application to cases of dangerousness due to mental illness.

Some years later, this administratively selected, criminally and clinically heterogeneous group was the subject of a widely acclaimed study conducted by two sociologists in the New York State Department of Mental Hygiene. They characterized this as a "natural experiment" of the psychiatric prediction of dangerousness, although, as they later acknowledged, they had no predictions of dangerousness for *any* of the patients.[49] The study's findings were widely and enthusiastically accepted in the forensic psychiatry and general psychiatry communities as proof that psychiatrists overpredict, or cannot predict, dangerousness.

Diamond was, of course, correct in his position that psychiatrists could not predict that specific individuals would commit specific violent felonies sometime in the future. In a discussion he and I had about this paper some dozen years later, we agreed that psychiatrists could identify people who, because of their mental illness, were dangerous at the time of the examination, but that too many psychiatrists did not limit themselves to this narrow time constraint. He was appalled by the record of one Texas psychiatrist who appeared to have consistently testified that young defendants who were allegedly sociopaths would remain dangerous to society for the rest of their lives, a prediction that persuaded several juries to recommend executions. That psychiatrist idiosyncratically ignored the generally accepted body of evidence that most sociopaths become far less dangerous as they get older.

Diamond's Role in the Establishment of
Standards of Forensic Psychiatry Expertise

In 1969, at the annual meeting of the American Psychiatric Association, a group of members with a concern for facilitating and improving the development and training of forensic psychiatrists formed the American Academy of Psychiatry and the Law (AAPL), a psychiatric organization dedicated to education in forensic psychiatry. Bernard L. Diamond was a major figure in that group. Soon after its formation, that organization, along with the American Academy of Forensic Sciences, sponsored the establishment of the American Board of Forensic Psychiatry. Bernard Diamond was one of the original directors of that body. It began administering examinations and issuing certificates to successful candidates in February 1979. There are now more than 200 forensic psychiatrists certified by the Board. To assist those persons preparing to become forensic psychiatrists, AAPL has established an annual review course in forensic psychiatry and a separate body for accrediting fellowship programs in that discipline.

In the early 1990s, at the behest of those of its members who were also members of AAPL, the American Psychiatric Association requested that the American Board of Psychiatry and Neurology administer examinations to certify successful applicants as having "added qualifications in forensic psychiatry." This established a nationwide standard examination for a credential supported by the entire medical profession through the American Board of Medical Specialties, which can be expected to provide minimum standards of knowledge for specialization and to encourage the psychiatric residency programs in the United States to provide some minimum education in forensic psychiatry. Bernard Diamond lived long enough to see that this was going to happen but died before the first examinations were given.

It is likely that with the existence of the American Academy of Psychiatry and the Law and the Psychiatric Section of the American Academy of Forensic Sciences and with the establishment of minimal criteria for expertise in forensic psychiatry, the development of the law as it relates to psychiatric issues will be more rooted in and more cognizant of clinical realities than it has been in the past.

Notes

[1]Diamond, B. L. (1938), Are clinical clerkships abused? J. Assn. of Med. Students, 2:206–208, 217.

[2]Diamond, B. L. (1938), The psychological abdomen—its surgical importance. West. J. Surg., Obstet., Gynecol., Div. I–46:416–425; Div. II–498–502.

[3]Correspondence from Bernard L. Diamond to Robert Weinstock, M.D., April 25, 1988.

[4]Diamond, B. L. & Ross, A. (1945), Emotional adjustment of newly blinded soldiers. Amer. J. Psychiat., 102:367–371.

[5]Ray, I. (1841), Second Report of the Superintendent of the Maine Insane Hospital, pp. 48–51.

[6]Diamond, B. L. (1953), Privileged communication and the clinical psychology. J. Clin. Psychol., 9:388–390.

[7]People v. Williams, 200 Cal. App.3d 838, at fn. 3, 19 Cal. Rptr. 743 (1962).

[8]Bernard L. Diamond Archives. Personal correspondence. Letter dated April 1, 1983, to Professor Phillip E. Johnson.

[9]Lambard, W. (1581), Eirenarcha; or of the Office of the Justices of Peace, in two Bookes; Gathered, 1579, and Now Revised, and Firste Published, in the 24, Yeare of the Peacable Reigne of Our Gratious Queene Elizabeth. Imprinted by Ra Newberry, and H. Byneman, by the ass. of Ri Tot. & Chr. Bar (First Book, chap. 21, p. 218).

[10]Diamond, B. L. (1983), Lecture to residents at St. Mary's Hospital and Medical Center. San Francisco, CA, October 18.

[11]Diamond, B. L. (1992), The forensic psychiatrist: Consultant vs. activist in legal doctrine. Bull. Amer. Acad. Psychiat. & Law, 20:119–132.

[12]Wade v. United States, 426 F 2d 64, at 72 (1970).

[13]Mosk, S. (1990), A giant in the field. *Cal. L. Rev.*, 78:1431–1432.

[14]Rush, B. (1811), *Sixteen Introductory Lectures to Courses of Lectures Upon the Institutes and Practice of Medicine, With a Syllabus of the Latter.* Philadelphia, PA: Bradford & Inskeep (contains his 16th lecture "On the Study of Medical Jurisprudence," delivered November 5, 1810, pp. 363–395).

[15]Ibid., pp. 363–364.

[16]McDade, T. M. (1961), *The Annals of Murder.* Norman: University of Oklahoma Press.

[17]Drake, D. (1829), Medical jurisprudence—Report of a trial for murder, in which the culprit was defended on the ground of his laboring under *mania à potu*, or delirium from intemperance. *West. J. Med. & Physical Sci.*, 3:44–65; (1829), Medical jurisprudence—Sequel to the case of John Birdsell, with remarks on feigned insanity. *West. J. Med. & Physical Sci.*, 3:215–221; (1830), Medical jurisprudence—*Mania à potu.* Birdsell's case. *West. J. Med. & Physical Sci.*, 3:598–602.

[18]Ray, I. (1853), *A Treatise on the Medical Jurisprudence of Insanity.* Boston: Little, Brown.

[19]Bracton, H. de, quoted in Sayre, F. B. (1932), *Mens rea. Harvard L. Rev.*, 45:985.

[20]Hale, M. (1736), *Historia Placitorum Coronae [The History of the Pleas of the Crown].* London: E. R. Nutt & R. Gosling, pp. 14–15.

[21]Ibid., p. 30.

[22]The adult authority in California is that state's major governmental correction agency, which sets the actual sentences for those convicted of indeterminate-sentence crimes.

[23]Hale, op. cit., sup. note 20, p. 30.

[24]Diamond, B. L. (1956), Isaac Ray and the trial of Daniel M'Naghten. *Amer. J. Psychiat.*, 112:651–656.

[25]The English Reports, Vol. 8: House of Lords Containing Clark & Finnelly 8–12 (1901). Edinburgh, pp. 718–724.

[26]Hale, op. cit., sup. note 20, p. 30.

[27]Diamond, B. L. (1983), Lecture to residents at St. Mary's Hospital and Medical Center, San Francisco, CA, October 18.

[28]Lecture #6, Legal Studies 181, Boalt Hall, University of California (Berkeley). March 2, 1989. Black Lightning Lecture Notes.

[29]The defense of diminished capacity was abolished in 1981 by P. C. 28, and again in 1982 by P. C. 25 (part of Proposition 8) (Witkin, B. F. & Epstein, N. L. [1988], *California Criminal Law*, Vol. 1. San Francisco: Bancroft-Whitney, p. 238). See also §§ 210, 211. Although the formal "diminished capacity defense" was abolished, the psychiatric issue of the actual presence or absence of the specific *mens rea* was still admissible, and prosecutorial proof remains integral to the criminal law of California.

[30]Diamond, B. L. (1980), Testimony before the California Assembly Criminal Justice Committee (relative to SB 2033 and 1314). Representing the California Psychiatric Association and speaking on behalf of the California Attorneys for Criminal Justice. June 23.

[31]State v. Mena (1981), 128 Ariz. 226 [624 P.2d 1274, 1722].

[32]People v. Shirley (1982), 31 C.3d 18, 66–67.

[33]Ibid., p. 63 n.45.

[34]American Psychiatric Association Fact Sheet, "Memories of Sexual Abuse," April 1994.

[35]Council on Scientific Affairs (AMA) (1985), Council report: Scientific status of refreshing recollection by the use of hypnosis. J. Amer. Med. Assn., 253:1918–1933.

[36]Ake v. Oklahoma 105 S. Ct. 1087, 1097 (1985): "We therefore hold that when a defendant demonstrates to the trial judge that his sanity at the time of the offense is to be a significant factor at trial, the State must, at a minimum, assure the defendant access to a competent psychiatrist who will conduct an appropriate examination and assist in evaluation, preparation, and presentation of the defense."

[37]"Finally, even if I were to agree with the Court that some right to a state-appointed psychiatrist should be recognized here, I would not grant the broad right to 'access to a competent psychiatrist who will conduct an appropriate examination and assist in evaluation, preparation, and presentation of the defense.' A psychiatrist is not an attorney, whose job it is to advocate. His opinion is sought on a question that the State of Oklahoma treats as a question of fact." (Ibid., pp. 1101–1102.)

[38]Diamond, B. L. (1973), From Durham to Brawner: A futile journey. Wash. Univ. L. Quart., p. 116.

[39]Diamond, B. L. Letter to Robert Weinstock, M.D., April 25, 1988.

[40]Diamond, op. cit., sup. note 38.

[41]See, for example, Diamond, B. L. (1980), Review of Taking Care of Strangers: The Rule of Law in Doctor–Patient Relations by R. A. Burt (New York: Free Press, 1979). Mich. L. Rev., 78:743–749.

[42]See, for example, Diamond, B. L. (1964), Review of Law, Liberty and Psychiatry by T. S. Szasz. Cal. L. Rev., 52:899.

[43]17 Cal. 3d 425, 551 P.2d 334, 131 Cal. Rptr. 14 (1976).

[44]Ibid. at 451, P.2d at 364, 331 Cal. Rptr. at 34.

[45]Ennis, B. J. & Litwak, T. R. (1974), Psychiatry and the presumption of expertise: Flipping coins in the courtroom. Cal. L. Rev., 62:693–752.

[46]Steadman, H. J. & Cocozza, J. J. (1974), Careers of the Criminally Insane: Excessive Control of Social Deviance. Lexington, MA: Lexington Books.

[47]American Psychiatric Association (1974), Clinical Aspects of the Violent Individual. Washington, DC: American Psychiatric Press.

[48]Baxstrom v. Herold 383 U.S. 107 (1966).

[49]"It was *necessary* for us to assume [they] were considered dangerous by the psychiatrists in the hospitals for the criminally insane" (Cocozza, J. & Steadman, H. [1976], The failure of psychiatric predictions of dangerousness: Clear and convincing evidence. *Rutgers L. Rev.*, 29:1074–1101 [italics added]).

Note on Citations

Unfortunately, several of Dr. Diamond's papers appeared with the citations in less than ideal form. Wherever possible, these citations have been improved and amended to provide more complete information, although this was not feasible in all cases. In every instance enough information has been provided so that the original legal source can be located in an academic law library and medical citations can be located through academic medical libraries.

Careful scrutiny of the original published versions of Dr. Diamond's papers revealed what were clearly typographic errors and unedited stylistic problems; these have been silently amended.

Legal citations begin with the title of the case or the article, followed by the volume number, the name of the journal or book and the page of the decision or the article, followed by the year.

Medical citations have the name of the author first; then the date of publication, the title of the chapter or article, the journal or book title, the volume number, followed by the page number, and, in the case of books, the city of publication and the publisher.

The Psychiatrist in the Courtroom

Psychoanalysis in the Courtroom

[1978]

I would like to begin with the date May 21, 1924. It was on that day that a fourteen-year-old boy by the name of Robert Franks was kidnapped from a very expensive private school in Chicago. His parents were sent, through the mail, a ransom note demanding $10,000 for the return of their son. The next day, before any contact with the kidnappers could be arranged, the police reported the discovery of the body of the boy hidden in a culvert in a swamp on the outskirts of Chicago. He had been brutally murdered, his head bashed in by what appeared to be a chisel. Near the body police found the only clue, a pair of eyeglasses. Within a week the crime was solved, and it turned out that the nineteen-year-old sons of two very wealthy families in Chicago were responsible for the murder.

The two murderers, Richard Loeb and Nathan Leopold, had gone to the school Robert Franks attended, which was familiar to them because Loeb had attended it when he was a child. Looking for a suitable victim, they waited outside the school at the close of the school day. Bobby Franks, who was a distant cousin of theirs, recognized them. They invited him into their car and said they would take him home. They drove off, and within a very short time, while they were driving, one of them hit the boy in the back of the head with a chisel and killed him. Later, each accused the other of delivering the fatal blow. They hid the body in a culvert in an area that was well known to Nathan Leopold, who was a bird watcher, a bird fancier. He had made many trips to the outskirts of Chicago looking for specimens and had suggested this as the logical place to hide the body.

The families, as would be expected, searched the country for the most prominent and most successful criminal defense lawyer, and they employed Clarence Darrow. Associated with Darrow was their family attorney, a Benjamin Bachrach. Bachrach had a younger brother Walter, also a lawyer, who had recently become totally engrossed in what was then a new psychology from Vienna, psychoanalysis. The younger Bachrach was in a

1

personal analysis and he recommended to Clarence Darrow that they seek out the foremost psychoanalytic experts of the day and use them in the defense of these two boys. The first psychiatrist Darrow thought of was Dr. Karl Bowman, who at that time was in Boston. Bowman was considered a national authority on endocrinology and neuroendocrinological states associated with mental disorders. Darrow had written a book on crime[1] and was convinced that the secret of criminal behavior somehow lay in the constitutional genetic and endocrinological makeup of the criminal. Darrow was eager to try out this theory. The younger Bachrach persuaded him, however, that a more suitable approach would be that of Freudian psychoanalysis. It was in this rather unusual trial, under these very unusual circumstances, that the first intensive effort was made to apply Freudian psychoanalytic concepts directly to a criminal trial in a court of law.

Many other psychiatrists and analysts were engaged in the case for the defense, as were psychiatrists for the prosecution. The basic task of assembling all the data was assigned to Dr. Bowman and to Dr. Culbert, a Chicago neuropsychiatrist. Their task was to produce what eventually turned out to be several thousand pages of psychiatric reports describing every conceivable feature of the two defendants and the circumstances of the crime. The strategy was then to bring in the big names to deliver the testimony in the courtroom. For the defense, three of the most prominent psychoanalysts in the United States at that time were employed. There was William Healy of the Judge Baker Foundation who was probably the most important authority on juvenile delinquency in the United States. There was Bernard Glueck, who was probably the first psychoanalyst to devote himself seriously to a study of prisoners and criminals within a prison situation. He had conducted research at and was a consultant to Sing Sing prison. The third member of the defense team, and its leading light, was William Alanson White who at that time was director of St. Elizabeths Hospital in Washington, D.C.

It quickly became apparent in the initial examinations by Dr. Bowman and Dr. Culbert that it was very unlikely that any amount of psychiatric scrutiny, or psychoanalytic investigation, could establish a defense of insanity—both boys were brilliant, rational, and free from any obvious manifestations of psychosis. Clarence Darrow adopted an unusual strategy. He decided that the best chance of saving the boys from execution by hanging was to plead them guilty to first-degree murder and then to introduce psychiatric testimony in the form of a plea for mitigation of sentence. The law in Illinois, as in most states, permitted introduction of any evidence having to do with the question of sentencing, specifically, whether a defendant convicted of first-degree murder should be sentenced to death or to life imprisonment.

The Trial of Leopold and Loeb

Darrow wished to avoid a jury trial because the circumstances of the crime, extreme wealth and prominence of the involved families, and the peculiar motivation for the crime had already attracted sensational publicity throughout the world. The Leopold-Loeb case is still regarded as the crime of the century, even though there was no television and very little radio in 1924. The sensationalism created by the media through daily detailed reports and screaming headlines in all the newspapers blanketed the world. I remember the events of that trial very clearly myself, and I would say that Patty Hearst's trial and its publicity were not even in the running in the competition for the trial of the century.

Darrow assumed that any jury selected would be so prejudiced that there would be no chance of avoiding the death penalty, and that the best strategy would be simply to plead for mercy before a judge. The defense hoped also to prevent the prosecution from making a case because theoretically if one pleads guilty to first-degree murder there is no need for the prosecution to introduce the gory details of the crime. The District Attorney, however, was not going to allow an opportunity like this to go by, so even though there was a plea of guilty and even though there really was not a trial but simply a hearing on the question of punishment, the District Attorney insisted on introducing all the prosecution evidence that would have been introduced if there had been an actual trial. Platoons of psychiatrists were called by the prosecution to testify that both defendants were thoroughly sane. Healy, Glueck, and especially White, however, made a most thorough analysis of the case in more or less Freudian concepts and testified in the spotlight of all this publicity. William Alanson White, in particular, took this occasion to introduce into the courtroom the dynamic concepts that he had learned well from his studies of Freud's writings and that he accepted as the new psychology, which he believed would eventually replace the stereotypic, static, diagnostic psychiatry that had been prevalent in courtrooms.

The psychiatric testimony in the case lasted over a month and the transcripts reached tens of thousands of pages. I shall not review the details, which are not important, except to mention the very strange motivation for the crime. It turns out that Loeb, who had originated the idea of the crime, was a brilliant, very charming student of philosophy, who had been very much impressed by Nietzsche's concept of the superman in the book *Beyond Good and Evil*. Loeb was fascinated by detective stories and read every one that he could get his hands on. He eventually came to the decision that the true mark of his intellectual growth would be his willingness to put his philosophical ideas to the test. The test would be to prove that he actually was the kind of superior intellect, the kind of superior human being that Nietzsche spoke of, and was above the normal restrictions of the human conscience. He decided that the way to do this would be to commit the most barbaric and cruelest, but perfect, crime. He concluded that this perfect crime must involve murder, kidnapping, and ransom, even though being independently wealthy he had no need of the money. He decided, however, that to execute this crime he would need an assistant, for one person alone could not accomplish the deed. So he revealed his plans to his closest friend, Nathan Leopold, who was an equally brilliant law student and who had a kind of complementary personality to Loeb's.

Where Richard Loeb was the innovator and saw himself as superman, Nathan Leopold saw himself as the loyal follower, the loyal believer who would demonstrate his own integrity by his willingness to follow blindly the dictates of a master to whom he related as the obedient slave. These ideas seemed bizarre at that time. Since then similar ideas have become better known through experiences in Nazi Germany and elsewhere, but at that time they existed only in the abstract writing of philosophers like Nietzsche. So even though Leopold felt a strong revulsion toward what he regarded as an ugly deed, he also found it to be an ugly necessity and agreed to participate. It was his glasses that were left near the crime. Evidently there was a very strong unconscious motivation to be detected. Theirs was very far from a perfect crime, and the two boys were quickly apprehended.

Healy, Glueck, White, Bowman, and others used all their rhetoric, ingenuity, and ability to teach and lecture from the witness stand in the courtroom. At the end of a month, the judge sentenced the boys to life imprisonment without possibility of parole. Judge Calvary stated: "The court is willing to recognize that the careful analysis made of the life history of the defendants and of the present mental, emotional, and ethical condition, has been of extreme interest and is a valuable contribution to criminology." But then he went on to say, "In choosing imprisonment instead of death the court is ruled chiefly by the consideration of the age of the defendants." Clearly, this exhaustive application of psychoanalysis to the courtroom had relatively little effect on the legal decision. The impact of this case outside the courtroom, however, was very great. Although Freud and psychoanalysis were well known to psychiatric professionals, the average man in the street had never heard of Freud and never heard the word *psychoanalysis* until it screamed from the newspaper headlines.

Freud's Refusal

During the trial strenuous efforts had been made to have Freud himself come to the United States and serve as an observer in the courtroom and write a daily article. Ernest Jones writes in his biography of Freud that Gilbert Seldes, who was reporter for the McCormick paper, the Chicago Tribune, was authorized to make a deal with Freud and was given authority to send the following telegram to Freud: "Offer Freud $25,000 or anything he names to come to Chicago and psychoanalyze the murderers."[2] When the Hearst papers got wind that the McCormick papers were trying to bring Freud to Chicago and learned that Freud declined because of ill health, the Hearst interests offered Freud any sum he would care to name and told him that they were prepared to charter an ocean liner on which he would be the sole passenger. Freud was not tempted. He already had his cancer of the palate and replied by letter to Seldes:

> Your telegram reached me belatedly because of being wrongly addressed. In reply I would say that I cannot be supposed to be prepared to provide an expert opinion about persons and a deed when I have only newspaper reports to go on and have no opportunity to make a personal examination. An invitation from the Hearst Press to come to New York for the duration of the trial I have had to decline for reasons of health.

I was a school boy in Fresno, California, in 1924, and I remember very clearly the summer this trial took place. It was the first time I had ever heard of Sigmund Freud, and I was enormously fascinated with the daily reports of the trial. I went so far, at the age of twelve, to go to the library to get Freud's *Interpretation of Dreams*[3] and attempt to read it. That September when the verdict was handed down, I entered seventh grade in junior high school. One of the first things we were required to do was to write what the teacher called a "career book." I had long had vague, but uncertain, ideas about becoming a doctor. In those days when a question like this arose I would go to my father's office and ask him. My father had a male secretary, Henry, who was a good stand-in for my father. If my father was busy I would talk over the problem with Henry, who was very free with his advice. That day I went to the office to speak to my father about what I should become and what I should write about in my career book. He was busy, so I talked to Henry. I told Henry I had been reading in the newspapers about Freud and the Leopold-Loeb trial and was so fascinated that I had even gotten a book by Freud from the library. Henry asked, why don't you become a psychoanalyst? That sounded like a wonderful idea, so I immediately went home and wrote in my career book that I wanted to become a psychoanalyst. My image of the psychoanalyst was not of Freud, but of William Alanson White, the psychoanalyst in the courtroom.

My teacher was appalled to receive a career book on psychoanalysis from a twelve-year-old boy. I'm sure she assumed that I had only a morbid sexual interest. Her immediate response was to assign me to a vocational program in the junior high school. The idea, I suppose, was to provide a better balanced view of life, and I spent the next three years in studies that have profited me greatly. I learned all about automobile mechanics, woodworking, basket weaving, typing, electrical work, and plumbing—skills which I can still use to this very day — while other students were wasting their time learning English composition, literature, and things of that kind. I really didn't experience this as oppressive, but I still had in the back of my mind the idea of becoming a Freudian psychoanalyst and eventually testifying in the courtroom like William Alanson White and Healy.

The actual impact of the Leopold-Loeb trial on the law itself was minimal. Trials seldom affect the course of the law. Whatever happens in an individual trial is legally binding only for that particular case. To introduce an innovation into the law, one must attempt the innovation in the trial, fail, and then appeal the failure. If the appellate courts support the innovation and overrule the trial court, then new law is made. For good or bad reasons Darrow had won his case in that the two youthful defendants were sentenced to life in prison and escaped the hangman. Of course there was no appeal, so no legal doctrine was created by the extensive psychiatric and psychoanalytic testimony. Because there was no appeal, the Leopold-Loeb trial did not set legal precedents.

The attempt of Darrow and the expert witnesses to deal not with the issues of insanity, but rather with the inner life, emotional experience, and motivation for the criminal act itself was not of great legal influence and was not incorporated in any formal legal doctrines. Also, I think White and Glueck, and perhaps less so Healy, were hopelessly idealistic in what they hoped to achieve. For one thing, they wanted a nonadversarial process in which the psychiatrists for the defense would get together in a sort of friendly consultation with psychiatrists for the prosecution and they would all reach a common ground of understanding. Thus a battle between the experts would be avoided. The prosecuting attorney objected very strenuously to this idea and forbade any such meeting between prosecution and defense psychiatrists.

Sigmund Freud and Criminal Responsibility

Freud himself had always been exceedingly cautious about the possible application of psychoanalysis to the law. The first paper in which he demonstrated any specific interest in the application of psychoanalytic concepts to the law was in the transcript of a lecture that Freud[4] delivered in June 1906 at the request of a Professor Laufler, professor of jurisprudence at the University of Vienna. Laufler was conducting an advanced seminar in criminal jurisprudence. A number of his students had learned about a new psychological technique that had been proposed by Carl Jung but that had originally come out of Wilhelm Wundt's famous laboratory of experimental psychology. This technique involved the so-called word association test, in which one would give a person a list of words; the time the person took to respond and the number of associations would be observed; and one could make certain inferences about the emotional content of the word for the subject. Students were very much interested in the possibility of using this test as a device for determining the truth and the credibility of defendants in a criminal trial, and they asked Freud to inform them about it.

In a most interesting lecture, Freud expanded the subject matter to include the new field of psychoanalysis. He pointed out that the phenomenon of free association, which he was using as a therapeutic instrument, was very closely related to the technique of Jung, but he was very cautious about the possibilities for truth-telling by such an instrument. This is the first paper in which Freud ever mentions the name of Jung. It is also the first of Freud's papers in which he speaks of complexes, a word that was used very frequently although not originated by Jung. Freud emphasized the difference between unconscious resistance and conscious resistance and noted that such techniques as word association and free association were devices for overcoming unconscious resistances but that they had no power to overcome a conscious deceit and a conscious withholding. He also warned that there is a possibility of being "led astray by a neurotic who, although he is innocent, reacts as if he were guilty because of a lurking sense of guilt that already exists in him which seizes upon the accusation made in the particular instance."[5] He went on to describe how guilt arising from early events in childhood may make one feel guilty about an extraneous event as an adult. This was an extremely advanced and sophisticated idea for his time. He suggested that an experiment be undertaken whereby all defendants in criminal trials would be subjected to such psychoanalytic scrutiny, but *"without [the] results being allowed to influence the verdict of the Court."*[6]

The next paper by Freud dealing with the subject is his famous short paper on "Some Character Types Met with in Psychoanalytic Work,"[7] the third section of which, containing only two pages, is entitled "Criminals From the Sense of Guilt." In a rather cursory manner Freud stated that he had patients who seemed first to have developed a sense of guilt and later to have committed a crime in order to be punished and to allay that sense of guilt. He said that although the normal sequence was to commit a crime and then feel guilty, some neurotic persons could reverse this order and feel guilty and could commit a crime because of the guilt. This was, I think, the earliest attempt to make a truly dynamic explanation of some criminal behavior.

In 1922, Freud was directly involved in a court case of some interest. The son of an old servant of Freud's shot his father, though not fatally, while the father was in the act of raping the youth's half-sister. This incident obviously called for psychoanalytic intervention, not only because of the direct connection with the Freud family, but because of the important oedipal implications. Freud did not know the son personally. He did know the father and was sufficiently interested to take it upon himself to pay all the legal expenses for the boy. He felt obliged to do so because he, himself, refused to go to court to testify on the boy's behalf, but instead engaged and paid a Dr. Valentin Teirich, who was then the leading authority on forensic psychiatry in Vienna, to defend the boy. Freud wrote a memorandum to Dr. Teirich saying that he hoped there would be no attempt to seek for deeper motives, which would only obscure the facts. He advised the doctor to leave the oedipal complex out of the defense and to deal solely with the traditional concepts of insanity. Temporary insanity was accepted by the court, and the boy was acquitted and discharged.

In 1925 Freud wrote another paper in which he dealt very briefly with responsibility, specifically with responsibility for dreams.[8] In answer to the question, should one be held responsible for the content of one's dreams? Freud wrote:

> Obviously one must hold oneself responsible for the evil impulses of one's dreams. What else is one to do with them? Unless the content of the dream (rightfully understood) is inspired by alien spirits, it is a part of my own being.[9]

He concludes by saying:

> The physician will leave it to the jurist to construct for social purposes
> a responsibility that is artificially limited to the metapsychological ego. It
> is notorious that the greatest difficulties are encountered by the attempts
> to derive from such a construction practical consequences which are not
> in contradiction to human feelings.[10]

Clearly, Freud held a very low opinion of the possibilities of psychoanalysis
in the administration of justice.

The last formal contribution of Freud to the medicolegal scene occurred
in 1931 in response to his being asked to comment about some psychoanalytic or pseudopsychoanalytic testimony in the Halsmann case.[11] Halsmann
was a young student who was convicted of the crime of parricide, killing
his father. The Innsbruck faculty of medicine had given an expert opinion
about this case, which involved a lot of garbled psychoanalytic interpretations of oedipal complexes and the like and which had no particular impact
on the jury. The boy was convicted; and after the conviction, one of the
professors of medicine, who was very fond of the student, started an active
campaign to try to have a new trial of the case. To support the possibilities
of a retrial, he asked Freud for his opinion of the testimony that had been
given by the various members of the Innsbruck faculty of medicine. Freud
declined to have an opinion and said,

> Precisely because it is always present, the Oedipus complex is not suited
> to provide a decision on the question of guilt. The situation envisaged in
> a well-known anecdote might easily be brought about. There was a
> burglary. A man who had a jemmy in his possession was found guilty of
> the crime. After the verdict had been given and he had been asked if he
> had anything to say, he begged to be sentenced for adultery at the same
> time—since he was carrying the tools for that on him as well.[12]

Because of Freud's skepticism of the possibilities for using psychoanalytic
testimony in the courtroom, all well-behaved psychoanalysts, except a few
of us sort-of freaky ones, have avoided the courtroom like the plague. The
others have not, however, avoided writing and thinking and theorizing
about criminal activity, and the list of psychoanalysts who have made many
important contributions to the understanding of the psychodynamics of
crime is extensive.

Contributions of Other Psychoanalysts

These contributions range from Aichorn's[13] pioneer work on the treatment
of juvenile delinquency to Alexander and Staub's[14] classic book *The
Criminal, the Judge, and the Public*, in which they attempt a systematic
classification of criminal behavior based on psychoanalytic concepts. The

literature on the subject is considerable and includes contributions from such men as Gregory Zilboorg, Karl Menninger, Philip Roche, Edward Glover, Kurt Eissler, Robert Waelder, Jay Katz at Yale, Andrew S. Watson at Michigan, and Fritz Redl. Stanislaus Szurek, the emeritus head of the Department of Child Psychiatry, University of California, together with Adelaide M. Johnson from the Menninger Clinic, made one of the most important contributions to the understanding of adolescent delinquency. They describe the possibilities for adolescents to incorporate into their conscience or superego, not only the traditional Ten Commandments they are taught, but also the repressed and forbidden wishes of the parents. Some children, then, are destined to act out those forms of delinquency which their parents did not dare commit.

Perhaps the true importance, or lack of it, of the Leopold-Loeb trial and the strenuous efforts of William Alanson White, Bernard Glueck, William Healy, and Clarence Darrow is portrayed in the book written by Jay Katz, a psychoanalyst on the Law School faculty at Yale, Joe Goldstein, and Allan Dershowitz, now on the Harvard Law School faculty.[15] A huge compendium of everything believed to be of significance in the law and psychiatry and psychoanalysis, it contains abstracts or portions of every conceivable article and legal case deemed relevant to the modern scene. I searched through the book most carefully, and there is no mention of Leopold, Loeb, Clarence Darrow, Healy, Glueck, or William Alanson White. It is as if they just vanished from the legal scene.

Nevertheless, psychoanalysis has been an active, moving force in the law, at least outside the courtroom. The highest recognition or award given for an interest in psychiatry and the law is the Isaac Ray Award of the American Psychiatric Association. That award is given each year to the psychiatrist, lawyer, judge, or other person who is believed to have made the most important contribution in recent years to the interface of the law and psychiatry. It is interesting to review the distribution of persons who have received that award. Three judges have received it, two law professors, and eleven psychiatrists. Of the eleven psychiatrists, six are card-carrying psychoanalysts; in proportion to their numbers, psychoanalysts have been prominently recognized.

Also of interest is that at four of the major law schools in this country, psychoanalysts who are not lawyers have been given full professorships of law. Jay Katz is a professor of law at Yale, Allan Stone is professor of law at Harvard, Andrew Watson is professor of law at Michigan, and I am professor of law at Berkeley. This is a very unusual thing, for nonlawyers are not usually appointed to law school faculties. Jonas Robitscher is a professor of law at Emory University; however, he is both a psychoanalyst and a lawyer.

An opportunity arose later in California to try to do what had not been accomplished in the Leopold-Loeb trial, that is, to alter the law in such a way as to permit the regular introduction of psychodynamic, psychoanalytic material into the courtroom. Psychiatric evidence had long been introduced into the courtroom. As a matter of fact, the concept of legal insanity is much more ancient than the profession of psychiatry. Even in ancient Rome and Greece, in many early societies in the Orient, and in Biblical Hebrew society an individual who was insane was exempt from punishment. The various ways in which this would be accomplished differed until the Middle Ages. In England such a person would be convicted of a crime and then pardoned by the King. Since the Middle Ages in England and throughout all the history of the United States, a person who was so insane as not to know the difference between right and wrong, not to be able to distinguish between good and evil, was exempt from any kind of punishment and was found to be not guilty by reason of insanity. Such a concept was essentially static, in that it had nothing whatsoever to do with the events of the crime. What interested the law was exclusively the severity of the defendant's disease. Thus, if a person was so far gone that he was suffering from delusions and hallucinations, or did not know right from wrong, then he was legally insane; if he did not suffer from delusions or hallucinations, or knew right from wrong, he was sane. Psychiatrists who participated in such trials at the level of the insanity defense had no occasion to inquire into the dynamics of the criminal act.

The Tragic Case of Wesley Robert Wells

In 1949 in an unusual trial of a San Quentin prisoner, Wesley Robert Wells, a change in the law came about almost inadvertently. Wells was tried under Section 4500 of the Penal Code, which was a very harsh and cruel law stating that any person undergoing life imprisonment who committed an assault on another human being, whether a prisoner or a guard, with what the law called "malice aforethought" was subject to a mandatory death penalty. There was, however, reason to believe that Wells was a particularly objectionable prisoner to the personnel of the Department of Corrections. He could, I think, quite properly be called the original black militant. He was a man of great force of personality, a natural leader in the prison situation, and he had many very significant underground connections.

At that time, in 1949, the California prisons were very much like those of the deep South. Blacks and whites were rigorously segregated and the blacks got the worst of everything. There was reason to believe that Wells was probably the source of the leakage of information about these barbaric ethnic discriminations to various outside left-wing political groups and to others interested in prison reform. The administration of the prison seemed determined to "get" him. One day at a disciplinary hearing following a fracas in the dungeon where Wells had been confined, Wells was sitting on the floor waiting to be admitted to the hearing. The guard who testified against him came out of the hearing room and Wells picked up a cuspidor, threw it at the guard, hitting him on the face, fracturing his cheek bone, but not otherwise injuring him. For this offense Wells was indicted under Section 4500 and was subject to the mandated death penalty if convicted.

The lawyers who handled the case were at a total loss as to how to defend him. In desperation they decided to call the prison psychiatrist who had seen Wells shortly before the cuspidor event when Wells created a disturbance, shouting and banging on the walls of his solitary confinement cell. The prison physician and the psychiatrist saw Wells and concluded that he was "in a state of emotional tension" for which was prescribed a Nembutal capsule (which Wells never received). The lawyers hoped that in some way this incident might sway the court toward mercy.

A law existed, and still exists, in California requiring that when a defendant pleads not guilty by reason of insanity, there must be two trials. First there is a trial on the issue of guilt and then a trial on the issue of sanity if the defendant is found guilty in the first trial. There is no possibility of using the psychiatric evidence of the sanity trial to mitigate guilt for the first trial because the degree of guilt, whether of first-degree murder, second-degree murder or manslaughter, has already been determined by the jury. So the sole issue is that of the classical right and wrong test of insanity.

In the Wells case the judge ruled that the evidence about the state of emotional tension could not be introduced because the split-trial law forbade any kind of psychiatric evidence concerning the state of mind of the defendant; such evidence belonged only in the insanity trial. Wells was found guilty. Then there was the sanity trial, which was meaningless since the doctors had to admit that a state of emotional tension could not meet the required test of insanity. Wells was found sane, and the judge had no discretion but to sentence him to death. An appeal was made to the California Supreme Court.

It is this appeal that is of interest, for the California Supreme Court affirmed the death penalty but also admitted that the judge had made an error in excluding the psychiatric testimony. The court ruled that the judge should have admitted the testimony about an emotional state of tension during the guilt phase of the trial, for it might have had some bearing on the mental state required by the definition of the charged crime. They also ruled, however, that it really would not have made any difference, for the evidence was so trivial that it could not possibly have affected the verdict, and they affirmed the death penalty.

There was a clemency hearing before Earl Warren, who was then Governor of California. Even though Warren was an outspoken opponent of capital punishment, he was persuaded by the prison authorities that Wells was personally and politically so dangerous that he had to be put to death. Governor Warren twice refused to commute the death penalty, and Wells was on his way to the gas chamber when an unforeseen event happened. Earl Warren was appointed by President Eisenhower to be Chief Justice of the United States Supreme Court and was replaced as governor by Lieutenant Governor Goodwin Knight.

Now, Goodwin Knight was a long-time political foe of Earl Warren. While Warren was an ultraliberal Republican who opposed the death penalty, Knight was an ultraconservative Republican who was very much in favor of the death penalty. But Knight could not resist the temptation to show Warren's inconsistency. His first public act when he got into office was to commute Wesley Robert Wells's sentence to life imprisonment. That was in 1949. In 1976, almost 30 years later, Wells was finally released from prison, a very old man, not at all able to deal with the realities of life after having spent some 46 years in prison, a tragic loss of an extraordinary personality. Since that Supreme Court decision, California law has permitted psychiatrists to testify in guilt trials on the mental state of defendants as well as on the issue of insanity. But this decision was of no help to Wesley Robert Wells.

Charles Garry had assumed responsibility for Wells's appeal, and efforts were made to appeal his case to the United States Supreme Court. The attorneys were eager to get some kind of medical support for the idea that psychiatrists have something to say about the mental states required by the definition of the crime. These mental states, such as premeditation and malice aforethought, are issues quite different from those concerned with insanity. Garry and his associates searched the medical literature but found little to support their position. They came to me and asked if I would write an article on the subject that they might then quote for purposes of appeal. I agreed at least to look at the issues. I interviewed Wells and did a lot of historical research on the legal concepts. I came to the conclusion that they had a valid point and that if this legal principle had been known earlier there might have been a more meaningful and dynamic inquiry into Wells's mental state. Such an inquiry might have resulted in more than the trivial evidence of a state of emotional tension. I wrote such an article (see "With Malice Aforethought," this volume), and the attorney quoted from it. The case, however, was not accepted by the United States Supreme Court.

The Doctrine of Diminished Capacity

There were cases in California in which efforts were being made to apply this new leeway enabling psychiatrists to address issues other than insanity. Most of these cases involved Charles Garry and his associates, Dreyfus and McTernan, for the defense. The first such case concerned an analyst, Meyer Zeligs, who testified about what is now called the "diminished capacity defense" in a case of a quarrel between two homosexual men. One struck the other, who fell and hit his head on a fireplace hearth, fractured his skull, and died. At the murder trial Dr. Zeligs carefully detailed the psychodynamics that had led to the quarrel and the death of one of the men. The verdict was manslaughter, which is all that one hopes for in such a diminished capacity defense. It is not at all clear what role the psychoanalytic testimony played in the decision of this case, inasmuch as in this type of case a manslaughter verdict is possible anyway.

In this case and in others in California, Garry and Dreyfus attempted to integrate modern psychoanalytic knowledge of criminal behavior and mental disorder with traditional, time-honored, well-established legal concepts. The law in England and in the United States traditionally defines crimes in a double way. Seldom, if ever, is an act alone a crime. It is no crime to kill people. There are many circumstances in which people are killed: in war people are killed; policemen kill people; people are killed in self-defense and killed accidentally in automobiles and the like. Thus killing a person does not constitute the crime of murder. The crime of murder is defined as the unlawful killing of another human being by someone else with certain mental states. These psychological states of mind must be proved by the prosecution in order to establish the crime of murder. Without these states of mind no crime exists. There is in the law a whole range of culpability of evilness that has fundamentally religious and theological bases. Anglo-American criminal law and the law of most Western civilizations is essentially based on the writings of Augustine and Thomas Aquinas, whose views were that one is punished not for the deed alone but for the deed coupled with a particular intent. To be punishable, one must have been capable of exercising the powers of free will in the commission of crime. This requirement of free will is expressed in the law in various complicated and technical ways. For instance, for a conviction of ordinary first-degree murder, it must not only be proved that one committed an unlawful killing, but it must also be proved that one did this killing with two particular states of mind—the state of mind called premeditation, and the state of mind called malice.

These terms, malice and premeditation, have very technical, legal meanings. Customarily, the law has evolved over the centuries by retaining its words and phrases but altering the meaning of these phrases. The word malice, for example, no longer means anything having to do with malice, as such, or evil, or enmity, or anger, or hatred; it is a technical term that refers to the rational act of making a free choice to commit what is called "a man-endangering act" at the very moment of the crime. If a person possesses only malice but not premeditation, then he can be guilty only of second-degree murder; and if there is no malice but there is still an unlawful homicide, he can be guilty only of manslaughter. If there is no intent whatsoever, he may not be guilty of any crime.

The door was opened by Wells's case to the possibility of using psychoanalytic and psychodynamic testimony to comment on these mental states, which relate to the criminal act itself. Such an abnormal mental state may be far short of insanity and quite different from the delusions, hallucinations, and other conventional symptoms of insanity. Now, the testimony for the defense is for the purpose of negating or canceling out the mental states specified by the definition of the crime, permitting conviction only for a lesser offense. The effect is to eliminate what has always been the worst feature of the legal concept of responsibility: its dichotomous, all-or-none quality. Thus, instead of a defendant's being found either sane or insane, responsible or not responsible, there can be degrees of responsibility, varying all the way from first-degree murder punishable by death to misdemeanor manslaughter, which may mean only a brief stay in jail or even probation.

The Case of Nicholas Gorshen

In 1959 it was possible to clarify and test this new approach in a case that is famous in legal circles: the case of Nicholas Gorshen. Again, Mr. Garry was the attorney for the defense, and I was the testifying psychiatrist. In this case, the dynamics involved something quite opposite to the traditional insanity defense. I was prepared to testify on the basis of my clinical examination, that Gorshen was a borderline psychotic who had certain paranoid schizophrenic tendencies but who was in good contact with reality, and that the commission of the murder was necessary, psychologically necessary, to prevent a psychotic disintegration. I was satisfied from my examinations and the clinical material that could be produced that this was a believable and realistic appraisal. The theoretical basis for this case was influenced by a paper written by two San Francisco analysts, Suzanne Reichard and Carl Tillman.[16] They described cases identical to that of Nicholas Gorshen. They described an unassuagable anger that arises when certain persons are confronted with heavily loaded keywords. The Gorshen case involved a homicide committed by a middle-aged man who was undergoing a sexual decline and who was also subject to very strange hallucinatory episodes, visions in which he was being put to the test by various demonological half-animal, half-human creatures. There was a rich variety of bizarre material—of distortions of body image and sexual peculiarities in the visions, which lasted only moments.

Gorshen was not in one of these psychotic states at the time he committed the crime. He had reported for work as a longshoreman. He had a boss named Red O'Leary. Gorshen was a Russian refugee, and O'Leary, who had many Russians on his longshoremen work staff had learned to curse and swear in Russian. When he got angry with his crew, he would often use these Russian words. When Gorshen reported for work, O'Leary accused him of being drunk, which he really was not, and insisted that he get off the ship and go home. Gorshen experienced this incident as a very severe blow to his masculinity, which was already in precarious shape, and he felt it necessary to strike out and fight back. There was a fist fight, and Gorshen was knocked out cold. At the moment he lost consciousness, he was aware of a particularly vulgar curse that O'Leary had hurled at him in—an untranslatable term implying that you're a bastard and a pervert and that all your ancestors were capable of perversions. When Gorshen came to, this word was on his mind, and he had an uncontrollable urge to kill O'Leary. Gorshen was a man who previously had been quite peaceful and was never involved in fights, drunkenness, or similar violence. Nonetheless, when he woke up, he went to the edge of the ship and announced to all his fellow workers that he was going home to get a gun and was going to come back and kill O'Leary. He left the ship and drove home.

In the meantime, the police had been called and when Gorshen returned to the docks the police were waiting for him. They asked him if he was the man who was going to kill O'Leary. He said yes, he was. They patted him down but did not find a gun. They decided they had better take him to the police station anyhow. Just at that moment O'Leary walked up, and Gorshen, with a policeman at each side of him, pulled out a gun he had hidden beneath his longshoreman's apron and shot and killed O'Leary in full view of everyone.

It was not an easy act to defend. Premeditation, malice, and motivation seemed to be well established. I testified, for what I believe to be good reasons, that this case very much fitted the Reichard-Tillman description of unassuagable anger. I said that Gorshen had killed not because he was insane, but because he needed to ward off a psychosis that might develop if he were to be revealed as the totally helpless, impotent, and perverted character that was described directly to his unconscious at the climax of the fight. The trial judge (this case was tried before a judge, not a jury) admitted the evidence on the basis of the previous Wells decision. There was no attempt to plead not guilty by reason of insanity, and I was perfectly willing to concede that Gorshen was fully sane under the traditional right and wrong test. He was found guilty of second-degree murder. The judge said that my explanation of the crime seemed to him valid but that his hands were tied, that such new approaches were not permitted by existing law. There was an appeal of this case, and this time the appeal was very carefully focused on the diminished capacity defense and the use of psychodynamic testimony. A clear distinction was made between this defense and the insanity defense in the appeal. A friend-of-the-court brief was drawn up by the attorneys and was endorsed by a very impressive group of psychiatrists and psychoanalysts. To make a long story short, the California Supreme Court approved this use of expert testimony and established what is now referred to as the Wells-Gorshen Doctrine of Diminished Capacity. Subsequent decisions of the California Supreme Court have modified the definitions of other mental states required by the statutory definition of homicide. Of particular interest is a 1964 decision in which the concept of premeditation was redefined to include the level of emotional maturity of the defendant. To be guilty of premeditation, not only did one have to plan the crime beforehand, but also the crime had to be planned in a mature and meaningful way.

The Wells-Gorshen doctrine is still being developed. It is now a kind of open door to psychiatrists and analysts to present the full clinical and psychodynamic facts relating to a criminal act. One could say that, at least in the State of California and to some degree elsewhere, there are no restrictions on the admissibility of psychiatric and psychoanalytic testimony concerning the motivation, thoughts, feelings, unconscious, background, or personality characteristics of the person on trial, regardless of and quite separate from the issue of insanity. No psychiatrist can ever complain in this state that he is thwarted in his willingness to present the full details to the judge and jury.

The problem now is quite different. The admissibility of psychiatric testimony has been well established; the credibility of psychiatric testimony is still an open question.

Notes

[1]Darrow, C. (1934), *The Story of My Life*. New York: Scribners.
[2]Jones, E. (1957), *The Life and Work of Sigmund Freud*, Vol. 3. New York: Basic Books.
[3]Freud, S. (1900), *The Interpretation of Dreams*. Standard Edition, 4 & 5. London: Hogarth Press, 1953.
[4]Freud, S. (1906), Psychoanalysis and the establishment of the facts in legal proceedings. *Standard Edition*, 9:99–114. London: Hogarth Press, 1959.
[5]Ibid., p. 113.
[6]Ibid., p. 114.
[7]Freud, S. (1916), Some character types met with in psychoanalytic work. *Standard Edition*, 14:311–333. London: Hogarth Press, 1957.
[8]Freud, S. (1925), Moral responsibility for the content of dreams. *Standard Edition*, 19:131–134. London: Hogarth Press, 1961.
[9]Ibid., p. 133.
[10]Ibid., p. 134.
[11]Freud, S. (1931), The expert opinion in the Halsman case. *Standard Edition*, 21:251–253. London: Hogarth Press, 1961.
[12]Ibid., p. 252.
[13]Aichorn, A. (1935), *Wayward Youth*. New York: Viking.
[14]Alexander, F. & Staub, H. (1931), *The Criminal, the Judge, and the Public: A Psychological Analysis*, trans. G. Zilboorg. New York: Macmillan. (Revised 1956, Glencoe, IL: Free Press.)
[15]Katz, J., Goldstein, J. & Dershowitz, A. (1967), *Psychoanalysis, Psychiatry and Law*. New York: Free Press.
[16]Reichard, S. & Tillman, C. (1950), Murder and suicide as a defense against schizophrenic psychosis. *J. Clin. Psychopath.*, 11(4):149–163.

The Origins and Development of the "Wild Beast" Concept of Mental Illness and Its Relation to Theories of Criminal Responsibility

with Anthony Michael Platt
[1956]

The object of this paper is to identify and trace the "wild beast" concept of mental illness with special reference to legal insanity and to historical materials, which include descriptive and definitive accounts of mental disorders. Legal historians have severely neglected the relationship between medicine and the law, and most information in this field has been assembled from secondary sources. The "wild beast" test of criminal responsibility has been treated with condescension and ridicule by so many writers that it has come to play a mythological role in the history of the behavioral sciences. In this paper, we shall first trace the "wild beast" test of criminal responsibility in a legal context and explain how it was introduced and perpetuated in the literature of the law. After commenting upon the etymology of this phrase, we shall speculate on the nature of those sociolegal labels which are applied in general to the mentally ill and which are more clearly viewed in an historical perspective.

The "Wild Beast" Test of Criminal Responsibility

The criminal law of England and the United States, from its earliest systematization in the middle of the thirteenth century until the present day, has always considered insanity as a mitigating or exculpating factor that exempts the accused from punishment.[1] The primary test of criminal responsibility in all English-speaking countries is the 1843 M'Naghten Rule,

19

which, *inter alia*, exempts from punishment those persons who do not know the difference between right and wrong at the time of committing a criminal act. As for tests of insanity before 1843, there has been little systematic research or even interest. Weihofen agreed with the English jurist Stephen that the early materials concerning insanity should be regarded as little more than "antiquarian curiosities."[2] The Royal Commission on Capital Punishment (1949–53) noted that "little need be said of the development of the law (of insanity) before the case of M'Naghten in 1843."[3] According to Hibbert, "it was not until the seventeenth century that the first legal decisions that have any relevance to the modern attitudes towards responsibility were taken in Europe."[4] The general thesis supported by lawyers and historians alike is that the "wild beast" test of criminal responsibility originated with the English judge Henry de Bracton in 1256, was developed and approved during the next five centuries, and was finally dogmatized by Judge Tracy at the trial of Edward Arnold in 1724. Thus, Guttmacher (1961) has suggested that "Bracton, in the first systematic treatise on English law, written in the 13th century, asserted that, an insane person should not be held morally accountable since he was not far removed from a *beast*"[5] (*italics* added).

Judge Biggs quoted Bracton as saying that "Such (mad)men are not greatly removed from *beasts* for they lack reasoning"[6] (*italics* added).

Sheldon Glueck also reported that Bracton supplied us with "the wild beast or wild brute test."[7] Moreover, Lloyd (1905) criticized Judge Tracy for citing the "primitive and crude . . . wild beast theory of the Roman Law and of Bracton."[8] Judge Bazelon (1960) noted that:

> As early as the thirteenth century, British law recognized that "a madman does not know what he is doing." In 1724 Judge Tracy held that insanity was exculpatory if the defendant "doth not know what he is doing, no more than . . . a wild beast." Thirty-six years later the "wild beast test" was abandoned in favor of the defendant's capacity to distinguish between "right and wrong"–the precursor of the M'Naghten Rules.[9]

Henry de Bracton and the "Wild Beast" Test

The criminal law of England was in a critical and nebulous state when Henry de Bracton wrote the first comprehensive legal treatise on the English system. Written in Latin, his work, *De Legibus et Consuetudinibus Angliae*, was finished by about 1256, and Reeves held that it was "a finished and systematic performance, giving a complete view of the law in all its titles, as it stood when it was written."[10] Much has been written about Bracton's "Romanism" and he has been accused of plagiarism and legal trickery. Maine even called him an inexplicable fraud and impostor. "When I rely on authority of Bracton," wrote Sir William Jones, "I am perfectly aware that he copied Justinian almost word for word."[11] In recent years, however, Bracton's originality and legal scholarship have been recognized, and Maitland said that "the substance of Bracton's work is English. He writes no less than five hundred decisions of the King's Judges."[12] It is true that Bracton made extensive use of English case materials but, in areas where the law was deficient or uncertain, he borrowed freely from the Romanists and Canonists. For example, his treatment of homicide was actually transplanted from a discourse by the distinguished canonist Bernard de Pavia, and many of his references to the civil liabilities of infants and the insane closely paralleled the ideas of Justinian and Gaius.

As well as being a Chief Justiciary of the highest court, Bracton was also a prominent ecclesiastic, and in 1264 he became Archdeacon of Barnstaple and Chancellor of Exeter Cathedral. His legal writings consequently reflected both the theoretical and the practical experiences of his career and demonstrated the constant interaction between Church and State. As Sayre has pointed out, "the early felonies were roughly the external manifestations of the heinous sins of the day."[13]

It is not only the worst kind of historical scapegoating but also a distortion of factual evidence to reduce Bracton's sophistication and scholarship concerning criminal intent and responsibility to a single glib maxim such as the "wild beast" test. Bracton's conceptualization of insanity did not rely on any such crude test; using the conceptual framework of Continental jurisprudence, he was the first English lawyer to classify and incorporate into working definitions the mental element in crime. In accordance with his religious training and reliance on canon law, Bracton (1569) emphasized subjective intent as a necessary criterion of criminal behavior. Corporal homicide may be committed

> by act in four ways, i.e., by [the administration of] justice, by misadventure or by desire. By justice, as when the judge or justiciar or his officer kills a criminal justly condemned. But it is homicide, if it be done from malignity or through delight in shedding human blood; although the criminal be justly killed, nevertheless because of the corrupt intent the judge commits mortal sin (*peccat mortaliter*).[14]

Although Bracton's book was an accurate statement of actual practices, it is evident that much of his conceptualization was not derived from English sources. For example, another text held that,

A crime is not implied unless the will to harm intervenes, and the will
and the purpose reveal malice (maleficium), and theft is not committed
without the disposition to steal. And this is in accordance with what
might be said of the infant or madman, since the innocence of judgment
protects the one and imbecility of the deed excuses the other.[15]

Bracton specifically excused madmen from criminal sanctions and civil
liability in another text dealing with suicide. He wrote:

But what shall be said of the madman who has no reason, and of
the lunatic and the raving, or of the child, or if he who labours in a
severe illness drowns himself, it is asked whether he commits a felony
against himself. It seems that they do not, nor do they forfeit their
inheritance or their chattels, because they lack sense and reason and can
no more do wrong or commit a felony than a *brute animal* (*brutum
animal*), since they are not far [from being] brutes (*brutis*), according to
what can be seen in the minor, if he kills someone while under age, he
will not suffer judgment.[16]

There are other important noncriminal references to insanity and
infancy, and in this respect Bracton closely followed Justinian. Despite this
plagiarism, Bracton was the first English lawyer to limn the legal concepts
of insanity and infancy:

A madman cannot make an agreement nor do any business because he
does not understand what he is doing. The same may be said of infants;
for they are not very different from madmen (*multu a furioso no distat*)
and cannot do any business unless this is done for their advantage and
by the authority of a tutor.[17]

Bracton also noted that contracts with madmen were not valid because
"such persons are not much different from brutes (*brutis*) which lack
reasoning, nor should anything which is done with such people be valid as
long as their madness lasts."[18]

The foregoing texts demonstrate that Bracton had a great deal to say
about the criminal responsibility of the insane, and nowhere did he
compare such persons to "wild beasts." Bracton was very sophisticated, even
by modern standards, in his description of the criminal offender who was
insane. Such a person could not be guilty of a crime because he did not
have a "corrupt intent" or the "will to harm" or "malice"; he was protected
by the "imbecility of the deed:" his lack of "reason," "sense," and "understanding;" and his likeness to a "young child" or "brute animal."

Bracton's reference to *brutis* was abstracted by later translators and
interpreters of *De Legibus*, and his numerous statements concerning the
criminal responsibility of the insane were reduced to the form of a maxim.

Although it is clear from the original text that Bracton did not have "wild beasts" in mind when he used the phrase *brutis*, it is possible to understand how this misinterpretation was incorporated into legal literature. Bracton's influence varied from century to century, and after 1350 his popularity waned. His broad cosmopolitan learning gave way to the technical science of procedure. From the end of the thirteenth century to the middle of the sixteenth century few comprehensive legal treatises were written, and it is necessary to rely on the *Year Books* for an account of legal proceedings during this period. Many reported cases demonstrate how the law was consolidated during these 300 years and how medieval legal science established a hard core of practical decisions from which the "common law" was not to emerge as a body of flexible principles until the seventeenth century. "In England," wrote Maitland, "the new learning (Renaissance) found a small, well-conquered, much governed kingdom, a strong legislating kingship. It came to us soon; it taught us much; and then there was healthy resistance to foreign dogmas."[19] During this interim period, there were no references to Bracton's so-called "wild beast" test, although there were numerous descriptions of the insane as *demens, furiosus, insanis,* and *non compos mentis.*[20]

Centuries after his death, the printing press reestablished Bracton's position in English literature. The first edition of his work in 1569 proved an antidote to theories of state absolutism that the later Tudors and Stuarts had proposed. The great English lawyer and politician Sir Edward Coke incorporated many of Bracton's ideas into his treatise on the criminal law. Coke (1777) was not an original legal thinker, but he was the first English jurist "who attempted anything like a scientific treatment of the subject of insanity."[21] He was also an excellent synthesizer and, in the *Beverly* Case, he condensed much of the law that appeared in the earlier law reports and dogmatized Bracton's writings concerning insanity. The *Beverly* Case, which was first published at the beginning of the seventeenth century, was essentially concerned with civil rights and liabilities, but included the following reference to the criminal law's attitude toward insanity:

> But the punishment of a man who is deprived of reason and understanding, cannot be an example to others. No felony or murder can be committed without a felonious intent and purpose . . . *"furiosus non intelligit quid agit et animo et ratione caret, et non multum distat a brutis,"* as Bracton saith, and therefore he cannot have felonious intent . . . [22]

This Latin abstraction from Bracton's work was not translated[23] until it reappeared in 1678 in the writings of Sir Matthew Hale, who was Lord

Chief Justice of the King's Bench from 1671 to 1676. Hale's *History of the Pleas of the Crown* included a comprehensive account of the law concerning insanity in which he noted that, if madmen, or *dementes*, are "totally depriv'd of the use of reason, they cannot be guilty of capital offenses, for they have not use of understanding, and act not as reasonable creatures, but their actions are in effect in the condition of *brutes*" (*italics* added).[24]

Hale's translation of Bracton's phrase as "brutes" was later developed by Judge Tracy at the trial of Edward Arnold in 1724. Many modern legal authorities, including the Royal Commission on Capital Punishment,[25] and Judge Bazelon in the *Durham* Case, have blamed Tracy for exploiting the "wild beast" test. This, in fact, is a cruel distortion and simplification of what the Judge actually said,[26] as the following extract from his summing up to the jury demonstrates:

> If he was under the visitation of God, and could not distinguish between good and evil, and did not know what he did, though he committed the greatest offense, yet he could not be guilty of any offense against any law whatsoever; . . . a mad man . . . must be a man that is totally deprived of his understanding and memory, and doth not know what he is doing, no more than an infant, than a *brute, or a wild beast*, such a one is never the object of punishment[27] (*italics* added).

Judge Tracy's opinion represented a medley of legal theories of responsibility mixed with popular superstition about mental illness. He was not a judicial innovator, and his use of the phrases "brute" and "wild beast" reflected his reliance on authoritative legal opinion. He was indebted especially to earlier jurists, and parts of his summing up in the *Arnold* Case improvised upon and paraphrased the writings of Coke and Hale.[28] However, Tracy certainly played an important role in perpetuating the "wild beast" myth, and U.S. jurists incorporated his account of the test (albeit in a simplified form) into the main body of U.S. law.[29]

Finally, it should be pointed out that between the times of Bracton and Coke, the criminal law made no references to either "brutis" or "wild beasts" and the usual legal description of a madman was by *demens et furiosus* or *demens et furiens*.[30] The "wild beast" concept emerged finally in the seventeenth century as a result of a mistranslation of *brutis*. It was not inherent in the early written law of insanity and it never appeared in any definition of insanity; moreover, it certainly was not part of Roman law, as some writers have suggested.[31]

Brutes and Beasts

The Latin word *brutis* was used by Bracton to distinguish human beings from dumb animals and to emphasize the lack of reason that is usually attributed to madmen; according to Bracton, the phrase did not connote "wildness" or "beastliness." However, Bracton was using the word in a specialized form and according to a particular intellectual tradition.[32] Bracton was not only a jurist who was familiar with the traditions and techniques of Continental jurisprudence; he was also a churchman, trained in ecclesiastical matters and comfortable with the philosophical disputes within the Church. Bracton's use of *brutis* was in fact shorthand for *brutis animalibus*,[33] which may be literally translated as "brute" or "dumb animals." This expression and idea was used particularly by the canonists to distinguish humans from animals. Bracton correctly observed that "animals which lack reason"[34] do not possess the will or intent to do harm; consequently, they are not to be considered legally accountable. It was quite legitimate for Bracton to include the insane in this conceptual framework because they, too, like dumb animals, were considered to be lacking in will and understanding. His reference to *brutis* was not meant to associate the insane with wild beasts but rather to place them in the category of animals (or beasts[35]) as opposed to rational human beings.

Bracton was using the notion of reason as a distinguishing criterion between human beings and animals in the same sense that it occurred to many leading philosophers and lawyers. Saint Augustine (353–430), for example, argued that the human will contains liberty of choice so that man cannot blame God for his own faults because he is "not like a horse or a mule, which have no understanding."[36] *Bruta* was first used in late Latin, in the sense of brute or dumb animals, by Pope Gregory in 604.[37] Catholic doctrine in effect downgraded animals in order to emphasize man's use of reason and understanding. Bracton was using *brutis* in the same way that his contemporary, Thomas Aquinas, had used it in the *Summa Theologica*:

> Man has free choice, or otherwise counsels, exhortations, commands, prohibitions, rewards and punishment would be in vain. In order to make this evident, we must observe that some things act without judgment, as a stone moves downwards; and in like manner all things which lack knowledge. And some act from judgment, but not a free judgment; as *brute animals*. For the sheep seeing the wolf judges it a thing to be shunned, from a natural and not a free judgment; because it judges, not

from deliberation, but from natural instincts, and the same thing is to be said of any judgment in *brute animals*. But man acts from judgment, because by his apprehensive power he judges that something should be avoided or sought (*italics* added).[38]

Bracton, like Aquinas, considered brute animals as lower creatures lacking in wit, discretion, and understanding. The category "brute animals" included wild and beastlike creatures, but the term itself had a much broader designation, symbolizing and distinguishing, by exclusion, the special human characteristics that God gave to humans.

Many of the moral treatises of the fourteenth and fifteenth centuries were instruction manuals that taught the layman how to live a godly life and how to make the fullest use of his human attributes:

> For there is nothing to distinguish between man and beast except understanding. Do not glorify in anything but that. You who are proudest of your strength, you shall be surpassed by animals. You who are proudest of your swiftness, you shall be surpassed by the slowest of the flies. You who are proudest of your beauty, see how much beauty there is in the feathers of a peacock. In what then are you worth more? In God's image. Wherein does God's image lie? In thought and understanding. Then if you are better than a beast it is because you have thought, whereby you understand that which a beast cannot understand. Therefore, in truth, a man is far better than a beast (*italics* added).[39]

The European legal scholar, Samuel Pufendorf, writing in 1688, acknowledged this use of "brute beasts" in the original sense of the phrase:

> And here we hold, that no man of mature years and possessed of reason, is too dull to comprehend at least the general precepts of natural law, especially those which are most commonly kept by society, and observe to what extent they accord with the rational and social nature of man. ... For these general precepts have been so fully set forth, and so interwoven with nature that *man can never descend so nearly to the level of brute beasts* as to be incapable of understanding and judging between them. Why, no outstanding mental ability is required for this or any special intellectual acumen, but the ordinary light of one's native wit is sufficient, provided the mind be not affected by some disorder (*italics* added).[40]

Bracton made his reference to "brutes" with this categorical division between "man" and "beast" in mind. "Beast," like "brute" was not used in the sense of "wild," "carnal," or "sensual" but merely to distinguish lower beings from rational beings. Furthermore, Bracton used the phrase to emphasize and elaborate his idea that the insane lacked reason and understanding; he did not, as many jurists and historians have suggested, make the phrase the focus of a test of responsibility for the mentally ill. Moreover, he did not use the phrase "wild beast," and, if he had so wished, a whole range of perfectly suitable Latin phrases were at his disposal.

Wildness, Beastliness and Madness

Until recent times, lay ideas of mental illness were strongly influenced by theological teachings concerning the nature of Man and his relationship with God. The social and economic power of the Church in the Middle Ages encouraged a theological (or supernatural) explanation of mental illness whereby the only permissible and legitimate means of relief from distress was through the offices of the Church, whose agents were solely empowered to perform healing rites and prescribe treatment. Consequently, the early psychology of the mentally ill explained "insanity" in terms of spirit possession and exorcism. Religious scholars devoted whole treatises to techniques and rituals of exorcism (*modus juvandi afflictos a daemone*) in much the same way that modern experts have overburdened the literature with textbooks on psychotherapy.[41]

Bracton's casual reference to the insane being like *brutis* has wider implications for extralegal writings in the Middle Ages; the literature of that age solidifies his analytical assessment into a more concrete and fundamental relationship, for animals and the insane were both considered embodiments of evil spirits. Underlying the "wild beast" myth is the notion that insanity is somehow related to Satanic agencies of evil and that the mentally ill are therefore supernaturally endowed with unpredictable and magical powers. The tendency to displace insanity onto bestial and animal forms may also signify the threatening, nonpersonal[42] characteristics that were attributed to the insane. Thus, one medieval treatise noted that in the insane "reason is dead and therefore they live like animals for their wisdom is all gone astray and perverted."[43] As a result of this status degradation, the mentally ill were often a source of entertainment and amusement,[44] as well as of fear and danger.[45] Thomas Bakewell, a nineteenth-century reformer of lunatic asylums commented how "a maniac confined in the room over my own . . . bellowed like a wild beast and shook his chain, almost constantly for several days and nights. . . . I therefore got up, took a hand whip and gave him a few smart stripes upon the shoulder. . . . He disturbed me no more."[46]

Catholic dogma distinguished human beings from animals by assigning to human beings the possibility of an immortal soul.[47] At the same time, animals were considered appropriate objects of punishment and excommunication. One means of reconciling these views—endowing animals with intelligence and souls without contradicting Christian dogmas—was to assume that they were incarnations of evil spirits. This notion seems to have been generally accepted in the Middle Ages. The fact that evil spirits are often mentioned in the Bible metaphorically or symbolically as animals and assumed to be incarnate, especially the adder, the asp, the serpent, and the swine, confirms this view. Bartholomew Chassenée, a distinguished French jurist of the sixteenth century, documented much literary and theological evidence to justify the policy of cursing and punishing animals. He noted, *inter alia*, that "the anathema then is not to be pronounced against the animals as such, but should be hurled inferentially at the devil, who makes use of irrational creatures to our detriment."[48] As a result of this philosophical trickery, it was possible to reconcile man's cruel treatment of animals with the goodness and omniscience of an all-wise God. Père Bougeant, an eighteenth-century Jesuit priest, explained that the Christian church did not consider it a duty to protect lower animals, for the good Catholic became an efficient coworker with God by maltreating brutes and thus aiding God in the punishment of devils.[49]

As irrational beings, the insane were also considered proper objects of diabolical intervention, who had to be carefully guarded and even "treated" in order to expel the devils. Since animals and the "insane" alike were considered peculiarly liable to diabolical possession, a relationship between these two categories was tacitly understood. This juxtaposition of animals with the mentally ill is clearly depicted in the Biblical story of Jesus and Legion.[50] The "insane" or "possessed" were compared only to dangerous and wild kinds of animals, for not all animals were regarded as diabolical incarnations. For example, a fifteenth-century treatise by Chambery distinguished between sweet beasts (*bestes doulces*) and stenchy beasts (*bestes puantes*). Chief among the stenchy or offensive beasts were the pig, the wolf, the fox, and the boar; it was especially in these animals, as well as in the "insane," that evil spirits sought refuge and cooperation.[51]

This tendency to equate the insane with animals was not only a product of medieval superstition and Church psychology, but also found its place in a more scientific age. Lombroso's theory of constitutional criminality openly embraced such a notion, obscuring and even obliterating the line of distinction between human beings and animals.[52] Some writers have exploited this concept to emphasize the social uselessness of criminals and the mentally ill.[53] Others have used the same argument to promote reformistic and welfare campaigns on behalf of social misfits and pariahs.[54]

Underlying most of these descriptions and social movements concerning mental illness is the assumption that insanity is the ultimate catastrophe to befall a human being; the rationale for this attitude appears to stem from the notion that the mentally ill are not really human beings at all but have regressed to a state of "animal appetency."[55]

The "Wild Beast" Myth of Mental Illness

The "wild beast" myth is a recurring motif in the history of the criminal law and has indirectly contributed to the development of attitudes toward mental illness. It is profitable to examine this test in the context of broader social implications, bearing in mind that it was generated by an historical accident. Some writers might explain the crystalization of this test in terms of an unconscious longing for a childlike world of myths and unreality or as an indication of underlying themes of magical and primary process thinking in the law.[56] Without taking such a speculative and unverifiable position it is still possible to understand the "wild beast" test as a significant archetype in the history of law and medicine. Modern surveys have confirmed the suspicion that most people regard "insanity" as extremely intolerable when it is manifested by unpredictably wild or inappropriate behavior in a social milieu.[57] The literature and folklore of mental illness contains numerous allusions to the "insane" as "ferocious," "uncontrollable," and "savage."[58] It is probably a mistake to take these phrases—or the "wild beast" test—as a literal indication of how the mentally ill were treated in the Middle Ages.[59] Sarbin pointed out that, in the Middle Ages, symbols that were already in existence to denote "distal events" (rain, sun, fire, people, and so on) were borrowed from metaphors to denote "proximal events" (aches, hurts, itches, for example).[60] He further hypothesized that the commonest forms of metaphors were composed through analogy; according to this construct, it might be posited that the earliest metaphors describing mental illness were borrowed from the physical, distal world and the linguistic constructs of the hunter. Thus, the insane, like wild beasts, were to be avoided, or segregated, or feared (or even eliminated).[61] Later, the term "wild beast" became reified and was used in the literature first as a metaphor and then as a myth.[62]

Wildness and Childishness

The "wild beast" myth has its "natural contrary"[63] in the immaturity concept of mental illness. The mentally ill have been popularly caricatured as either wild or idiotic, raging or withdrawn, uncontrollable or unresponsive. As Samuel Farr, a nineteenth-century physician noted, "The insane are either furious or melancholic."[64] These two labels symbolize the extremes of behavior that society has designated "mentally deviant"; both definitions have played major roles in legal theories of criminal responsibility. Outside the law, the immaturity concept has been generally used to describe those persons who either regress to infantile modes of behavior or fail to develop adult modes of behavior.

Children and the insane have usually been exempted from punishment and treated as nonpersons by the law. This association may be partly explained as a result of the doctrine of moral blameworthiness, which assumes the criminal offender to be endowed with free will and the ability to discriminate rationally between right and wrong. Children and the insane are alike in that they are considered to be morally blameless in the eyes of the law.[65] The law does not explicitly recognize any other similarities between these two categories, although the "right and wrong" test of insanity developed out of much older tests of infant capacity.[66] Moreover, the paternalistic approach of the mental hospital toward its patients demonstrates a more fundamental relationship between these two social groups. Thomas Bakewell, an important nineteenth-century reformer, urged "a sweeping legislative measure, that should recognize every Lunatic as a Child of the State."[67]

The "infancy" concept of mental illness finally emerged from the reform movements as an antidote to cruder and less humanitarian approaches; it was adopted by reformers as a slogan and propaganda tool. This metaphor is no longer popular because the cause for which it was developed is not of immediate concern to laypeople or reformers.[68] Its influence, however, is still felt because the status of the mentally ill has not been radically transformed during this century. The logical implications of treating and labeling the insane as though they were children is that the wider society also relates to the mentally ill paternalistically. In many respects, this social policy is to be encouraged because it encompasses all the compassionate and tolerant aspects of social welfare. In contrast to the absolutely illegitimate and negative connotations of the "wild beast" role for mental patients, the "child" role has become sufficiently institutionalized to allow mental patients partial legitimacy and interaction with other members of the community. The "child" role exposes the patient to reintegrative forces because it is not as threatening to the community as the "wild beast" role.[69]

There is a real danger in oversimplifying this construct by regarding the two definitions as somehow antithetical, for the successful institutionalization of the "child" role was due partly to its ability to incorporate and modify some aspects of the "wild beast" model. The stereotype of childlike behavior includes uncontrolled and uninhibited activity as well as innocence and naiveté. Myths about childhood are full of accounts of children's relationships with animals and wild beasts.[70] The idea that children left to themselves will soon become like animals played a significant part in the notorious reports of the "Wild Man" or "*Homo Ferus.*"[71] Freud analyzed the same concept in more sophisticated terms while at the same time contributing to the folklore. Moreover, it should be noted that the "child" model of mental illness symbolizes the fixed, irremediable position of such persons and excludes for them the developmental capacities of "normal" children. Underlying the definition of madness as a kind of innocent childishness are the dramatic and fearful connotations of the "wild beast" myth. This unresolved tension has far-reaching implications for the labeling and treatment of the mentally ill.

Notes

[1] Under Section 26 of the California Penal Code, "lunatics and insane persons" are not considered persons "capable of committing crime." The criminal responsibility of the mentally ill in California is defined by the Rules from *M'Naghten's Case*, 10 Clark and F. 200: 8 Eng. Rep. 718, 1843. The earliest comprehensive and systematic reference to criminal responsibility in English law may be found in Bracton, H. de (1569) *De Legibus et Consuetudinibus Angliae, Libri Quinq* . . . London: Richard Tottel, at Cap. 17 and Cap. 31. Bracton completed this work around 1256.

[2] Weihofen, H. (1933), *Insanity As A Defense in Criminal Law.* New York: Commonwealth Fund.

[3] Royal Commission, (1949–53), *Report on Capital Punishment.* Cmd. 8932.

[4] Hibbert, C. (1963), *The Roots of Evil.* Westport, CT.

[5] Guttmacher, M. S. (1961), A historical outline of the criminal law's attitude toward mental disorder. *Arch. Crim. Psychodynamics,* 4:648–670.

[6] Biggs, J. (1955), *The Guilty Mind.* New York: Harcourt, Brace.

[7] Glueck, S. (1925), *Mental Disorder and the Criminal Law.* Boston: Little, Brown.

[8] Lloyd, J. H. (1905), Insanity: Forms and medicolegal relations. In: *Medical Jurisprudence,* ed. F. Wharton & M. Stillé. Rochester. New York: Lawyers' Cooperative.

[9] Bazelon, D. L. (1960), The awesome decision. *Saturday Evening Post,* January 23. Judge Bazelon expresses the same opinion in *Durham v. U.S.,* 214 F. 2d 682, 874 (D.C. Cir. 1954). See also Leifer, R. (1964), The psychiatrist and tests of criminal responsibility. *Amer. Psychologist,* 19:825. In 1724, Judge Tracy formulated the "wild beast" test according to which an offender was not responsible for his actions if he could not distinguish good from evil more

than a wild beast. This test held that it was the function of reason that distinguished man from beast.

[10]Reeves. (1869), *History of the English Law*, Vol. 11. London, p. 86.

[11]Quoted by Lloyd, op. cit., sup. note 8, p. 509.

[12]Quoted in Maxwell, W. H. (1925), *Complete Law Book Catalogue: A Bibliography of English Law to 1650*. London: Sweet & Maxwell, p. 38. See also Allen, C. K. (1958), *Aspects of Justice*. London, p. 289: ". . . Bracton was for long looked down on as a mere plagiarist, or even impostor. Modern scholarship has crushed this slander. Bracton was, in truth, English of the English, and though he chose a Romanistic pattern, his work is full of native doctrines which would have startled Justinian."

[13]Sayre, F. B. (1931–32), Mens rea. *Harvard L. Rev.*, 45:994–1026.

[14]Bracton, H. de. op. cit., sup. note 1, Fol. 120b; translated by Sayre, op. cit., sup. note 13, p. 984.

[15]Ibid., Lib. iii, Cap. 17. Bracton took the latter part of this quotation, almost word for word, from Justinian's *Digest*, XLVLII, 8, 12: "Infans, vel furiosus, si hominem occiderunt, lege Cornelia non Tenetur: cum alterum consilii tuctur, alterum fati infelicitas excusat."

[16]Ibid., Fol. 150, Cap. 31. Unless otherwise stated the passages from De Legibus et Consuetudinibus Angliae were translated by Jerry R. Craddock, Department of Romance Philology, University of California, Berkeley.

[17]Ibid., Fol. 100 Bracton extracted this text from Justinian 3, 19, 8; 3, 19, 1): "A madman can transact no business, because he does not understand what he is doing . . . an infant and one almost an infant do not differ much from a madman (non multum a furioso distant), because pupils of this age have no understanding (nullum intellectum habent)."

[18]Bracton, op. cit., sup. note 1, Lib. V, Cap. 20.

[19]Maitland, F. W. (1900), *The Law Quart. Rev.*, 14:33.

[20]A Coroner's Case in 1396 reported that "it happened . . . that Edith Rogers of Wick, who was demented and insane (demens et insania), was drowned in a little well filled with rainwater on the highway . . . and was found dead" (Select Coroner's Roll, Roll of John Trye. *Selden Society*, Vol. 5, p. 49). See also Select Coroner's Rolls, Hundred of Dengie. Great Maldon, Essex. *Seldon Society*, p. 46.

[21]Lloyd, op. cit., sup. note 8, p. 515.

[22]Coke, E. (1777), *The Reports of Sir Edward Coke*, Vol. 2, ed. G. Wilson, p. 124.

[23]This quotation was not accurately abstracted but represented a synthesis of two widely separated phrases. See Lloyd, op. cit. sup. note 8, p. 510.

[24]Hale, M. (1736) *Historia Placitorum Coronae [The History of the Pleas of the Crown]*. London: E. & R. Nutt & R. Gosling.

[25]*Royal Commission on Capital Punishment*, op. cit., sup. note 3, p. 75.

[26]Sheldon Glueck was the first to absolve Judge Tracy of this charge. See Glueck, op. cit., sup. note 7, p. 139.

[27]Howell, T. B., compiler (1816), The trial of Edward Arnold. In: A *Complete Collection of State Trials*, 15:465. London: T. C. Hansard.

[28]Tracy noted that "punishment is intended for example, and to deter other persons from wicked designs; but the punishment of a mad man . . . can have no example." This was a paraphrase of Coke's statement that "the punishment of a man who is deprived of reason and understanding, cannot be an example to others."

[29]See, for example, *State v. Jones*, 50 N. H. 369; 9 Am. Rep. 242, 1871.

[30]An entry from the Roll of Kent Eyre of Edward II, in 1313, reported that one Geoffrey *"lanquam demens et furiosus occidit predictum J. et non per feloniam" (Selden Society,* vol. 24, p. lxxi).

[31]Lloyd, op. cit., sup. note 8, p. 524. Justinian referred to "wild beasts" as *"ferae bestiae"* (Institutes, 2, 1, 12).

[32]The Latin word *"brutus"* has a Greek origin, coming from "brithus" which was used in the sense of "heavy" or "unwieldly." In classical Latin, it had the same literal significance of "heavy or immovable," but it was used figuratively to describe "dull," "stupid," "insensible," or "unreasonable." It was also used figuratively of animals in the sense of the Greek *anaisthelos,* which signified "irrational" or "lacking perception." It was used only in late Latin as a general designation of animals or beasts as opposed to men, in the sense of "brute" or "dumb animals." In the English language, "brute" has been used generally but perhaps remains nearest to distinguishing the difference between man and beast. "Brutish" means "uncultured" or "crude." whereas "brutal" implies "cruelty" of "lack of feeling." "Beastly" expresses that which is "disgusting" in human conduct and "bestial" is applied to that which is "carnal," "sensual" or "lascivious."

[33]Bracton, op. cit., sup. note 1, Fol. 150, Cap. 31.

[34]Ibid., Lib. V, Cap. 20.

[35]The word "beast" carries the added implications of "ferocity," "strangeness," and "carnality." Simply to observe that Bracton compared the insane with "beasts" is misleading because it exploits an ambiguous linguistic symbol.

[36]Augustinus, Saint Aurelius, *On Grace and Free Will,* Chap. 4.

[37]Maximus, Pope Gregorius, *Job,* 10, 13, 23, 17, 30, 46: quoted in *Harper's New Latin Dictionary* 1907), revised by C. T. Lewis & C. Short. New York: Harper, p. 253.

[38]Aquinas, Saint Thomas, *Summa Theologica,* Question 83, Article 1: published in Pegis, A. C., ed. (1945) *Basic Writings of Saint Thomas Aquinas.* New York.

[39]Michel, D. (1340), *Ayenbite of Inwyt [Remorse of Conscience],* ed. by R. Morris, (Trans. M. B. King, Dept. of Comparative Literature, University of California, Berkeley). London: The Early English Text Society, p. 270, 1866. Robert Burton, in his classic treatise on melancholy, developed this theme more systematically: "three differences appear between a man and a beast; at first, the sense only comprehends 'singularities,' the understanding 'universalities;' secondly, the sense hath no innate notions; thirdly, brutes cannot reflect upon themselves. Bees indeed make neat and curious works, and many other creatures besides: but when they have done, they cannot judge of them"

(Burton, R. [1927], *The Anatomy of Melancholy*, ed. F. Dell & P. Jordan-Smith. New York: Farrar & Rinehart, 1941, p. 144; reprinted by Tudor, 1951).

[40]Pufendorf, S. (1688), The law of nature and nations. In: *The Classics of International Law*, ed. J. B. Scott (1907). Washington, DC: Carnegie Institution of Washington, p. 40. Thomas Hobbes also uses this expression in a discussion of "naturall witte" or "sense": "By Naturall, I mean not that which a man hath from his Birth: for that is nothing else but Sense; wherein men differ so little from one another, and from brute Beasts as it is not to be reckoned amongst Vertues" (Hobbes, T. [1651], *Leviathan*. London, p. 32).

[41]As late as 1851, one Catholic scholar maintained that most so-called nervous diseases and milder forms of mental illness were caused or greatly aggravated by diabolical agencies. See, for example, Lobhauer, Pater F. X. (1851), *Rituale ecclesiasticum ad usum clericorum S. Francisci*, Munich.

[42]This term has been used by sociologists (especially Erving Goffman) to describe those persons who are not acknowledged within an institutional system. The insane and infants are "nonpersons" when they are not treated as a reference for decisions concerning their own interest and welfare; they are outside "a defined cultural territory." See Erikson, K. T. (1962), Notes on the sociology of deviance. *Social Problems*, 9:307.

[43]Michel, op. cit., sup. note 39, p. 29.

[44]The laws of Henry I (1118) discussed the problem of criminal liability. "if someone should be brought [to see] the show of a wild beast or lunatic and should suffer any harm from them . . ." (*Leges Henrici Primi*, c. 90, 11: translated by Sayre, op. cit., sup. note 13, p. 979).

[45]"[T]he madman wills, but his reason being disturbed by his actions, are not suitable to the usual relations of society. . . . The prevailing complexion of maniacs is swarthy, with dark or black hair" (Dease, W. [1815], *Remarks on Medical Jurisprudence*. Philadelphia).

[46]Bakewell, T. (1815), A letter, addressed to the chairman of the Select Committee of the House of Commons appointed to enquire into the state of madhouses. In: *Three Hundred Years of Psychiatry, 1535–1860*, ed. R. Hunter & I. Macalpine. London: Oxford University Press, 1963, p. 705.

[47]It was a maxim of medieval jurisprudence that animals devoid of understanding cannot commit crimes (*nec enim potest animal injuriam fecisse quod sensu caret*). Aquinas, who endorsed this doctrine, asked whether it was therefore permissible to curse such irrational creatures, for curses and blessings could be pronounced only upon those who were capable of distinguishing and receiving good and evil impressions. Catholic logic evaded this assumption by justifying the punishment of irrational beings according to their relationship with rational beings. Thus God was able to curse the earth because it was considered essential to Man's existence. Further, it was not considered blasphemous to curse animals if they were the work of the devil and not creatures of God. See Evans, E. P. (1906), *The Criminal Prosecution and Capital Punishment of Animals*. New York: Dutton.

[48]Chassenée, B. (1531), Consilium Primum: *De excommunicatione animalium insinsectorum*, France (1531) 1, 75, trans. by Evans, ibid., p. 55.

[49]Bougeant, Pére G. H. (1739), Amusement Philosophique sure le Language des Bestes, trans. by Evans, ibid, p. 82: "[W]hatever pain is inflicted is felt, not by the physical organism, but by the animated spirit. It is the embodied demon that really suffers, howling in the beaten dog and squealing in the butchered pig" (p. 82).

[50]Legion was a madman who "had often been bound with fetters and chains, and the chains had been plucked asunder by him . . . neither could any man tame him." Jesus exorcised the evil spirits and transferred them into wild animals: "Now there was nigh unto the mountains a great herd of swine feeding. And all the devils besought him, saying, Send us into the swine, that we may enter to the swine: and the herd ran violently down a steep place into the sea." (*The Holy Bible* of King James, St. Mark Chap. 5).

[51]Chambery (1486), *Le Livre du Roy Modus et de la Reyne Racio*, trans. by Evans, op. cit., sup. note 47, p. 55.

[52]According to Lombroso, criminals are born with many of the characteristics of animals ("*i delinquenti nati fra gli animali*") (Lombroso, C. [1881], *L'Uomo Delinquente*. Torino). See also Evans, op. cit., sup. note 47, p. 55.

[53]"Criminals are organically inferior. . . . It follows that the elimination of crime can be effected only by the extirpation of the physically, mentally and morally unfit, or by their complete segregation in a socially aseptic environment" (Hooton, E. A. [1939], *The American Criminal*. Westport, CT: Greenwood, p. 309).

[54]"There is not one of any age who may not be made more of a man and less of a brute by patience and kindness directed by energy and skill" (Howe, S. G. [1848], Report to Massachusetts legislature. In: *Basic Considerations in Mental Retardation*, Group for the Advancement of Psychiatry, Report No. 43, p. 6).

[55]Robert Burton dramatically likened a madman to a person "inferior to beast: Man in honour that understandeth not, is like unto beasts that perish . . . a monster by stupend metamorphosis, a fox, a dog, a hog, what not? How much altred from that he was." (Burton, op. cit., sup. note 39, p. 113).

[56]See Frank, J. (1963), *Law and the Modern Mind*. New York: Peter Smith. Part I, chs. 1 & 3.

[57]Star, S. A. (1962), The public's ideas about mental illness. In: *Criminal Law*, ed. R. C. Donnelly, J. Goldstein, & R. D. Schwartz. New York: Free Press.

[58]Future historians and linguists will have to cope with such colorful metaphors as "out of one's mind," "not all there," "unhinged," "unbalanced."

[59]The mistranslation of *brutis* was primarily due to careless reporting and an unnecessary reliance on secondary sources. The only known correct translation is to be found in Collinson, G. D. (1812), *A Treatise On The Law Concerning Idiots, Lunatics, And Other Persons Non Compotes Mentis*, London: W. Reed, p. 472. Collinson's interpretation, however, was not made with sufficient lucidity or directness to affect the more authoritative, if less

accurate sources. Twentieth-century writers have avoided his reference because it conflicts with their evolutionary and progressive theory of law (see, for example, Hibbert, C. [1963], *The Roots of Evil*. Westport, CT: Greenwood; Guttmacher, M. S. [1961], A historical outline of the criminal law's attitude toward mental disorder. *Arch. Crim. Psychodynamics*, 4:648–670; and Lloyd, op. cit., sup. note 8).

[60]Sarbin, T. R. (1964), Anxiety: Reification of a metaphor. *Arch. Gen. Psychiat.*, 10:630–638.

[61]The inability to predict the actions of wild beasts and the mentally ill may have constituted the real threat. See Star, op. cit., sup. note 57.

[62]"[T]he metaphor of one generation becomes the myth of the next. . . . A myth has the force of literal truth until it's exploded and replaced by a currently more useful metaphor" (Sarbin, op. cit., sup. note 60, p. 632).

[63]Ibid., p. 633.

[64]Cooper, I. (1819), *Medical Jurisprudence Including Farr's Elements of Medical Jurisprudence; Dease's Remarks on Medical Jurisprudence; [Male's Epitome of Judicial or Forensic Medicine; and Haslam's Treatise on Insanity with a Preface, Notes and a Digest of the Law Relating to Insanity and Nuisance. To Which is Added an Appendix containing Erskine's Speech. . . .] Report of the Trial of Kessler . . . and a memoir of the Chromat of Pot-ash*. Philadephia: James Webster.

[65]"The legal and moral traditions of the western world require that those who, of their own free will and with evil intent, commit acts which violate the law, shall be criminally responsible for those acts. Our traditions also require that where such acts stem from and are the product of mental disease or defect, moral blame shall not attach" (Judge Bazelon in *Durham v. U.S.*).

[66]Platt, A. M. (1965), The criminal responsibility of the mentally ill in England, 1100–1843, Unpublished Master's Thesis, University of California, Berkeley.

[67]Bakewell, op. cit., sup. note 46, p. 707.

[68]"[T]he test of whether one metaphor is better than another is the pragmatic one. Modern scientists and practitioners must ask: Which metaphor leads to implications that are useful, which helps one to achieve his purposes?" (Sarbin, op. cit., sup. note 60, p. 634).

[69]Parsons, T. *The Social System*. Reprinted in Donnelly, Goldstein, & Schwartz, op. cit., sup. note 57, pp. 503–505.

[70]Chamberlain, A. F. (1896), *The Child and Childhood in Folk-Thought*. New York, p. 172. The mythological relationship between children and wildness is reflected in the common fallacy that regards cultural primitives as the "apparent infancy of humanity, where people seem to us, to be at one moment as naive as children, at another as possessed as lunatics" (Erickson, E. [1963], *Childhood and Society*. New York: Norton, p. 111).

[71]See Itard, J-M. G. (1963), *The Wild Boy of Aveyron*, trans. G. & M. Humphrey. New York: Prentice-Hall.

The Origins of the "Right and Wrong" Test of Criminal Responsibility and Its Subsequent Development in the United States: An Historical Survey*

with Anthony Platt

[1966]

O ne of the earliest sources of the "right and wrong" test of responsibility, the core of the M'Naghten rules, is Genesis:[1]

> And out of the ground the Lord God made to grow every tree that is pleasant to the sight and good for food, the tree of life also in the midst of the garden, and the tree of the knowledge of good and evil. And the Lord God commanded the man, saying, "You may freely eat of every tree of the garden; but of the tree of the knowledge of good and evil you shall not eat, for in the day that you eat of it you shall die."

> But the serpent said to the woman, "You will not die. For God knows that when you eat of it your eyes will be opened, and you will be like God, knowing good and evil."

> Then the Lord God said, "Behold, the man has become like one of us, knowing good and evil; and now, lest he put forth his hand and take also of the tree of life, and eat, and live for ever"—therefore the Lord God sent him forth from the garden of Eden, to till the ground from which he was taken.[2]

There are, as far as we can ascertain, only six other places in the Old and New Testaments where the phrase, "knowledge of good and evil," or a synonym, can be found.[3] The meaning of this phrase, as it is used in the

*This research was supported in part by grant number 449 of the Institute of Social Sciences, University of California, Berkeley, from funds derived from the National Science Foundation.

Bible and the criminal law, is not at all clear and has traditionally been subject to ambiguous interpretations. In its original idiomatic sense it meant the "knowledge of all things, both good and evil" and was not intended to depict people's capacity for moral choice. One Biblical commentator has observed that "the ordinary explanation of the phrase good and evil in the literal sense, assumes that God would for any reason withhold from man the ability to discern between what is morally right and wrong—a view which contradicts the spirit of the scripture."[4] This interpretation is supported by the fact that Adam's decision to eat from the tree was in itself a morally significant act.

Although "good and evil," as originally used, signified perfect wisdom, the phrase as subsequently used refers more specifically to moral capacity. Thus Solomon asked God to grant him "an understanding mind to govern thy people, that I may discern between good and evil" and in *Hebrews*, righteousness is said to be found in "those who have their faculties trained by practice to distinguish good from evil." This double meaning of the phrase, one idiomatic and the other literal, is reflected in the modern law of criminal responsibility, which to this day perpetuates the conflict.[5] This chapter outlines how the "good and evil" test of responsibility found its way into Anglo-American jurisprudence from Hebrew law, and traces, in greater detail, its subsequent development in American criminal law during the early part of the nineteenth century.

Ancient Doctrines of Responsibility

The earliest legal ideas of responsibility were generalized in Hebrew law, which distinguished between crimes committed intentionally and those committed unintentionally. The archetypal examples of criminal incapacity were accidental homicide and crimes committed by children or insane persons. With respect to major crimes, ignorance of the law was a good defense, and proof of "forewarning" had to be demonstrated for a successful prosecution.[6] Whether the wrongful act had been done intentionally or inadvertently was also an important consideration when determining the appropriate punishment. Children and the insane were not legally obligated to compensate the victims of their harmful acts.[7]

The doctrine of criminal responsibility was further elaborated in Greek philosophy and Roman law. Among the Greeks, as elsewhere, most primitive laws treated intentional homicide more harshly than they did unintentional homicide. The moral philosophers reflected the assumptions and practices of the courts by recognizing the different kinds of impulses that might motivate harmful acts.[8] Although Plato argued that the distinction between voluntary and involuntary wrongs was philosophically unsound because unjust acts were always done unwillingly, he nevertheless acknowledged the pragmatic benefits of such a concept and conceded that harms committed with some degree of calculation deserved severer punishments than those committed in the heat of passion.[9] Plato attributed to human beings "an element of free choice, which makes us, and not Heaven, responsible for the good and evil in our lives."[10]

For Aristotle, the distinction between voluntary and involuntary acts was more important that it was to Plato; Aristotle believed moral virtue to be the state of character that allows humans to function well in accordance with their nature. Aristotle held that an action is voluntary only if it is not done under compulsion or owing to ignorance; man, therefore, has the capacity to choose, and this choice is defined as the "deliberate desire of things in our own power."[11] To Aristotle, knowledge, rather than forethought, was the real test of responsibility: a person is morally responsible if, with knowledge of the circumstances and in the absence of external compulsion, he deliberately chooses to commit a specific act.[12] Children, therefore, can act voluntarily, but because they do not have the capacity to premeditate their acts, they, like animals and the insane, are not to be considered morally responsible.[13]

Roman law contained only vague allusions to responsibility for crimes, but the concept of accountability was implicit in such analogous areas as contractual and delictual obligations. The earliest Roman legal sources, such as the Twelve Tables (c. 450 B.C.) referred only briefly to the legal incapacities of children and the insane.[14] In the third century B.C., however, the Lex Aquilia, which dealt with delictual obligations arising from wrongful damage to property, contained more specific references on accountability: "[A] man who, without negligence or malice, but by some accident, causes damage, goes unpunished."[15]

The Lex Cornelia of the time of Sulla provided a criminal or quasi-criminal remedy for injuries to person, property, or reputation. The essence of the action was, according to Buckland, "outrage or insult or wanton interference with rights, any act, in short, which showed contempt of the personality of the victim or was of a nature to lower him in the estimation of others, and was so intended."[16] Persons lacking the ability to form the intent requisite for willing a harmful act were exempt under the law. Thus, if a child or an insane person committed homicide, he was not to be held accountable because "the one is excused by the innocence of his intentions, the other by the fact of his misfortune."[17]

Delictual obligations of children were determined according to age as well as capacity. Infants were children under seven years, and puberty was usually reached at fourteen in males and twelve in females.[18] Children under seven were considered doli incapax, or incapable of evil intent, whereas those between the ages of seven and fourteen could be held accountable only if proof of intention was clear and certain. Gaius, in his compilation of the second century A.D., noted that at one time there had been a dispute as to the capacity of a young child to incur delictual obligations for theft. "Most lawyers," Gaius noted, "hold that, since theft depends on intention, the child is only liable on such charge if he is approaching puberty and so understands that he is doing wrong (*intellegat se delinquere*)."[19]

By the time of Justinian's codification of the law in the sixth century A.D., there was considerable evidence to support the privileged legal status of children and of the insane in their delictual and contractual obligations. With regard to the former, Justinian's lawyers observed that "punishment is to be mitigated of one who committed homicide in a brawl by accident rather than of his own free will."[20] As for contractual liability, children and the insane enjoyed similar protection, for they were generally regarded as deficient in discretion and intellectual capacities. A child, reported Justinian, was "not very different from a madman,"[21] though he was allowed to make contracts that were to his advantage; in other cases, a child could not make a contract without his tutor's authority. An insane person, however, was completely incapable of contracting, because "he does not know what he is doing."[22] Moreover, he was not responsible for his harmful acts and was "excused by his madness."[23]

Medieval Concepts of Responsibility

The doctrine of *mens rea* in modern criminal law presupposes a dualism of mind and body and the existence of "mental states" that cause external acts. In law this concept is usually expressed in terms of freedom of the will. The definition and boundaries of "free will" were expounded in the Middle Ages, and many writers argue that the genesis of the doctrine of *mens rea* "is to be found in the mutual influences and reactions of Christian theology and Anglo-Saxon law."[24] On the other hand, it is probably more accurate to say that the idea of *mens rea* has its intellectual roots in Hebrew or Talmudic law and in the moral philosophy of Plato and Aristotle, but that it remained for Christian ethics to extend and elaborate on its metaphysical and pragmatic ramifications.

The social control of criminals and deviants during the medieval period was guided by the moral dogmas reflected in theological literature. Early English law reports very few cases of criminal incapacity, but those who promulgated the principles of law had no difficulty finding religious concepts to justify and validate a unique role for children and the insane.

Children, especially, were the subject of great interest and concern: medieval theology contains descriptive and doctrinal accounts of baptism, the moral development of children, parental responsibility, and the socialization of young persons by way of religious institutions. This concern for the child's "innate ignorance" was a function of the Church's political interest in recruiting and controlling new members rather than of benign paternalism. As an indirect result of this emphasis on induction ceremonies, however, the Church established different standards of treatment for children, which ultimately affected socioethical concepts of responsibility.[25]

It is in this period's theological speculation concerning the nature of childhood that one again finds reference to the concept and phrase "knowledge of good and evil." Children, according to medieval moral theology, are incapable of personal sin, although tainted by original sin. According to Augustine, all men are born with the guilt of original sin and are therefore incapable of acting without sin; they can, however, choose to do good through divine grace, and God does not require man to do that which is impossible for human volition. Man is expected to overcome evil by overtly consenting to do good; "it is one thing to be ignorant, and another thing to be unwilling to know."[26]

Augustine held that children, although capable of sin, are incapable of voluntarily acknowledging and freely pursuing sin. They are protected and excused by their "profound ignorance, their great weakness of mind and body, their perfect ignorance of things, their utter inability to obey a precept, the absence in them of all perception and impression of either natural or written law, the complete want of reason to impel them in the direction of either right or wrong." They are immune to sanctions or rewards until "they are of age to know their father and mother"; they are "incapable of moral government" and "completely involved and overwhelmed in a cloud of darkness and ignorance."[27]

Bede and other contemporary writers of the Church emphasized the mental elements of crime, with special reference to the nature of conscience and the benefits of confession. Children, Bede wrote, are not capable of "inner depravity" in their early years because they can "will nothing of good or ill."[28] This concept was uniformly accepted by the Patristic Fathers, the writers of moral treatises, the followers of Abailard and Aquinas, and eventually the judges and jurists of England in the fourteenth century. By the twelfth century, there was growing support for the view that man is a free individual, morally and rationally autonomous, and unaffected by an inherent attachment to general humanity. Abailard and Aquinas, for example, stressed man's subjective capacity to make moral distinctions and further argued that children are incapable of personal sin until they reach the age of intellectual and moral discernment. One influential moral treatise of the fourteenth century included the observation that both children and the insane are unable to understand the nature and effects of their harmful acts:

> The first [kind of freedom] is a free-will whereby he [man] can choose and freely do either good or evil. This freedom he has freely [gratuitously] from God so that no one can [make him] do wrong nor can all the devils of hell strengthen man's will to do one sin against his will. For if man did that sin against his will, it would not be a sin. For one does not sin because he cannot escape; as St. Augustine says: All men have freedom but it is restrained in children, in fools, and in the witless who do not have reason whereby they can choose the good from the evil.[29]

The "Good and Evil" Test in English Law[30]

The first known use of the "good and evil" test of responsibility in English criminal law came in the early fourteenth century; since the phrase appears without explanation or justification, one must assume that it was commonly used by judges of that period and that its meaning was commonly understood. The source of the phrase must have been either the Bible, particularly *Genesis*, or any of the numerous secondary theological sources that were familiar to the English judges of the fourteenth century. The case is reported in the Eyre of Kent for the year 1313: "An infant under the age of seven years, though he be convicted of felony, shall go free of judgement, because he knoweth not of good or evil (conisaunt de bien ne de mal). . . ."[31]

In early English law, children over twelve years were held to be as responsible as any adult for their crimes; children under seven years, however, were considered legally incapable of committing a crime. Children under twelve but over seven years could be found guilty if malice and discretion were proved.[32] Thus in 1338, Judge Spigurnel "found that an infant of ten years of age killed his companion and concealed him; and he caused him to be hung, because by the concealment he showed that he knew how to distinguish between evil and good. And so malice makes up for age (malitia supplet aetatem)."[33]

During the fourteenth, fifteenth, and sixteenth centuries, the rules of infant capacity remained constant in English law; the "good and evil" test was regularly cited by judges and legal commentators.[34] By the time of Elizabeth I (c. 1581), there existed a legal rationale for the exclusion of special groups from criminal responsibility. Infants and the insane both generally failed to possess the necessary mental capacity to commit a crime;

they were treated as "nonpersons" because of their supposed lack of understanding, intelligence, and moral discretion. Moreover, they were not considered fit subjects for punishment since they did not comprehend the moral implications of their harmful acts. Children, the insane, and idiots enjoyed a privileged position in English civil law as well, especially in regard to the laws of guardianship and contractual liability.

Very few cases of insanity were reported in English criminal law before the seventeenth century, and it is reasonable to infer that only the most gross and dramatic kinds of mental illness were acknowledged in mitigation of responsibility (see "Wild Beast Concept," this volume). The criminal law generally perceived the insane person as resembling a young child in terms of his moral development and cognitive abilities. According to the Elizabethan writer Lambard:

> If a mad man or a naturall foole, or a lunatike in the time of his lunacie, or a childe y apparently hath no knowledge of good nor evil, do kil a ma, this is no felonious acte, nor any thing forfeited by it . . . for they cannot be said to have any understanding wil.[35]

Edward Coke writing in the early part of the seventeenth century, did not mention the "good and evil" test but did compare the mental deficiencies of madmen with the mental capacity of children; he also noted the age of responsibility was 14 years.[36] Coke was the first English jurist to attempt anything like a scientific treatment of the criminal law, and his partial codification of the common law encouraged other commentators to remedy existing conceptual gaps. The rules of responsibility for the insane were extremely inadequate compared with those for children. It was not difficult, however, for judges to rectify this deficiency by analogy to the "good and evil" test, which had long been used to distinguish between the infant, who was innocent of moral guilt, and the older child, who was *doli capax*.

By the end of the sixteenth century, the courts had begun to apply the test of "knowledge of good and evil" to the insane. Michael Dalton's legal manual, *The Countrey Justice*, first published in 1618, contains the first known written acknowledgment of the "new" test for the insane. Dalton was not an important judge, and his treatise is not a recognized judicial authority;[37] either he made a mistake in copying the precedents or he was just reporting accepted practice. In view of the steady legal development of the "good and evil" test and the close jurisprudential relationship between the concepts of infancy and insanity, the latter view is more likely correct. Dalton reported that

> if one that is *"non compos mentis"* [mad], or an ideot, kill a man, this is no felony; for they have not knowledge of good and evill, nor can have a felonius intent, nor a will or minde to doe harm. . . . An Infant

. . . may commit Homicide, and shall bee hanged for it, viz. if it may appeare . . . that he had knowledge of good and evill, and of the perill and danger of that offence.[38]

After Coke, Matthew Hale is perhaps the most significant figure in English legal history. In a lengthy discussion of infant capacity, he approved the earlier decisions and mentioned the "good and evil" test five times; for example, he noted that "it is clear that an infant above fourteen and under twenty-one is equally subject to capital punishments, as well as others of full age; for it is *praesumptio juris*, that after fourteen years they are *doli capaces*, and can discern between good and evil."[39] As for insanity, Hale improved upon earlier definitions, stating that "such a person as labouring under melancholy distempers hath yet ordinarily as great understanding, as ordinarily a child of fourteen hath, is such a person as may be guilty of treason or felony."[40] This definition of insanity relied on analogy to the "good and evil" test, a fact that critics have failed to observe. Hale's test was neither revolutionary, nor unsupported by any authority,[41] nor based on personal ignorance.[42] On the contrary, it was something of an improvement on earlier definitions, and it was certainly an appropriate interpretation in the light of contemporary legal knowledge. The English legal scholar, William Blackstone, whose contributions are discussed in the section on U.S. criminal law, approved Hale's test of responsibility.

In the eighteenth century, the "good and evil" test was regularly used in insanity and infancy cases.[43] In *Rex v. Arnold* (1724), the jury was instructed that the defendant was not to be held insane if he "was able to distinguish whether he was doing good or evil. . . ."[44] The same test was used in *Rex v. Ferrer*[45] (1760), *Parker's Case*[46] (1812), *Bellingham's Case*[47] (1812), *Rex v. Bowler*[48] (1812), *Martin's Case*[49] (1829), *Offord's Case*[50] (1831), and *Oxford's Case*[51] (1840). The "good and evil" test was momentarily abandoned in *Hadfield's Case* (1800) as a result of the brilliance and oratory of the defense counsel, Thomas Erskine,[52] but this decision had no lasting effect on the rules of criminal responsibility for the insane. By the time M'Naghten was tried for the murder of Edward Drummond in 1843, the earlier test of responsibility had been reestablished.

Although M'Naghten was acquitted and committed to a mental hospital, the case provoked public anger and political repercussions. Governmental pressure, aggrandized by the righteous indignation of Queen Victoria, who feared that the acquittal might encourage cranks and radicals to make attempts on her life, was brought to bear upon the judges in the House of Lords.[53] Consequently, the "Law Lords" reexamined the rules of responsibility and the "anti-M'Naghten Rules," as Koestler called them,[54] resulted. In essence, the judges held that:

[T]o establish a defence on the ground of insanity, it must be clearly proved that, at the time of committing of the act, the party accused was labouring under such a defect of reason, from disease of the mind, as not to know the nature and quality of the act he was doing: or, if he did know it, that he did not know he was doing what was wrong. The mode of putting the latter part of the question to the jury on these occasions has generally been, whether the accused at the time of doing the act knew the difference between right and wrong.[55]

During the early nineteenth century, the phrases "good and evil" and "right and wrong" were used interchangeably and synonymously. The first known substitution of "right and wrong" for "good and evil" was in *Parker's Case*[56] (1812), in which the Attorney General argued that "before it could have any weight in rebutting a charge [treason] so clearly made out, the jury must be perfectly satisfied, that at the time when the crime was committed, the person did not really know right from wrong." In *Bellingham's Case*[57] (1812), both phrases were used, and Lord Chief Justice Mansfield instructed the jury that "the single question was, whether, at the time this fact [murder] was committed, [the defendant] . . . possessed a sufficient degree of understanding to distinguish good from evil, right from wrong." In the United States, these two phrases were also used synonymously in both infancy and insanity cases.[58]

Concepts of Responsibility in the United States

Criminal Responsibility of Children, 1800–1900

The responsibility of children in the United States during the nineteenth century was formulated according to traditional common-law principles and especially the works of William Blackstone. His *Commentaries* contain a systematic treatment of the criminal law, and his summary of the criminal incapacity of children was, in effect, incorporated into U.S. law. The *Commentaries* served as a model for contemporary jurists; judges also cited his theoretical statements to justify specific decisions:

By the law, as it now stands, and has stood at least ever since the time of Edward the Third, the capacity of doing ill, or contracting guilt, is not so much measured by years and days, as by the strength of the delinquent's understanding and judgment. For one lad of eleven years old may have as much cunning as another of fourteen; and in these cases our maxim is, that "*malitia supplet aetatem.*" Under seven years of age indeed an infant cannot be guilty of felony; for then a felonious discretion is almost an impossibility in nature: but at eight years old he may be guilty of felony. Also, under fourteen, though an infant shall be *prima facie* adjudged to be *doli incapax*; yet if it appear to the court and jury that he was *doli capax*, and could discern between good and evil, he may be convicted and suffer death. Thus a girl of thirteen has been burnt for killing her mistress; and one boy of ten, and another of nine years old, who had killed their companions, have been sentenced to death, and he of ten years actually hanged; because it appeared upon their trials, that the one hid himself, and the other hid the body he had killed; which hiding manifested a consciousness of guilt, and a discretion to discern between good and evil. And there was an instance in the last century, where a boy of eight years old was tried at Abingdon for firing two barns; and, it appearing that he had malice, revenge, and cunning, he was found guilty, condemned, and hanged accordingly. Thus also, in very modern times, a boy of ten years old was convicted on his own confession of murdering his bedfellow; there appearing in his whole behavior plain tokens of mischievous discretion; and as the sparing this boy merely on account of his tender years might be of dangerous consequence to the public, by propagating a notion that children might commit such atrocious crimes with impunity, it was unanimously agreed by all the judges that he was a proper subject of capital punishment.[59]

U.S. case law on the criminal responsibility of children was more elaborate and sophisticated than its English counterpart. Additionally, some of the same cases developed rules of evidence for the protection of young offenders.

In *State v. Doherty*[60] (1806), a young girl between 12 and 13 was indicted for the murder of her father. When challenged by the court she remained mute, and a plea of not guilty was entered on her behalf. During the trial, "the defendant stood up erect in the bar several hours, her countenance was ghastly pale, without the least expression, or indication of understanding."[61] On the question of responsibility, Judge White instructed the jury that

their inquiry was, whether the prisoner was the person who took the life of the deceased, and, if they were of that opinion to inquire whether it were done with malice aforethought. If a person of fourteen years of age does an act, such as stated in this indictment, the presumption of law is that the person is "*doli capax*." If under fourteen and not less than seven, the presumption of law is that the person cannot discern between right and wrong. But this presumption is removed, if from the circumstances it appears that the person discovered a consciousness of wrong.[62]

The jury returned a verdict of not guilty.

In *State v. Aaron*[63] (1818), a young Negro slave of 11 years was accused of murdering another young child. Although there was circumstantial evidence that the defendant had known the victim as a playmate and had been working in the field where the murder took place, he at first denied the crime. Following the inquest, "he was taken apart by one or more of the jurors and told that he had better confess the whole truth, and he did then confess that he had thrown the child into the well, in which the body had been found, and from which he had seen it taken. . . ."[64] At the trial he again denied the crime but was convicted and sentenced to death. On appeal to the Supreme Court of New Jersey, counsel for the defendant claimed that the prosecution had failed to rebut the presumption that a child of 11 years is incapable of committing a crime. Chief Justice Kirkpatrick ordered a new trial on the grounds that the defendant had been convicted by a mere naked confession, uncorroborated, and obtained by pressure, which should not have been admitted as evidence. (The trial judge had justified the extortion of the confession on the grounds that "it was the anxiety only of a moral and religious community, seeking to discover the perpetrator, that it might be purged from the guilt of shedding blood."[65]) The Chief Justice held that the presumption of innocence on the part of the defendant could only be rebutted "by *strong* and *irresistible* evidence that he had sufficient discernment to distinguish good from evil." Were it demonstrated that the defendant could "comprehend the nature and consequences of his act, he may be convicted and have judgment of death. . . . With respect to confessions in general," the judge continued, "and especially with respect to the confessions of infants, it is necessary to be exceedingly guarded."[66] Confessions obtained "by the flattery of hope or by the impression of fear, *however slightly the emotion may be implanted,* [are] not admissible evidence."[67]

In *State v. Bostick*[68] (1845), the defendant, a white girl of twelve years, was indicted for arson. Mary Bostick had been a servant of Mrs. Ann Fisher, who described her as a "very shrewd, artful girl; not intelligent, or very capable of learning; but smart to work, and shrewd in mischief." The defendant had confessed to her mistress that she had set fire to the house on purpose. Two young children in the charge of the defendant had been burned to death, and the prosecution sought to establish the malicious motivation of Mary Bostick. The defendant appealed on the ground that the confession had been improperly obtained, "as being brought about by promises, or inducements of favor." A majority of the court agreed, ruled out the confession, and acquitted the defendant.

> One or two unavailing attempts had been made, to induce her to confess. Afterwards her mistress took her into another room, and questioned her

whether she did the act. The child at first denied it. Her mistress then told her, "that she was suspected of the offence, and if she confessed it, the suspicion would not be stronger, that she [the mistress] did not expect to do anything with her, but was going to send her home." The prisoner then confessed, that when she went upstairs in the evening, she placed the candle under the clothes which hung from the bed. Here then is an inducement to confess; a promise of favor held out by a person in authority, and a hope raised in the mind of the child, that she would be sent to her home. Hence, a doubt and uncertainty arise, whether the confession was not made more under the influence of hope, than from a consciousness of guilt.[69]

In *Walker's Case*[70] (1820), a young boy just over seven years was indicted for petit larceny. The boy's mother said that "his senses were impaired," and the prosecutor offered no evidence to demonstrate the boy's mental capacity to commit a criminal act. The defense submitted that

> as a child of seven was held incapable of crime, and between that age and fourteen it was necessary to show his capacity; and that, in proportion as he approached to seven, the inference in his favor was the greater, and as he approached to fourteen the less, that there was not sufficient evidence in this case to support the prosecution, especially as strong evidence of incapacity had been produced on his part.[71]

On this principle, the mayor charged the jury, who immediately acquitted the defendant.

Stage's Case[72] (1820) involved a group of children, between the ages of seven and fourteen, who were indicted for grand larceny. George Stage, eight years old, was arrested while trying to escape from a private house with a stolen bear skin. In convicting and sentencing the defendant to three years in the state prison, the court held that

> with regard to an infant, between the age of seven and fourteen, the jury should be satisfied that he had a capacity of knowing good from evil. And proof of this may be given either by extrinsic testimony, or it may arise from the circumstances of the case. In this case, the fact of concealment, and of an attempt to escape, appear; and it will rest with the jury to determine, whether this boy did not know, at the time he stole this property, that he was doing wrong.[73]

In *People v. Davis*[74] (1823), William Davis, fifteen, and James McBride, thirteen, were indicted and pleaded not guilty to a charge of grand larceny. The recorder instructed the jury that

> the presumption of law was in favor of an infant under 14 years of age, that under seven the law supposed the infant incapable to commit a

crime. He is supposed to want discretion to judge between right and wrong; but from that age to fourteen, the law still supposed him innocent, and in order to show his liability for crimes, it was necessary to prove his capacity, that it was the province of the jury to say, from all the evidence before them, whether James McBride was guilty or not guilty; that he was present, and assisted in felony, was satisfactorily proved, but whether liable on account of his tender years, was the point for them to decide, no proof of his capacity or incapacity had yet been given; the presumption was therefore in his favor up to the period the law supposed he has attained his capacity.[75]

The jury rendered a verdict of guilty against Davis, and not guilty for McBride.

In *People v. Teller*[76] (1823), Jason Teller, thirteen, and William Teller, who was over fourteen, were indicted for petit larceny after the stolen property had been found in their possession and both had confessed to the crime. The evidence of Jason's capacity was unsatisfactory; some of the police officers, who knew the boy, thought him active, shrewd, and intelligent, while others had a different opinion of his capacity. The jury returned verdicts of guilty against William Teller and of not guilty for Jason Teller. In a note to this case, the reporter reviewed English and U.S. law on the subject of the criminal responsibility of children. Quoting Hale, Hawkins, and Blackstone, he noted that their "principles have long been established in Great Britain and have been adopted in this country. Their decisions, therefore, upon this subject are good authority here." The reporter then summarized the principles of capacity:

> Infancy is a satisfactory excuse for the commission of any crime up to the period of seven years, and may or may not extend to fourteen. But upon the attainment of that age, the person of an infant is placed precisely upon the same footing as the rest of mankind, as it respects their accountability for crimes; for at and after this period, the law supposes the party has attained a judgment capable, and a conscience willing to decide between right and wrong.[77]

> If the circumstances under which a felony is committed by an infant between seven and fourteen years of age, indicate that he was doing wrong while stealing, this is tantamount to evidence of his capacity.[78]

In *State v. Guild*[79] (1828), a Negro slave, aged twelve, was accused of beating an old woman to death. The defendant confessed to the crime, but the question of his capacity to form intent was disputed. The prosecution sought to establish that the defendant was "a cunning smart boy," "full of mischief," "smarter than common black boys of his age," and "ingenious," and "acute in many things."[80] A witness for the defense admitted that "he knows the difference between good and evil" and had "intelligence enough to know when he did wrong [and] capacity enough to distinguish between right and wrong."[81]

In the trial court, Judge Drake instructed the jury as to the presumption in favor of persons between seven and fourteen and told them that, to find the defendant guilty, they must realize that

> at the age of this defendant, sufficient capacity is generally possessed in our state of society, by children of ordinary understanding, and having the usual advantages of moral and religious instruction. You will call to mind the evidence on this subject; and if you are satisfied that he was able, in a good degree, to distinguish between right and wrong; to know the nature of the crime with which he is charged . . . his infancy will furnish no obstacle, on the sense of incapacity, to his conviction.[82]

On appeal, the Supreme Court of New Jersey upheld the verdict of the lower court and, apparently, ignored the principles relating to confessions established in State v. Aaron.[83] The court approved Blackstone's opinion that "mischievous discretion" was sufficient proof of criminal capacity and held that the defendant was a rational and moral agent who should be judged by his act and motives.[84] The defendant was subsequently sentenced to death and executed.

In Godfrey v. State[85] (1858), a young Negro slave, about 11, was indicted for the murder of a four-year-old child who had been in his charge. The defendant claimed that "an Indian had done it; that they hunted for Indians, but could not find any." Several witnesses for the prosecution testified that "the [dead] child was on the floor, all bloody; that he was cut on the face and head, three cuts, and a bruise as if with the head of a hatchet; . . . his brain was projecting from his skull." There was further evidence against the defendant that he had been wet and covered with blood; the hatchet had been found in a bucket of water. One witness testified that Godfrey had said on the evening of the killing that he had killed Lawrence because he had broken his kite, and he would do it again if they did not hang him. There was conflicting evidence as to the character and intelligence of the defendant: one neighbor observed that he was "a smart, intelligent boy, heap smarter than boys of twelve years generally are"; another described him as "kind and gentle" and probably not yet eleven years old.

The jury was informed of the presumption in favor of the defendant because of his age and further instructed that

> they must take into consideration his condition as a negro and a slave, with all the evidence in the case; and that unless [they were satisfied

> from the evidence] . . . that he was fully aware of the nature and consequences of the act which he had committed, and had plainly shown intelligent malice in the manner of executing the act, they should render a verdict of not guilty. . . .[86]

The jury returned a verdict of guilty, but the presiding judge, doubting the propriety of passing sentence under the circumstances of the case, reserved the question for the decision of the appellate court. On appeal, the Supreme Court of Alabama affirmed the judgment, citing State v. Guild[87] in which "a negro slave, of less than twelve years was convicted of murder and executed," and approving the good and evil test, as stated in State v. Aaron.[88]

In State v. Learnard[89] (1869), the defendant, a male adult, was charged with a burglary and larceny that had been effected by his two children, a boy of about sixteen and a girl of about thirteen. The boy had been prosecuted in a prior term and, on his plea of guilty, was sentenced to the reform school. The defendant pleaded that he was not a principal to the offense because "a girl thirteen or fourteen years old, of good size, and ordinarily intelligent, who was capable of working away from home for wages, and who had done so, is of sufficient discretion to be responsible for what crimes she commits."[90] For the defendant, one witness testified concerning the girl's capacity to commit a crime: "She worked for me; I think she earned one dollar per week; she appeared to have intelligence; think she could distinguish between right and wrong. Don't think she ever attended sabbath school; don't think her morals very good."[91] The jury returned a verdict of guilty, stating that the daughter "was under the age of discretion and had not sufficient discretion to be responsible for this act, that she entered the store, and took the goods, by direction of the respondent, that the respondent by said threats compelled his daughter to enter the store and take the goods, and that she committed the act through fear of loss of her life. . . ."[92]

On appeal, the defendant claimed that there was sufficient evidence to demonstrate that the girl "could distinguish right from wrong" and therefore had a "sufficient degree of discretion" to render her guilty of a crime. In dismissing the appeal, the court held that any doubt should operate in favor of a young child in "the dubious stage of discretion"; the law "has never undertaken to say that any defined physical dimensions or strength, and being ordinarily intelligent, and working away from home for wages, constitute the capacity for crime, or the criterion of such capacity."[93]

In Angelo v. People[94] (1880), Theodore Angelo, eleven, was charged with homicide. He was convicted of manslaughter, and the jury sentenced him to the penitentiary for six years. A motion for a new trial was overruled by the court, and he was resentenced to the reform school for four

years. On appeal to the Supreme Court of Illinois, the defendant said that
his capacity and malice had not been proved "beyond a reasonable doubt."
In Illinois, a child under ten years was legally incapable of committing a
crime, and between the ages of ten and fourteen he was prima facie
incapable and deemed *doli incapax.*

In a highly sophisticated and compassionate opinion by Justice
Walker,[95] the court reversed the decision of the trial court on the grounds
that there was no evidence as to the defendant's capacity.

> [T]he rule required evidence strong and clear beyond all doubt and
> contradiction, that he was capable of discerning between good and evil;
> and the legal presumption being that he was incapable of committing the
> crime, for want of such knowledge, it devolved on the People to make
> the strong and clear proof of capacity, before they could be entitled to a
> conviction. This record may be searched in vain to find any such proof.
> There was no witness examined on that question, nor did any one refer
> to it. There is simply evidence as to his age. For aught that appears, he
> may have been dull, weak, and wholly incapable of knowing good from
> evil. It does not appear, from even the circumstances in evidence, that he
> may not have been mentally weak for his age, or that he may not have
> even approached idiocy.[96]

In *State v. Toney*[97] (1881), Lawrence Toney, about twelve, and others,
were charged with malicious trespass. The jury determined that the
defendant, "a well-grown boy, apparently at least over twelve years," was
guilty because "he was conscious that his act was wrongful" and "he could
discern between right and wrong." On appeal, the Supreme Court of South
Carolina affirmed: the "evidence of malice was strong and clear, beyond all
doubt and contradiction."[98]

In *State v. Adams*[99] (1882), a Negro boy of twelve was indicted for
murder in the first degree, having killed another youth, aged 17, by
stabbing him in the heart with a pocket knife. Witnesses for the prosecution testified that the two boys often fought and that the defendant
killed the deceased after being attacked with a pitchfork. The jury found
the defendant guilty of first degree murder. The Morgan Circuit Court of
Missouri reversed the judgment; the higher court held that a lesser degree
of homicide would have been more appropriate, aside from the fact that
"no effort seems to have been made at the trial to show the defendant
possessed criminal capacity."[100]

The criminal responsibility of children in the United States during the
nineteenth century was determined according to traditional principles of
English law and by the elaboration of rules of procedure and evidence,
which leaned toward the protection and benefit of the defendant. There

seems to be no justification for the proposition that children were regularly executed; on the contrary, the courts were extremely hesitant to sentence a child under fourteen to death and, where such a case arose, it was either appealed by the defense counsel or certified by the trial judge to the state supreme court. According to contemporary judicial records and legal textbooks, it appears that only two children under fourteen were judicially executed between the years 1806 and 1882.[101]

In both cases, the defendants were Negro slaves and, in one case, the victim was the son of a white property owner.[102]

In the 14 cases[103] on the criminal responsibility of children in the United States between 1806 and 1882, the "good and evil" or "right and wrong" test was used 10 times and, in one other case, *Godfrey v. State*,[104] a similar test was substituted. In one case, *State v. Bostick*,[105] no specific test was mentioned because the appeal rested on the issue of the admissibility of confessions; in the two remaining cases, no particular test was used. Of the fourteen children tried, seven were indicted for murder, one for manslaughter, five for various degrees of larceny, and one for malicious trespass. In ten instances the jury returned a verdict of not guilty; two children, aged eleven and twelve, were executed, and the remaining child, aged eight, was sentenced to three years in a state prison.

Criminal Responsibility of the Insane, 1800–1843

Much has been written in criticism of the *M'Naghten* rules since their pronouncement in 1843, but few historians have considered the legal development of the "good and evil" or "right and wrong" test prior to *M'Naghten's Case*.[106] James Hendrie Lloyd dismissed this test as a common law doctrine of no great antiquity.[107] Weihofen agreed with the legal historian Stephen that early legal materials concerning the responsibility of the insane should be treated as "antiquarian curiosities."[108] The Royal Commission on Capital Punishment further noted that "little need be said of the development of the law before the case of M'Naghten in 1843."[109]

The four leading works on the history of criminal responsibility in the United States generally endorse this view and attach no historical or legal significance to pre-1843 tests of legal insanity. The historical chapters in these works usually begin with the incorporation of the *M'Naghten* rules into U.S. case law after 1843 and do not account for the legal climate that facilitated the acceptance of these rules. Lloyd,[110] Glueck,[111] Weihofen,[112] and Deutsch[113] discount any historical justification for the "good and evil" and "right and wrong" tests. According to Glueck, for example, "there is nothing inherently sacred in the origin of these tests, nothing absolutely authoritative in them, nothing very consistent in them, and no very good reasons why they should not be changed."[114]

Inquiry into the origins of criminal responsibility has been extremely limited and has relied, for the most part, on secondary sources. The standard and most widely used reference in the United States is the fifth edition of Wharton and Stillé's *Medical Jurisprudence*, which includes the first comprehensive survey of the historical development of tests of responsibility for the insane.[115] In this treatise, James Hendrie Lloyd observed that the "right and wrong" test was a "brand new formula," which was "adopted arbitrarily by the courts" in the United States after 1843.[116] Both Weihofen and Deutsch modeled their historical chapters on Lloyd's survey and consequently accepted his initial premise. Glueck, however, did go beyond existing knowledge and suggested that the "good and evil" test was "well established in New York and in some, if not all, the states" before 1843.[117] Glueck's impression, based on the evidence of only two cases, was in fact correct although he did not attempt to systematize his findings or evaluate their historical implications.

The culpability of the criminally insane in U.S. law during the nineteenth century was determined according to the traditional principles of English law, reinforced by the ideas and emerging expertise of medical jurisprudence. Many of the earliest U.S. commentaries on criminal law, such as Bishop's *Commentaries on the Criminal Law*,[118] and *The Crown Circuit Companion*,[119] were merely abridgments of English works by Coke, Hale, Hawkins, and Blackstone. As early as 1792, one such commentary included a reference to the "good and evil" test in a discussion of principles relating to the insane offender.[120]

The traditional assumptions underlying tests of criminal responsibility were approved both by lawyers and by physicians. The stereotypic definitions of insanity were not peculiar to legal reasoning but were also implicit in the ideas of professionals from medicine and related disciplines who supported the philosophy of deterrence and the strict control of social deviants; the "right and wrong" test was considered bad medicine but good law.

Such writers as Highmore, Collinson, Farr, Cooper, Dease, Prichard, Haslam, and Wood, who founded the discipline of medical jurisprudence in England, generally were agreed that there existed a wide range of mental illnesses that lay outside the scope of the traditional legal tests of responsibility. Dease, for example, noted that

[t]here are . . . many instances of decided insanity, where the patient cannot write and read, but converse and argue closely and accurately on

every subject, except that on which he is insane. . . . It is a false notion
that madmen cannot reason; they often reason with accuracy on many
subjects, and carry into execution plans, which require subtlety and
long-continued dissimulation. . . .[121]

It was felt, however, that such a mental illness should excuse an offender
only if, "at the period when he committed the offense," he was "wholly
incapable of distinguishing between good and evil."[122] Dease, a surgeon, felt
that punishment was a valuable deterrent whose utilitarian functions
precluded clinical interests. He argued that the "improper extension [of the
right and wrong test] would become a cloak for crimes, which would
ultimately tend to the injury of the community and the subversion of social
order."[123] Another physician, William Wood, echoed these sentiments and
"totally repudiated the doctrine that an insane person is necessarily
irresponsible":

[W]hilst we are tenderly alive to the frailties of our common nature, and
feel it to be a Christian obligation to shield from man's vengeance one
already withering under the chastening hand of God, we yet, as good
citizens, have a solemn duty to perform towards society, and our
responsibility is immensely increased when, as members of a learned and
honourable profession, we are called upon to assist, with our experience,
in deciding whether or not the evidence adduced in defence of a criminal
is sufficiently clear to justify the administrators of the law in departing
from the course which is essentially necessary for the safety of society,
and the protection of the lives and property of individuals.[124]

It is likely that U.S. judges of the nineteenth century were familiar with
the English literature of medical jurisprudence (which, if anything,
supported and encouraged the use of the right and wrong test of criminal
responsibility), as there were few comparable U.S. resources.[125] Benjamin
Rush's classic treatise, Diseases of the Mind, first published in Philadelphia
in 1812, did not deal with the problem of criminal responsibility but was
more concerned with the treatment of deviant behavior. The first
comprehensive U.S. text on medical jurisprudence was written by Theodric
Beck in 1823.[126] It cited Bellingham's Case as the leading authority on
English law. In so doing, it approved the use and assumptions of the "right
and wrong" test. "By these principles [of Bellingham's Case]," he wrote,
"the criminal jurisprudence of England and this country has been guided,
and decisions conformable to them have repeatedly been made. They are
doubtless correct, and conducive to the ends of justice."[128]

Before M'Naghten's Case[129] we find almost no criticism of the "right
and wrong" test in the United States; only the renowned forensic

psychiatrist Isaac Ray pointed out that such a test was inconsistent with psychological knowledge of human behavior. He characterized the criminal law as clinging to "crude and imperfect notions" of insanity.

> In their zeal to uphold the wisdom of the past, from the fancied dese-crations of reformers and theorists, the ministers of the law seem to have forgotten that, in respect to this subject, the real dignity and respectability of their profession is better upheld by yielding to the improvements of the times and thankfully receiving the truth from whatever quarter it may come than by turning away with blind obstinacy from everything that conflicts with long-established maxims and decisions.[130]

Ray's main objection to the "right and wrong" test of responsibility was based on the "well-established" proposition that "the insane mind is not entirely deprived of [the] . . . power of moral discernment, but on many subjects is perfectly rational and displays the exercise of a sound and well balanced mind."[131] Ray's objections, however, had little effect on U.S. criminal law during the nineteenth century.

U.S. courts accepted the "right and wrong" test long before 1843, as the following cases, reported between 1816 and 1838, demonstrate. The cases also give clues as to how insanity was pleaded and proved and the criteria used by judges and juries. These cases were considered authoritative by leading contemporary commentators, and they were cited in textbooks on criminal law in the latter part of the nineteenth century.

In *Cook's Case*[132] (1816), the defendant was indicted for grand larceny. His counsel claimed that the defendant was an idiot, a fact that could be ascertained by "ocular demonstration." The defense counsel introduced no supporting expert testimony but "informed the jury that he possessed a knowledge of physiognomy and that madness itself was stamped on every lineament of the prisoner's countenance by the hand of nature." "I do aver," he said, "every movement of that head, every glance of that vacant, staring eye—nay his whole exterior, indicates downright madness." Under questioning, the defendant "answered with peculiar facial gestures," which the court did not accept as "positive proof of madness." The jury quickly pronounced him guilty, and he was sentenced to the state prison for three years.

In *Clark's Case*[133] (1816), Richard Clark, indicted for petit larceny, was described by the prosecution as "one of the many foreigners who come to this country with an exalted idea of their own consequence, and with a certain haughty demeanor, not adapted to the simplicity of our manners. Such an one, we admit, may live in this country, should he have the means to buy." After a plea of insanity had been entered, the mayor charged the jury that

> [s]uch was the humanity of the law, that no man could be held re-
> sponsible for an act committed while deprived of his reason. . . . [A]
> madman [is] . . . generally considered, in law, incapable of committing a
> crime. But it is not every degree of madness or insanity which abridges
> the responsibility attached to the commission of crime. In that species of
> madness, where the prisoner has lucid intervals, and when capable of
> distinguishing good from evil, he perpetrates an offense, he is responsible.
> The principal subject of inquiry, therefore, in this case, is whether the
> prisoner, at the time he committed this offense, had sufficient capacity to
> discern good from evil.[134]

The jury accordingly found the defendant guilty, but the court suspended
sentence for the purpose of "speedily sending the prisoner back to his
native country."

Traux's Case[135] (1816) demonstrates how the insanity defense could
be used as a fiction to disguise discriminatory findings. Unlike the
defendant in the previous case, Isaac Traux was a "gentleman of good
breeding," and "it clearly appeared that he was a young man of property
and respectable connexions in the city of Albany, but that his senses had
been impaired, and his moral faculties totally ruined by the excessive use
of ardent liquor." He was immediately acquitted by the jury and the
presiding judge suggested that "he ought to be taken from the city to his
friends, in whose custody he ought to remain."

In *Sellick's Case*[136] (1816), in which the defendant was indicted for
murder by poisoning and pleaded insanity, there was "the absence of all
motive." The judge instructed the jury that "the evidence of insanity should
not only be conclusive, but overwhelming":

> Insanity is a defence often resorted to, and in most cases, when
> every other ground of defence has failed. . . . In my view, such a defence,
> in such a case, ought to be scrutinized by the jury with no ordinary
> degree of caution. It does not follow, by any legitimate rule of reasoning,
> that because we are unable to penetrate into the motive which induced
> the act, that we are therefore to attribute the act to insanity. In her
> examination she says she was possessed with the devil, and knew not
> what she did. Can we reasonably look for any other motive than that
> laid in the indictment?[137]

Following this instruction, the jury quickly found the defendant guilty and
the judge, "in a solemn, pathetic address," sentenced her to "be hanged by
the neck until dead."

In *Ball's Case*[138] (1817), the defendant was indicted for willfully and
maliciously setting fire to a dwelling house. In his defense, it was pointed
out that he was an old man "with habits of brutal intoxication and violent

vindictive passions." The mayor instructed the jury that revenge or despair was not a sufficient defense. "It did not necessarily follow," he said, "that the act of which he had been charged was the result of insanity because, from its nature, it was horrid and unnatural." The only question to be determined in the case, continued the mayor, "is whether, at the time he committed the offence, he was capable of distinguishing good from evil." The defendant was accordingly found guilty and fined by the court.

In *Pienovi's Case*[139] (1818), an Italian immigrant was indicted for an assault and battery; he was charged with maiming his wife by biting and tearing off the tip of her nose. The case created a great deal of public excitement, for the court reporter described Mrs. Pienovi as a "woman remarkable for her beauty. Considering the ideas entertained by the sex in general relative to their personal appearance, this was certainly one of the most insidious acts of revenge that was ever conceived and perpetrated." The defendant pleaded insanity, and his counsel argued that, at the time of the offense, he had exhibited every "symptom of derangement" and "an air of wildness, indicative of phrensy." After at least seven witnesses testified that the defendant was either greatly "disturbed" or "deranged," the defense counsel asked the jury to acquit the prisoner because "at the time he committed the act charged in the indictment, he had not a mind capacitated for distinguishing good from evil."[140]

In response, the prosecution observed that he could "distinguish good from evil," a fact demonstrated by his "cunning and intelligence." The mayor, in his instructions to the jury, emphasized the "good and evil" test of responsibility and stated:

> A man should never suffer himself to be hurried into a state of temporary insanity by any of the violent passions. It is the universal language of the law—Govern your passions: for if you do not, you shall be punished. . . . The jury . . . will determine whether at the precise point of time in which the act was perpetrated, he was capacitated for distinguishing good from evil.[141]

The jury found the defendant guilty but recommended mercy, which was not granted by the mayor. According to the court reporter,

> after a most impressive address to the prisoner on the shocking deed of which he had been convicted, wherein his honour said that a crime of this precise description had never before . . . been perpetrated in the United States, and he trusted in God never might be committed by any of its citizens, the prisoner was sentenced to the penitentiary for two years.[142]

In *Meriam's Case*[143] (1810), the defendant who previously had been adjudged insane and "committed to the house of correction, as one too dangerous to go at large," was indicted for murder. The court found the defendant "not guilty by reason of insanity." A court reporter, commenting on *Meriam*, restated the rules of responsibility for the insane offender: (1) insanity is a defense of last resort; (2) insanity should be clearly proved when relied on for a defense; (3) shocking or "unnatural" crimes do not presuppose insanity; (4) "frenzy" and "violent passions" are not synonymous with insanity; (5) a defense of insanity is to be strictly examined; and (6) the only question to be determined is whether the defendant, at the time of the crime, was "capable of distinguishing good from evil."[144]

In *United States v. Clarke*[145] (1818), the defendant was indicted for the murder of his wife. In his defense it was claimed that he suffered "from long and settled habits of intemperance, had become disordered both in body and mind, and subject to fits which affected both his mind and body." The presiding judge instructed the jury that

> if they should be satisfied, by the evidence, that the prisoner at the time of committing the act charged in the indictment, was in such a state of mental insanity, not produced by the immediate effects of intoxicating drink, as not to have been conscious of the moral turpitude of the act, they should find him not guilty.[146]

The jury found the defendant guilty, and he was sentenced to death.

In *People v. Tripler*[147] (1822), the defendant, who was charged with stealing five silver spoons, entered a plea of insanity on the grounds that her head was "affected by a fall" and "her conduct was strange." The court's instructions to the jury departed from the traditional principles of evidence by placing the burden of proof on the prosecution:

> Although the defence has not been satisfactorily made out, yet there was quite enough made out to raise a doubt in the mind of the court, of the prisoner's being a person of a sound mind; and where a doubt exists, it would always be the safest way to acquit: insanity itself is calamity enough, without inflicting the pain of a conviction and its consequences. The witnesses have not shown any particular act whereby we could discover derangement, yet it is sufficient to say that a doubt has been raised, and that doubt ought to operate in favour of the prisoner.[148]

Hadfield's Case[149] was the first English decision to reject explicitly the "good and evil" test of responsibility for insane offenders. In the United States, the court reporter in *Tripler*[150] and the defense counsel in *People v. De Graff*[151] argued for the incorporation of the principles of *Hadfield's Case* into U.S. law. This would have had a liberalizing effect on the traditional tests of responsibility by allowing broader interpretations of the "good and evil" test.

De Graff, who was indicted for forgery, entered a plea of insanity on the grounds that he had "for the last six months, acted as if he were 'shattered,' and conducted himself very strange, [and] was different from what he used to be." Counsel for the defense contended that the prisoner was "apparently insane," and he introduced the testimony of neighbors who "were unanimous in the opinion that he was crazy." The defendant was "a member of the church," he continued, "and it was extremely improbable that a man in his situation would voluntarily plunge himself into such a depth of guilt." In conclusion, the defense admitted that the plea of insanity was not made out to the complete "satisfaction of the Court, yet but if there was a doubt of his insanity, that doubt ought to be put in the scale of mercy."

The prosecution argued that the insanity defense was too readily made and that he saw in the defendant "no indication of a defective mind: his whole demeanour was shrewd and acute. His conduct, from the beginning to the end, was indicative of his criminal intent, and not of unsound mind." The presiding judge concurred with the prosecution, and the jury returned a verdict of guilty against the prisoner. The court reporter referred to the Tripler case and, noting the conflict as to quantum of proof created by this case, restated the law, suggesting that the "good and evil" test was still the prevailing test of criminal responsibility.[152]

In *Commonwealth v. Miller*[153] (1838), the defendant, aged 23, was indicted for murder in Pennsylvania. The prosecution established that William Miller had stationed himself by the side of a public highway and waited for his victim; "a pedlar soon made his appearance and while he was stooping down to take some articles out of his pack to exhibit to Miller, the latter killed him with his axe." The defense, "in their anxiety to do all in their power to save the prisoner's life," argued that their client was insane as a result of "monomania" and, to this effect, they introduced the expert testimony of "a celebrated phrenologist," O. S. Fowler.[154]

In his instructions to the jury, Judge Ellis Lewis equated "moral insanity," the irresistible propensity for violence arising from "an undue excitement of the passions," with "vice" and held that "it is not generally admitted in legal tribunals as a species of insanity which relieves from responsibility for crime, and it ought never to be admitted as a defence until it is shown that these propensities exist in such violence as to subjugate the intellect, control the will, and render it impossible for the party to do otherwise than yield." The judge questioned the scientific validity of the expert testimony of O. S. Fowler concerning the defendant's "moral insanity."[155] The court suggested that "monomania" might constitute a successful defense:

It was stated to the jury, that the court could perceive no sufficient evidence of *delusion* or hallucination on any subject to establish the existence of *monomania*, still, if the jury believed that the prisoner was, at the time of committing the act charged, "incapable of judging between right and wrong, and did not know that he was committing an offence against the laws of God and man," it would be their duty to acquit. . . . [156]

The jury found the defendant guilty of murder, and the court sentenced him to death. Judge Lewis, in a letter to the *American Phrenological Journal* in 1839, reported that the prisoner "made a full confession, appeared much affected with his situation in reference to a future world, seemed truly penitent, and met death with great firmness, even assisting the sheriff in some of the last sad offices of the melancholy scene."[157]

Thus, in 12[158] cases on the criminal responsibility of the criminally insane offender in the United States between 1816 and 1841, the "right and wrong" (or "good and evil") test was used seven times, and various synonyms were used on three other occasions. As for the two remaining cases, one was based on a plea of drunkenness and the other did not explicitly refer to any test of responsibility. Five cases involved an indictment for murder; four for larceny; and one each for arson, forgery, and assault and battery. According to the judicial records, the plea of insanity was successful only in three cases and, of the remaining nine prisoners who were found guilty, three were sentenced to death and executed. This evidence suggests that U.S. courts were already using a "right and wrong" test of responsibility for the insane long before 1843 and that they were willing to acknowledge the *M'Naghten Case* as something not too foreign to their own experiences. The *M'Naghten* rules, therefore, offered an opportunity to U.S. courts to solidify and legitimate, rather than change, standard practices.

The history of the "right and wrong" test in the United States after 1843 has been well documented in the literature. Following the emergence of the juvenile court system at the end of the last century, this test became obsolete with regard to children. There is, nonetheless, considerable debate as to whether such a test should be revived on the grounds either that it guarantees the constitutional rights of the defendant or that it increases the criminal law's effectiveness as an instrument of moral education.[159]

As far as insanity is concerned, most states formally adopted the "right and wrong" test of responsibility after the trial of Daniel M'Naghten in 1843. Chief Justice Shaw, in *Commonwealth v. Rogers*[160] (1844), generally has been acknowledged as the first U.S. judge to cite *M'Naghten's Case* as an authority for the "right and wrong" test, which was first cited in California in *People v. Coffman* (1864).[161]

In some states the "right and wrong" test has been supplemented by other derivative rules, notably the "irresistible impulse" test. New Hampshire, under the influence of Isaac Ray, rejected the "right and wrong" test and substituted a doctrine that exempted from responsibility a defendant whose crime "was the offspring or product of mental disease."[164] Despite numerous attempts to modify the *M'Naghten* rules, the "right and wrong" test continues to be the traditionally accepted test of responsibility. The *Durham* rule[163] the test proposed by the American Law Institute,[164] the *Currens* rule,[165] and other recent formulations have been accepted in only a few jurisdictions.[166]

Conclusion

The evolution of the "right and wrong" test of criminal responsibility can be traced from Hebrew law, Greek moral philosophy, Roman law, the literature of the Church in the Middle Ages, and English common law to its final elaboration in U.S. case law. There is substantial evidence to suggest that the role of children, as prospective members of adult society, was an expedient and ideologically meaningful reference for rules of criminal responsibility for insane criminal offenders. The "right and wrong" test was used in England to determine the criminal capacity of children as early as the fourteenth century and of the insane probably by the seventeenth century. It has been used widely in the United States for both children and the insane since 1800.

It is clear that the "right and wrong" test of criminal responsibility did not arise in 1843, either in England or in the United States. The "knowledge of right and wrong" test, in the form of its earlier synonym ("knowledge of good and evil"), is traceable to the *Book of Genesis*. The famous M'Naghten trial of 1843 and the subsequent opinion of the judges provided only the name, "*M'Naghten* Rule." The essential concept and phraseology of the rule were already ancient and thoroughly embedded in the law.

TABLE I

Leading Cases on the Criminal Responsibility of Children in American Law, 1806–1882

	Case	Date	Offense	Test of Responsibility & Age	Verdict	Sentence
1.	Doherty's Case (Tennessee)	1806	Murder	Right and Wrong (12)	Not guilty	Acquittal
2.	Aaron's Case (New Jersey)	1818	Murder	Good and Evil (11)	Guilty. Reversed on appeal	Acquittal
3.	Walker's Case (New York)	1820	Petit Larceny	None (7)	Not guilty	Acquittal
4.	Stage's Case (New York)	1820	Grand Larceny	Good and Evil (8)	Guilty	3 years in state prison
5.	Davis's Case (Fed.)	1823	Grand Larceny	Right and Wrong (13)	Not guilty	Acquittal
6.	Teller's Case (Fed.)	1823	Petit Larceny	Right and Wrong (13)	Not guilty	Acquittal
7.	Guild's Case (New Jersey)	1828	Murder	Right and Wrong (12)	Guilty	Death
8.	Elliott's Case (Fed.)	1834	Murder	None (12)	Not guilty	Acquittal
9.	Bostick's Case (Delaware)	1845	Murder & Arson	None (12)	Guilty. Reversed on appeal	Acquittal
10.	Godfrey's Case (Alabama)	1858	Murder	Aware of nature and consequences of act (11)	Guilty	Death
11.	Learnard's Case (Vermont)	1869	Burglary & Larceny	Right and Wrong (13)	Not guilty	Acquittal
12.	Angelo's Case (Illinois)	1880	Manslaughter	Good and Evil (11)	Guilty. Reversed on appeal	Acquittal
13.	Toney's Case (S. Carolina)	1881	Malicious Trespass	Right and Wrong (12)	Not known	Not known
14.	Adams's Case (Missouri)	1882	Murder	None (12)	Guilty. Reversed on appeal	Acquittal

TABLE II

Leading Cases on the Criminal Responsibility of Insane Offenders in American Law, 1818–1841

	Case	Date	Offense	Test of Responsibility	Verdict	Sentence
1.	Cook's Case (New York)	1816	Grand Larceny	None	Guilty	3 years in state prison
2.	Clark's Case (New York)	1816	Petit Larceny	Good and Evil	Guilty	Deportation
3.	Traux's Case (New York)	1816	Grand Larceny	Moral faculties affected by liquor	Not guilty	Acquittal
4.	Sellick's Case (New York)	1816	Murder	Knowledge of Act	Guilty	Death
5.	Ball's Case (New York)	1816	Arson	Good and Evil	Guilty	Fine
6.	Pienovi's Case (New York)	1818	Assault and Battery	Good and Evil	Guilty	2 years in state prison
7.	Meriam's Case (Massachusetts)	1810	Murder	Good and Evil	Not guilty	Commitment
8.	Clarke's Case (Fed.)	1818	Murder	Knowledge of moral turpitude of act	Guilty	Death
9.	Tripler's Case (New York)	1822	Grand Larceny	Understanding of a fourteen-year-old child	Not guilty	Acquittal
10.	De Graff's Case (New York)	1822	Forgery	Good and Evil	Guilty	Not known
11.	Miller's Case (Pennsylvania)	1838	Murder	Right and Wrong	Guilty	Death
12.	Abbot's Case (Connecticut)	1841	Murder	Right and Wrong	Not known	Not known

Notes

[1]See Graves, R., Patai, R. (1966), *Hebrew Myths.* New York: McGraw Hill.

[2]Genesis 2:9, 2:16–17, 3:4–5, 3:22–23 (Revised Standard Version) (italics added).

[3]*Deuteronomy* 1:39; *2 Samuel* 14:17; *1 Kings* 3:9; *Isaiah* 7:14–16; *Jeremiah* 4:22; *Hebrews* 5:14.

[4]Hertz, J. H. (1956), *Pentateuch and Haftorahs.* New York: Bloch. See also Graves & Patai, op. cit., sup. note 1, p. 81, para. 13.

[5]See, e.g., *People v. Wolff*, 61 Cal. 2d 795, 800, 394 P.2d 959, 961–62, 40 Cal. Rptr. 271, 273–74 (1964).

[6]Horowitz, G. (1953), *The Spirit of Jewish Law.* New York: Central Book Co., pp. 167–70.

[7]"A deaf-mute, an idiot and a minor are awkward to deal with, as he who injures them is liable [to pay], whereas if they injure others they are exempt" (*The Babylonian Talmud: Baba Kamma* [1935] London: Soncino Press, pp. 501–02.) "To clash with a deaf-mute, an imbecile, or a minor is bad, seeing that if one wounds one of these, he is liable, whereas if they wound others, they are exempt. Even if a deaf-mute becomes normal, or an imbecile becomes sane, or a minor reaches majority, they are not liable for payment inasmuch as they were legally irresponsible when they caused the wound" (Code of Maimonides, Book 11: Book of Tort [1954], trans. H. Klein. New Haven, CT: Yale University Press).

[8]"During the fifth century there had clearly been a greater emphasis on fault as the basis of liability, and in the fourth Demosthenes puts the completely different attitude shown to intentional and unintentional injuries among the unwritten laws of nature supported by the universal moral sense of mankind" Jones, J. W. (1956), *The Law and Legal Theory of the Greeks.* Oxford: Clarendon, p. 264.

[9]Plato, *Laws*, Book 9, trans. Taylor (1931), p. 256.

[10]Plato, *The Republic* (trans. F. M. Cornford). New York: Oxford University Press, 1945, p. 350. See also Agretelis (1965), Mens rea in Plato and Aristotle, *Issues in Criminology*, 1:19.

[11]Aristotle, *The Nichomachean Ethics* (trans. W. D. Ross, 1954) p. 58.

[12]"[I]f the acts that are in accordance with the virtues have themselves a certain character it does not follow that they are done justly or temperately. The agent also must be in a certain condition when he does them; in the first place he must have knowledge secondly he must choose the acts, and choose them for their own sakes, and thirdly action must proceed from a firm and unchangeable character" (Ibid., p. 34).

[13]Jones, op. cit., sup. note 8, p. 273.

[14]For a general discussion of the Twelve Tables, whose authorship and content are subject to question, see Buckland (1963), *A Text-Book of Roman Law*, 1–2.

[15] The Institutes of Gaius (trans. F. de Zulueata) 1:223. Oxford: Clarendon Press, 1946. For a discussion of the *Lex Aguilia*, see Buckland, op. cit., sup. note 14, pp. 580–82.

[16] Buckland, op. cit., sup. note 14, p. 585.

[17] Justinian, *Digest*, 48.8.12.

[18] Moyle, J. B. (1955), *Imperatoris Justaniani Instutionum*. Oxford: Clarendon Press, pp. 416–17.

[19] Institutes of Gaius, op. cit., sup. note 15, p. 223.

[20] Justinian, *Digest*, op. cit., sup. note 17, 48.8.3.

[21] Justinian, *Institutes*, 3.19.9..

[22] Ibid.

[23] Justinian, *Digest*, op. cit., sup. note 17, 48.8.12. In English law this maxim was commonly written as *furiosus solo furore dunitur*,

[24] Levitt, (1922), The origin of the doctrine of mens rea, *Ill. Law Rev.*, 117:136.

[25] For a general view of how Christian ethics permeated the whole human fabric, see De Wulf (1922), *Philosophy and Civilization in the Middle Ages*.

[26] Augustine, *The Anti-Pelagian Works*. On "Grace and Free Will," ch. 5: "We sin either because we do not know what we ought to do, or because we do what we already know we should not do. The first, that of sinning without knowing the wrongness of a thing, is the sin of ignorance. The second, that of sinning while knowing a thing to be wrong, is the sin of weakness." Augustine, *Enchiridion*, ch. 81. (The works of Augustine cited in notes 26 and 27 were translated by Jerry R. Craddock, Dept. of Romance Philology, University of California, Berkeley, in June 1965.)

[27] Augustine, *On the Forgiveness of Sins and Baptism*, Book 1. ch. 66–67.

[28] The Venerable Bede, in *Cantica Canticorum Alleogirca Exposition* lib. 1, 1070.

[29] Michel, D. (1340), *Auenbit of Inwyt [Remorse of Conscience]*, ed. R. Morris (Trans., M. B. King, Dept. of Comparative Literature, University of California, Berkeley). London: The Early English Text Society, 1866.

[30] The development of the "good and evil" test in English criminal law is traced more systematically in Platt, A. M. (1965), The Criminal Responsibility of the Mentally Ill in England, 1100–1843 (unpublished thesis, University of California, Berkeley, School of Criminology).

[31] Y.B., 6 & 7 Edw. II, in *Selden Society* (1909) 24:109.

[32] See Kean (1937), The history of the criminal liability of children. *Law Quart. Rev.*, 53:364.

[33] Y.B., 11 & 12 Edw. III, 626 (Horwood ed. 1883). 31.

[34] See Platt, op. cit., sup. note 30, pp. 53–78.

[35] Lambard, W. (1581), *Eirenarcha: or of the office of the Justices of Peace in two Bookes: Gathered. 1579. and Now Revised, and Firste Published, in.the. 24. Yeare of the Peaceable Reigne of Our Grations Queene Elizabeth.* Imprinted by Ra: Newberry, and H. Byneman, by the ass. of Ri. Tot. & Chr. Bar. (First Book, Ch. 21, p. 218).

[36]Coke, E. (1719), *Institutes of the Laws of England, or A Commentary Upon Littleton*, 2:247. In the Savoy [London], printed for Eliz. Nutt & R. Gosling . . . , pp. 247b, 247a. See also Kean, op. cit., sup. note 32, p. 370.

[37]Dalton does not cite Lambard, but it seems likely that he was familiar with Lambard or at least with some other (now unknown) Elizabethan legal source. It is hardly possible that he would have presumed to have initiated his own formulation without reference to previous authoritative sources. Assuming that he knew Lambard's writing, it is conceivable that he failed to note that Lambard's qualifying phrase, "y apparently hath no knowledge of good nor evil," could be interpreted as applying only to the child and not to "mad man, or a naturall foole, or a lunatike in the time of his lunacie." He (or some other legal writer or judge) may have assumed that the good and evil phrase applied equally to all, as did Biggs, J., Jr. (1955), *The Guilty Mind*. New York: Harcourt Brace.

[38]Dalton, M. (1630), *The Countrey Justice*. In the Savoy [London], printed by E. & R. Nutt & R. Gosling, p. 244.

[39]Hale, M. (1736), *Historia Placitorum Coronae. The History of the Pleas of the Crown . . . Now first published . . . with . . . notes by Sollom Emlyn*. In the Savoy [London], printed by E. & R. Nutt & R. Gosling.

[40]Ibid., p. 30.

[41]Perkins, R . M. (1957), *Criminal Law*. Brooklyn, NY: Foundation Press, p. 740.

[42]Stephen, J. F. (1883), *A History of the Criminal Law of England*, 3 vols. London: Macmillan.

[43]But those that are to be esteemed guilty of any offences must have the use of their reason, and be at their own disposal or liberty. For those that want reason to distinguish betwixt good and evil (as infants under the age of discretion (viz.), under the age of fourteen years, idcots, lunaticks etc.) ought not to be prosecuted for any crime" (Wood, T. [1728], *An Institute of the Laws of England*. In the Savoy [London]: E. & R. Nutt & R. Gosling, 4th ed. corrected, p. 339).

[44]Trial of Edward Arnold (1812). In: *A Complete Collection of State Trials and Proceedings for High Treason and other Crimes and Misdemeaners, 1722–1725*, Vol. 15, compiler T. B. Howell. London: T. C. Hansard, p. 465.

[45]Trial of Lawrence, Earl Ferrers. In Howell, op. cit., sup. note 44, Vol. 19, p. 885.

[46]Collinson, G. D. (1812), *A Treatise on the Law Concerning Idiots, Lunatics, and Other Persons Non Compotes Mentis*. London: W. Reed, p. 477.

[47]Ibid., pp. 636, 657.

[48]Ibid., p. 673.

[49]Shelford, L. (1833), *Lunatics, Idiots, and Persons of Unsound Mind*. London: S. Sweet, and Stevens & Sons, p. 465.

[50]5 Car. & P. 168 (1831); Lloyd, J. (1905), Insanity: Forms and Medicolegal Relations. In: *Medical Jurisprudence*, ed. F. Wharton & M. Stillé, 498 (5th ed.). Rochester, NY: Lawyer's Cooperative, §498.

[51] 9 Car. & P. 525 (1840); Wharton & Stillé, op. cit., sup. note 50, p. 500.

[52] Howell, T. B., ed. (1800), p. 1281. See *The Speeches of the Hon. Thomas Erskine* (1813). Ridgeway ed., p. 495.

[53] Diamond, B. L. (1956), Isaac Ray and the trial of Daniel M'Naghten, *Amer. J. Psychiat.*, 112: 651, 655.

[54] Koestler, A. (1957), *Reflections on Hanging*. New York: Macmillan, p. 75.

[55] Regina v. M'Naghten, 10 Clark and F. 200, 8 Eng. Rep. 718 (1843).

[56] Collinson, op. cit., sup. note 46, p. 477.

[57] Ibid., p. 657.

[58] In an important California murder case, Judge Dwinelle instructed the jury that "a person sometimes insane, who has lucid intervals, or is so far sane as to distinguish good from evil, right from wrong, may commit a crime and be legally held responsible" (*Offical Report of the Trial of Laura D. Fair, for the Murder of Alex P. Crittenden Including the Testimony, the Arguments of Counsel. . . . and the Entire Correspondence of the Parties . . . From the Shorthand Notes of Marsh & Osbourne . . .* [1871], San Francisco: San Francisco Cooperative Printing. Both of the phrases, "good and evil" and "right and wrong," were also used in cases of infant incapacity. See, e.g., *State v. Gain*, 9 Humph. 118 [Tenn. 1848]).

[59] Blackstone, W. (1962), *Commentaries on the Laws of England: Of Public Wrongs*, Vol. 4. Boston: Beacon Press, pp. 23–24.

[60] 2 Tenn. 79 (1806).

[61] Ibid., p. 82.

[62] Ibid, p. 87.

[63] N.J.L. 263 (1818).

[64] Ibid., pp. 272–73.

[65] Ibid., p. 278. The trial judge subsequently restated the rules of responsibility for children: "The great subject of inquiry in all cases, ought to be, the legal capacity of the prisoner; and this is found in some, much earlier than others. The real value of the distinctions is to fix the party upon whom the proof of this capacity lies. There is indeed an age so tender that the nature and consequences of acts cannot be comprehended, and every uncorrupted feeling of the heart, as well as every moral and legal principle, forbids punishment. But after we pass this age and progress towards maturity, there have been periods settled, which ascertain the presumption of law, as to the existence of this capacity. If under fourteen, especially under twelve years, the law presumes that it does not exist and if the state seek to punish, it must conclusively establish it. If above the age of fourteen, the law presumes its existence, and if the accused would seek to avoid punishment, he must overcome that presumption by sufficient evidence. But wherever the capacity is established, either by this presumption of law, or the testimony of witnesses, punishment always follows the infraction of the law. If the intelligence to apprehend the consequences of acts; to reason upon duty; to *distinguish between right and wrong*; if the consciousness of guilt and innocence be

clearly manifested, then this capacity is shown: in the language of the books, the accused is *capax doli,* and, as a rational and moral agent, must abide the results of his own conduct" (Ibid., p. 279; italics added).

[66]Ibid., p. 271.

[67]Ibid., p. 272.

[68]4 Del. (4 Harr.) 563 (1945).

[69]Ibid., p. 565.

[70]City-Hall Recorder (New York City) (1820), 5:137.

[71]Ibid., p. 138.

[72]Ibid., p. 177.

[73]Ibid., p. 178.

[74]Wheeler (1823), *Criminal Law Cases,* vol. 1, p. 230.

[75]Ibid., pp. 230–31.

[76]Ibid., p. 231.

[77]Ibid., pp. 231–32.

[78]Ibid., pp. 233–34. In *Commonwealth v. Elliot,* 4 Law Rep. 329 (1842), a boy of twelve years was acquitted of a charge of murder. "The defense . . . rested mainly on the entire want of any adequate motive for so malignant an act; on the youth and inexperience of the prisoner. . . ."

[79]N.J.L. (1828), 10:163.

[80]Ibid., p. 170.

[81]Ibid.

[82]Ibid., p. 174.

[83]See sup. note 63. The court, in *Guild,* said that "although an original confession may have been obtained by improper means, subsequent confessions of the same or of like facts may be admitted, if the court believes from the length of time intervening, from proper warning of the consequences of confession, or from other circumstances, that the delusive hopes or fears under the influence of which the original confession was obtained, were entirely dispelled" (N.J.L.[1828], 10:180–181).

[84]The Chief Justice approved the following statement from Leach's edition of Hawkins: "[F]rom this supposed imbecility of mind, the protective humanity of the law will not, without anxious circumspection, permit an infant to be convicted on his own confession. Yet if it appear, by strong and pregnant evidence and circumstances, that he was perfectly conscious of the nature and malignity of the crime, the verdict of a jury may find him guilty and judgment of death be given against him" (Ibid., p. 189).

[85]31 Ala. 323 (1858).

[86]Ibid., pp. 326–27.

[87]10 N.J.L.(1828), 10:163.

[88]N.J.L (1818), 4:263.

[89]41 Vt. 585 (1869).

[90]Ibid.

[91]Ibid.

[92]Ibid., p. 587.

[93]Ibid., p. 589 (italics added).

[94]96 Ill. 209 (1880).

[95]Justice Walker criticized the prosecution counsel for proposing to the jury that the defendant's refusal to take the witness stand should be taken as evidence of his guilt. "We can not conceive that any member of the bar could deliberately seek by such means to wrongfully procure a conviction and the execution of a fellow being, when his highest professional duty to his client only requires him to see that there is a fair trial according to the law and evidence" (Ibid., p. 213).

[96]Ibid., pp. 212–13.

[97]15 S.C. 409 (1881).

[98]Chief Justice Simpson held that "out of tenderness to infants—the ease with which they may be misled—their want of foresight and their wayward, disposition, no doubt, the evidence of malice, which is to supply age, should be strong and clear beyond all doubt and contradiction; . . . but we find no authority for the position that this evidence must be outside of the facts of the offence itself. . . ." (Ibid., p. 414).

[99]16 Mo. 355 (1882).

[100]Ibid.: "But we are very clearly of opinion that the court erred in its view of the law touching the age of defendant. We refer to the third and seventh instructions given at the instance of the State. Those instructions virtually told the jury that the defendant's age should not affect the conclusion at which they should arrive, any more than if he had been of mature years. This is not the law" (p. 358).

[101]Godfrey v. State, 31 Ala. 323 (1858); State v. Guild, 10 N.J.L. 163 (1828).

[102]There is a possibility that in the other case, State v. Guild, sup. note 102, the victim was also white.

[103]See summary of cases in Table 1, in Appendix.

[104]31 Ala. 323 (1858).

[105]4 Del. (4 Harr.) 563 (1845).

[106]Psychiatric dissatisfaction with the M'Naghten rules has been well summarized in Allen, F. A. (1964), The Borderland of Criminal Justice. Chicago: University of Chicago Press, pp. 109–13.

[107]Lloyd, op. cit., sup. note 50, p. 535.

[108]Weihofen, H. (1933), Insanity as a Defense in Criminal Law. New York: Commonwealth Fund, p. 17.

[109]Royal Commission on Capital Punishment 1949–1953. (1953), Report 397. London: H. M. Stationery Off.

[110]Lloyd, op. cit., sup. note 50, p. 554.

[111]Glueck, S. (1925), Mental Disorder and the Criminal Law: A Study in Medico-Legal Jurisprudence with an Appendix of State Legislation and Interpretive Decisions. Boston: Little, Brown, p. 153.

[112]See Weihofen, op. cit., sup. note 108, pp. 14–44.

[113]Deutsch, A. (1949), *The Mentally Ill in America*. New York: Columbia University Press, 1960, p. 387.

[114]Glueck, op. cit., sup. note 111, p. 157.

[115]The earlier editions of Wharton and Stillé's *Medical Jurisprudence*, published in 1855, 1860, 1872, and 1882, do not include a comprehensive survey of the history of legal insanity. In the fifth edition (1905), according to the preface, "the whole subject of the medical jurisprudence of insanity has been written by Dr. James Hendrie Lloyd. This is therefore an entirely new work, not a mere edition of the former volume."

[116]Lloyd, op. cit., sup. note 50, p. 556.

[117]Glueck, op. cit., sup. note 111, p. 154.

[118]Bishop, J. P. (1856), *Commentary on the Criminal Law*. Boston: Little, Brown.

[119]*The Crown Circuit Companion* (1816), 1st Amer. Ed. New York: R. McDermott & D. D. Arden. See also Brown (1892), *The Elements of Criminal Law*.

[120]Burn, R. (1792), *Burn's Abridgement, or the American Justice*, 2nd ed., Dover, NH: Eliphalet Ladd, p. 300.

[121]Male (1819), Epitome of juridical or forensic medicine. In: *Tracts on Medical Jurisprudence*, ed. T. Cooper. Philadelphia, PA: James Webster, pp. 251, 254.

[122]Collinson, op. cit., sup. note 46, p. 474.

[123]Male, op. cit., sup. note 121, p. 255.

[124]Wood, W. (1852), *Remarks on the Plea of Insanity and the Management of Criminal Lunatics*. London: Longman, Brown, Green & Longman, pp. 4–5.

[125]Halleck, S. (1965), American psychiatry and the criminal: A historical review. *Amer. J. Psychiat.*, 121 (suppl.):i–xxxi.

[126]Beck, T. R. (1823), *Elements of Medical Jurisprudence*, Albany, NY: Websters & Skinners.

[127]Collinson, op. cit., sup. note 46, p. 657. See text accompanying sup. note 57.

[128]Beck, op. cit., sup. note 126, pp. 369–70.

[129]10 Clark & F. 200, 8 Eng. Rep. 718 (1843).

[130]Ray, I. (1853), *A Treatise on the Medical Jurisprudence of Insanity*, 3rd ed. Boston: Little, Brown, p. 13.

[131]Ibid., p. 32.

[132]City-Hall Recorder (New York City) (1816), 5:1.

[133]Ibid., p. 176.

[134]Ibid., p. 177.

[135]Ibid., p. 44.

[136]Ibid., p. 105.

[137]Ibid., p. 190.

[138]City-Hall Recorder (New York City) (1817), 2:85.

[139]City-Hall Recorder (New York City) (1818), 3:123.

[140]Ibid., p. 126.

[141]Ibid., pp. 126–27.

[142]Ibid., p. 127.

[143]7 Mass. 168 (1810).

[144]City-Hall Recorder (New York City) (1822), 6:162.

[145]25 Fed. Cas. 454 (C.C.D.C. 1818).

[146]Ibid.

[147]City-Hall Recorder (New York City) (1822), 7:48

[148]Ibid., p. 49.

[149]Howell, T. B. (1800), State Trials, op. cit., sup. note 44.

[150]City-Hall Recorder (New York City) (1822), 48, 7:5.

[151]Ibid., p. 203.

[152]Ibid., p. 218.

[153]Lewis (1848), An Abridgment of the Criminal Law of the United States, pp. 399–401.

[154]Fowler described the defendant as "of the lymphatic temperament; and stated that persons of this temperament are more apt to be deranged upon the animal passions than upon the intellectual or moral faculties. He also, among other things, described the prisoner's phrenological developments as they appeared to him on an examination some days previously in the prisoner's cell. The organs of 'Destructiveness, Secretiveness and Acquisitiveness' were stated by Mr. Fowler to be immense, the head measuring about seven and a quarter inches in diameter from ear to ear" (Ibid., p. 400).

[155]The scientific authenticity and medical proof of phrenology in the nineteenth century raised the same kind of doubts for judges and juries as does the concept of psychopathy today.

[156]Lewis, op. cit., sup. note 153, p. 401.

[157]In an interesting postscript to this case, the editors of the Phrenological Journal reconstructed a crude case history of William Miller to explain his "vicious and criminal conduct and the gradual process by which he became so hardened and cruel." Miller's parents were poor, but "not in absolute poverty," and they had "never shown as much attention to education as people generally do, and their unhappy son was said to be exceedingly illiterate. His mother died when he was quite young. He was subject to little, if any, parental restraint and government; received, comparatively, no education, nor moral and religious instruction; early gave way to his 'evil passions'; was greatly encouraged by bad associates; was not restrained by the ties of family affection, nor influenced much by any relations to friends and acquaintances, either in regard to his business or his character; first commenced stealing little things, then lying; persevered constantly in such offences for nearly fifteen years, till he finally committed robbery and murder. But it appears that he had planned several murders, and even that of his 'own' brother, before the execution of his last fatal deed. Let every reader observe that Miller grew up with his intellectual faculties uneducated,' his moral sentiments unenlightened, his domestic feelings 'but little exercised', and his selfish propensities and sentiments 'unrestrained'. We need not say, that these facts involve important principles in the true physiology of the brain and the silence of mind."

[158]The twelfth case, *People v. Abbot* (1841), is cited by Ray, op. cit., sup. note 130, p. 55. See summary of cases in Table II in Appendix.

[159]This conflict between the "legal moralists," represented by Stephen, Denning, Devlin, Goddard, and Wigmore, and the "constitutionalists," represented by Francis Allen, Matza, Rubin, Jeffery, and Tappan, has been partially analyzed by Hart (1963), *Art, Law, Liberty and Morality.*

[160]48 Mass. 500 (1844). 161 24 Cal. 230 (1864).

[162]*State v. Jones,* 50 N.H. 369 (1871); *State v. Pike,* 49 N.H. 399 (1869).

[163]*Durham v. United States,* 214 F.2d 862 (D.C. Cir. 1954).

[164]American Law Institute, (1954), *Model Penal Code* §4.01.

[165]*United States v. Currens,* 290 F.2d 751 (3d Cir. 1961).

[166]For a discussion of these tests and also California's experience with the test of diminished responsibility, see "Criminal Responsibility of the Mentally Ill," this volume. See also Diamond, D. L. (1962), *From M'Naghten to Currens, and beyond. Calif. L. Rev.,* 50:189.

Criminal Responsibility of the Mentally Ill

[1961]

The father of modern psychiatry was a Rhenish-German physician, Johann Weyer (1515–1588). In his great book, *De Praestigiis Daemonum*, published in 1563,[1] Weyer vigorously attacked the superstition of witchcraft and made the daring assertion that the supposed witches prosecuted and burned to death by the Inquisition were innocent victims of melancholia and delusions.

The criminal code of Saxony, published nine years later, in 1572, states:

> In the course of the past few years many books have appeared in which sorcery is considered not a crime but a superstition and a melancholy, and these insist violently that it should not be punished by death. The *Wieri rationes* [Weyer's reasonings] are not very important, for he is a physician and not a jurist.[2]

I am a physician and not a jurist, so my reasonings may not be very important. Further, I am a psychiatrist and a psychoanalyst. To some this will mean that my reasonings are not only unimportant, but impudent and presumptuous as well. To the latter two judgments I will agree. For the subject of *mens rea* and criminal responsibility is, in the words of Weihofen: "one of the most difficult concepts in Criminal Law. . . . The problems . . . have taxed the ingenuity of jurists for hundred of years. They are inordinately complex and involve a great many ramifications."[3] Yet to me, a psychiatrist and psychoanalyst, the legal concept of *mens rea* offers so much promise of a rational bridge between the science of medical psychology and that of jurisprudence that I feel impelled to be as presumptuous and as impudent as is necessary to make my point.

For psychiatry to make a significant contribution to the law, there must be a bridge between medicine and the law that the psychiatrist may cross. And when he arrives at the other side, there must be room for him to move about—to function within the framework of his familiar values and goals. Perhaps in Rome one must do as the Romans do, but in the courtroom the psychiatrist must never do as the lawyer does. In the courtroom, no less than in his own office and hospital, the psychiatrist can apply only his own skills and knowledge and be oriented by his own medical values and goals. If he does otherwise, he is no longer an expert; instead he is an amateur. The instant he takes the witness stand he will change from a competent clinician into an incompetent lawyer, or a sophomore philosopher, or a pious moralist. Worst of all, he will deserve the title that to a physician is the most denigrating of all—that of quack.

Psychiatry, like all medicine, is dedicated to the preservation of life and health; it is humanistic and individualistic; its goals are cure and rehabilitation, protection of the individual, and protection of society; it is nonjudgmental, amoral (but not unethical), and impious, in that it must treat all alike, friend or enemy, good citizen or criminal, believer or heretic; it is scientific, by which I mean that it is reality oriented and deals with human beings instead of with abstractions, fictions, philosophical syllogisms, or theoretical moralities; its method is that of all sciences—experimentation, statistical analysis, and trial and error within a framework of its own hypotheses; finally, it must perpetually put to practical test its theories, abandon those which fail to meet the test, and adopt new theories and practices as they become of evident usefulness.

I believe that most of the mutual dissatisfaction between psychiatry and the law is the result of a lack of a common, theoretical bridge between the two professions. Such a bridge is required for effective communications and responsible interchange of ideas. Within the law, the psychiatrist must find an area within which he can operate without changing his values and goals. The legal rules and procedures for the determination of insanity and criminal responsibility do not provide such a bridge, and so in this area of the criminal law there has been no effective communication and interchange of ideas, with sporadic exceptions, in hundreds of years of contact between medicine and law.[4]

Whenever a psychiatrist is called upon to testify, under the M'Naghten Rule of a knowledge of right and wrong, as to the sanity or insanity of a defendant, the psychiatrist must either renounce his own values with all their medicohumanistic implications and thereby become a puppet doctor, used by the law to further the punitive and vengeful goals demanded by our society; or he must commit perjury if he accepts a literal definition of the M'Naghten Rule. If he tells the truth—stating on the witness stand that just about every defendant, no matter how mentally ill, no matter how far advanced his psychosis, knows the difference between right and wrong in the literal sense of the phrase—he becomes an expeditor to the gallows or gas chamber.

To illustrate what I call perjury: very recently I testified for the defense in the murder trial of a very nice and respectable middle-class woman, the young mother of two children. The defendant had, with care and precision, strangled her second child when he was eight weeks old. He had been crying incessantly, and the mother thought that she was not able to care properly for the child and that it would be better off dead. At the time the deed was committed, the mother knew perfectly well what she was doing. She was not suffering, at that time, from delusions or hallucinations, nor was there any grossly visibly evidence of mental abnormality. She knew the nature and quality of her act and that it was wrong. Nevertheless, at the moment of the killing she believed it to be the only course of action open to her.

There was no difficulty in convincing the court that the defendant was legally insane and did not know right from wrong because of mental disease. The three court-appointed psychiatrists agreed with my testimony that she was legally insane. All of us had arrived at approximately the same clinical findings. Four years earlier, with the birth of the first child, she had developed a severe postpartum psychosis characterized by several weeks of overt delusions, hallucinations, and psychotic behavior. Although she had similar destructive thoughts toward her first baby, she was so psychotically disorganized that she was not able to translate these into action. Within a few weeks she had recovered, having experienced a delusional ecstasy of rebirth herself, and until the birth of her second child lived a relatively normal life with no obvious evidence of mental abnormality. The first child thrived normally with the loving care of her mother.

Remarkably, there was a family history of the defendant, father, two brothers, and two sisters suffering from schizophrenic psychoses, and all had been repeatedly hospitalized in a state mental institution. Psychological testing of the defendant shortly after the killing revealed that, despite the absence of any gross signs of mental illness, there was sufficient abnormality of thought and emotion for a diagnosis of a still-existing schizophrenia; and all the clinical facts taken together left no doubt that the slaying of her child was a direct consequence of her mental illness. This case is typical, for seldom do mentally ill persons commit crimes at the height of their psychotic disorganization. They are much more apt to act out a suicidal or murderous impulse when they are in better control of their faculties and able to translate their disturbed emotions into real actions. Yet it is at those times of relative recovery that they know, within the strictures of *M'Naghten*, right from wrong.

This perjury can be justified and explained away by all sort of rationalizations: the defendant really did not know what she was doing; her act was so totally deviant from any normal maternal behavior and the evidence of mental disease so conclusive that she just could not have known the "nature and quality" of her act; or, the word "know" in the M'Naghten formula does not mean what it says, but rather means "to appreciate" or "to comprehend" or "to realize in its full meaning." Professor James Hall[5] and Dr. Gregory Zilboorg[6] both endorse this widening of the scope of the word "know." I endorse this too, but I do not like having to take refuge in such semantic devices.

Central to the difficulties with any definition of legal insanity is the all-or-none conceptualization of the law. A defendant is either sane and totally responsible, or insane and not at all responsible. Such all-or-none concepts are foreign to modern psychiatric thinking. Neither normal persons nor mentally disturbed persons are ever "all-or-none" in their psychological functioning. When such an arbitrary division is required of a psychiatric expert, he is liable to testify capriciously and not in accord with all the psychological facts of the case.

Psychiatrists have permitted themselves to be used in varied ways by the law, law enforcement agencies, and penal institutions. Psychiatrists have been used to extort illegal confessions through hypnotic suggestion.[7] Psychiatrists have administered shock treatment to prisoners awaiting execution so that the prisoners could be brought back into sufficient contact with reality to be put to death.[8] Psychiatrists have testified, under oath, that defendants were sane and mentally normal—even when those experts had absolute medical evidence to the contrary—because they believed "the defendant was too dangerous to be allowed to escape execution."[9] There have been instances where a psychiatrist has concealed from the defendant that he was a psychiatrist, deceitfully using his status as a physician who wants to help and cure, as a means of obtaining information.[10] These deplorable examples inevitably follow from psychiatrists' abandonment of medical values and goals.

The great majority of psychiatrists, and nearly all psychodynamic and therapeutically oriented psychiatrists and psychoanalysts, avoid medicolegal work like the plague. They would never be willing to depart from their humanistic, therapeutic value system, and they feel incapable of coping with the all-or-none fictional abstractions of M'Naghten.

Sigmund Freud was exceedingly cautious about the possible application of psychoanalysis to the legal process,[11] despite the fact that he was intensely interested in law and in criminal behavior. He had, in fact, very seriously considered becoming a lawyer instead of a physician.[12] As early as 1906, Freud had been a guest lecturer at a University of Vienna seminar in jurisprudence. He discussed the use of psychoanalysis for obtaining legal evidence. He strongly emphasized the highly experimental nature of such a method and insisted that it be used only in the spirit of research and that the results must never be allowed to influence the verdict of the court. He said, "It would, indeed, be best if the Court were never informed of the conclusion which you had drawn from your examination on the question of the defendant's guilt."[13]

In 1922, the son of an old servant of Freud's shot his father, although not fatally. The father had attempted to rape the boy's half-sister. Freud personally paid all the legal expenses and engaged the leading forensic psychiatrist to participate in the defense. Freud wrote a memorandum saying that any attempt to seek for deeper motives would only obscure the plain facts. The boy was acquitted on a verdict of temporary insanity.[14]

In 1924, during the Leopold-Loeb trial, Freud was offered $25,000 by Colonel McCormick of the *Chicago Tribune* to come to Chicago and psychoanalyze the defendants from the courtroom. The Hearst papers offered any sum Freud would name as well as a chartered ocean liner so that he could travel undisturbed by other company. He declined both offers.[15] Freud strongly deprecated any "half-baked" application of psychoanalytic theories in legal proceedings, and his only other excursion into the medicolegal field was a short paper published in 1931 commenting upon the expert testimony in a prominent trial.[16]

Following Freud's example, psychoanalysts have remained remote from the courtroom, although still intensely interested in what is happening in law and criminology. Some, like Alexander,[17] have made a penetrating analysis of the judicial process and the psychological implications of the public trial and the institutionalized vengeance upon the criminal. Zilboorg wrote brilliantly and extensively on the need for legal reform in the handling of the mentally ill offender.[18] Roche, having practiced as a prison psychiatrist for over ten years, had considerable direct experience in the psychoanalytic investigation of crime; yet he shares with Freud a pessimism as to the application of psychoanalytic concepts to the trial procedure. He believes that it is more appropriate to the pre- and posttrial phases.[19] Szasz is convinced that there is no place for the psychiatrist and his theories in the courtroom[20] and that attempts at rapprochement between psychiatry and the law are neither possible nor desirable.[21]

Thus, psychoanalysts and dynamically oriented psychiatrists, although vociferous in their demands for legal reform, by and large have been unable or unwilling to participate in the only ways in which the law could be altered—either by actual participation in the criminal trial and subsequent appellate procedures in order to influence directly the higher courts toward decisions that would reflect modern psychiatric attitudes or by direct appeal to the legislature. I fear that much of what is written and said by our leading psychiatric authorities is dismissed by the courts and the legislature as heckling from the sidelines and is not even considered as grounds for legal reform.

I have had occasion to review both the psychiatric and the legal literature, as well as the major court decisions, dealing with the responsibility of mentally ill criminal offenders. I have covered a period of well over 150 years and even much further back in history in terms of the few original sources that are available. There does not appear to have been any particular resolution of the breach between medicine and the law. For a hundred years and more the arguments have been monotonously the same on both sides. The judges are critical and skeptical of the physicians, and the physicians are scornful and deprecating toward the law and the courts. The arguments are depressingly the same whether one is reading books in the early nineteenth century or in the mid-twentieth century. It is discouraging that the best of all books in the English language on forensic psychiatry was written over 120 years ago. It is, of course, Dr. Isaac Ray's *A Treatise on the Medical Jurisprudence of Insanity*, published five years before the M'Naghten trial.[22]

The M'Naghten trial in 1843, which is not to be confused with the subsequent "Opinion of the Judges" promulgating the *M'Naghten* Rules, was a model of good trial procedure. The medical testimony was unanimous that M'Naghten was insane, and the arguments of counsel provided a scholarly debate between the traditional legal concepts of insanity as laid down by Coke and Hale in the seventeenth and eighteenth centuries and the modern medical concepts proposed by Isaac Ray in the nineteenth century. Dr. Ray, through defense counsel's use of his book, clearly won the day, for Justice Tindal appropriately directed a verdict of not guilty by reason of insanity. This triumph for the psychiatric point of view was short lived. Within a few months the public furor over the verdict led to a parliamentary investigation, and the judges retreated under political pressure back to the medieval formula of a "knowledge of good and evil" as the test of criminal responsibility.[23]

Today we have Judge Bazelon's decision in *Durham*.[24] It has been greeted with as much enthusiasm by psychiatrists and enlightened juries in 1954 as was Isaac Ray's contribution in 1838. Yet such enthusiasm cannot be sustained. I cannot agree with the optimism of my very good friend Watson, who writes: "While no major jurisdiction has yet adopted *Durham*, many have had to exert strong pressure to resist it. These courts have gone to great length to prove why they should not abandon

M'Naghten. Psychiatrists should recognize this as the earliest stage of acceptance. . ."[25]

Is there a way out of this stalemate? Is there a way of outflanking the unbridgeable gulf that separates the thinking of the jurist and that of the psychiatrist? Does there exist within the law a conceptual framework that is, or could be made to be, in closer correspondence to the conceptualizations and value systems inherent in modern psychiatry, particularly psychoanalytic psychology?

I believe there is and that the key to the development of a state of rapport between psychiatry and the law exists within the ancient doctrine of *mens rea.* I am convinced that within the jurisprudence of the criminal law there is a nuclear concept—*mens rea*—that is capable of an evolutionary development which will provide an effective bridge of communication between psychiatry and the law and will provide ample room within the judicial process for psychiatrists to move about freely without offense to the values and goals inherent in medical psychology. And of even greater importance is the probability that such evolutionary development will correspond closely to the intrinsic logic and tradition of the common law. I will even go so far as to declare that any evidence to the contrary—any past trends in the law that deny the crucial psychological implications of *mens rea*, or that relegate *mens rea* to a subordinate position in the criminal law—represents legal aberrations and deviations inconsistent with the common law's own philosophy, logic, and values. Out of this ancient doctrine of *mens rea*—of criminal intent—has finally evolved the modern principle of *diminished responsibility* of the mentally ill. This principle, I believe, will form the keystone of the bridge between psychiatry and law. Inexorably it will lead to a fusion of criminal jurisprudence and penology with all the behavioral sciences.

The historical background of *mens rea*, as the requisite mental element without which there can be no crime, condenses within itself the entire history of civilized morality, ethics, philosophy, and religion.[26] I confess that I become impatient with some of the involved discussions about whether exceptions to the legal maxim *Actus non facit reum, nisi mens sit rea* ever existed or do exist today. It is to me quite irrelevant whether or not any particular primitive society punished mere accidents as if they were crimes. And I cannot regard the mental element of criminality as representing exclusively the grafting of a theological concept of sin onto the law. Granted that in ancient and medieval times ethics and morality were so intimately bound together with theology that a separation, in retrospect, cannot be made. But I do not believe it is correct to assume that without

Biblical and Church law there would have been no historical development of the ethical values reflected in this legal maxim. It is a common prejudice existing even today to assume that without theology there can be no morality. Hence, it is always surprising to some persons to discover that the atheist is not also a criminal by definition. To me it is sufficient that there existed from the days of the Mosaic Law a manifest distinction between a crime with intent and a slaying done intentionally. This is expressed in *Deuteronomy* 19:4-6:

> And this is the case of the slayer, which shall flee thither [to a city of refuge] that he may live: Whoso killeth his neighbor ignorantly, whom he hated not in time past; as when a man goeth into the wood with his neighbor to hew wood, and his hand fetcheth a stroke with the axe to cut down the tree, and the head slippeth from the helve, and lighteth upon his neighbor, that he die; he shall flee unto one of those cities, and live: Lest the avenger of blood pursue the manslayer, while his heart is hot, and overtake him, because the way is long, and slay him; whereas he was not worthy of death, inasmuch as he hated him not in time past.

I am astonished that this early concept of *mens rea* has been overlooked by most writers on the subject. It is of great significance, particularly because it establishes as clearly as could possibly be that the Mosaic *Lex Talionis*—an eye for an eye, a tooth for a tooth—was a maximum, not a mandatory, punishment. The *Lex Talionis*, in its historical context, was a most humane concept, restricting the maximum punishment that could be inflicted, under any circumstances of evilness of crime, to an amount proportional to the injury done. It was only much later that it was perverted into authority for obligatory vengeance and retaliation.[27] Granted, as Sayre states, that there is substantial evidence that prior to the twelfth century in England the element of intent was not a requisite to crime. But this might very well reflect no more than the primitive state of the existing society and signify only that the ancient Judeo-Christian ethicomoral values had not yet been formally incorporated into the simple legal records of the time. It is known for certain that numerous technical devices were employed in medieval England to produce the effect of such a mental element, for example, use of the King's pardon, permitting escape through technicalities in the wording of the indictment, or other contrivances of the judges.[28]

Modern arguments against the universality of *mens rea* in criminal law revolve about the issues of libel and criminal negligence. This is thoroughly discussed by Mueller[29] and I am impressed with his demonstration of the fallacy of the opposing assertions that in certain crimes there need be no mental element. I believe that the abandonment of *mens rea* in favor of an objective liability, as formulated by Oliver Wendell Holmes, would mean an abandonment of all the ethical values inherent in our civilization and would be compatible only with a totalitarian form of government. Holmes stated:

> In the characteristic type of substantive crime acts are rendered criminal because they are done under circumstances in which they will probably cause some harm which the law seeks to prevent.

> The test of criminality in such cases is the degree of danger shown by experience to attend that act under those circumstances.

> In such cases the *mens rea*, or actual wickedness of the party, is wholly unnecessary, and all reference to the state of his consciousness is misleading if it means anything more than that the circumstances in connection with which the tendency of his act is judged are the circumstances known to him. . . . In some cases, actual malice or intent, in the common meaning of these words, is an element in crime. But it will be found that, when it is so, it is because the act when done maliciously is followed by harm which would not have followed the act alone, or because the intent raises a strong probability that an act, innocent in itself, will be followed by other acts or events in connection with which it will accomplish the result sought to be prevented by the law.[30]

Imagine, if you please, a society in which objective liability is truly the law of the land. There could be no valid distinction between deliberate murder and a death resulting from an automobile accident. Morality, as an element of an individual's conscience, would be irrelevant to interpersonal relationships. It would be a barbaric nightmare of a society in which expediency would be the only effective motivating force. There would be nothing to prevent the powers in legal authority from deciding that the mere existence of certain classes of persons, in the words of Holmes, "cause[s] some harm which the law seeks to prevent"; in which case, the liability of those classes of persons would be clearly established and their legal elimination condoned. This, of course, is the state of affairs that exists in totalitarian societies. In short, I assert that the very essence of the ethicomoral values of our civilization lies within the legal maxim *Actus non facit reum, nisi mens sit rea*.

In recent years, a new approach to the doctrine of *mens rea* has appeared. *Mens rea*, as an essential requisite of criminality, is rejected in the name of psychological enlightenment. This approach is typified by Judge John Biggs, Jr. If I sense his thesis correctly, Biggs regards *mens rea* as a relic of the past and as an obstacle to the application of modern psychological and psychiatric principles to criminal law and penology. He states:

> We must stop laying so much emphasis on guilt—on the "guilty mind" of the criminal. We must reappraise our concept of guilt. We look *now* only to the events in connection with commission of the crime. . . . We must look *now* and in the *future* beneath the surface of the events immediately surrounding the commission of the crime and analyze the social and psychological background of the criminal. . . . We must look to the causes of the criminal's state of mind rather than to the fact that he possessed a guilty mind, as a guide to the disposing of him. The fact that he is guilty and possessed *mens rea* is a superficial fact when it comes to the determination of the kind and nature of the sanction to be imposed upon him. . . .[31]

In the battle lines between psychiatry and the law, between what we psychiatrists egotistically call "enlightened progressiveness," as opposed to "punitive legal conservatism," Judge Biggs, like Judge David Bazelon, of *Durham* fame, is on our side. But I think Judge Biggs has missed the point of *mens rea*. To me, the doctrine of *mens rea* is not the obstruction to a psychologically enlightened law. It is the compromise with the doctrine, the failure to sense its true meaning and the substitution of mechanistic formulae of practical expediency for the ethicomoral substance of the concept, which has brought about the state of affairs deplored by Judge Biggs.

Implied malice, in reference to the definition of murder, is the best illustration of this compromise. To demand that the mental state of a defendant be known before a conviction for murder can be obtained created enormous difficulties for the early law. It is infinitely easier to prove that a defendant killed under particular circumstances than it is to prove the state of mind that accompanied the killing. In the days of Coke and Hale, unless the defendant confessed or unless a great deal was known about the preexisting relationship between the slayer and the victim, there was no objective way of determining the existence of *mens rea*. Furthermore, certain crimes, such as poisoning or a slaying accomplished by lying in wait, by every commonsense point of view demonstrated by their very nature the existence of malice and premeditation. It was a natural and, for the time, a logical extension of the law to attempt to make objectively revealed that which was so easily subjectively concealed. So in Coke[32] in Hale[33] and in Blackstone[34] we find precise statements as to when, and under what circumstances, malice is implied. The ultimate extension of this is demonstrated by the modern "felony murder" where the psychological element insofar as the killing is concerned may not exist at all.[35]

My quarrel is not with the principle of inferring the existence of malice from the nature and circumstances of the crime; not even a psychiatrist of today is capable of learning anything about the content of another person's mind without resorting to inference. My objection is that, for what were probably good and sufficient reasons of the time, the early formulations were far too rigid, mechanistic, and stereotyped. It was only too easy for the seventeenth-century courts to slip away entirely from any consideration of the subjective psychology of the defendant and use eminently practical definitions of malice that could easily be proven by objective circumstances.

As Perkins points out, the difference between express and implied malice did not refer originally to any difference in the malice itself as a form of *mens rea*. It meant only that a different means was used to demonstrate the existence of that malice. But already by Hale's time, implied malice had come to mean something quite different; malice could be implied even though it was conceded that no such actual state of mind existed. Thus, the distinction between "malice in fact" and "malice in law."[36] Such implied malice no longer had any relevancy to psychological phenomena, but was truly objective liability.

I would like to call attention to a rather subtle difference between Coke and Hale. Both great authorities of English law wrote at length about malice and *mens rea*. The legal substance of what each wrote is almost identical. Yet throughout Coke are interspersed comments indicating that he was acutely sensitive to the possible abuses and misuses of too rigid legal formulations. For example, in writing about madness and high treason, he referred to the statute[37] that provided for the trial *in absentia* of defendants charged with high treason and who claimed to have fallen into madness after their apprehension; that statute had been repealed as contrary to the common law. He labeled this statute as "cruel and inhumane" and noted that it was repealed because execution of a madman is "a miserable spectacle, both against the law, and of extreme inhumanity and cruelty, and can be no example to others."[38] No such compassion exists on the pages of Hale's *Pleas of the Crown*. There was a vast difference in personality between Coke and Hale. Coke was a most colorful character who had lived fully and had suffered adversity, including imprisonment.[39] Hale, on the other hand, was an incredibly rigid, pious moralist, a writer of sermons, an amateur scientist, and an ardent believer in witchcraft.[40]

In Hale one finds a complete list of those conditions which render an individual incapable of committing a crime. The list is divided into three classes—natural, accidental, and civil incapacities. Natural refers to infancy; accidental to dementia, casualty, chance, and ignorance; civil defects, to civil subjection, compulsion (external), necessity, and fear.[41] Hale discusses each of these classes in detail, with an approach typical of the compulsively rigid personality. Each incapacity is considered only as an all-or-none affair, and the possibility of subtle variations, of in-between states of responsibility, escapes him. Hale recognized the existence of partial insanity and even made the remarkable observation that "for doubtless most persons, that are felons of themselves, and others are under a degree of partial insanity, when they commit these offenses. . . ."[42] Yet he cannot take the step of correlating partial insanity with partial responsibility.

The real question here is whether it was logical and necessary for the criminal law to have evolved into this all-or-none attitude toward the *mens rea* of the mentally ill offender. I cannot see that it was either necessary or was it logical. I think that if Hale had been a different sort of person he might easily have introduced the concept of diminished responsibility; the influence of his authority was so great that the idea would have had no difficulty becoming imbedded in subsequent decisions.

If it is asking too much to expect a seventeenth-century judge to have accomplished this, certainly the mid-nineteenth century judges of England might have done so in formulating the *M'Naghten* Rule, had they not been under overwhelming social pressure arising out of the political implications of M'Naghten's acquittal. For only shortly thereafter, in 1867, the concept of diminished responsibility was originated in Scotland and has persisted in the common law of that country ever since.[43]

The principle of diminished responsibility because of mental illness is in every way compatible with the true implications of *mens rea*. If, as Sayre insists, there are innumerable kinds of *mens rea*,[44] then there must exist innumerable degrees of any particular *mens rea*. We thus arrive at a legal spectrum of an infinitely graduated scale of responsibility that corresponds, or could be made to correspond closely, to the psychological reality of human beings as understood by twentieth-century medical psychology.[45]

Modern psychoanalytic knowledge does not support the legal fiction of an absolute dichotomous distinction between the responsible and the irresponsible. Freud's great caution as to the application of psychoanalysis to the law was fully justified as long as the law clung to its rigid all-or-none formulations. But with the development of the legal doctrine of diminished responsibility, for the first time it has become possible for the law to utilize intelligently the central truth of psychoanalysis: that all human behavior—be it mentally sick or healthy, be it good or evil, be it based on love or on hate—is distributed on an infinite spectrum of fine gradations. There is no "all-or-none" in human psychology.[46]

In California, the principle of diminished responsibility of the mentally ill offender was introduced by two decisions of the California Supreme

Court:[47] *People v. Wells* in 1949, and *People v. Gorshen* in 1959. The legal situation in California was particularly ripe for extension of the doctrine of *mens rea* because of the peculiar split-trial system used in criminal trials when the plea of not guilty by reason of insanity was made. Since 1927, California has used two separate trials to determine, first, the issue of guilt or innocence; then, if the defendant is convicted, a separate trial is held to determine his sanity or insanity.[48] Until the *Wells* decision in 1949, trial judges had consistently excluded any psychiatric testimony from the first trial in determining guilt or innocence. This exclusion was based on the reasoning that anything a physician might have to say about the mental state of the defendant was pertinent only to the question of legal insanity and thus such testimony must be deferred until the second trial. The split-trial statute specified a conclusive presumption of sanity during the first trial. Trial judges assumed that there was an equally conclusive presumption that the defendant possessed the mental capacity to have intent, malice aforethought, or other required elements of *mens rea*. By the time the psychiatrist was permitted on the witness stand at the second trial, a verdict had already been reached as to all elements of *mens rea*. The degree of the offense had been fully determined, and anything that the psychiatrist had to say now had only to do with total exculpation under the right-and-wrong test of M'Naghten. Under such a system, psychiatric testimony was hardly more than a ritualistic formality, a static, all-or-none formulation that had little connection to the defendant's actual psychology in relation to the crime.

In *Wells*, the potentiality for a much more dynamic use of psychiatric testimony was established (see "With Malice Aforethought," this volume). In effect, the California Supreme Court ruled that even though the split-trial system prevailed in California, the defendant had the right to introduce in the primary trial any type of evidence, including expert medical testimony, to disprove the existence of any mental element of the crime. Just as the prosecutor must prove the existence of premeditation or malice aforethought, so the defendant must be allowed to disprove them.

The full impact of the *Wells* decision on trial law practice was not immediately felt. Few lawyers and no psychiatrist recognized, at the time, the far-reaching implications that presaged a new role for psychiatrists in the determination of criminal justice. I doubt that the attorneys who tried and appealed the *Wells* case to the California Supreme Court had any intention of introducing revolutionary reform into the criminal law. It was more an instance of using any device possible to save from the gas chamber a doomed defendant who had been convicted under an impossibly rigid statute that made the death penalty mandatory for all life prisoners who committed an assault with malice aforethought.[49] Wells had not committed murder. During a prison altercation he had thrown a cuspidor at a guard, who though he had been injured, fully recovered. Yet the law permitted only the sentence of death upon conviction.[50] In addition, there were racial, social, and civil liberty aspects of the case which aroused a great deal of public interest and which overshadowed the theoretical implications of the decision. Wells, himself, had not benefitted by the appeal, in that the California Supreme Court decided that even though the trial judge had erred in excluding the medical testimony, the error did not justify interference with the judgment of death.[51]

Very slowly, in a few trials from 1953 onward, psychiatric testimony was used to disprove premeditation, malice, and criminal intent; and there were several trials in which psychiatric testimony was the prime factor in reducing the verdict from first-degree murder to manslaughter.[52] Because these few trials resulted in the lowest possible verdict, that is, manslaughter, no appeals were made and there was no specific judicial confirmation of the principle of diminished responsibility of the mentally ill offender until People v. Gorshen[53] in 1959.

In contrast to the Wells trial, the trial of Nicholas Gorshen was carefully planned from the very beginning to utilize to the fullest possible extent psychiatric evidence to disprove premeditation and malice aforethought. From the start it was recognized by the attorneys that the case had unusual possibilities for appeal, and every effort was made during the trial and during the appeals to restrict the central issues to those directly concerned with the use of psychiatric testimony, short of legal insanity, to contradict evidence of premeditation and malice aforethought. It was hoped that the ambiguities in the Wells decision would be eliminated and that the dynamic formulations of psychoanalytic psychiatry representing a finely graduated scale of psychological responsibility could be engrafted onto the traditional legal scale of criminal responsibility represented by the definitions of first-degree murder, second-degree murder, and manslaughter.

By this time, a number of other states had with various degrees of clarity acknowledged in their judicial decisions the relevancy of psychiatric evidence to questions of criminal intent,[54] and the United States Court of Military Appeals had made a particularly fine decision extending this principle to the courts-martial of all the armed services.[55] The English Homicide Act of 1957 established by statute a related principle of diminished responsibility.[56] As early as 1947, Weihofen and Overholser in a critique of the United States Supreme Court decision in Fisher v. United States,[57] concluded that

[t]he theory that mental disorder, though not so pronounced as to come within the tests of criminal insanity, may nevertheless negative the particular intent requisite to the crime charged, will continue to make progress in the courts. This is so because it rests upon basic principles "long established and deeply rooted." Its logic has not yet been refuted by any court, and it will not permanently be disposed of by mere summary rejection.[58]

So when Nicholas Gorshen shot and killed his longshoreman boss, Red O'Leary, at 2:00 AM on Saturday, March 9, 1957, the lawyers and the psychiatrists were, so to speak, ready and waiting for him. And a theoretical and judicial matrix in which the principle of diminished responsibility could be developed was ready-made.

Nicholas Gorshen was born in Russia in 1901. He escaped to Korea with the White Russian Navy and came to the United States by way of Shanghai in 1923. He led an exemplary family life, worked steadily as a longshoreman, and was deeply religious in the Russian Orthodox Church. One of his two sons was killed in action on Guadalcanal. Gorshen was no ordinary murderer, nor was he suffering from any ordinary form of mental illness.

The killing followed a quarrel at the pier. Gorshen had reported for work at 7:00 the evening before. He felt nervous and upset and drank about a half pint of sloe gin before going on the job. This was unusual for him, as he seldom drank to excess. The gang boss, Red O'Leary, accused him of being too drunk to work and ordered him off the ship. Gorshen insisted that he was able to work. The boss insisted that he could not. They quarreled, then fought, and Gorshen was left unconscious on the deck. When he came to he could think of only one thing—kill O'Leary . . . kill O'Leary! Gorshen announced to everyone on the dock that he was going home to get his gun and would return to shoot O'Leary.

He left, and when he returned later with the gun the police were waiting for him. Gorshen was arrested and was about to be taken to the police station in a squad car. The police had searched him but had failed to find a gun. As he stood there with a policeman at each elbow, Red O'Leary came into sight. Gorshen pulled out his gun, which he had hidden in his longshoreman apron, and shot and killed his victim.

By all conventional rules of law, a conviction of first-degree murder was inevitable. The fight was hardly sufficient provocation for murder; the evidence for malice and premeditation was overwhelming. Although the requirement of the "policeman at the elbow" test of the irresistible impulse defense was doubly fulfilled, California has never recognized that defense.

When I examined Gorshen, there was virtually no evidence of mental illness. But I was alerted by two facts: one, that the crime was completely out of keeping with the defendant's usual personality; and two, that his nickname had been for many years "Sleepy." Out of these simple clues there developed a strange and fascinating story of a secret mental illness, which had never before been revealed to even his closest friends or family.

He was called Sleepy by his friends because he was frequently observed to flutter and close his eyes, appear to be asleep for a few moments, and then resume whatever he was doing as if nothing had happened. Naturally, I thought of the possibility of *petit mal* epilepsy, but this was not confirmed by neurological electroencephalographic studies. He had had these sleepy spells for at least 20 years, perhaps once or twice a week. With great reluctance, he finally revealed to me what took place during those few moments of trance. He entered into a different world, populated by demons, strange animals, and bizarre and deformed people. In reality the trance would last only a few minutes; subjectively, he would experience it as hours and days during which he would have many strange adventures and visions. Invariably, in these trance states he would be subject to incredibly bizarre sexual temptations, inhuman surgical experiments, and mystical transformations of body organs, both of himself and of other creatures in his visions. The theme of perverse sexual temptation, sexual transformation, and bodily disfigurement was always present. Because of the strange sexual character of his trances, he had never dared to tell anyone about them, not even his priest. He knew that the trance experiences were not real, but he also was convinced of the existence of the devil. He believed that these trances were inflicted on him by supernatural agencies in order to test him and that the devil could influence the glands in his head to cause him to have unnatural thoughts.

These trances fitted the classical description of paranoid schizophrenia. Yet the overt manifestations of Gorshen's schizophrenia existed for only a few moments a few times each week. At all other times, he seemed free from mental illness. Particularly, he was frank in stating that he had not been in a trance when he quarreled with or killed O'Leary. He claimed he knew full well what he was doing and very deliberately planned to kill.

The connection with the murder became clear when he revealed that the last thing he remembered before losing consciousness was a sexually perverted name O'Leary had called him during the fight. The name stung him viciously because O'Leary had shouted the obscenity in Russian. (O'Leary, though Irish, had learned that Russian swear words were more effective with longshoremen of Russian background.)

For the previous two years, Gorshen had been having progressive difficulty with his sexual potency, and he was beginning to doubt his capacity to return from his world of visions and devils. Slowly his confidence in his masculinity and his confidence in his ability to withstand the perverse sexual temptations of his trances were lessening, and he was becoming more dependent on being able to work hard as a longshoreman. When the gang boss ordered him off the ship, it was the climax of his worst fears. In the dazed emotional confusion of the fight, the Russian obscenity was too much for him. He returned to consciousness with only one thought, one emotion: the overwhelming compulsion to kill O'Leary. Only by killing could he retain his sanity and avoid eternal incarceration in the hell of his visions. He was correct. For following the slaying, he felt normal again, far better, in fact, than he had felt in years.

The essence of my testimony was that Gorshen killed not because he was insane, but rather as a defense against insanity. Although he knew right from wrong in the sense of M'Naghten, and although he appeared to have premeditated, deliberated, and to have had the requisite criminal intent of malice, he was, nevertheless, not a free agent. He was suffering from an uncontrollable compulsion, the consequence of mental disease; he did not meet the legal requirements established by the *mens rea* for murder and could be guilty only of manslaughter.

There was no supporting testimony for the defense other than the defendant's own testimony concerning the slaying. The trial judge conceded that "up till the time that Dr. Diamond testified in this case, there was no explanation of why this crime was committed. . . . [The doctor is] the first person that has any reasonable explanation. . . . I'm willing to go on the record, that in all probability his theories are correct . . . that he [the defendant] had no particular intent to commit this crime." But he said also, "I like to be advanced. But it seems to me that my hands are tied with legal jurisprudence as it stands today. . . ."[59] The verdict was murder in the second degree. It was appealed solely on the issue of the use of psychiatric testimony to negate premeditation and malice, thus establishing a principle of diminished responsibility because of mental illness.

This appeal to the California Supreme Court represents, I believe, an extraordinary example of collaborative effort between the professions of law and psychiatry. It is only too true that most of the criticism of the law by the medical profession has been heckling from the sidelines. For rarely do doctors have the opportunity to participate actively in the juridical process of appeal and thus directly contribute to the evolution of the law toward the reforms they advocate. However, in *Gorshen* it was different. Eighteen outstanding psychiatrists from different areas of the country joined together in writing an amici curiae brief. In this brief they firmly established the basic soundness of this type of psychiatric evidence. Particularly, they emphasized the need for reform of the fundamental relationship between psychiatry and the law; the need to move on from the static purely diagnostic and legalistic formulations of the past to the newer concepts of dynamic psychology in which all-or-none fictions must be abandoned. They concluded:

> The use of psychiatry in this dynamic relationship to the law will also stimulate far greater interest by psychiatrists in the law. It will attract the best of well-trained dynamic psychiatrists of the highest ethical standing who will correctly perceive their role as allies of our legal institutions, as advisors, not usurpers of the law, as protagonists, not antagonists of the administration of criminal justice.[60]

In their decision in *People v. Gorshen*, the California Supreme Court largely accepted the reasoning offered in the amici curiae brief. The court declared that

> on the trial of issues raised by a plea of not guilty to a charge of a crime which requires proof of a specific mental state, competent evidence that because of mental abnormality not amounting to legal insanity defendant did not possess the essential specific mental state is admissible.[61]

They went on to say that

> a plea of not guilty to a charge of murder puts in issue the existence of the particular mental states which are essential elements of the two degrees of murder and manslaughter . . . [and] defendant should be allowed to show that in fact, *subjectively*, he did not possess the mental state or states in issue.[62]

And again:

> While the insanity of defendant is not in issue under the general plea, yet this does not preclude evidence tending to establish his mental condition . . . at the time the offense was committed for the purpose of showing lack of criminal intent, malice or premeditation.[63]

In this they disapproved the inconsistent implications in thirteen previous California decisions.

Of particular interest is the court's ruling that even though the California statutes declare that "a malicious and guilty intent" is conclusively presumed "from the deliberate commission of an unlawful act, for the purpose of injuring another," this "conclusive presumption" has little meaning, either as a rule of substantive law or as a rule of evidence, since the facts of deliberation and purpose that must be established to bring the presumption into operation are just as subjective as the presumed fact of malicious and guilty intent.

We who worked on the case would have like to see Gorshen himself profit from this decision. Unfortunately, the court did not choose to reduce the verdict of second-degree murder to manslaughter. With what appears to me to be very tortuous reasoning, the court thought that the trial judge really did not mean what he said—"that [defendant] had no particular intent to commit this crime"—and that the evidence concerning negation of premeditation could be accepted without at the same time accepting the evidence against intent and malice.[64]

The immediate impact of the *Gorshen* decision has been a sharp increase in the use of psychiatric testimony of this type in almost all murder trials throughout California. It is much too early to gather statistics, but I think that in a sizable number of cases, a death penalty has been avoided even when the jury verdict was first-degree murder. In other cases, the use of this defense has resulted in a verdict of second-degree murder or of manslaughter where formerly a verdict of first-degree murder would have been inevitable.

Of more importance to the science and art of forensic psychiatry has been the shift away from static, diagnostic, and classification psychiatry toward dynamic descriptions of the particular mental mechanisms that up to the crime. Psychiatric examinations have had to be much more detailed, and many more hours have had to be spent with defendants to uncover such psychological mechanisms and to interpret them in the psychodynamic framework of each defendant's life history. I believe that this is the first major step toward a radical alteration in the way mental and emotional illness of the criminal offender is considered by the law.

I am aware that I am not entirely correct in applying the term "diminished responsibility" to these decisions. As observed by Weihofen and Overholser, this is not really diminishment of the responsibility, but rather the defendant is held fully responsible for a lesser crime.[65] This is a valid distinction but also a highly technical one that is beside the point insofar as the net effect on the defendant is concerned. "Partial responsibility" is not a good phrase, for it is often confused with "partial insanity"—a meaningless and archaic concept. To avoid confusion, I suggest that the *Wells-Gorshen* type of defense be termed "limited responsibility."

I concede that this whole business of lack of mental capacity to premeditate, to have malice, or to entertain intent is a kind of sophistry that must not be allowed to remain an end in itself. Right now we must use these legal technicalities to permit the psychiatrists to gain entrance into the trial court and to allow the judge and jury to give full consideration to the deeper and more complex mental and emotional facets of the defendant. I think it would even be improper and unnecessary for a psychiatrist to attempt to precisely fit his psychiatric knowledge into the technical and legalistic distinctions made by the law between these various elements of the *mens rea*. I myself could be accused of such impropriety, for I have testified in such legalistic terms in some cases. But it was necessary in these cases before we had the benefit of *Gorshen*. Now that the principle behind this type of testimony has been accepted, the psychiatrist should stick to his clinical approach. It is his job to describe the mental and emotional abnormalities of the defendant—the psychopathology of the crime—as he sees them as a psychiatrist and a doctor. And he can safely let the court worry about the niceties of premeditation and malice. It is for this reason there can be no rules or formulae for the psychiatric evaluation of malice, premeditation, and intent (see "With Malice Afore-thought," this volume).

The good practice of modern psychodynamic psychiatry demands a total approach toward each patient. We are interested in and find significant everything that has happened to the patient, starting with his ancestors and going through the entire life history right up to the present moment. This same totalistic approach should be carried over into the courtroom. The psychiatric expert should not give a direct or limited response to the legal questions of intent, premeditation, and malice. Instead, he should use this opportunity to tell everything that he knows about the defendant. But this testimony must be in meaningful, psychodynamic terms, never in static diagnostic, sterile formulations that contribute nothing to the understanding of the particular criminal act. It has been possible in every recent case to testify very freely, giving all the clinical facts without restriction and without preoccupation with the legal technicalities. In each case, I believe, this has allowed the judge and jury to understand better the human complexities of the individual whom they must judge. The result inevitably must be greater justice for all.

The next step after *Gorshen* is to expand the principle of limited or diminished responsibility of mentally ill offenders to include all definitions of crime. It was easier to introduce this principle in the crimes of homicide because there already existed the legal structure of graduated responsibility for homicide. But when the courts, and particularly the public, get used to the idea of giving full consideration to the mental and emotional abnormalities of homicide offenders, there will be little difficulty in applying the same principles and practices to all crimes. Diminished responsibility, in its true meaning, would then extend throughout the penal code and no longer be bound by the technicalities of the degrees of homicide.

The effect will be, I am certain, to encourage psychiatrists to practice as good medicine in the courtroom as they do in their own offices and hospitals. In essence, the court will say to the expert witness:

> Forget about the legal definitions and the technicalities; forget about sanity and insanity; premeditation, malice, and *mens rea*—that is our concern. Tell us everything that you, as a medical expert, know about this defendant. What kind of a person is he? What is wrong with him emotionally and mentally? How did he get to be the way he is now? What made him do what he is accused of? What hidden mechanisms in his mind caused him to behave in the way he did? What kind of treatment does he need to ensure his rehabilitation? Is he likely to respond to treatment? What kind of protection does society require to prevent something like this happening again? Tell us all that you know about this defendant, and we will give full consideration to what you have said; we will put it together with all the evidence from other sources: then we will decide what is best for society to do with this defendant.

This is what I mean by a radically new relationship between psychiatry and the law. It is a relationship in which each profession respects the basic tenets of the other, and neither usurps the functions of the other.

It is important to realize that the impact of diminished responsibility does not stop with the verdict and sentence of the trial court. It will have, I believe, a most significant impact upon the correctional institutions to which convicted, mentally ill offenders are sent. It is a matter of common knowledge that our prisons contain large numbers of mentally ill inmates. Psychoses, psychoneuroses, character disorders, and perversions abound in the prison population. Yet the average correctional institution makes little or no provision for the treatment of such inmates. They are allowed to mingle indiscriminately, untreated and uncared for. Many of the most pressing administrative problems in a correctional system arise out of this mass of inadequately treated and improperly segregated group of mentally ill prisoners. It may sound paradoxical to recommend that even more such mentally ill offenders to be sent to correctional institutions under a rule of diminished responsibility, but there is an important difference here. Because of the strictness of our laws defining legal insanity, the courts have always committed large numbers of the mentally ill to prison. But there has never been any official acknowledgment of the existence of their mental illness. Most of the public still naively believes that if a prisoner is really mentally sick, he is hospitalized in a mental institution. Even many judges, who should know better, scoff at the idea that mental illness is widely prevalent among the prison population. But when an offender is convicted with diminished or limited responsibility because of mental illness, *he is now officially labeled as sick and the courts have publicly acknowledged his need for treatment.* The correctional institution to which he is confined can no longer evade the moral and legal responsibility for providing such treatment and rehabilitation. Informed public and professional groups, such as mental health organizations, penal welfare societies, and medical and bar associations, have a sound foundation to demand that their state provide such facilities within the correctional system.

The State of California has traveled a long way in this direction. The California Medical Facility at Vacaville, an integral part of the correctional system, is able to provide excellent psychiatric treatment for at least a limited number of prisoners. The doctors who work in this hospital need not concern themselves about who is sane and who is insane. Treatment can be provided according to the needs of their patients without regard for legal technicalities. This hospital represents a pilot organization of very high order. I do not hesitate to say that Vacaville provides a higher standard of psychiatric treatment than does the corresponding hospital for the criminally insane at Atascadero, which is operated by the California Department of Mental Hygiene. So there is no doubt that good psychiatric treatment can be given within a department of corrections. Of course, their limitations are severe because of restricted budgets, lack of bed space, and too few trained personnel. But these limitations are even worse for many hospitals for the criminally insane that are outside a correctional system. What is still worse, such hospitals for the insane may often be only prisons in disguise—barbaric institutions operating behind a façade of medical respectability but without even a pretense of adequate therapy. I believe that the official and public acknowledgment of mental illness of convicted offenders who have been legally determined to have only partial responsibility for their crimes will do much to eliminate the shame and hypocrisy of both our prisons and our so-called hospitals for the criminally insane.

I do not make this recommendation for every state. The majority of our states have prisons that are not fit for animals, let alone mentally ill persons. Yet progressive programs, such as the pilot programs of psychiatric treatment carried on by California and the federal government, can be encouraged to expand in every direction. They must become centers for research and training of professional personnel. From such centers will flow a spirit of treatment and rehabilitation, as well as social protection, that will permeate every aspect of our penal system. Once the philosophy of rehabilitation is introduced into a correctional system its progress is inevitable. Such progress is often slow, for our knowledge of effective rehabilitation methods is very limited, but it cannot be stopped by reactionary, punitive opposition.

The ultimate step will be the extension of the treatment principle to all prisoners—sane, insane, fully responsible, and partially responsible–to each according to need and to none according to legal classification. In the prison of the future, consideration will be given to only two principles: what will insure the maximum rehabilitation potential of the individual prisoner, and what will provide the greatest protection to society against crime. In such a future institution, the psychiatrist will be one member of the penologic research and treatment team (and certainly not the most important member).

I do not feel I exaggerate when I claim that all of this springs out of the ancient doctrine of *mens rea*. It has been the perversion of *mens rea*– its misinterpretation, its evasion, and its distortion that has produced a system of justice emphasizing the deed rather than the doer; that punishes the crime, but neglects the criminal. Mens rea was mankind's earliest attempt to acknowledge the human psychological element of every crime. It is a most precious heritage whose full benefits are yet to be reaped.

Notes

[1]There is now a scholarly English translation of this book, which Dr. Diamond considered one of the ten greatest in the history of psychiatry; Weyer, J. (1563), *Witches, Devils, and Doctors in the Renaissance*. ed. G. Mora & B. Kohl. trans J. Shea from the original *De praestigiis daemonum, et incantationibus, ac veneficis, etc.* Binghamton, NY: Medieval & Renaissance Texts & Studies, 1991.

[2]Zilboorg, G. & Henry, G. W. (1941), *A History of Medical Psychology*. New York: Norton, 1967, p. 233.

[3]Weihofen, R. (1956). Personal communication.

[4]The most important exceptions are Isaac Ray-Justice Doe correspondence, resulting in the New Hampshire doctrine laid down in *State v. Pike*, 49 N.H. 399 (1869) and *Durham v. United States*, 214 F.2d 862 (D.C. Cir. 1954). See Reik, L. (1959), The Doe-Ray Correspondence: A Pioneer collaboration in the jurisprudence of mental disease. *Yale L. Rev.*, 63:183.

[5]Hall, J. (1958), *Studies in Jurisprudence and Criminal Theory*. New York: Ocean, p. 289.

[6]Zilboorg, G. (1939), Misconceptions of legal psychiatry. *Amer. J. Orthopsychiat.*, 9:540, 553.

[7]*Leyra v. Denno*, 347 U.S. 556 (1954).

[8]*McCracken v. Teets*, 41 Cal. 2d 648, 262 P.2d 561 (1953).

[9]Personal communication from the psychiatrist involved.

[10]*Leyra v. Denno*, sup. note 6; *People v. Nash*, 52 Cal. 2d 36, 41, 338 P.2d 416, 418 (1959).

[11]Freud, S. (1906), Psycho-analysis and the establishment of the facts in legal proceedings. *Standard Edition*, 9:99–114. London: Hogarth Press, 1959.

[12]Bernfeld, S. (1949), Freud's scientific beginnings. *Amer. Imago*, 6:163–196; see also Jones, E. (1953), *The Life and Work of Sigmund Freud*, Vol. 1. New York: Basic Books, pp. 27–38

[13]Freud, op. cit., sup. note 10, p. 114. Ten years later, in an astonishingly brief paper of only two pages, Freud introduced a revolutionary explanation of criminal behavior: that some criminals first have their sense of guilt and then commit crimes in order to fulfill their guilt feelings. See Freud, S. (1916), Some character types met with in psychoanalytic work. *Standard Edition*, 14:311–333. London: Hogarth Press, 1957.

[14]Jones, E. (1957), *The Life and Working of Sigmund Freud*, Vol. 3. New York: Basic Books, p. 103.

[15]Ibid.

[16]Freud, S. (1931), The expert opinion in the Halsmann case. *Standard Edition*, 21:251–253. London: Hogarth Press, 1961.

[17]Alexander, F. & Staub, H. (1931), *The Criminal, the Judge, and the Public*. Glencoe, IL: Macmillan.

[18]Zilboorg, G. (1943), *Mind, Medicine, and Man*. New York: Harcourt Brace. See also Zilboorg, G. (1954), *The Psychology of the Criminal Act and Punishment*. Westport, CT: Greenwood, 1968.

[19]Roche, P. (1958), *The Criminal Mind*. Westport, CT: Greenwood, 1974.

[20]Szasz, T. (1956), Some observations on the relationship between psychiatry and the law. *Arch. Neurol. & Psychiat.*, 75:297–315.

[21]Szasz, T. (1957), Psychiatric expert testimony—Its cover meaning and social function. *Psychiat.*, 20:313–316.

[22]Ray, I. (1853), *A Treatise on the Medical Jurisprudence of Insanity*. Boston: Little, Brown.

[23]Diamond, B. (1956), Isaac Ray and the trial of Daniel M'Naghten. *Amer. J. Psychiat.*, 112:651–56.

[24]*Durham v. United States*, sup. note 2.

[25]Watson, A. (1959), Durham plus five years: Development of the law of criminal responsibility in the District of Columbia. *Amer. J. Psychiat.*, 116:289–297.

[26]Biggs, J. Jr. (1955). *The Guilty Mind*. Baltimore, MD: Johns Hopkins University Press. See also Sayre, F. (1932), Mens rea. *Harv. L. Rev.*, 45:975.

[27]Goldin, H. E. (1952), *Hebrew Criminal Law and Procedure: Mishnah, Sanhedrin, Makkot*. New York: Twayne.

[28]Sayre, op. cit., sup. note 26, p. 986.

[29]Mueller, G. (1958), On common law mens rea. *Minn. L. Rev.*, 42:1043.

[30]Holmes, O. W. (1881), *The Common Law*, Boston: Little, Brown, 1984.

[31]Biggs, op. cit. sup. note 25, pp. 192–193. My criticism of Judge Biggs is inappropriate in view of the *Currens* decsions of May 1, 1961, in which Judge

Biggs employed the historical develolpment of *mens rea* to establish a new rule of criminal responsibility that promises to be of great significance in reform of the attitude of the criminal law toward mentally ill offenders (*United States v. Currens*, 290 F.2d 751 [3d Cir. 1961]).

[32]Coke, E. (1644), *Institutes of the Laws of England*, Part 3. London: W. Rawlins for Thomas Bassett, 1680.

[33]Hale, M. (1736), *Historia Placitorum Coronae [The History of the Pleas of the Crown]*, Vol. 1. London: E. & R. Nutt & R. Gosling.

[34]Blackstone, W. (1769), *Commentaries on the Laws of England*, Vol. 4. Boston: Beacon Press, 1962.

[35]Perkins (1934), A re-examination of malice aforethought. *Yale L. Rev.*, 43:537, 556–557.

[36]Ibid., pp. 546–552.

[37]Statute of 1541, 33 Hen. 8, c. 20.

[38]Coke, op. cit., sup. note 21.

[39]James, C. W. (1929), *Chief Justice Coke*. New York: Scribner's Sons.

[40]Hale, M (1677), *The Primitive Origination of Mankind Considered and Examined According to the Light of Nature*. London: W. Godbid for William Shrewsbury. See also Hale, M. (1682), A Tryal of Witches at the Assizes Held at Bury St. Edmonds. London: William Shrewsbury.

[41]Hale, sup. note 30, p. 15.

[47]Ibid., p. 30.

[43]Royal Commission (1949–53), *Report on Capital Punishment*, pp. 131–133.

[44]Sayre, op. cit., sup. note 25, pp. 974, 1016–1026.

[45]For a discussion of diminshed responsibility in England, see Hughes (1959), The English homicide act of 1957. *J. Crim. Law, Criminol. & Police Sci.*, 49: 521, 525–528.

[46]As Professor Walter Kaufman of Princeton states, "No man before Freud had given equal substance to one of the most striking sayings in the Gospels . . . 'He that is without sin amongst you, let him first cast a stone.' Nothing that Freud has done, and little that anyone else has done, is more relevant to ethics than his success in breaking down the wall between the normal and the abnormal, the respectable and the criminal, the good and the evil. Freud gave, as it were, a new answer to the Gospel query, 'Who is my neighbor?' The mentally troubled, depressed, hysterical, and insane are not possessed by the deville but essentially 'as thyself.' Freud made men seek to understand and help where previous ages despised and condemned" (see Kaufman, W. [1956], Sigmund Freud. In: *Encyclopedia of Morals*. Westport, CT: Greenwood, pp. 171, 178.

[47]*People v. Wells*, 33 Cal. 2d 330, 202 P.2d 53, cert. denied, 338 U.S. 836 (1949); *People v. Gorshen*, 51 Cal. 2d 716, 725, 336 P.2d 492, 497 (1959).

[48]Cal. Pen. Code § 1026.

[49]Cal. Stats. 1941, ch. 106 § 4500, at 1124.

[50]The mandatory death penalty was subsequently repealed. Cal. Pen. Code § 4500.

[51]I believe the first attorney to recognize the full psychiatric implication of the *Wells* decision was Charles Garry of San Francisco. Garry entered the *Wells* case after the California Supreme Court decision in 1949 and attempted to appeal to the United States Supreme Court. It was in connection with this final attempt at appeal that I became involved in the case. I examined Wells at San Quentin in 1953. In discussions with Garry and later with his associate, Benjamin Dreyfus, the possibilities for this type of psychiatric testimony became apparent.

The United States Supreme Court denied certiorari, and Wells's death sentence was commuted to life imprisonment by the governor.

[52]Typical of these trials was that of Lewon Melkonian, described in "With Malice Aforethought," this volume

[53]*People v. Gorshen,* sup. note 47.

[54]The most recent decision acknowledging the relevancy of this evidence was that of the Supreme Court of New Mexico (*State v. Padilla,* 66 N.M. 289, 347 P.2d 312 [1959]). Weihofen lists Colorado, Connecticut, Indiana, Ohio, Rhode Island, Tennessee, Utah, Virginia, Wisconsin, and perhaps Kentucky, Montana, and Oregon, as holding the evidence admissible. In addition, Maryland and New York have indicated in dicta their willingness to accept this type of testimony (Weihofen, H. [1956], Procedure for determining defendant's mental condition under the American Law Institute's model penal code. *Temp. L. Q.,* 29:235, 245, n.28).

[55]*United States v. Dunnahoe,* 6 U.S.C.M.A. 745, 21 C.M.R. 67 (1956).

[56]See Hughes, op. cit., sup. note 45.

[57]*Fisher v. United States,* 328 U.S. 463 (1946).

[58]Weihofen, H. & Overholser, W. (1947), Mental disorder affecting the degree of a crime. *Yale L. J.,* 56:959, 981.

[59]*People v. Gorshen,* sup. note 47.

[60]Brief by Amicus Curiae, ibid., p. 54.

[61]51 Cal. 2d at 726, 336 P.2d, p. 498.

[62]Ibid. at 733, 336 P.2d, p. 502 (italics added).

[63]Ibid. at 725, 336 P.2d, p. 498.

[64]As with all expert testimony, the trial judge or jury is free to reject any or all of the psychiatric evidence in favor of contradictory factual evidence. This was made abundantly clear in a subsequent California decision (People v. Ritter, 54 Cal. 2d 720, 730, 355 P.2d 645, 650, 7 Cal. Rep. 901, 906 [1960]) and should put to rest the fears of those who think that psychiatrists are taking over in legal areas where they do not belong.

[65]Weihofen & Overholser, op. cit., sup. note 55, p. 960.

With Malice Aforethought

[1957]

Lhe most fundamental concept in Anglo-American criminal law is the principle of *mens rea*—literally, guilty mind—or criminal intent.

It is a general principle of our criminal law that there must be as an essential ingredient in a criminal offense some blameworthy condition of mind. Sometimes it is negligence, sometimes malice, sometimes guilty knowledge, but as a general rule there must be something of that kind which is designated by the expression *mens rea*.[1]

The full definition of every crime contains expressly or by implication a proposition as to a state of mind. Therefore, if the mental element of any conduct alleged to be a crime is proved to have been absent in any given case, the crime so defined is not committed; or, again, if a crime is fully defined, nothing amounts to that crime which does not satisfy that definition.[2]

Of the greatest interest to the psychiatrist is that all legal rules providing for the relief of criminal responsibility of the insane and the mentally deficient, and, more recently, for the mitigation of responsibility for the intoxicated and others who suffer from disturbances of emotion and will, arose, not as an act of humanity toward the mentally ill, but because those conditions, among others, impaired the individual's capacity to form the intent—the *mens rea*—held requisite for the commission of a crime. Only very occasionally did early legal authorities express belief that punishment could have no deterrent effect on such individuals and hence would be futile and inhumane. By and large, the criminal law has had no interest in the mental condition of the accused except insofar as his capacity to entertain intent is concerned. There is not now, and never has been, any legal objection to the conviction and execution of a mentally ill defendant, provided he was, at the time of the crime, able to entertain the necessary *mens rea* required by the definition of the particular crime.[3] This is, of course, the basis for all the rules defining legal insanity. A man who does not know right from wrong is not able to commit, of his own free will, a criminal act. But an insane person who does know the difference between right and wrong is considered to be capable of forming the necessary intent and is treated like any other person under the law. It is from this basic principle of *mens rea* that the long-standing, seemingly irreconcilable difference between "medical insanity" and "legal insanity" has arisen.

Ever since the *M'Naghten* rules for the determination of legal insanity were formulated in 1843, psychiatrists have studied, written, and advocated voluminously and vociferously concerning this difference. Yet, surprisingly, they have paid little attention to the legal issues involved in the evaluation of the state of mind of the noninsane. This is unfortunate, for it is probable that in these latter cases psychiatry might have the greater contribution to make to the administration of justice.

The determination of sanity or insanity is essentially a static procedure based on static concepts of psychology. The psychiatric evaluation of the state of mind in reference to the *mens rea* of the noninsane opens the legal door to a genuine, dynamic psychology based on modern psychodynamic principles. It is the purpose of this paper to discuss this application of dynamic psychiatry to such legal problems in the light of recent court decisions that, I believe, foreshadow an entirely new type of relationship between psychiatry and the law—a relationship based not on static diagnostic labels and legal "tests," but on a real desire of the law to understand and to judge with full consideration given to unconscious factors and ego mechanisms. In short, a courtroom in which psychiatrist and psychoanalyst can feel at home and be certain that the special insights they can contribute concerning human behavior will be given full recognition.

Historical Background of *Mens Rea*

Biblical law clearly introduced the concept of *mens rea* when distinguishing between those slayers who are to be put to death and those who are to be permitted to escape to cities of refuge. Deuteronomy, Ch. 19, v. 4–6, states:

> Whoso killeth his neighbor ignorantly, whom he hated not in time past
> . . . he shall flee unto one of those cities, and live: Lest the avenger of
> blood pursue the manslayer, while his heart is hot, and overtake him . . .
> and slay him; whereas he was not worthy of death, inasmuch as he hated
> him not in time past.

Bracton, writing in the thirteenth century, was the earliest English authority to attempt to define legal insanity: "*Furiosus . . . non intelligit quid agit* [a madman does not know what he is doing]."[4] He also emphasized the mental element in his definition of homicide as a slaying done "intentionally, as if any one with certain knowledge and with a premeditated assault, through anger or hatred, or for the cause of gain."[5] Again he stated: "A crime is not committed unless a guilty intention (*nocendi voluntas*) intercedes."[6]

In the sixteenth century, Plowden, the most accurate of the old reporters of the common law,[7] wrote:

> So if a Man *non sanae memoriae* kills another, although he has broken the Word of the Law, yet he has not broken the Law, because he had no Memory or Understanding, but mere Ignorance, which came to him by the hand of God; and therefore it is called involuntary Ignorance, to which the law imputes the Act, inasmuch as there is no Fault in him, and for that Reason he shall be excused, seeing he is ignorant by Compulsion. . . . But where a man breaks the Word of the Law by voluntary Ignorance, there he shall not be excused. As if a person that in drink kills another, this shall be Felony and he shall be hanged for it, and yet he did it through Ignorance, for when he was drunk he had no Understanding nor Memory; but inasmuch as that Ignorance was occasioned by his own Act and Folly, and he might have avoided it, he shall not be privileged thereby.[8]

Coke, whose *Institutes* and *Reports* of the seventeenth century were most fundamental to the development of English common law, also closely linked the definition of insanity with the concept of intent. He wrote:

> For in Criminal Causes, as Felonie, &c., the Act and Wrong of a mad Man shall not be imputed to him, for that in those Causes, *Actus no reum, nisi mens sit rea* the act does not make the criminal unless the mind, or intention, is criminal; and he is *Amens (id est) sine mente*, without his Minde or Discretion; and *Furiosus solo furare punitur*, a mad Man is only punished by his Madness.[9]

Like Plowden, Coke asserted that intoxication is no defense: "as for a Drunkard, who is *Voluntarius Daemon*, he hath . . . no privilege thereby; but what Hurt or Ill soever he doth, his Drunkenness doeth aggravate it".[10]

Matthew Hale, writing in the latter half of the seventeenth century, was the first to make the clear distinction between that degree of insanity which will relieve from criminal responsibility and that which will not. His chapter "Concerning the Defect of Ideocy, Madness and Lunacy, in Reference to Criminal Offenses and Punishments" is only part of a broader discussion of criminal intent and the various conditions and circumstances which impair will and intention. He wrote: "For it is the will and intention that regularly is required, as well as the act, and event, to make the offense capital."[11] Hale wrote the first systematic treatise on *mens rea*, and his ideas have had very great influence on the common law, even to the present day. Hale's definitions of the distinction between murder and manslaughter in terms of "malice" have been crucial to the development of modern homicide statutes.

Blackstone, in the 18th century, followed Hale closely in regard to *mens rea* as well as the tests of insanity. His contribution to these subjects was to give further examples.[12] It was through Blackstone, who became the authority of early American law, that these definitions were transmitted to the United States. Modern penal statutes on homicide, in most states, differ only slightly in language from that of Coke, Hale, and Blackstone.

The Definition of Malice Aforethought and the Degrees of Homicide

The legal term "malice aforethought" refers to the particular type of *mens rea* necessary to establish the crime of murder and sometimes other crimes involving bodily harm, such as assault.[13]

Malice aforethought is a special type of criminal intent that has nothing to do with ill will, hatred, enmity, or the ordinary meaning of the word "malice." Furthermore, contrary to the conventional meaning of "afore-thought," there is no implication of premeditation.

This semantic quirk in the phrase "malice aforethought" is an excellent illustration of the danger of a psychiatrist's failing to familiarize himself with the precise technical definitions of the words and concepts to which he proposes to apply his professional knowledge. The expert witness who presumes to deal with these legal concepts without full awareness of their specialized technical meanings is no expert. Indeed, he will quickly make a fool of himself on the witness stand. These specialized legal terms have changed in meaning throughout the centuries, and it is only by our understanding them in their genetic (i.e., historical) development that they make sense. In this respect the historical study of the law is closely analogous to the analysis of our patients, where symptoms that are seemingly contradictory and incomprehensible become fully meaningful through the genetic approach.

The earliest use of the term "malice aforethought" or "malice prepense," as it was called in Old English, was to distinguish murder from a slaying that had occurred in self-defense. In the latter case, the jury brought in the special verdict that the homicide had not occurred with malice prepense. This concept was incorporated into the English law in 1390, by statute that established the distinction between excusable and felonious homicide.[14]

William Lambard, respected as an authority in Elizabethan times and whose manual for the guidance of justices of the peace was widely used, defined murder as "that willful manner of sleying w[ith] malice prepensed long since and most properly called *Felonie*, because it was done *Felico anima*, in malicious heate & displeasure." Manslaughter, on the other hand, "is taken to be a speciall manner of wilfull killing without any malice forethoughte off."[15]

Although Coke described malice aforethought as being an essential element of the crime of murder and said that the malice could be either express or implied, it remained for Hale, later in the same century, to lay down precise rules for the implication and determination of malice aforethought. Hale defined express malice as follows:

> Malice in fact is a deliberate intention of doing any bodily harm to another, whereunto by law he is not authorized. The evidences of such a malice must arise from external circumstances discovering that inward intention, as lying in wait, menacings antecedent, former grudges, deliberate compassings, and the like which are various according to variety of circumstances. It must be a compassing or designing to do some bodily harm.[16]

Note that in Hale's definition, although evidence of preexisting hostility or of premeditation is used to prove the existence of malice, such hostility or premeditation is not actually part of the definition, which states only that malice is a deliberate intention. This distinction was to become of critical importance as the law came to disregard motivation in favor of intention as a criterion of guilt.

Holt, in 1707, crystallizing this distinction further, decided in *Regina v. Mawgridge*:

> Some have been led into mistake by not well considering what the Passion of Malice is; they have construed it to be a Rancour of Mind lodged in the Person killing, for some considerable time before the commission of the Fact, which is a mistake arising from the not well distinguishing between Hatred and Malice. Envy, Hatred and Malice are three distinct Passions of the Mind. . . . Malice is a design formed of doing mischief to another.[17]

Since Holt's decision, both English and American common law and statutes continue to use malice aforethought as the essential distinction between manslaughter and murder and to insist on its being defined as a special type of intent, rather than as implying hatred and premeditation, as it did in the earlier law. Thus in California, which is similar to most states in these statutes, malice aforethought is defined as follows:

> Such malice may be express or implied. It is express when there is manifested a deliberate intention unlawfully to take away the life of a fellow-creature. It is implied, when no considerable provocation appears, or when the circumstances attending the killing show an abandoned and malignant heart.[18]

The words "malice aforethought" do not imply deliberation or the lapse of considerable time between the act and the malicious intent to take life or cause bodily harm. Rather, malice aforethought denotes purpose and design in contradistinction to accident and mischance.[19] In other words, today, it means a "man-endangering state of mind" at the actual time of the criminal act.[20]

The first United States statute to divide murder into two degrees was enacted in Pennsylvania in 1794.[21] This division is not made in every state, but the California distinction is typical:

> All murder which is perpetrated by means of poison, or lying in wait, torture, or by any other kind of wilful, deliberate, and premeditated killing, or which is committed in the perpetration or attempt to perpetrate arson, rape, robbery, burglary, mayhem, or any act punishable under Section 268 [sex crimes], is murder of the first degree; and all other kinds of murders are of the second degree.[22]

Murder is defined as "the unlawful killing of a human being with malice aforethought."[23] Manslaughter is defined as "the unlawful killing of a human being, without malice."[24]

To summarize: First-degree murder is homicide committed with premeditation and with malice aforethought. Second-degree murder is homicide committed without premeditation, but with malice aforethought. Manslaughter is homicide committed without premeditation and without malice aforethought. The element of time is central to these distinctions. Premeditation, as the word applies, means that some time must have elapsed, even though very short, between the planning and the execution of the crime. Malice aforethought, like all criminal intent, refers only to the state of mind at the actual instant of the slaying or assault and has nothing to do with preexisting behavior, except that its existence at the moment of the crime may be implied by certain behavior and attitudes that existed before the crime was committed.[25]

Deriving from the concept of implied malice (to be discussed further) penal statutes have been enacted in which the psychological element of malice aforethought does not enter into the definition of first-degree murder. This is the case with the so-called felony murder, where a slaying committed during the course of certain specified felonies is designated as first-degree murder. Thus, for example, in many jurisdictions today, a killing unintentionally committed during an armed robbery does not require any consideration of malice aforethought in order for the offense of first-degree murder to be established.

Intent vs. Motive and the Expert Witness

Clearly, the traditional formulations of criminal law define guilt in terms of a state of mind. I believe that few psychiatrists would quarrel with the basic idea that criminality is a problem of psychology, rather than of act and circumstance. Unfortunately the law sharply restricts psychological concerns by eliminating consideration of motivation in determining guilt. As Hall wrote: "For hardly any rule of penal law is more definitely settled than that motive is irrelevant."[26] Malice aforethought refers to *how* the mind functions in the act of crime, not why the mind functioned in that particular way. Thus, the law is interested in whether a certain act is good or evil (i.e., lawful or unlawful); whether the act was performed out of conscious volition (i.e., intentionality); and whether the individual had the mental capacity to exercise such volition. But the law is not interested—or so it says—in the reasons for which the crime was done.

For example, it is murder in the first degree to kill a man for the purpose of robbing him. It is also murder in the first degree for a physician to kill a patient dying of cancer by administering an overdose of morphine in order to put him out of his pain and suffering. That one act is performed for bad reasons, the other for good, does not alter the identity of the crimes.

Anyone who has ever witnessed a trial knows that this distinction is fictional and that these two offenses would not be dealt with in the same way as a matter of practical legal procedure. Furthermore, in every trial, witnesses and attorneys are constantly talking about motivation in nearly everything they relate about the events of the crime and the person of the defendant. But such interest in motivation must be disguised or rationalized by various legal devices. This may be done by the introduction of evidence concerning motivation so as to establish premeditation of intent. Motivation may be used to build up a chain of circumstantial evidence to prove that the defendant was the one who committed the crime. Or motivation may be used at length by the attorneys in an attempt to convince the jury, through logic or emotional exhortation, of the guilt or innocence of the defendant. But, technically speaking, the jury is supposed to bring in its verdict without regard to the *why* of the crime. That, in actuality, juries do not restrict themselves as they are instructed is a tribute to their own common sense, for such a fictional distinction has no meaning in the ordinary experience of human beings.

This necessity for a devious introduction of the motives of the crime may, however, sharply restrict the type of evidence that reaches the jury's ears, and consequently grave injustices have been done in certain cases. Almost always such a restriction prevents the defendant's life history—all the events leading up to the commission of the crime—from being presented to the jury in a coherent, meaningful way. Instead the jury is given fragments of this information, some from this witness and some from that, but seldom in a logical, whole pattern that accurately reflects the true nature of the defendant and the alleged criminal action.

It is inconceivable that a psychiatrist could form any opinion about a defendant if he were to disregard motivation. And he certainly could not communicate any valid information about the defendant to the jury without talking about motives. Fortunately, psychiatrists are not subject to this limitation: they are legally permitted to give full consideration to motivation and to communicate their considerations without restriction to the jury. This is possible because of their status as expert witnesses. The expert witness differs from the ordinary witness in fact, in that he is asked to testify about his own opinion, rather than about facts relevant to the crime that he may have observed. Having given his opinion, the expert witness must then explain to the jury the facts and other bases on which his opinion is based. Technically, restrictions concerning hearsay evidence apply to expert witnesses, as well as to witnesses in fact, but often a trial judge will allow considerable latitude in the expert's use of clinical material gained from sources other than the direct examination of the defendant. Testimony about the clinical history is admissible provided it is relevant to the formation of the expert's opinion in accordance with the sound clinical judgment expected of the medical expert.[27]

Karpman described very well the difficulty of this problem of intent versus motive:

> From the standpoint of law and the treatment of the offender, the intent to commit the act is more important than the motivation back of it. And as for motivation, the law is primarily concerned with the immediate surface, conscious motivation. Psychodynamics, however, goes beyond

that, for it recognizes that without intent there would have been no deed, and without motivation there would have been no intent. It further believes that every deed, however brief and spontaneous, is never fully the result of immediate, preceding circumstances, but has a long life history and cannot be understood without it. We have also long learned that behind an overt conscious motivation there is universally a deep-seated unconscious motivation. Intent, therefore, is meaningless unless we understand the motivation that prompted it, and we cannot understand motivation unless we understand its history, and especially its relation to other motivations in the personality.[28]

The expert witness must constantly bear in mind that such concepts as malice aforethought and all other concepts of intent are simply legal abstractions that have no psychological meaning unless integrated with motivation, both conscious and unconscious. Although the law is restricted by its own need for such abstractions, the psychiatrist need not be. He may give full weight to motivation in his analysis of the personality of the defendant, provided only that he employ the legal expedient of asserting his need to consider motivation in order to arrive at his opinion as to the criminal intent.

Unfortunately, some psychiatrists mistake their function to be that of a legal expert rather than a clinician; and they unduly restrict the clinical material on which they base their opinions. Such pseudo-expert witnesses become a caricature of a doctor—talking in legal jargon that they do not understand and leaving their clinical knowledge, judgment, and experience behind them when they take the witness stand. For their own unconscious reasons, they may try to "out-legal" the lawyers and forcibly compress their testimony into the narrowest possible interpretation of the legal principles involved. Something like this seems to happen with psychiatrists who will testify that a chronic, deteriorated, delusional schizophrenic knows the difference between right and wrong just because the unfortunate defendant is able to mumble in a parrotlike fashion that he knew that to kill is against the law.

It is to be emphasized that the medical expert is expected to use his best possible clinical skill in arriving at his opinion and that there are no legal restrictions on his medical abilities. What is more, he has the right and obligation to communicate his opinion in full to the jury, provided that his testimony as to his opinion is legally admissible in the first place and that a proper foundation has been laid for his testimony by establishing its relevancy through other evidence. Thus, if a psychiatric expert is permitted to testify at all, he must be permitted to testify in full about everything that he used to form his clinical opinion. And, within the bounds of good medicine and subject to the discretion of the trial judge, he is the sole judge of what is relevant to the formation of his own opinion. He must keep in mind, however, that the jury is free to accept or reject both his opinion and the evidence upon which it is based.[29]

This provides a unique opportunity for psychodynamically oriented psychiatrists in those cases where such medical evidence is admissible. The psychiatrist can present the full history of the patient/defendant together with all his psychodynamic interpretations and conscious and unconscious material, both directly observed and deduced through his clinical judgment. This can be done in a manner very similar to what would take place in a well-run clinical conference, except that the psychiatrist must remember that the jury is composed of laymen and that everything must be expressed in words and concepts that are understandable to the nontechnically trained. In my own experience, juries have been surprisingly receptive to such clinical information when it was properly presented to them. The lay public is often a good deal more sophisticated about modern psychological knowledge than psychiatrists give them credit for being, and it is quite possible to communicate to the average intelligent layperson ideas concerning the unconscious and other basic psychodynamic principles.

In this way the psychiatrist enters the courtroom as a powerful ally in the administration of justice, placing the full measure of modern psychiatric knowledge at the service of the law.

The full measure of modern psychiatric knowledge has become possible in California through a 1949 decision of the California Supreme Court in the *Wells* case.[30] This case involved the admissibility of psychiatric evidence concerning malice aforethought, where the question of insanity was not at issue. The decision has already produced a radical improvement in the use of psychiatric testimony, and although the direct effect of this decision applies only in California, it is reasonable to suppose that similar decisions may be won in other jurisdictions as well. To properly understand this decision, however, it is necessary to review the legal history regarding crimes committed in a state of intoxication.

Intoxication

The admissibility of psychiatric testimony as evidence of lack of capacity or impairment of ability to premeditate or to entertain malice aforethought, thereby reducing a murder to manslaughter, has its historical roots in the legal conflict over alcoholic intoxication.

As indicated in the quotations given earlier from legal authorities on *mens rea*, intoxication was not accepted as grounds for exculpation of guilt during the fifteenth to eighteenth centuries and, at least by Coke, was regarded as an aggravating factor. This is very surprising, for such an attitude is totally inconsistent with the basic premise of criminal law. If, to establish the crime of murder, there must be volitional premeditation and intent to kill, a heavily intoxicated man should have been considered in the same light as a somnambulist, an infant, or an insane person. One who acts through drunkenness can hardly be considered to possess the attribute of free will. If there is no free will, there is no malice aforethought and there may not be any possibility of premeditation in the sense of conscious deliberation.

In ancient times, drunkenness was an aggravation of a crime; according to Aristotle, it doubled the punishment for any given offense.[31] But in the middle ages, at least in ecclesiastical law, a more rational view was held. Thomas Aquinas wrote:

> One sin added to another makes more sins, but it does not always make a sin greater, since it may be that the two sins do not coincide, but are separate. It may happen, if the first diminishes the second, that the two together have not the same gravity as one of them alone would have; thus murder is a more grievous sin if committed by a man when sober than if committed by a man when drunk, although in the latter case there are two sins, because drunkenness diminishes the sinfulness of the resulting sin more than is implied in the gravity of drunkenness itself.[32]

Such a view of intoxication is logically airtight; but the legal indignation toward the alcoholic offender was such that authority after authority twisted and turned the legal reasoning of Aristotle and Aquinas into all sorts of specious arguments to deny intoxicated criminals their rights under the doctrine of *mens rea*. These decisions, over a period of 300 years, provide amazing examples of how far a jurist will go in forcing the law to express irrational moral indignation even though all logical consistency is violated.[33]

In 1838, in England, in a case of assault with intent to murder, for the first time a jury was instructed that gross intoxication might disprove the intention required for this aggravated offense.[34] Very gradually, throughout the nineteenth century, both in England and in this country, there was an increase in the number of cases where intoxication, at least of severe degree, was held to impair the capacity to premeditate or to entertain malice aforethought; consequently verdicts of second-degree murder or of manslaughter, rather than first-degree murder, were brought in.

In 1890, in a case involving a homicide committed by a man in a state of alcoholic hallucinosis, this principle was extended into the general statement:

> [T]he conclusion logically follows that murder in the first degree, in which, under our statute, premeditated malice is the distinguishing ingredient, can only be committed by one possessed of the mental capacity to deliberate and premeditate, and that a homicide committed by one who was at the time, *for any reason*, incapacitated to think deliberately or determine rationally as to the quality, character, and consequences of the act, cannot be murder in the first degree.[35]

In 1930, it was held that

> [it] is not necessary that a defendant's reason be dethroned to mitigate a killing to manslaughter. . . . If the excitement and passion adequately aroused obscured the reason of the defendant, the killing will be reduced to manslaughter. . . . A defendant acting under such temporary mental stress is presumed to be incapable of malice, an essential ingredient of murder.[36]

In the often cited New York case of *People v. Caruso*, a similar principle was sustained in a case not involving intoxication.[37]

Thus, slowly but surely, the criminal law was forced by its own need for internal consistency to adopt a more humane attitude toward alcoholic offenders. In doing so, the foundation for the *Wells* case was laid.

It is unfortunate that, in 1946, when the Supreme Court of the United States had the opportunity to rule on the question of intent in the case of *Fisher v. United States*, the major issues were evaded and the affirmation of the death sentence was based on other technical considerations. The dissenting opinion of Justice Murphy is of great interest to psychiatrists, as it contains a most enlightened awareness of the contribution that psychiatry could make to the law:

> It is undeniably difficult, as the Government points out, to determine with any high degree of certainty whether a defendant has a general mental impairment and whether such a disorder renders him incapable of the requisite deliberation and premeditation. The difficulty springs primarily from the present limited scope of medical and psychiatric knowledge of mental disease. But this knowledge is ever increasing. And juries must constantly judge the baffling psychological factors of deliberation and premeditation. . . . It seems senseless to shut the door on the assistance which medicine and psychiatry can give in regard to these matters, however inexact and incomplete that assistance may presently be.

. . . Only by integrating scientific advancements with our ideals of justice can law remain a part of the living fiber of our civilization.[38]

The Wells Case

In 1949 the Supreme Court of California, in effect, invited the assistance of psychiatry in every case of murder where there was any question as to the mental capacity of the accused to entertain premeditation, deliberation, intent, or malice. This decision eliminated in California the absurd restriction on psychiatric testimony to only those few mental conditions that fulfill the narrow restrictions of the 1843 M'Naghten rules. The court held without equivocation that mental and emotional abnormalities, even "tension states," are pertinent to the determination of the degree of homicide and that the testimony of a psychiatrist must be admitted in evidence.[39]

The *Wells* decision profoundly influenced the use of psychiatric testimony in California murder trials. Formerly, trial judges had tended to exclude all testimony of psychiatric experts unless there was a plea of not guilty by reason of insanity, and then it was only admissible in the second trial.[40] There was no opportunity for juries to take into consideration any evidence of mental or emotional abnormality in reaching a decision as to guilt and degree of the offense.

From the point of view of the psychiatrist, the decision in the *Wells* case is the most enlightened and most comprehensive of the various opinions on these matters. Accordingly, it deserves detailed discussion here.

Wesley Robert Wells[41] was a 46-year-old Negro who had spent practically all his life, since the age of twelve, in California reformatories and prisons.

He was born in Texas, the second of three children. His mother left his father when he was still very young, and shortly afterward the mother died. The children were taken care of by an uncle in Colorado for a short period and then shipped to an aunt in California. The three children were raised together with the aunt's own three children under conditions of poverty and emotional deprivation. The aunt was separated from her husband. She was a very slight, ineffectual, but well-meaning person, hardly able to act as a stabilizing influence on the children. At the age of twelve, Wells was sent to reform school for two years for stealing a car. Again at sixteen he was returned to reform school for the same offense. After 18 months he was released on parole, only to be returned within a month's time on a technical parole-violation charge.

In 1928 he was convicted of receiving stolen property and was sentenced to one to five years in San Quentin Prison; he was then transferred to Folsom Prison for disciplinary reasons. In 1931, while at Folsom, he was involved in a "free-for-all" that resulted in the death of another prisoner. He was convicted of manslaughter and sentenced to ten more years. In January 1941 he was released on parole, only to be returned to Folsom within a few weeks for an attempted car theft. Throughout his prison career he was in disciplinary trouble on the average of 10 to 15 times a year and as a result served repeated long stretches in solitary confinement. In 1944 he struck a prison doctor. Also in 1944 he seriously injured another prisoner in a knife fight. In 1945 he assaulted several guards with an iron rod torn from his bedstead. In the same year he struck a guard with his fist.

In 1947, following a period of solitary confinement of more than three months, he became very irritable, tense, and very preoccupied with the failure of the Adult Authority to determine his sentence at a definite number of years.[42]

Wells heard through the grapevine that a letter had been sent from the District Attorney's Office to the Adult Authority, advising them not to fix his sentence, so that he would be technically eligible for capital punishment if he should ever commit another assault. Such a letter had actually been sent to the Adult Authority.

Wells was seen by the prison physician and by a consulting psychiatrist, who found him to be in an abnormal "state of tension." It was recommended that he receive sedation and be taken out of solitary. However, this was not done. Later, at checkup time, Noble Brown, a guard, flashed a light in Wells's face. Wells awoke and reacted with an outburst of fury, shouting and screaming at the guard. Two days later, at a disciplinary hearing in the warden's office, Wells became angry, insolent, and hysterical, and the warden directed him to leave the hearing room. In the hall outside, while the guards were trying to quiet him down, an altercation ensued, and Wells threw a cuspidor, which hit Brown, injuring him.

Wells was indicted for malicious assault. At the trial, an attempt was made by his defense to introduce medical and psychiatric testimony to the effect that he had been suffering from a

> state of tension, i.e., a condition in which the "whole body and mind are in a state of high sensitivity to external stimuli, and the result of this state is to cause the victim or patient to react abnormally to situations and external stimuli. *One of the characteristics of this state is that the patient possesses an abnormal fear for his personal safety and that an external stimulus apparently threatening that personal safety will cause*

the patient to react to it more violently and more unpredictably than the same stimulus applied to a normal person. In other words, that the threshold of the fear of the patient is lower to the extent where stimuli which would normally cause no fear in the patient will cause fear in the patient suffering from this state."

The purpose of such testimony was to prove that the defendant had acted through fear, even though abnormal and unreasonable, rather than from malice.

This testimony was excluded by the trial judge and Wells was convicted and sentenced to death.[43]

On appeal, the California Supreme Court held that the medical and psychiatric testimony should not have been excluded. The court stated that:

[h]ere, the offer was to show not insanity, not a lack of capacity to have malice aforethought, but rather, the fact of nervous tension and that the particular tension was directly relevant to the issue of "purpose, motive, or intent"; i.e., to the critical question as to whether defendant's overt act was done with "malice aforethought" or was actuated by fear, genuine although unfounded in ultimate truth. This evidence was admissible for reasons similar to those which fundamentally make evidence of intoxication admissible.

Ironically, Wells did not directly benefit by this decision. Although the court held that the exclusion of psychiatric evidence was erroneous, they also determined that such evidence would not have altered the verdict of the jury, and thus affirmed the judgment of the lower court.

In rejecting a new trial for Wells, the California Supreme Court weighed the excluded testimony of the physicians who had examined him two days before the offense against the implication of malice as judged by his previous conduct and enmity toward guards as a class and decided that such medical testimony would not have influenced the decision of the jury.

When executive clemency was refused Wells on the grounds that he was "incorrigible," the case became a *cause celebre* in California. In 1953, when I had the opportunity to examine Wells, I felt that it was most unfortunate that the proffered psychiatric testimony considered by the court was not the full story of Wells's emotional disorder. Experience in subsequent cases shows that where more detailed testimony regarding the psychiatric elements responsible for the crime is presented in a meaningful way to the jury, it may carry much greater weight than the traditional criterion of implied malice.

I was impressed by Wells's great strength—both physical and mental. Though he had had little formal education, his I.Q. was over 120. He showed remarkable shifts of identity. One moment he was angry, belligerent, and threatening, an almost animal-like person; confused, acting on impulse, and having utter disregard for consequences. Almost instantaneously he would acquire a smug, self-satisfied demeanor; he arrogantly discussed with the captain of the guards his idea of how an efficient prison should be run. At another time he appeared to be a sincere, friendly, and wholly rational person who was able to discuss intelligently the problems of racial discrimination in the prison system. But at times he reacted with whining, hypochondriacal complaints almost paranoid in nature.

Before Wells was sent to death row, he became notorious for his acts of sadistic cruelty toward certain other prisoners; yet he also was very protective in a kindly way to others. Some of the prison guards seemed to have been intimidated by him and responded to his aggression with anger and counter-aggression. Other guards and prison officials who had known him for many years acquired a certain fondness and respect for him, despite all the trouble he caused them. One senses that strong qualities of leadership lay beneath his gross emotional instability.

One can infer that his major areas of unconscious conflict involved problems of latent homosexuality, aggression toward authority figures, and narcissism, combined with overwhelming self-destructive urges. His ego identity was shifting and unstable. His chief defense mechanism against total loss of ego identity and self-destructive annihilation appeared to be the formation of an aggressive, "bad" identity, rebellious and defiant, revolving about the central idea of "I will never submit to authority. I am strong, I am dangerous. No prison will ever break my spirit. It is not true that I am not potent and masculine." These are not his actual words, of course, but are his castration fears expressed in the language of his behavior.

Wells is an excellent reminder of the close similarities between the traumata of military life and prison confinement. And in prison there are none of the compensatory self-esteem mechanisms of patriotism, group identification with a common good cause, and public recognition. It is true that in both the military and the prison situation the passive-dependent person who forms his ego identity around submissive patterns has the least difficulty. But it is the extraordinary prisoner who, lacking in passive qualities, can still preserve his integrity as well as his sanity under years of prison confinement. Far more frequently we meet the type of problem of which Wells was an extreme example. Wells's symptoms were strikingly similar to those of soldiers whose "evil," aggressive identity may be a last stand against total psychotic disintegration.

Erickson described them:

The boundaries of their ego have lost their shock absorbing delineation: anxiety and anger are provoked by everything too sudden or too intense, whether it be a sensory impression or self-reproach, an impulse or a memory. A ceaselessly "startled" sensory system is attacked by stimuli from outside as well as by somatic sensation: heat flashes, palpitation, cutting headaches. Insomnia hinders the nightly restoration of sensory screening by sleep, and that of emotional synthesis by dreaming. Amnesia, neurotic pseudologia, and confusion show the partial loss of time-binding and of spatial orientation. What definable symptoms and remnants of "peace-time neuroses" there are have a fragmentary and false quality, as if the ego could not even accomplish an organized neurosis.

The American group identity supports an individual's ego-identity as long as he can preserve a certain element of deliberate tentativeness; as long as he can convince himself that the next step is up to him and that no matter where he is staying or going he always has the choice of leaving or turning in the opposite direction if he chooses to do so. . . . For many men, then, the restraint and discipline of army life provides few ideal prototypes. To quite a few, it represents instead the intensely evil identity of the sucker; one who lets himself be sidetracked, cooped up, and stalled while others are free to pursue his chance and his girl. But to be a sucker means to be a social and sexual castrate; if you are a sucker, not even a mother's pity will be with you. . . . In their struggle . . . their traumatized ego fights and flees an evil identity which includes elements of the crying baby, the bleeding woman, the submissive nigger, the sexual sissy, the economic sucker, the mental moron—all prototypes the mere allusion to which can bring these men close to homicidal or suicidal rage. . . . Therapeutic efforts as well as attempts at social reform verify the sad truth that in any system based on suppression, exclusion, and exploitation, the suppressed, excluded and exploited unconsciously believe in the evil image which they are made to represent by those who are dominant.[44]

Eventually the death sentence imposed on Wells was commuted by the Governor of California to life imprisonment. Shortly afterwards, Wells performed an act of considerable heroism during a prison fire. He was transferred to a prison medical facility for treatment and adjusted quite well.

It is of utmost importance that psychiatrists understand clearly the basis on which the *Wells* decision was made, particularly in relation to insanity. It may be summarized thus: (1) The *Wells* decision in no way altered existing rules governing *legal insanity* as a defense. If there is any question as to the legal sanity of the defendant, customary legal procedures are applicable. The insanity of a defendant cannot be used for the purpose of reducing his crime from murder in the first degree to murder in the second degree, nor is there any degree of insanity sufficient to acquit of murder, but not of manslaughter. The legal presumption of sanity still holds true. (2) The issue in the *Wells* case did not involve *lack of capacity* for malice aforethought, but rather that the defendant *did not* have malice afore-thought because of his nervous tension and fears, and that the medical testimony concerning the tension and fears was relevant to the determina-tion of this. (3) Regardless of the statutory restrictions that exist as to the admissibility of testimony concerning insanity, medical, psychiatric and other evidence pertinent to the existence of premeditation, deliberation, intent and malice aforethought must be admitted and can be considered by the jury in determining the question of guilt. Thus, in California, psychiatrists who were formerly excluded from testifying in the main portion of the trial (being able to testify only *after* a verdict of guilt was reached), can now bring evidence to bear on these basic elements of guilt itself.

The issue, then, is not the existence of any particular mental condition or disease that is empirically or theoretically believed to preclude malice, but that the case must be decided on the actual psychodynamics of the particular defendant. The issue must be whether this individual, under the special circumstances of the crime, in his particular frame of mind, *did or did not* have the necessary design or intent, that is, malice. If it can be shown that the defendant acted out of fears, tensions, delusions, impulses, or in any other manner except with full, conscious, deliberate intention, then, I believe, the *Wells* decision is appropriate.

From experience with subsequent trials, I also believe it is permissible to use psychiatric evidence of a lack of capacity to entertain malice aforethought as proof that the defendant did not have malice aforethought, even though the lack of capacity itself is not at issue. I could well, though, imagine a very strict judge insisting that the question of capacity not be discussed at all.

Another point settled by this decision is that the conclusive presump-tion of sanity is not a conclusive presumption of legal capacity to commit crime. Although the burden of proof of insanity rests on the defense, the burden of proof of the existence of premeditation and malice aforethought rests on the prosecution. Just as the prosecution has the right to introduce evidence attempting to establish these elements of the crime, so the defense has the right to bring contrary evidence, including psychiatric testimony that denies these elements.

The Melkonian Trial

In 1953 the opportunity arose to apply the *Wells* decision in the trial of Lewon Melkonian, a Russian-Armenian displaced person who, in an acute confusional state, killed his wife and the man he supposed to be her lover. Because this case is such an excellent illustration of the use of psychiatric testimony to exclude malice aforethought, with a consequent manslaughter verdict rather than first- or second-degree murder, it is presented in some detail here.

Numerous witnesses testified as to the events immediately preceding the slayings, and much evidence was produced to prove premeditation and criminal intent. The defendant took the stand on his own behalf and freely admitted everything that had occurred. The defense was based mainly on expert psychiatric testimony, which was used to prove that the defendant, because of his mental illness, did not possess the elements of premeditation and malice aforethought required for the crime of murder; hence, he could be found guilty only of manslaughter. As the defendant understood very little English, the psychiatric examination, as well as most of the trial, had to be conducted through interpreters.

Melkonian was a very small man. During the trial he was excitable, visibly tense, and most of the time appeared very depressed. His appearance unquestionably impressed the jury with both his sincerity and his emotional instability. The man whom he killed was very tall, heavy, and strong, and the jury had no difficulty in appreciating the reality of the fear that had obsessed Melkonian prior to the slayings.

There was the prosecuting attorney's expected objection to the admission of psychiatric evidence. Evidently the prosecution had not anticipated such a defense tactic: during the cross-examination the prosecuting attorney admitted that he had never heard of a similar attempt to use medical evidence to rebut evidence of malice aforethought.[45] There was no psychiatric witness for the State. No plea of insanity had been made, and the District Attorney's office had not seen fit to have the defendant examined by its own psychiatrist prior to the trial.

The *Wells* decision was cited by the defense counsel as justification for the expert testimony, and, after considerable legal argument, the trial judge permitted me to testify in full. The frequent objections of the prosecution were consistently overruled, and I experienced no difficulty in presenting to the jury a very complete report of my psychiatric findings, including the full story of the defendant's life and social background. On cross-examination, the prosecuting attorney attempted to challenge my right as an expert to give an opinion on what he considered to be a purely legal matter. I was interrogated in considerable detail as to the precise legal definitions of insanity, malice aforethought, and the statutory laws dealing with homicide. I was questioned about historically significant cases and their bearing on this trial. The prosecution made much of the fact that none of the prominent alienists in California had ever raised questions of malice before, and I was asked to account for this, including giving an opinion about those physicians. At one point in the trial, a prosecution witness had testified at length about certain details of Melkonian's behavior that did not agree with my history. I was asked for, and allowed to give, the opinion that I did not think this witness was truthful. Before taking the witness stand, I had carefully studied the testimony of all the preceding witnesses. It seemed evident that because the trial judge was relatively unfamiliar with this type of defense, he had permitted considerable latitude to both the defense and the prosecution insofar as the expert testimony was concerned.

The following case history is essentially as it was given to the jury. Lewon Melkonian was born in Russia in 1914, of Armenian parentage. When he was an infant, his father was killed in World War I. His mother died soon afterward, and in early childhood Melkonian was raised under very unfavorable conditions in an orphanage. Later he was cared for in a rather indifferent way by relatives. His entire childhood was spent in an atmosphere of extreme poverty, emotional deprivation, and social turmoil. He tried to become a house painter, but at the age of 20 he was drafted into the Russian Army, where he served in a menial capacity. After three years' service, he was released, only to be drafted again, three years later, in 1940. He was in combat near Stalingrad for a little less than a year and was captured by the Germans. After 11 months in a prison camp, he escaped in 1944. He took refuge with an Armenian family, and it was their daughter with whom he fell in love and married. Shortly after the marriage, he and his wife were taken by the Germans and placed in a concentration camp, where he witnessed and experienced much horror and brutality. They were released by the Allies in 1945 and taken to a displaced persons camp. It was in the D.P. camp that their three children were born.

All his life he had planned and dreamed of an idealized marriage and home life. His prison, concentration camp, and D.P. camp experiences were of intolerable frustration, and his constant daydreaming of the happy life to come was his sole comfort. He developed severe symptoms of nervousness, tension, irritability, startle reactions, and moody depression from which he would escape into his idealized fantasies. He was particularly affected by witnessing the shooting of several hundred Jewish inmates of the concentration camp. He became very panicky, and he felt that this experience left an ineradicable mark on him. It was even harder to bear the frustrations of the D.P. camp. He had naively expected quick release, and as the years went by his tension and depression increased.

Finally in 1949, through the mediation of a refugee organization, he and his family were brought to the United States for settlement in an Armenian colony in Fresno, California. The trip to America was anticipated as the entrance into paradise: now would come the ideal marriage and happy home life. But on the voyage he discovered his wife with a strange man in their stateroom. He was stunned by this shattering of all his hopes. His wife protested her innocence, and it may well be that Melkonian built up a harmless incident into something much more than it actually was. Because of the language barrier, it was never possible for me to evaluate accurately just what was reality and what might have been paranoid attitudes, possibly even delusions. I admitted this difficulty frankly to the jury, and I did not attempt to distinguish sharply between what might have really happened and what might have only been built up in the defendant's mind. It was this impossibility of evaluating the reality situation that made an insanity plea unsuitable in the first place. The two persons who might have shed light on this matter were dead—killed by the defendant. It was my impression that most of what Melkonian claimed was true in reality, but that he had also elaborated small details of his wife's behavior into paranoid fantasies. There was some reason to believe that his wife, in reaction to his accusations of infidelity, deliberately taunted him and told him things that had not happened.

In any event, Melkonian and his wife were reconciled during the voyage, and they settled in Fresno, he working as a painter. Very soon he became suspicious that his wife was interested in an Armenian journalist who was paying considerable attention to her. He reacted with a recurrence of all his old symptoms. He was very depressed and suspicious and evidently had some ideas of reference at times, including thoughts that people were trying to harm him. His wife would try to prove her innocence. They would reconcile, and then it would happen all over again.

Finally he decided that the solution was to move to San Francisco and take his wife away from this man, which he did in the fall of 1952. He and his wife lived with an old friend, Usunian, and his wife. Melkonian described Usunian as his best friend—a "blood brother," but he did not get along well with Usunian's wife. Almost immediately he developed a fear that his own wife and Usunian were interested in each other. This fear precipitated more tension and depression, and there was a recurrence of the severe panic of the type he had experienced in the concentration camp. He bought a gun for protection. He entreated his wife, Usunian, Usunian's wife, and eventually all the leaders of the Armenian group in San Francisco for help.

He would hide under the house or under the bed to eavesdrop on his wife. About a week prior to the killing, he hid under the bed and claimed to have overheard his wife and Usunian plotting to get rid of him, of poisoning him, of marrying his wife off to a rich Russian emigre. There is some reason to believe that such a conversation with these threats actually took place between his wife and Usunian, but that it was a joking, facetious exchange, the two having no idea that they were overheard. Melkonian became even more fearful. He could not eat or sleep and would refuse to go to bed at night. He lay on the couch in the living room, fully dressed, with the gun conspicuously in his belt.

On Sunday morning, January 23, 1953, he left the house to go to church. Having forgotten his cigarettes, he returned home in a few minutes to find his wife and Usunian in an embrace. He reacted, in his words, by going "bereft of my mind, my lid was raised" (the Russian equivalent of "blowing my top"). "My blood was boiling, and I was like a drunken man. I was shaking and the house was going around and around." Most of all, he was frightened—he felt sure that Usunian would now kill him. He claimed that Usunian made a gesture as if to choke him. Melkonian ran to the kitchen, got his gun, and shot both his wife and Usunian. Then he shot himself in the neck.

Several hours later he regained consciousness when awakened by his youngest child, who had been at Sunday school. The neck wound was superficial, and he crudely bandaged himself. He and the child walked to the church to get the other two children. He left all the children at a friend's home and then returned to his own home. The police were there already, and he admitted the double killing to them. During his brief hospital stay he showed no evidence of delusional or confused behavior, although he continued to be anxious and depressed. He could not account for his actions except that he was jealous and afraid.

When I first saw him, five months later, his clinical picture resembled more a tension state with depression than it did a paranoid psychosis. He was very voluble, and it was difficult for the translator to convey everything that he would say. Facial expressions and affective responses were exceedingly labile. He would weep and storm, argue, and insist on certain details. There seemed little remorse specifically for the killings, but instead he showed a sort of overall remorse for his entire life and its misfortunes and frustrations. He felt that the deaths were inevitable and that he should have died too. But, having recovered, he now wanted to live to take care of his children and build a new life and a "happy home." He did not feel that he deserved punishment; he believed the tragedy was already sufficient punishment.

It is no easy task to reach a diagnosis in a case such as this. That he was paranoid in his thinking seemed self-evident. Yet there was a good deal of reality basis to all his fears and suspicions, and these were superimposed on a lifetime of hardship, poverty, deprivation, and frustration. Then there were the traumata of combat, the horrors of concentration camps, and the miserable years in D.P. camps. All this he survived with an ego intact except for the paranoid trends. The pressing symptoms were always anxiety and depression in response to the failure of his dreams to materialize. His suspicious jealousy was clearly in response to repressed homosexual fears. He had lived in a world of violence and aggression, and his castration fears were never quiet. He felt inadequate, sexually and in all other ways. Yet he had a tremendous capacity for self-preservation despite the overwhelming odds against him. It did not seem to me that his paranoid projections were his major means of keeping his ego intact. His dream of the happy home seemed more important as a self-preservatory function. Undoubtedly his fantasy of a happy life was more oral than phallic, and its regressive quality probably stood in the way of what little possibility there was of achieving his dream. But his latent homosexuality was his Achilles heel. The sight of his "blood brother" with his wife drove him to kill. I think if it had been anybody else he would not have shot but would have survived it as he had all the other traumata of his life. (In his own curious way, he even survived this; he made an excellent adjustment to prison life and looked forward to his parole and the happy life to come.)

I considered that he had had a psychotic break—an acute, confusional, paranoid psychosis—and I had no hesitation in telling the jury that the killings were the result of his abnormal mental state and that there had been no conscious voluntary, deliberative action. I also testified that the purchase of the gun and the threats he had made were of similar origin, being the result of mental disease rather than volition. The verdict was manslaughter, and he was sentenced to two consecutive prison terms.

The question can be asked, why was a defense of insanity not used in this case? The defense counsel, and I agreed, believed that it would be very difficult to fit him into the rigid California rule of right and wrong. It would have been very hard to prove to the jury the existence of his paranoia, in view of the impossibility of knowing for certain what was delusional and what was real. Just before and just after the crime he had appeared to be in contact with reality. The preponderance of reactive and situational factors spoke against an endogenous psychosis. It was assumed that if there had been the usual court appointed psychiatrists, they would have found him to be legally sane, and no consideration would have been given to the impairment of criminal intent. A failure to establish the plea of insanity would have resulted in a conviction of first-degree murder and the possibility of the gas chamber.

The Psychiatric Evaluation of
Malice Aforethought

If trials such as that of Melkonian are going to be more prevalent—if it becomes a matter of common practice to seek the help of psychiatrists to evaluate the elements of criminal intent, thus participating in the administration of criminal justice to a much greater degree than formerly—it would seem desirable, at first glance, that there be constructed some type of basic psychodynamic formulation to define the evaluation of malice aforethought.

I believe, however, that there are cogent reasons why such basic formulations should be avoided. In the first place, the central issue, that of the age-old philosophical abstraction of free will versus determinism, is itself undetermined. Freud brilliantly demonstrated by analysis of slips of the tongue, forgetting, and trains of association that what we call free will or voluntary choice is merely the conscious rationalization of a chain of unconsciously determined processes. Each act of will, each choice presumedly made on a random basis, turns out to be as rigidly determined as any other physiological process of the human body.[46] Yet all of us continue to live our lives, make our choices, exercise our "free will," and obey or disobey the law as if we actually had something to say about what we were doing. Criminal law could not exist were it not for this posit that each normal person intends to do the act he does and that such intention is based on the exercise of free will.

Medical psychology has embarrassingly few answers to this question in which the criminal law is most interested. It does no good to proclaim to the jurist that scientific evidence proves that there is no such thing as free will. There is a subjective phenomenon that the normal person experiences as free will. Illusory or not, free will remains the basis of all criminal law simply because free will is the basis of all normal social behavior.

In truth, today we do not have a sufficient foundation of scientific knowledge about the ego functions of decision, choice, and determination of action to justify the formulation of any general principles that could be applied to the law. As Gitelson stated:

Modern neuroanatomy, neurophysiology, cybernetics, animal psychology and the other natural sciences create the climate in which psychoanalysis exists today. Inevitably this affects its context, or, as some might say, the "field" of its operation. We can now have hope that the more recent advances in psychoanalysis, particularly in ego psychology, against this background, may bring us really fundamental insights into the individual nature of men and particularly into the problem of adaptation as it is related to determinism and free will. To the extent to which we do this we are also brought closer to a real solution of the living problems whose present insistence evokes our hectic improvisations.[47]

At the present time we must rely on the scientific philosophers, such as Reichenbach, who, by the use of the devices of logical positivism and probability theory, are able to construct an understandable working hypothesis concerning the quandary of apparent free will in a deterministic world.[48]

As a Freudian analyst, I find Jones's approach more interesting. He concedes that the problem of free will is "most profound and baffling," and so he sensibly leaves it alone. Instead he concerns himself with what is a more proper subject of psychoanalytic investigation: how it happens that this problem has possessed such an extraordinary interest for the thinkers of all ages; why some persons feel compelled to believe in the existence of free will, yet others feel as strongly compelled to deny its existence.

Jones points out the astonishing fact that

in practical daily life it does not seem to make any difference whether a given person, community, or religion adopts one or the other belief, in free will or determinism. . . . Here we have a question on the answer to which the most momentous and vital matters depend, and which one would suppose must affect profoundly the whole outlook of a man. And yet we cannot detect any difference it makes to his life or conduct according as he adheres to one answer or to its very opposite.

He concludes that

psychoanalysis of the unconscious shows that, whatever the conscious attitude towards the matter may be, there exist in the deeper layers of the mind the strongest, and probably ineradicable, motives creating what may be called the "sense of free will," closely connected with the sense of personality itself and retained so long as this is retained, i.e., until insanity, delirium or death dissolve it. That from the point of view of scientific objectivity this belief is illusory is irrelevant to the fact of its existence, and in a way to the necessity of its existence.[49]

Jones's analysis of this problem can be wisely applied, I think, to the issues of the criminal law. The task then becomes to understand the motivations, intent, and actions of the person who deviates from the common-sense posit of free will. This can be accomplished without specious generalizations that would attack the very structure of the law itself and would compel nonacceptance by the juridical mind. In the Melkonian trial, the judge and jury had no difficulty following my evidence, which demonstrated that the defendant had not acted out of free, voluntary will, despite the defendant's own assertion that he had. Similar evidence could be produced in many cases of neurosis and probably also of psychopathic personality. It is likely that in a good many cases such evidence would not be forthcoming, despite a meticulous clinical investigation. In these instances the defense of psychiatric impairment of malice aforethought would, accordingly, not be appropriate. Each case should be judged on its own clinical merits, and I see no need to attempt to decide arbitrarily that this or that diagnosis, or this symptom complex and not that one, affects the element of criminal intent. - To do otherwise is to lose the dynamic quality of modern psychoanalytic psychiatry. We would then be back in the static, nosological psychiatry of the nineteenth century, trying to substitute psychiatric abstractions for legal abstractions. There is little to choose between the two; neither has much to do with living, breathing, thinking, feeling people.

Hence, I believe that a psychiatrist's job in cases of this type is to make as thoroughgoing an investigation of the defendant as possible, search for the hidden psychodynamics that will explain the unique act of criminal behavior. The clinical information that is obtained can then be formulated in terms of the vast body of psychoanalytic knowledge, and particularly with the ever-growing fund of scientific observations dealing directly with delinquent and aggressive behavior.[50] These formulations must then be translated into terms that are meaningful to the judge and jury.

Actually, the law is not interested in psychiatrists' speculations about free will. Nor is it interested in the medical categorizing of who does or does not have malice aforethought. What it wants to know is whether, in the case of the particular individual on trial, the criminal action resulted from a voluntary, deliberate choice such as normal, reasonable persons appear to make in their daily lives, or whether it was the result of pathological forces arising far below the conscious level over which the defendant had little control. If it was the latter, then a psychiatrist is fully justified in using his professional skill and knowledge in seeking diminution of criminal responsibility, irrespective of the diagnostic categories that are fashionable at the moment.

I am concerned that, because there are no M'Naghten rules to serve as criteria for malice aforethought as there are for legal insanity, some timid, insecure psychiatrist may wish to have such rules provided. I can imagine that, if this type of defense comes into widespread use as more jurisdictions accept its logical place in criminal law, there will be assertions in the psychiatric literature that, for example, a diagnosis of psychopathic personality does not justify testimony of impairment of malice aforethought; or that a diagnosis of acute homosexual panic with paranoid projections does justify it. And thus there would evolve a set of psychiatric rules for evaluating malice.

Such rules, no matter how they were rationalized, would reflect only the timidity and lack of dynamic thinking on the part of those who formulated them. It is safer to take refuge in rules. Furthermore, it shortens the whole procedure: one has only to spend a half hour examining the defendant, decide what symptom complex he has, and easily and rapidly reach a conclusion about the existence of malice aforethought. The harder way, which requires more time, patience, and courage, is to study each case exhaustively, individualizing the medicolegal conclusions on the particular psychodynamics of the defendant.

One hundred and eleven years—from 1843 to 1954—separates the M'Naghten trial from the *Durham* case.[51] It took this length of time to crack the rigidity of the rules governing legal insanity. And it is only a tiny crack, as the jurisdiction over which the *Durham* decision prevails is small indeed. Fortunately, there is every indication that the crack will widen and the whole ridiculous structure of rules of psychopathology will crumble. It would be very wrong, indeed, if forensic psychiatry were to be burdened with a new set of rules for evaluating malice aforethought; and it would be ironic if the rules were the psychiatrists' own creation. It might take another 111 years to get out from under them.

Psychoanalytic knowledge of ego psychology and criminal psychodynamics is progressing far too rapidly to allow the development of arbitrary rules and principles that might come back to haunt us for generations to come. And it is a mistake to think that the legal mind demands such a compulsive approach. Many modern jurists and legal authorities have a far greater knowledge and appreciation of dynamic psychiatry than the best psychiatrists have of the law. They also seek the scientific, the rational, and the humane, as do we, and they are prepared to accept it in terms of the fluid psychodynamic processes of the individual rather than static rules and concepts. To prove this statement, one has only to read the writings and decisions of such jurists as Glueck,[52] Weihofen,[53] Biggs,[54] Sobeloff,[55] and Bazelon,[56] to name only a few.

Antipsychological Trends in the Criminal Law

Although the legal limitations against the consideration of motivation in determining guilt are restrictive, they are, nevertheless, not basically antipsychological. Malice aforethought, as limited an abstraction as it is, still takes into account the mental state, hence the psychology, of the defendant as well as the act itself. But certain other trends in the law can be categorically labeled as antipsychological in that they attempt to eliminate entirely any consideration of the mental processes of the defendant.

Implied Malice

The most important, and the most difficult, trend for psychiatrists to cope with is the traditional concept of implied malice. Quite early in legal history, difficulty arose in determining the actual state of mind of a defendant. Unless there were witnesses who overheard the planning of the murder or expressions of hatred and ill will, or unless the defendant confessed and acknowledged his mental attitude, there was no reliable way for the jury to determine the existence of malice aforethought. As so often happens in the law, when there is no precise way of realistically dealing with a difficult problem, the law will still insist on a dichotomy of opposites. It seems not to matter that human psychology and conduct are never black or white, but only exist in infinitely varying shades of grey. In the courtroom, a decision must be reached. A defendant must be found guilty or not guilty. A man is sane or insane. There is or is not malice aforethought. And so the necessary legal rules are evolved to permit such definite decisions, and these will then be rationalized in one or another specious manner.

The doctrine of implied malice was a simple and direct solution to this difficult problem of evaluating a subjective state of mind: certain criminal acts, by their very nature, were presumed to be proof of the existence of malice aforethought. The first such encroachment on the psychology of the law was an English statute in 1530 that declared that homicide by poisoning was always high treason, punishable by boiling to death.[57] The mere act of poisoning was considered, with some logic, to prove the existence of premeditation and malice. It is interesting that then, as now, such statutes, which tend toward a more punitive law, arise out of particular cases of a sensational nature that incite a powerful surge of public and judicial revenge. This 1530 statute was enacted to punish a man by the name of Richard Roose, a cook for the Bishop of Rochester. One day

Richard the cook put poison in a cauldron of porridge, and 17 members of the Bishop's household died. The punishment of boiling in oil was intended, I suppose, to strike particular terror into the hearts of all cooks who might in the future decide to poison their masters.

By the 17th century Hale included in the growing list of crimes that, by the deed alone, implied malice such offenses as any killing without provocation, the slaying of any minister of justice in the execution of his office, a slaying occurring during the course of a robbery, or the incidental killing of an innocent bystander during an attempt to kill another. The last instance clearly established the principle of transference of malice. One catches a glimpse of the bare beginnings of a concern for the welfare and protection of prisoners in Hale's rules that malice is implied "if a prisoner die by reason of duress and hard usage by the gaoler, it is murder in the gaoler. . . . So if a sheriff have a precept to hang a man for felony, and he beheads him, it is murder."[58]

The trend of the law toward the omission of the psychological factor was well described by the Law Revision Commission of the State of New York in its 1937 Communication to the Legislature:

It is self-evident that the state of mind, being subjective, is capable of proof only by objective manifestations of conduct. Thus the common law, upon the premise that persons intend the natural consequences of their acts, drew the inference that where dangerous weapons were used or where wounds were inflicted in vital organs or where the assault was violent or brutal, the fatal consequences that invariably ensued were actually intended by the perpetrator. This inference hardened into a presumption so that in every instance of a homicide committed in the ways just enumerated, malice was implied. The result was that the doctrine of implied malice placed upon persons accused of homicide an often insuperable burden of disproving malice. Again the dangerousness of the act rather than the killer's intent or state of mind in a specific case was the controlling consideration.

The extension of the doctrine of malice aforethought to cases where in fact it did not exist marked the final step in the development of malice as a medium of the punishment of dangerous acts. Where a person by reason of extreme negligence or recklessness caused death or in the course of certain unlawful acts committed homicide, it was said that malice was implied in law; that is, an absolute presumption that malice had existed in the mind of the perpetrator was raised as a matter of law. This presumption was irrebuttable; and though the facts overwhelmingly revealed a total absence of actual malice, the presumption prevailed. The logical extreme of the objective attitude of the common law was reached in this rule which totally disregarded the actual state of mind of the perpetrator and imposed liability solely on the basis of the act committed. This development, however, was of relatively recent date in the history of the common law. Indeed, so harsh would the logical implications of the fiction of malice implied in law be, that this rule has proved to be the focal point of attack of critics of the common law rules of homicide. It has even been greatly doubted whether the rule of implied malice as formulated by Coke and adopted by Blackstone was ever actually the law. "Malice aforethought" had been distorted out of all relation with its literal and natural meaning.[59]

I know of no attempt that has been made to introduce psychiatric evidence concerning malice in a case that would fall under the rule of implied malice aforethought. I can conceive how this might be done, however. For example, in a bank robbery where an accidental killing results, malice in the killing is implied and could not be refuted by psychiatric evidence. But if such medical evidence showed that there was no *mens rea* possible in the robbery itself, it seems to me that this would exclude the resultant homicide from the rule of implied malice. Whether this opinion would hold up in court remains to be seen.

By the very nature of their humanistic profession, all psychiatrists must oppose any tendency of the law that ignores the *doer* and considers only the *deed.* As Karpman said:

No deed can be understood unless the psychology of the doer is understood. And society, which is concerned with the abolition of deeds, will never accomplish that as long as it deals with the deed only. Hence, because of the system of punishing the deed and not the doer, crime has never abated and goes on from year to year, increasing in severity. A most radical change is needed: one must reach the deed through the doer.[60]

Probably, psychiatrists are not able at the present time to do much with the antipsychological and antihumanistic doctrine of implied malice. Yet some day the law may be revised and psychiatrists may be called on to aid in the formulation of a more rational substitute.

Objective Liability

A second trend in the criminal law that I think should be opposed by dynamic psychiatry was first formulated by the distinguished jurist Oliver Wendell Holmes in his famous lectures on *The Common Law.* Holmes asserted that the trend of the law was toward the development of "objective liability," that is, where motive and intent are completely disregarded or at most retained as fictional cliches. In this light, *mens rea* and malice aforethought have no real relationship to state of mind but refer only to the special circumstances of the criminal act and the probability of harm arising from certain acts which society wishes to prevent. Holmes stated:

> In the characteristic type of substantive crime acts are rendered criminal because they are done under circumstances in which they will probably cause some harm which the law seeks to prevent.
>
> The test of criminality in such cases is the degree of danger shown by experience to attend that act under those circumstances.
>
> In such cases the *mens rea*, or actual wickedness of the party, is wholly unnecessary, and all reference to the state of his consciousness is misleading if it means anything more than that the circumstances in connection with which the tendency of his act is judged are the circumstances known to him. . . . In some cases, actual malice or intent, in the common meaning of these words, is an element in crime. But it will be found that, when it is so, it is because the act when done maliciously is followed by harm which would not have followed the act alone, or because the intent raises a strong probability that an act, innocent in itself, will be followed by other acts or events in connection with which it will accomplish the result sought to be prevented by the law.[61]

As an example of objective liability, consider what happens when one receives a parking ticket. It matters not who actually parked the car and under what circumstances it was parked or what the mental state of the driver was. The owner of the car is liable for the fine simply because it is his car and it was found in a wrong parking zone.

Fortunately this mechanical, dehumanized concept of criminal responsibility has made only limited inroads into the law. But the idea of objective liability as a practical expedient has great appeal to many legislators and jurists, and one may expect that further efforts will be made to expand the principle to many different criminal offenses. Psychiatrists should, I believe, offer their objections to such a trend at every opportunity. Objective liability may be a useful way of coping with traffic problems, but if extended to major crimes it could result in a dehumanized legal structure suitable only for a totalitarian society.

A description of the ways in which objective liability has already encroached on the legal structure of our society is beyond the scope of this paper. The reader is referred to the excellent discussion by Hall, who has compiled a mass of material concerning this.[62]

I have heard psychiatrists argue in favor of a kind of objective liability. In their desire to rid the law of its primitive elements of revenge, scapegoating, and theological morality, the idea of punishing individuals only for objective damage to society seems to them to be an easy solution. This is a dangerous fallacy: a mechanical, objective criminal law is contrary, I think, to everything that has been learned from psychodynamic psychiatry. A better, but much more difficult, solution is to strive for the creation of a body of law that gives the fullest possible consideration to the psychology of the individual, yet still is free from archaic concepts of revenge and theology.

Statutory Law and Vested Interests

There is no question that the majority of statutory laws were made for immediate reasons of expedience in response to the pressure of vested interests, and not because of their meaning in any overall philosophical system of criminal law. For example, in the instance of the 1530 statute punishing poisoners with boiling in oil, it is reasonable to assume that Henry VIII, who instigated this statute, had a decided vested interest in it. He must have constantly feared that he might be poisoned, as the Bishop of Rochester was, and so it was to his personal advantage to invoke the strictest possible punishment for this offense. Nowadays, vested interests are more likely to be economic rather than to involve personal physical danger. But the principle is the same, and a great many laws, criminal as well as civil, are passed by legislative bodies in response to pressure groups who have a specific, self-serving interest in the laws.

It could be argued that because such statutes result from sociological and economic forces, and because such statutes have supplanted so much of the traditional common law, today the criminal law is no longer psychological. Rather it must be viewed as a synthesis of socioeconomic factors in which such individualistic considerations as "state of mind" are merely archaic relics of a long-dead moralistic tradition. Obviously, if this were true, there would be no room in the courtroom for a psychiatrist.

Granted that many statutes arise out of such objective forces, it still seems to me that once a crime is given a more severe or more certain punishment, even though that change was brought about for economic or other reasons, an alteration occurs in the prevalent ethical and moral values of the members of the entire community. This must occur on both the conscious, rational level and on the unconscious, emotional level. Hence, alterations in laws and in the nature of punishment change the conscious moral standards and the unconscious guilt responses of each person in the community, and these changes, in turn, must affect the administration of the criminal law. Statutory provisions that once were purely matters of expediency or of vested interest may become enmeshed in a moral and psychological matrix that requires perpetuation of the particular law, irrespective of the continued existence of the original necessity. Thus archaic laws that once were dictated by practical considerations cannot be changed without coming up against powerful emotional resistance from members of the community, who now feel a psychological necessity—usually imposed by unconscious emotional conflicts and strivings to oppose the change. When this happens, the law becomes a subjective issue, a problem in group dynamic psychology, not an economic or objective expediency.

How accurately these statutory changes reflect the prevailing views of the community will determine the extent to which, and how quickly, they acquire their psychological and emotional values. Particularly they will determine the degree to which the practical, expedient origin is obscured and replaced by deep emotional attitudes of guilt and morality. This process of moralization undoubtedly varies according to the heterogeneity and submissiveness of members of the community, but especially it will vary according to how well it fits in with preexisting attitudes and prejudices.

Take, for example, the distinction made in most southern states between grand theft and petty theft. The theft of a chicken is usually made the major offense even though the value of the chicken is far below the minimum limit for grand theft. Chicken stealing, in the south, is associated with Negroes and is consciously and unconsciously linked with powerful emotional prejudices. A southern juryman sharing these prejudices would have no difficulty in feeling that chicken stealing is a far greater crime than would be the theft of another article of similar value. His moral indignation would be greater, and the laws that inflict the more severe punishment on the chicken thief would meet with his approval.

On the other hand, in California special economic interests have inserted in the penal code the provision that the theft of $50 worth of avocado pears is grand theft, whereas the theft of most other property to the value of $200 constitutes grand theft.[63] It is doubtful that the California juryman, unless he is an avocado pear grower, feels any emotional resonance with this law. He may follow the instructions of the judge in bringing in the proper verdict, but his emotional reaction—his moral indignation—will be less, and he may even seek ways to reach a verdict of acquittal, despite the guilt of the defendant, simply because he does not emotionally subscribe to the law. Such a law does not become incorporated into the prevailing morality of the community but remains an isolated, special instance, a matter of socioeconomic expediency, rather than a moral issue.

Statutory laws such as these tend to confuse the basic issues of criminal law and often result in a penal code that is a hodgepodge of inconsistencies. The day is coming, though, when enlightened legislative bodies will consult with psychiatrists, sociologists, penologists, and criminologists about the formulation and anticipated effect of proposed statutes. If consultation with such experts is to be valuable—if each professional group is to contribute its own special knowledge in a pertinent and constructive way—the members of these professions must be prepared with a consistent philosophy based on a background of scientific knowledge. In the past, psychiatrists have avoided consideration of any penal statutes that did not directly deal with insanity or sex offenses. They must realize that all penal laws involve fundamental problems of abnormal psychology, concerning not only individual offenders, but all members of the community as well.

Psychodynamically oriented psychiatrists should be especially able to contribute to the progressive molding and growth of the law as enacted in our statutes. More than anyone else, they are in a position to appreciate the social dangers of laws that are formulated only in terms of act and circumstance and that diminish the basic worth of the individual through omission of mental and emotional factors.

Psychiatry and the Law

Criminal law, which occupies the very core of our system of ethics and morality, has until recently reflected practically nothing of Freud's great discoveries. This lack has existed despite the fact that since 1915, when Freud first described a psychodynamic mechanism in criminals—the criminal acting out of a neurotic guilt[64]—a tremendous scientific literature on criminal psychodynamics has accumulated. The existence of the *Archives of Criminal Psychodynamics* testifies to the rapid growth in this field. Very little of this knowledge has entered the courtroom, and that little only through the back door by way of probation and presentencing reports.

Now there are two very important legal decisions: the *Durham*[65] case for the insane where there should be no criminal responsibility, and the *Wells*[66] decision for the legally sane who are held to be only partially accountable. These decisions promise a warm welcome for psychodynamically oriented psychiatrists to bring their skill and knowledge directly into the courtroom and be active participants in the administration of justice. Forensic psychiatry need no longer be left, by default, to the organically minded, descriptive nosologist.

The welcome is also a challenge. It is not sufficient that this body of psychoanalytic literature exist in the books and journals—it must be taken directly to judge and jury and applied to specific cases through expert testimony.

Justice Benjamin Cardozo, in an address to the New York Academy of Medicine in 1928 on "What Medicine Can Do for Law," said:

> I think the students of the mind should make it clear to the lawmakers that the statute [of criminal intent in homicide] is framed along the lines of a defective and unreal psychology. . . . The present distinction is so obscure that no jury hearing it for the first time can fairly be expected to assimilate and understand it. I am not at all sure that I understand it myself after trying to apply it for many years and after diligent study of what has been written in the books. Upon the basis of this fine distinction with its obscure and mystifying psychology, scores of men have gone to their death. I think it is time for you who speak with authority as to the life of the mind to say whether the distinction has such substance and soundness that it should be permitted to survive. . . . The resources of the two professions [of law and medicine] can be pooled in matters such as these where society has so much to gain from cooperative endeavor.[67]

The use of psychiatric evidence for the evaluation of malice afore-thought affords an outstanding opportunity for such a cooperative endeavor. It is unlikely that the criminal law will abandon completely the abstract concept of *mens rea*. But the law has a way of clinging to ancient phraseology while allowing the meaning of the words to undergo radical changes. Thus, the phrase "malice aforethought" has drastically altered through centuries of legal evolution. It can be anticipated that further changes will occur, although the old words will persist.

Psychiatrists must not restrict themselves only to criminal insanity procedures. They should take active roles in all cases in which their knowledge of psychodynamics has a bearing on the determination of criminal intent. In this way they will influence the future evolution of these legal concepts in a direction compatible with psychological reality.

This discussion of the historical development and legal definitions of *mens rea* and malice aforethought can, by no means, be considered complete or authoritative. The origin and meaning of these legal issues are subject to widely varying opinions, and considerable controversy exists about even fundamental principles. Some of the crucial court decisions are confusing or evasive; others are contradictory. "The problems . . . have taxed the ingenuity of jurists for hundreds of years. They are inordinately complex and involve a great many ramifications."[68] Intensive research and study on an active, multi-disciplinary, collaborative level will be required to clarify these issues to a point where a rational, effective, and humane criminal law can be anticipated. And then will come the even more difficult task of educating public and legislative opinion to the point where such a rational criminal law would become emotionally acceptable.

Summary

The most fundamental concept in Anglo-American criminal law is the principle of *mens rea*—literally, guilty mind—or criminal intent. The full definition of every crime contains expressly or implicitly a proposition as to a state of mind. Therefore, if the mental element of any conduct alleged to be a crime is proved to have been absent in any given case, the crime so defined has not been committed.

This concept of criminal intent is very ancient, going back at least to biblical law, which distinguished murder from a killing done "ignorantly, whom he hated not in time past." The development of *mens rea* in relation to the crime of murder is sketched from a historical point of view, with quotations from the early authorities of English law.

American and English common law and most penal statutes in the United States specify *malice aforethought* as the particular criminal intent required to establish the crimes of murder and assault. Originally, malice aforethought, as the words imply, meant hatred or enmity preexisting the criminal act. Through centuries of legal evolution, this phrase now refers only to the state of mind existing at the instant of the criminal act, and pertains to design or purpose in contradistinction to accident and mischance. Many states now provide for two degrees of murder: first-degree murder when there exists both premeditation and malice aforethought; second-degree murder when there is malice aforethought but not premeditation. Manslaughter is a slaying done with neither premeditation nor malice aforethought.

Although this basic principle of *mens rea* is essentially a psychological concept, there are certain trends in the law toward the development of a nonpsychological, even antipsychological basis for the definition of certain crimes. These trends are:

1. Implied malice, that is, the presumption of malice aforethought upon the acts and circumstances of the crime, rather than upon the actual state of mind or intention of the defendant. This has evolved to the point where in some penal statutes the crime of murder is defined solely in terms of

behavior and circumstance and omits all reference to a state of mind: the so-called felony murder.

2. The theory of objective liability, first proposed by Holmes, in 1881, emphasizes the fictional quality to the legal definition of *mens rea*. He proposed that crimes be defined in terms of the acts committed under circumstances in which they will probably cause some harm that the law seeks to prevent. The test of criminality then becomes the degree of danger shown by experience to attend that act under those circumstances. Malice aforethought, as a subjective element, would no longer be pertinent.

3. Vested interests have caused the enactment of many statutes defining crimes in nonpsychological terms. In some instances, these statutes become integrated into the emotional matrix of the community and influence the prevailing moral values and attitudes; in other instances they remain isolated from the emotional life of the community.

It is my opinion that these antipsychological trends in the criminal law tend toward a dehumanized law contrary to the values inherent in psychodynamic psychiatry.

Criminal law is interested primarily in intent, rather than motive: the *how* of the crime rather than the *why*, although consideration of motivation is appropriate to the proof or disproof of malice aforethought and other types of criminal intent. The psychiatrist, as an expert witness, need not restrict his clinical investigations only to considerations of intent. Every clinical fact bearing on the total psychology of the defendant, including the entire life history, is pertinent to the formation of his expert opinion, and he may present this clinical material as testimony in order to define the bases on which he has formed his opinion as to the element of intent.

The admissibility of psychiatric testimony as evidence of lack of premeditation or malice aforethought, thereby reducing murder to manslaughter, has its historical roots in the legal conflict over intoxication. Because a severely intoxicated person is not ordinarily able to act with the voluntary free will that is *implied* in the definitions of premeditation, deliberation, intent and malice aforethought, such a person should logically not be found guilty of murder for a slaying done in such a state. But because of the moral repugnance against mitigating the responsibility of an individual who has supposedly voluntarily made himself drunk, a sin in itself, the law has resisted for centuries the use of intoxication as a defense in the crime of murder. Sporadically in the nineteenth century and more generally in the twentieth century it has become possible to use evidence of severe intoxication as evidence of lack of premeditation or malice aforethought.

In 1949, in the *Wells* decision in California, this principle was extended to any condition, including mental illness short of insanity, tension states, abnormal fear conditions, and the like, that now can be introduced as evidence to rebut a contention of premeditation and malice aforethought. Before this decision, in California psychiatric evidence was not admissible in the main portion of the trial. It was held that evidence concerning the mental illness of the defendant had to do only with the question of insanity or sanity, and a split trial was required in which the psychiatric evidence was presented only after the question of guilt had been decided by the jury. The *Wells* decision now concedes that psychiatric evidence has an important part in the actual determination of guilt, insofar as premeditation and malice aforethought are concerned, and the psychiatrist must be permitted to testify, even though there is no plea of insanity.

The clinical background of *Wells* is presented, together with the psychiatric evidence in the case of *Melkonian*, where such evidence resulted in a verdict of manslaughter.

The psychiatric evaluation of malice aforethought is discussed with reference to the age-old problem of free will versus determinism. The undesirability of "rules," psychiatric or legal, for the determination of malice aforethought is maintained. The psychiatrist's job is to make a thoroughgoing investigation of the defendant, searching for the hidden psychodynamics that will explain the unique act of criminal behavior, without restriction as to diagnosis or arbitrary rules. The clinical information thus obtained can then be formulated in the light of psychoanalytic and other scientific knowledge concerning delinquent and aggressive behavior. These formulations must then be translated into terms which are meaningful to the judge and jury.

Forensic psychiatry, in relation to the question of legal insanity, has been a static, nondynamic psychiatry. The questions raised by the elements of premeditation and malice aforethought offer a special opportunity for the application of psychodynamic psychiatry. If decisions such as the *Wells* decision and trials such as that of *Melkonian* become more prevalent, psychodynamic psychiatry will truly become an important ally of the law in the more rational and humane administration of criminal justice. The psychiatrist, by participation in the criminal proceedings, can be of influence in directing the future evolution of these legal concepts towards psychological reality.

Notes

[1]Cave, J. In *Chisholm v. Doulton*, (1888), 22 Q.B.D. 736.

[2]Stephen, J. In *Regina v. Tolson* (1889), 23 Q.B.D. 168.

[3]If a prisoner awaiting execution is found to be insane, his execution may be postponed until such time as his sanity is restored.

[4]Bracton, H. de. (1569), *De Legibus & Consuetudinibus Angliae Libri Quinq* . . . London: Richard Tottell, p. 101b.

[5]Ibid., p. 121.

[6]Ibid., p. 101b.

[7]According to Bouvier, J. (1914), *Law Dictionary and Concise Encyclopedia*. Kansas City, MO: Vernon Law Book Co., p. 2898.

[8]Plowden, E. (1761), *The Commentaries or Reports*. London, p. 19, *Reniger v. Fogossa*.

[9]Coke, E. (1628), *The First Part of the Institutes of the Laws of England or, a Commentary Upon Littleton* . . . *the Eleventh Edition.* . . . In the Savoy [London], printed for Eliz. Nutt and R. Gosling . . . , 1719, pp. 247b, 247a.

[10]Ibid., p. 247a.

[11]Hale, M. (1736), *Historia Placitorum Coronae. The History of the Pleas of the Crown* . . . *Now first published* . . . *with* . . . notes by Sollom Emlyn. In the Savoy [London], printed by E. and R. Nutt and R. Gosling, Vol. 1, pp. 29–27, 38.

[12]Blackstone, W. (1769), *Commentaries on the Laws of England*. IV. Oxford: Clarendon Press, p. 24.

[13]It is essential that the psychiatrist who intends to testify in the type of defense proceedings to be described in this paper be fully acquainted with the precise statutory definitions laid down in his particular state.

[14]13 Richard II, Sec. 2, Ch. 1 (1390).

[15]Lambard, W (1581), *Eirenarcha: or of the Office of the Justices of Peace.* . . . London, imprinted by Ra: Newbery, and H. Bynneman . . , p. 212. It is of interest that Lambard's book, published in 1581, also contains the earliest known definition of insanity in terms of good and evil (i.e., right and wrong) (p. 218).

[16]Hale, op. cit., sup. note 11, p. 451.

[17]Holt, J. In *Regina v. Mawgridge* (1707). In: Kelyng, J. A. (1708), *Report of Divers Cases in Pleas of the Crown Adjudged and Determined; in the Reign of the Late King Charles II* . . . *to which is Added the Reports of Three Modern Cases.* . . . London, printed for Isaac Cleave, p. 126.

[18]*The Penal Code of the State of California* (1951). San Francisco: Bender-Moss, sect. 188.

[19]Bouvier, op. cit., sup. note 7, p. 4068.

[20]Weihofen, H. Personal communication.

[21]Derby, A. (1930), *Cases on Criminal Law*. Indianapolis: Bobbs-Merrill, p. 587n.

[22]California Penal Code, sup. note 18, sect. 189.

[23]Ibid., sect. 187.

[24]Ibid., sect. 192.

[25]Bouvier, op. cit., sup. note 7, p. 2068.

[26]Hall, J. (1947), *General Principles of the Criminal Law*. Indianapolis: Bobbs-Merrill, p. 153.

[27]*People v. Shattuck* (1897), 109 Cal. 673.

[28]Karpman, B. (1955), Criminal psychodynamics: A platform. *Arch. Crim. Psychodynam.*, I:3–100.

[29]Weihofen, H. (1933), *Insanity as a Defense in Criminal Law*. New York: The Commonwealth Fund, p. 222.

[30]*People v. Wells* (1949), 33 Cal. 2nd. 330.

[31]Aristotle (1952), Nicomachean Ethics. In: *Great Books of the Western World*, Vol. 9. Chicago: Encyclopaedia Britannica, p. 359.

[32]Aquinas, T. (1952), Summa Theologica. In: *Great Books of the Western World*, Vol. 20. Chicago: Encyclopaedia Britannica, p. 144.

[33]For a full account of these arguments, see Hall, op. cit., sup. note 26, ch. 13.

[34]*Regina v. Cruse*, 8 C. & P. 541, 173 Eng. Rep. 610 (N.P. 1838), cited by Hall, op. cit., sup. note 26, p. 432.

[35]*Aszman v. State* (1890), 173 Ind. 347; 24 N.E. 123 (italics added).

[36]*Davis v. State* (1930), 161 Ten. 23; 28 S.W. 2nd. 993.

[37]*People v. Caruso* (1927), 246 N.Y. 437; 159 N.E. 392. See also the record on appeal in this case in Hall, L. & Glueck, S. (1951), *Cases on Criminal Law and Its Enforcement*. St. Paul: West, pp. 15–58.

[38]*Fisher v. United States* (1946), 328 U.S. 463; 66 S. Ct. 1318.

[39]*People v. Wells*, sup. note 30.

[40]California statutes provide a special procedure for trials where the question of insanity is raised as a defense. If only the plea of not guilty by reason of insanity is made, this is considered to be an admission of the offense charged. Hence, the double plea of not guilty and not guilty by reason of insanity is invariably made. This requires a double trial, and at the first trial no evidence whatsoever pertinent to the person's alleged insanity is admissible in evidence. It is only after a conviction on the first plea can such evidence be introduced to sustain the claim of irresponsibility.

[41]I am deeply indebted to Warden Harley Teets and Dr. David Schmidt of the California State Prison, San Quentin, and to Mr. Charles R. Garry, attorney for Wesley Robert Wells. All of the prison, medical, and legal records were placed at my disposal, and it was possible for me to examine Wells personally in May 1953.

[42]In California, the Adult Authority is given the responsibility for fixing the maximum sentence in a case where the trial judge has sentenced a prisoner to a

certain minimum number of years. Before such a maximum is set by the Adult Authority, however, the prisoner is technically under a life sentence.

[43]Section 4500 of the California Penal Code provides that "every person undergoing a life sentence in a State prison of this State, who, with *malice aforethought,* commits an assault upon the person of another with a deadly weapon or instrument, or by any means of force likely to produce great bodily injury, is punishable with death."

[44]Erikson, E. H. (1947), Ego development and historical change. In: *The Psychoanalytic Study of the Child,* 2:359–396. New York: International Universities Press.

[45]There had actually been at least one previous murder trial in California in which a similar defense was used to achieve a verdict of manslaughter. Dr. Meyer Zeligs of San Francisco was the expert witness. As far as I know, Zeligs was the first psychiatrist to give this type of testimony.

[46]Freud, S. (1901), *The Psychopathology of Everyday Life. Standard Edition,* 6. London: Hogarth Press, 1960.

[47]Gitelson, M. (1956), Psychoanalyst, U.S.A. *Amer. J. Psychiat.,* 112:700–705.

[48]Reichenbach, H. (1951), *The Rise of Scientific Philosophy.* Berkeley: University of California Press.

[49]Jones, E. (1951), Free will and determinism. In: *Essays in Applied Psychoanalysis,* Vol. 2. London: Hogarth Press, pp. 178–189.

[50]Diamond, B. I. (1955), Review of *The Annual Survey of Psychoanalysis* in *Arch. Crim. Psychodynam.,* 1:445–450.

[51]*Durham v. United States* (1954), 214 F. 2nd. 2862.

[52]Glueck, S. (1925), *Mental Disorder and the Criminal Law; A Study in Medico-Sociological Jurisprudence.* Boston: Little, Brown.

[53]Guttmacher, M. S. & Weihofen, H. (1952), *Psychiatry and the Law.* New York: Norton.

[54]Biggs, J. Jr. In United States ex rel. *Smith v. Baldi* (1951), 192 F. 2nd. 540. See also Biggs, J. Jr. (1955), *The Guilty Mind, Psychiatry and the Law of Homicide.* New York: Harcourt, Brace.

[55]Sobeloff, S. E. (1955), Insanity and the criminal law: From McNaghten to Durham, and beyond. *Amer. Bar Assn. J.,* 41:793.

[56]*Durham v. United States,* sup. note 51.

[57]22 Henry VIII, ch.9 (1530).

[58]Hale, op. cit., sup. note 11, pp. 455–466.

[59]Law Revision Commission of the State of New York, Communication to the Legislature, Legislative Document (1937) No. 65, pp. 536–540. Quoted by Hall & Glueck, op. cit., sup. note 37, pp. 60–63.

[60]Karpman, op. cit., sup. note 28, p. 71.

[61]Holmes, O. W. (1881), *The Common Law.* Boston: Little, Brown, pp. 75–76.

[62]Hall, op. cit., sup. note 26, ch. 6.

[63]California Penal Code, sup. note 18, sect. 487.

[64]Freud, S. (1961), Some character-types met with in psycho-analytic work. *Standard Edition*, 14:309–333. London: Hogarth Press, 1957.

[65]*Durham v. United States*, sup. note 51.

[66]*People v. Wells*, sup. note 30.

[67]Cardozo, B. (1931, *Law, Literature and Other Essays and Addresses*. New York: Harcourt, Brace, pp. 86–101.

[68]Weihofen, H. Personal communication.

The Psychiatric Prediction
of Dangerousness

[1974]

Several horrendous cases of multiple murders have been committed in California by persons who had either been "cleared" by psychiatrists or been discharged from mental institutions as "no longer dangerous."[1] Such cases invariably result in strong demands by law enforcement officials and by the public for psychiatrists to "do something" to protect against such irrational killings.

In 1964, Edmund E. Kemper III, a 15-year-old boy, shot and killed his grandmother and grandfather. He was committed to Atascadero State Hospital, where he was confined and treated for five years. He was returned to the jurisdiction of the California Youth Authority and in 1970, being 21, was released. In September 1972 he applied to the court to have his records sealed.[2] Feeling some uncertainty about Kemper's mental condition, the court appointed two psychiatrists to examine him. Both psychiatrists reported that he was not dangerous or otherwise a threat to society. It later was revealed, however, that he had murdered and dismembered six young girls, his mother, and one of his mother's friends during the course of a year. One of the murders had occurred four days before the psychiatric examinations that declared him harmless.[3]

Such cases, understandably, greatly alarm the public and hardly inspire confidence in the ability of psychiatrists to predict dangerousness. Nevertheless, the courts rely heavily upon such psychiatric predictions both in criminal cases and in civil commitments for involuntary hospitalization. With the growing emphasis on civil rights of the mentally ill, the state of being dangerous to oneself or others may be the only ground for involuntary hospitalization under progressive statutes.[4] Rubin estimates that "[a]pproximately 50,000 mentally ill persons per year are predicted to be dangerous and preventively detained for society's and their protection as well as treatment."[5]

Can psychiatrists predict danger with reasonable accuracy? Are there well-established clinical symptoms that if present, can be relied on to indicate potential danger? Can one be reasonably sure that persons who are not dangerous will not be labeled as such and unnecessarily confined? I believe the answer to all these questions is an emphatic *no*.

This chapter discusses the psychiatrist's difficulty in predicting dangerousness to others and proposes procedural changes in the handling of potentially dangerous persons. The problem of dangerousness to self will not be discussed here, as it involves quite different clinical and legal problems.

The Clinical Prediction of Dangerousness

Because of the urgent need for protection against mentally ill persons who are dangerous, and because of the almost universal reliance on expert psychiatric advice for the preventive detention of such persons, one would suppose that there existed a sizable amount of valid clinical and research information concerning the prediction of dangerousness. However, there are remarkably few such studies in the scientific literature, and those that do exist have many deficiencies which impair their reliability.

Studies concerning prediction of dangerous behavior fall into two broad categories: those that tend to substantiate clinical predictors and those demonstrating the unreliability of such clinical predictions. Among the former is an article by Malmquist, who examined 20 adolescents charged with murder.[6] Malmquist was specifically interested in the possible existence of premonitory signs and symptoms that could be used to predict violence in other cases. Definite clinical findings were of considerable help in understanding the dynamic process that led to the homicidal acts. The clinical findings were summarized under the rubrics of behavioral changes prior to the homicidal act; a "call for help" by the juvenile; use of drugs; object losses[7]; threats to manhood; somatization, hypochondriasis, or a recurrent medical problem; an emotional crescendo; and homosexual threats. But, as Malmquist states, "Certain premonitory signs and symptoms culminating in a homicide appeared consistently. But a major difficulty is the prevalence of similar signs and symptoms in people who never commit a violent act."[8]

MacDonald followed up 100 consecutive threat-to-kill admissions to the Colorado Psychopathic Hospital.[9] Within five to six years of the original admission, three of these patients had taken the lives of others and four had committed suicide. Obviously, these seven fatalities are of significance;

yet one can hardly justify a preventive detention procedure when over 90% of the suspected persons do not commit dangerous acts. In fairness to the clinicians who predicted the dangerousness, it should be noted that it is impossible to estimate how many of those patients might have committed dangerous acts if there had not been the intervention of hospitalization.

Hellman and Blackman have described a triad of symptoms—enuresis, firesetting, and cruelty to animals—that, if exhibited in childhood, they claim are predictive of aggressive violent crimes in the adult.[10] This triad is well known and widely employed by clinicians in the prediction of dangerousness. Reference to the original report reveals that of 31 prisoners charged with aggressive crimes 23 had the full triad. Of 53 nonaggressive prisoners, only seven had the full triad, and eight more had a history of part of the triad. This is a very significant clinical difference, but not of a sufficient magnitude and consistency to justify involuntary detention on the basis of such predictive criteria. Further, a subsequent study by Climent, Hyg, and Ervin, comparing 40 emergency room patients brought in because of violent behavior with a matched group of control cases, failed to show a consistent difference in regard to the triad.[11]

Bach-y-Rita and his colleagues have reported an association between head injury and aggressive criminal behavior.[12] However, Climent and Ervin were subsequently unable to confirm a correlation between severe head injury and adult violence.[13] Nonetheless, they concluded that there is some relationship between childhood head injury and violent adult behavior, a finding that corresponds to my own clinical experience. Such an uncertain clinical relationship, of course, should not be used as a predictor when the consequence of a false-positive prediction is loss of liberty and the social stigmatization of a harmless individual.

Various authors have set forth in a pragmatic fashion what they believe are danger signs of potential violence. Usually such assertions claim to be based on study of hundreds of persons who have killed or threatened to kill. A typical assertion of this sort has been made by the psychiatrist David Abrahamsen.[14] In addition to more obvious signs, such as excessive aggressiveness, temper tantrums, and intense and recurrent fantasies of revenge, Abrahamsen cites such qualities as loneliness, withdrawal, isolation, and even "speech and spelling errors."[15] He claims that, when there is a pronounced incidence of two or more of his 14 signs, acting out of violent impulses is to be suspected. The absurdity of this claim is demonstrated by the fact that, by Abrahamsen's own criteria, spelling errors, loneliness, and excessive truancy would, as three such signs, be evidence of dangerousness.

A similar, though more complex, claim is made by Hartogs.[16] He lists 12 characterological signs, 13 developmental signs, 14 sociological signs, and

9 organic (physical) signs, a total of 48 predictors of violence. He gives no statistical or clinical data to support his claim that these 48 signs are valid predictors. Like Abrahamsen's signs, some are simply tautological statements that the individual is dangerous, and others are characteristics so widespread that they lose all predictive value in discriminating between the dangerous and the harmless. For example, Hartogs asserts that "[l]ack of family interest, love, support, or acceptance"[17] and "[c]onflict over basic identity"[18] are signs of potential violence.

It would be difficult for an objective observer to take such claims seriously if similar pseudoscientific descriptions had not been reiterated so often that they have become part of the accepted mythology of clinical practice. I am sure that many patients have been labeled as dangerous and have been institutionalized for long periods of time on the basis of such flimsy clinical criteria.

The lack of definitive predictive criteria does not mean that there is not valid scientific evidence for assuming a causative relationship between adult violence and certain psychological and sociological childhood experiences. Further, there is increasing interest in biomedical research on the brain and aggressively violent behavior.[19] Some claimed discoveries, such as the XYY chromosomal abnormality and its supposed association with crime, aroused great interest, only to be invalidated by further investigations.[20] Other studies, in connection with psychosurgery, are surrounded by intense controversy, both scientific and political.[21]

Goldstein's comprehensive review of brain research and violence[22] was based in part on evaluation discussions of a large group of experienced clinicians. They concluded: "Some of the already agreed upon predictive factors [of an act leading to murder] are a childhood history of maternal deprivation, poor father identification, or both; nocturnal enuresis; possibly fire setting; violence towards animals; and brutalization by one or both parents."[23]

This conclusion corresponds to my own clinical experience with mentally ill and supposedly healthy persons who have committed or attempted murder. I would even say that the conclusion of those clinicians represents the sum total of our present scientific knowledge concerning predictive factors of murderous violence. Yet I have repeatedly found some, and sometimes all, of these predictive factors in individuals who had never committed even the slightest harmful act, let alone assault or murder. And I have examined offenders who have committed the most extraordinarily brutal acts of great violence and lethality who possessed none of these factors.

I know of no reports in the scientific literature that are supported by valid clinical experience and statistical evidence that describe psychological or physical signs or symptoms that can be reliably used to discriminate between the potentially dangerous and the harmless person. That certain signs may sometimes be associated with violent behavior—as, for example, certain types of abnormal brain waves—or that persons who have committed acts of violence tend to reveal in their past histories certain common features—such as an unusual exposure to violence in early childhood, or a higher than average incidence of childhood head injuries—in no way meets the legal need for criteria that will discriminate between the potentially violent and the harmless individual.

Statistical Studies

A number of statistical studies amply demonstrate that the predictions of dangerousness by psychiatrists are unreliable.[24] Some of the studies are described in only casual fashion by their authors, but the findings so consistently demonstrate that psychiatrists over-predict dangerousness by huge amounts that the reports must be taken seriously.

Jonas Rappeport, director of the pioneer psychiatric court clinic in Baltimore, has reported:

> In 1960 we studied patients who requested sanity hearings or habeas corpus hearings. These were patients committed to one of our state mental hospitals. All had asked to be released, and all had been refused by the hospital and subsequently asked the court to release them. In essence, the hospital had said, we feel you are too dangerous to yourself or the person and property of others to leave. The court released one-third of them after the hearing. Of the remaining two-thirds remanded, one-third subsequently ran away, eloped as we say. The members of the remaining one-third either died, were eventually discharged or are still there. Not one of any of these patients got into any serious difficulty with the law within the 1 to 10 year follow-up period.[25]

Rubin provides a detailed report on the so-called Menard patients.[26] Seventeen mental patients had been labeled dangerously mentally ill and had been confined to the psychiatric division of the Menard State Penitentiary in Illinois. A series of administrative mix-ups and errors resulted in these 17 men spending a cumulative 425 years in prison after legislative changes had required their reassignment to treatment or community settings. Rubin describes the shocking story of how these men had been labeled as dangerous as a consequence of an original accusation of a violent crime, a stereotype of dangerousness, and a reaffirmation of the dangerousness, rather than on the basis of any realistic appraisal or clinically competent examination. Rubin personally examined each of the 17 men and found that in no case was the prediction of dangerousness valid.

The most important statistical study reflecting on the psychiatric prediction of dangerousness is concerned with the Baxstrom patients.[27] New York law permitted prisoners who had completed their maximum sentences and who were believed to be still mentally ill and dangerous to be retained indefinitely in maximum security hospitals for the criminally insane.[28] The United States Supreme Court, in *Baxstrom v. Herold*[29] held that such confinement violated the equal protection clause; as a consequence, 967 such patients were transferred to ordinary, civil mental hospitals.

Steadman, a research sociologist for the New York Department of Mental Hygiene, has, with others, made very careful follow-up studies of the 967 Baxstrom cases.[30] Four and one-half years after the transfer approximately one-third of the *Baxstrom* patients were free in the community.[31] Of the entire 967 patients, only 26 committed acts serious enough to warrant their return to a maximum security hospital for the criminally insane.[32] Of these 26 returnees, 15 were returned because of behavior in the hospital defined by the staff as dangerous.[33] One of these fifteen had made an assault resulting in death; six had made assaults against persons. The remaining eleven returnees had been rearrested after their release. Six of these were found incompetent to stand trial, and were returned to the maximum security hospital for that reason. The remaining five had been tried, convicted, and then transferred to the institution as psychiatrically disordered criminal. Two of these last five had committed homicides and a third committed a second-degree assault.[34]

Steadman attempted to differentiate the 26 returnees from the other 941 patients. He found that the returnees were much younger than the others; their average age was 33, as opposed to 47 for the nonreturnees. He also found that the returnees' scores on a "Legal Dangerousness Scale" (based on the history of criminal behavior prior to institutionalization) were significantly higher than the nonreturnees'. This finding, however, could not be used for prediction of the necessity for return, for over 90% of the patients with such a high score did not have to be returned.[35]

I believe it is clear from the *Baxstrom* studies that of the 967 persons who had been convicted at one time of serious crimes and who were designated as mentally ill and dangerous to others in order to justify their further confinement, only a very few were actually dangerous. One can only conclude that psychiatrists who make such judgments overpredict dangerousness greatly, by a factor somewhere between 10 and 100 times the actual incidence of dangerous behavior. It is understandable why this should be so. If a psychiatrist underpredicts danger, and clears a patient who later commits a violent act, he will be subjected to severe criticism. If, on the other hand, he overpredicts danger, he will suffer no consequence from such a faulty prediction, for his prediction might have come true had there been no intervention (such as institutionalization). In general, if a psychiatrist predicts that there is no danger, the feedback from an erroneous prediction is real and immediate. If he predicts that there is danger, there may be no feedback, or, if there is, it may not be possible to interpret it in ways that would improve the predictive ability of the psychiatrist. Inevitably, this will result in all concerned doing the "safe" thing: predicting dangerousness, if there are even the most minimal reasons to justify it.

Mental Illness and Dangerousness

One factor that has impeded the ability of psychiatrists to predict the dangerousness of mentally ill persons accurately is the lack of a clear-cut association between mental illness (or any particular form of mental illness) and dangerous behavior. Rappeport and Lassen were able to determine the posthospitalization arrest rates for all male patients over 16 years of age discharged from all but one of Maryland's psychiatric hospitals during the fiscal years 1947 and 1957.[36] Their data, when compared with the arrest rates of the similar male population of the state as a whole, revealed that the rate for robbery was significantly higher in the mental patients; the data also suggested that there may have been a higher incidence of rape by the mental patients before their hospitalization; but there was no evidence that murder, negligent manslaughter, or aggravated assault offenses were more common among the discharged hospital patients than in the general population.[37] Other studies[38] show a lesser involvement in criminal behavior by the mentally ill than is true for the general population.

Guze and his associates at Washington University published many reports on the possible relationship of mental illness and crime.[39] Their studies demonstrate that those conditions which are most clearly recognized as mental illness, such as schizophrenia and the other psychoses, are not found significantly more often in the criminal population.[40] On the other hand, psychiatric conditions such as sociopathy, alcoholism, drug dependence, and (among women offenders) hysteria, were frequently associated with adult criminality.[41] But these latter conditions are precisely those psychiatric states which are less easily definable and less generally agreed to be illnesses at all. "[E]xcept for [these conditions] and for sexually deviant behavior leading to arrest and conviction, other psychiatric disorders are infrequently associated with felonies."[42]

Psychiatrists as well as courts tend to perceive dangerousness as an attribute of an individual, as a quality one ought to be able to define, detect, and measure. Important decisions are made on the basis of the presence or absence of this quality of dangerousness, decisions that may result in the lifetime incarceration of a person so designated. If the quality of dangerousness is determined to be absent, as in the Kemper case cited earlier, the lives of many others may be jeopardized.

Theodore Sarbin, a psychologist and criminologist, has argued that the concept of danger and the concept of violence are not coterminous, that danger always denotes a relationship. He concludes that danger must not be construed as the expression of a personality trait, but rather as a relationship of relative power.[43] Sarbin has emphasized the process of reification, by which action or behavior becomes translated into an attribute of the person. This is an extremely important concept. For example, stealing is an action. To label a man who steals as a thief is to reify the action into an attribute. It implies that the man will continue to steal no matter what the situation and that his thieving behavior is a consequence only of factors within him. For the same reason, one should not label a man who acts violently and causes harm as dangerous, for by so doing one has transformed an action into an attribute and has knowingly or unwittingly made the prediction that there will be future acts of violence and that these future acts will be determined by qualities of the individual, not by the relationship or the circumstances. Although it may be convenient to label persons, to reify behavior into attributes, and thus to predict future conduct, it must be recognized that such a process has no scientific or logical basis and that there is no reason to expect that such predictions will come true.

Even if one accepts a simplistic concept of dangerousness, such as a propensity to commit criminal acts, should one regard dangerousness to property as being of the same social significance as violence to the person of others? It is remarkable that discussions of dangerousness so often fail to specify the nature of the danger. Clearly, it makes a difference to society if an offender is dangerous to property because of his need to write graffiti on subway walls or if he is dangerous because he molests little children or has an uncontrollable impulse to murder. Yet some statutes completely ignore such distinctions, and give the forensic psychiatrist no guidance.[44]

Restricting the definition of dangerousness to the propensity for violence is of no help, for violence itself is extremely difficult to define.

No definition of violence has ever proved completely successful. Although everyone "knows what violence is" no one has ever been able to define it adequately so that every possible instance of violent behavior is included within the definition while all the excluded behavior is clearly nonviolent. The working definition that has been adopted for the purposes of this Task Force is that acts of violence mean the "overtly threatened or overtly accomplished application of force which results in the injury or destruction of persons or property or reputation, or the illegal appropriation of property"[45]

Such definitions are either so vague or so all-inclusive that no reliance can be placed on them in seeking to differentiate the harmless from the dangerous. When such difficulties are coupled with the even greater problems of defining mental illness, sanity, and insanity,[46] it is no wonder that gross confusion exists and that the psychiatric predictions are devoid of validity and reliability.

No Means of Prediction Exist

There is an unfortunate tendency in the psychiatric literature to imply that the scientific answers to pressing social problems not now capable of solution would be available in the very near future if only there is were a bit more research. Optimistic statements such as the following abound: "Elaboration of methods for recognizing and understanding aggressive patients may enable us to manage them or treat them in ways which will reduce or eliminate their dangerousness and thus permit the restoration of their liberty."[47]

Realistically, it is more likely that growth of our scientific knowledge of human behavior, derived from both psychological and sociological sources, will increase, rather than decrease, the difficulty in applying such knowledge to legal issues. Increased knowledge brings complexity rather than simplicity, uncertainty rather than certainty, frequently blurring distinctions rather than clarifying them. This knowledge thus becomes less helpful to the all-or-none, two-valued decision-making process of the law.[48]

The evidence, as well as the consensus among responsible scientific authorities, is now unequivocal. At a recent international conference there was general agreement by psychiatrists and sociologists from many nations with the views expressed by N. Christie, Professor of Criminology at the University of Oslo: "There seems to be no convincing study to show that we can predict really dangerous behavior with any amount of acceptability."[49]

Finally, the Alcohol, Drug Abuse, and Mental Health Administration of the Department of Health, Education, and Welfare stated in a press release dated August 8, 1974: "Although the psychiatric profession is frequently called upon to predict the potential dangerousness of persons brought before the courts, no scientifically reliable method for predicting dangerous behavior exists."[50]

Neither psychiatrists nor other behavioral scientists are able to predict the occurrence of violent behavior with sufficient reliability to justify the restriction of freedom of persons on the basis of the label of potential dangerousness. Accordingly, I recommend that courts no longer ask such experts to give their opinion of the potential dangerousness of any person and that psychiatrists and other behavioral scientists acknowledge their inability to make such predictions when called upon to do so by courts and other legal agencies.

When appropriate legal authority has declared a person dangerous, on the basis of evidence of demonstrated violent behavior, psychiatrists and other experts on human behavior may be called upon to give their opinion whether the dangerous behavior is a consequence of, or related to, the existence of mental or emotional illness. Such experts may also be called upon to give their opinions about whether the so-called institutional or treatment program "medical model" is appropriate for remedying the dangerous condition and protecting society against the danger. They should not be asked to do more.

Notes

[1]See, e.g., *Newsweek*, June 4, 1973, p. 69.

[2] Cal. Penal Code,§1203.45 (West Supp. 1974) provides for the sealing of records of persons who were under the age of 18 at the time of the arrest. "Thereafter such conviction, arrest, or other proceeding shall be deemed not to have occurred, and the petitioner may answer accordingly any question relating to their occurrence" (Ibid., § 1203.45[a]). This section was not intended to apply to minors convicted of felonies, but Kemper had not been so convicted because of his mental condition.

[3]See sup. note 1.

[4]See, e.g., the Lanterman-Petris-Short Act. *Cal. Welf. & Inst. Code* §§ 5000–150 (West 1972).

[5]Rubin, B. (1972), Prediction of dangerousness in mentally ill criminals. *Arch. Gen. Psychiat.,* 27:397.

[6]Malmquist, C. (1971), Premonitory signs of homicidal aggression in juveniles. *Amer. J. Psychiat.,*128:461.

[7]In dynamic psychiatry, "object loss" refers to the loss of the object of one's love, such as a lover or mother, and not to the loss of an object as a "thing."

[8]Malmquist, op. cit., sup. note 6, p. 46.

[9]MacDonald, J. (1967), Homicidal threats. *Amer. J. Psychiat.*, 124:475.

[10]Hellman & Blackman (1966), Enuresis, firesetting and cruelty to animals: A triad predictive of adult crime. *Amer. J. Psychiat.*, 122:1431.

[11]Climent, C. & Ervin, F. (1972), Historical data in the evaluation of violent subjects. *Arch. Gen. Psychiat.*, 27:621, 624. But see Wax & Haddox (1974), Enuresis, firesetting, and animal cruelty in male adolescent delinquents: A triad predictive of violent behavior. *J. Psych. & Law*, 2:45. This report of six dangerously assaultive adolescent boys who exhibited all three symptoms of the triad seems to support the original Hellman & Blackman study (sup. note 10). However, the claim by Wax and Haddox that the triad has predictive value is weakened by their failure to present any information as to the frequency of the triad in non-aggressive children.

[12]Bach-y-Rita, G., Lion, J., Climent, C. & Ervin, F. (1971), Episodic dyscontrol: A study of 130 violent patients. *Amer. J. Psychiat.*, 127:1473.

[13]Climent & Ervin, op. cit., sup. note 11, p. 624.

[14]Abrahamsen, D. (1970), *Our Violent Society*, p. 218.

[15]Ibid.

[16]Hartogs, R. (1970), Who will act violently? The predictive criteria. In: *Violence: Causes and Solutions*, ed. R. Hartogs & E. Artzt, p. 332.

[17]Ibid., p. 335.

[18]Ibid., p. 333.

[19]For a thorough, up-to-date review of this biomedical research, see Goldstein (1974), Brain research and violent behavior. *Arch. Neurol.*, 30:1. Goldstein is meticulous in his documentation; hundreds of references to the scientific literature are included.

[20]Center for Studies of Crime and Delinquency, National Institute of Mental Health (1970), Report on the XYY Chromosomal Abnormality (Public Health Service Pub. No. 2103), pp. 33–34.

[21]Compare Mark, V. & Ervin, F. (1970), *Violence and the Brain.* New York: Harper & Row, with Breggin, P. (1972), The return of the lobotomy and psychosurgery. *Cong. Rec*, 118:5567 (extension of remarks of Rep. Gallagher).

[22]Goldstein, op. cit., sup. note 19.

[23]Ibid, p. 27.

[24]For a bibliography of such studies see Rubin, op. cit., sup. note 5, p. 407.

[25]Rappeport, J. (1968), Dangerousness and the mentally ill criminal. *S. CA L. Rev.*, 21:23, 27.

[26]Rubin, op. cit., sup. note 5, p. 401.

[27]The cases were named after *Baxstrom v. Herold*, 383 U.S. 107 (1966).

[28]Law of April 2. 1929, ch. 243, § 384, [1929] N.Y. Laws 599 (repeated 1966). The statute currently in force authorizes retention of such individuals in

ordinary, civil mental hospitals upon completion of their sentence. NY Correc. Law. § 385 (McKinney 1968).

[29] 383 U.S. 107 (1966).

[30] See Halfon, David & Steadman, H. (1971), The Baxstrom women: A four-year follow-up of behavior patterns. *Psychiat. Quart.*, 45:518; Steadman, INITIAL? (1973), Follow-up on Baxstrom patients returned to hospitals for the criminally insane. *Amer. J. Psychiat.*, 130:317; Steadman, H. & Halfon (1971) The Baxstrom Patients: Backgrounds and Outcomes, *Sem. Psychiat.*, 3:376; Steadman, H. & Keveles (1972), The community adjustment and criminal activity of the Baxstrom patients: 1966–1970. *Amer. J. Psychiat.*, 129:304; Hunt, R. & Wiley, E. (1968), Operation Baxstrom after one year. *Amer. J. Psychiat.*, 124:974.

[31] Steadman, op. cit., sup. note 30, p. 317; Steadman & Keveles, op. cit., sup. note 30, p. 305. Of a different sample of 246 Baxtrom patients, 17% were arrested at some time (Ibid., pp. 307–308).

[32] Steadman, op. cit., sup. note 30, p. 317.

[33] Ibid., p. 318.

[34] Ibid., p. 319.

[35] Ibid., pp. 31–37.

[36] Rappeport, J. & Lassen (1965), Dangerousness–arrest rate comparisons of discharged patients and the general population. *Amer. J. Psychiat.*, 121:776, 777.

[37] Ibid., p. 779.

[38] Cited and summarized in Ibid., p. 776.

[39] See, e.g., Cloninger, C. & Guze, S. (1970), Psychiatric illness and female criminality: The role of sociopathy and hysteria in the antisocial woman. *Amer. J. Psychiat.*, 127:303; Guze, S., Goodwin & Crane (1969), Criminality and psychiatric disorders. *Arch. Gen. Psychiat.*, 20:583; Guze, S., Tuason, Gatfield, Stewart & Ricker (1962), Psychiatric illness and crime with particular reference to alcoholism: A study of 223 criminals. *J. Nerv. Ment. Dis.*, 134:512; Guze, S., Woodruff & Clayton, P. (1971), Hysteria and antisocial behavior: Further evidence of an association. *Amer. J. Psychiat.*, 127:957; Guze, S., Woodruff & Clayton (1971), The medical and psychiatric implications of antisocial personality (sociopathy). *Dis. Nerv. Sys.*, 32:712.

[40] Guze, Goodwin & Crane, op. cit., sup. note 39; Guze, Tuason, Gatfield, Stewart & Ricker, op. cit., sup. note 39; Guze, Woodruff & Clayton (1969), op. cit., sup. note 39.

[41] See Cloninger & Guze, op. cit., sup. note 39; Guze, Goodwin & Crane, op. cit., sup. note 39; Guze, Tuason, Gatfield, Stewart & Ricker, op. cit., sup. note 39; Guze, Woodruff & Clayton (1969) op. cit., sup. note 39.

[42] Guze, Woodruff & Clayton (1969), op. cit., sup. note 39, p. 641.

[43] Sarbin, T. (1967), The dangerous individual: An outcome of social identity transformations. *Brit. J. Crim.*, 7:285.

[44]See, e.g., *Cal. Welf. & Inst. Code* §§ 5150(West 1972), which specifies "danger to others, or to himself" as grounds for involuntary hospitalization. Even when statutes define the general area of dangerousness, as is true for most "sexual psychopath" laws, they are still so vague as to preclude any rational distinction between those who should be confined and those who should not. California, for example, defines a "mentally disordered sex offender" as "any person who by reason of mental defect, disease, or disorder, is predisposed to the commission of sexual offenses to such a degree that he is dangerous to the health and safety of others" (Ibid. § 6300).

[45]Megargee, E. (1969), A critical review of theories of violence. In: *Three Crimes of Violence: A Staff Report Submitted to the National Commission on the Causes & Prevention of Violence*, pp. 1037, 1038.

[46]See Rosenhan, D. (1973), On being sane in insane places. *Science*, 179:250.

[47]Scott, P. (1973), Violence in prisoners and patients. *Medical Care of Prisoners and Detainees (Ciba Foundation Symposium 16)*. New York: Associated Scientific Publishers, pp. 143, 152. I am equally guilty of making such optimistic predictions as to the ability of psychiatric science to discover new information of great value to the law (see "From M'Naghten to Currens," this volume).

[48]See Diamond, B. (1973), From Durham to Brawner, a futile journey. *Wash. U. L. Quart.*, 109:111–115.

[49]Cited in Scott, op. cit., sup. note 47, p. 153. Rappeport, Lassen & Hay make a similar statement: "[T]here are no articles that would assist us to any great extent in determining who might be dangerous, particularly before he commits an offense" (Rappeport, J., Lassen & Hay [1967]. A review of the literature on the dangerousness of the mentally ill. In: *The Clinical Evaluation of the Dangerousness of the Mentally Ill*, ed. J. Rappeport. Springfield, IL: Charles C. Thomas, pp. 72, 79).

[50]U.S. Dept. of Health, Education, and Welfare, *HEW News* (News Release. Aug. 8, 1974).

The Simulation of Sanity

[1956]

There is a considerable literature on the subject of malingering, particularly the simulation of mental disease. Yet very little has been written about the simulation of sanity, even though the pretense of mental health seems to be a much more frequent and more important problem than is malingering.

Physicians in the military and prison services, prosecuting attorneys, and judges are all very alert to the possibility of a defendant's attempting to escape criminal responsibility by simulating mental unsoundness. Perhaps the medicolegal emphasis on the feigning of mental illness can be attributed in part to the graphic description of such a case in the Bible:

> And David arose, and fled that day for fear of Saul and went to Achish the king of Gath. And the servants of Achish said unto him, Is not this David the king of the land? Did they not sing one to another of him in dances, saying, Saul hath slain his thousands, and David his ten thousands? And David laid up these words in his heart, and was sore afraid of Achish the king of Gath. And he changed his behavior before them, and feigned himself mad in their hands, and scrabbled on the doors of the gate, and let his spittle fall down upon his beard. Then said Achish unto his servants, Lo, ye see the man is mad: wherefor then have ye brought him to me? Have I need of madmen, that ye have brought this fellow to play the madman in my presence? Shall this fellow come into my house?[1]

It is interesting, too, that the earliest statute in English law to deal with criminal responsibility of the insane is concerned mostly with the problem of malingering. In 1542, during the reign of Henry VIII, a law was passed that complains bitterly that

> for as muche as sometyme some personnes beinge accused of hyghe treasons, haue after they haue benne examined before the kinges maiesties counsayle, confessed theyr offences of hyghe treason, and yet neuer the lesse after the doynge of theyr treasons, and examinations and

157

confessions thereof, as is afore saide, haue falled to madness or lunacye, wherby the condygne punyshemente of theyr treasons, were they neuer soo notable and detestable, hath been deferred spared and delayed, and whether theyr madnes or lunacy by them outwardly shewed, were of trouth or falsely contriued and counterfayted, it is a thinge almost impossible certainely to iudge or try.

This statute then goes on to provide the solution for such a difficulty: all such cases are to be tried as if *in absentia*, and the madness, real or feigned, shall not stand in the way of execution of sentence.[2] Upon the accession of Edward VI, in 1547, this and many other criminal statutes contrary to the common law were repealed.

To this day, whenever insanity is introduced as a defense, the question is always raised: Is this defendant trying to escape punishment by malingering? Admittedly, the plea of "not guilty by reason of insanity" is frequently introduced under circumstances that hardly justify its serious consideration. But this is a legal maneuver by the defense attorney and does not imply that the defendant has actually attempted to malinger mental illness. It has been my experience that the faking of insanity is a very rare occurrence, and when it does happen it is likely to be a sign of serious psychopathology. S. Weir Mitchell, writing about his Civil War experiences with malingerers, stated that malingering of mental illness was very rare and that "anyone who would feign insanity and submit to its restraints and associations to avoid work and obtain ease, must be in reality a monomaniac."[3]

On the other hand, it has also been my experience that the willful concealment of existing mental illness, that is, the simulation of sanity, is very frequent, even in persons accused of serious crimes where mental illness would be an adequate defense.

During World War II, I saw an interesting case of a soldier who, just before he was scheduled to be shipped overseas, reported to sick-call with a mysterious discoloration of his eye. His entire right eye was colored bright purple, the color infiltrating even the aqueous humor. It was soon discovered that he had inserted small pieces of indelible lead into his conjunctiva with the intent of causing a mild inflammation that would prevent his being shipped out. There were many special circumstances surrounding this case, but none of them seemed to account adequately for his actions. There was no obvious evidence of mental illness, and he consistently denied any delusions of hallucinations. Yet after three months' observation he broke down and revealed an elaborate system of paranoid delusions that had existed for a long time, and he gradually deteriorated into a chronic schizophrenia.

During the war I also had the opportunity to examine a sizable group of draftees, all of whom had attended a school for malingering. For payment of a large fee, they had been systematically coached in faking mental illness at their draft examinations. Their "professor," a long-time swindler and confidence man, taught them very carefully, drawing from his extensive experience as an attendant in a mental hospital. Unfortunately for the students, he kept careful records of his pupils, and when the school was raided by the F.B.I. they found a card file with all the names of his graduates, and these were tracked down and arrested. A number of them had already successfully failed their induction examinations, but the interesting thing was the amount of genuine psychopathology that these malingerers exhibited. Several were undoubtedly schizophrenics who carefully concealed their real delusions relating to sexual matters in favor of the less embarrassing delusions that had been taught to them.

The Marcus Kidnapping Case

Sometime between 3:45 and 4 o'clock on the afternoon of September 19 [1955] a blowsy, ill-kempt blonde walked into the fourth floor nursery of San Francisco's Mount Zion Hospital, snatched up two-day-old Robert Marcus from his bassinet and disappeared into a void.

Eight days later the woman and the baby were found—the latter, happily, healthy and unharmed—but not before the greatest search in the area's history, a search at times involving some 1,500 police officers and citizens.[4]

On October 15, 1955, I had the opportunity to examine the kidnapper, Betty Jean Benedicto. Following her apprehension, she made several suicide attempts and had been given a brief period of psychiatric observation and reported as sane and returned to the jail. However, Dr. Michael Agron of Palo Alto reexamined her at the request of the defense attorney. Dr. Agron succeeded, after very great resistance on the part of the patient, in eliciting an elaborate delusional system, and he was able to make a tape recording of the patient's statements. Prior to my examination, I had had the benefit of listening to the recording and hence had less difficulty in obtaining the full story of the kidnapping from her.

Originally she had told a simple story: she had thought that she was going to have a baby, then found out that she was not pregnant and, in her frantic wish to have a child, she had decided to steal one from a hospital and tell everybody, including her husband, that it was her own. During her initial psychiatric examinations she appeared entirely rational, although emotionally upset and depressed, and firmly denied any delusions, hallucinations, or other symptoms. She maintained the kidnapping was done of her own free choice and that she had planned it that way. No thought of ransom, or harming the baby, had entered her mind, and she denied that there was any significance to the choice of the particular baby she had taken. She asserted no defense for her actions other than that she had wanted a baby very badly.

When I examined her she appeared very agitated and depressed and had made numerous suicidal gestures, such as swallowing pins. The jail matrons and other inmates regarded her as mentally ill and were very protective of her. They felt that it was impossible to care for her properly in the jail, yet each time she was sent to the psychopathic ward she was quickly returned as not a mental case. She had not eaten anything for three or four days.

She described how she had wanted to have a baby and some six months prior to the kidnapping she had been delighted to learn she was pregnant. Her abdomen enlarged and she had all the signs of pregnancy. Then a month or so before she anticipated giving birth she received a message from the Virgin Mary telling her that she was going to give birth to a baby of immaculate conception. Mary promised her that the baby would be a new Messiah, but that she must keep this secret from the world until she received the proper sign. About a week before the kidnapping, it seemed to her that she no longer had a baby inside her. Then she received another message from Mary, who told her that the Messiah baby was not to be born in the ordinary way, but was to be born immaculately, i.e., without contact with her body, and that she would be told when and where to find the baby.

For days she wandered around, mostly at the bus station, waiting for the sign to be given her. Then the thought came to her, as if by divine inspiration, to go to a hospital nursery and there she would find her baby, who would be marked with a sign that would indicate that it was hers. She went to the Mount Zion nursery and looked over the babies. When she saw one with the name "Marcus," she knew this was the supernatural sign, for her own husband's name was Mark. Awaiting an opportunity, she snatched the baby, took it to her home in a nearby city and announced to her husband that she had given birth to the child herself. Evidently she had made her story credible enough so that no suspicions were raised for over a week, despite the screaming headlines in the daily papers, dramatic appeals for the return of the child over the radio and TV and the offer of sizable rewards for information leading to the apprehension of the kidnapper.

She now still maintained that the baby was actually hers, that Mrs. Marcus was not the mother of the little boy but was only a kind of agent of Mary, a means of bringing this divine child into the world without the degradation of physical birth. Mrs. Benedicto felt certain that if the Marcuses knew the truth they would give the baby back to her, but that she was being prevented from seeing them. She assumed that this, too, was of supernatural significance and probably meant that when the baby's parents returned the baby to her this would be the proper sign that it was all right to reveal the secret birth of the Messiah to the world. She would be patient and await this sign.

When questioned as to why she refused to eat, she at first would give no explanation. But upon persistent interrogation, she finally revealed, in a most reluctant manner, her reasons. The psychodynamics immediately became clearer. She would not eat because all food was nasty and dirty. Food contained energy, and energy entered your body and gave one sexual thoughts. All of her life, because she had taken in food, she had been dirty, sexual, contaminated, and evil. The Messiah must be immaculately born from an immaculate mother, which she could become only through not eating. When confined to jail, her hair had been cut short and she attributed this to the efforts of the authorities to degrade her. By putting her in jail and cutting her hair, they had degraded her as Christ had been degraded, and this proved her divine mission.

This delusional system was related with intense affect and facial expressions, tears and agitation, and there has been no doubt, at least in my mind, of the authenticity of the material. She regarded the psychiatrist who first examined her as a policeman in disguise and hence had carefully concealed her true story from him. Actually, it was possible to elicit her delusional beliefs only by implying that we were also agents of Mary and were there to help her carry out her mission.

At the court hearing she was found to be presently insane and was committed to a state hospital for observation. She adjusted well to her hospitalization, denied all her delusions, and insisted upon her original story of simply having wanted a baby. After three weeks' observation she was returned as sane. In April, 1956, she withdrew her plea of insanity, and pleaded guilty, and was sentenced to a year in jail.

Her background history revealed a lifelong record of delinquency and disturbed behavior. Her parents had been divorced when she was eight years old and her father was killed in an accident a few years later. From eight to thirteen she was in a convent. She frequently ran away and was in perpetual difficulty with the school. Throughout her childhood there had been stealing, lying, and compulsive fire-setting, and her mother was unable to manage her. As an adolescent she had been committed by her mother to a state hospital as "incorrigible." Her first husband had divorced her when she deserted him. She had a girl by that marriage, but grossly neglected the child and seemed to have no ability to have any sustained interest in her own baby. Her second husband also divorced her and she ran away to Mexico. There she made repeated suicide attempts and was hospitalized. During the Mexican hospitalization, in 1954, she developed a pseudopregnancy. She married her third and present husband in October, 1954. In March, 1955, he committed her to a state hospital because she was "so hysterical." She was released in a week, and she claimed to be pregnant. It is of interest that even as a child she showed a peculiar interest in babies. She would collect four or five babies of the neighborhood and bring them home, putting them together on her bed.

Discussion

The case of Betty Jean Benedicto illustrates very well the medicolegal difficulties that arise from the concealment of mental symptoms and the pretense of sanity. Because the burden of proof of insanity lies with the defendant, if the defendant chooses not to reveal mental illness a grave miscarriage of justice may result. It seems to me that the forensic psychiatrist has a heavy responsibility in this type of case. If there is any possibility that mental unsoundness exists, it should be his responsibility to uncover it, and he should be prepared to use all of his technical skill as well as auxiliary aids, like the Rorschach and the Thematic Apperception Tests, to follow up any clues that might reveal major psychopathology. Too often the examining psychiatrist conducts a brief interview under unfavorable circumstances with haste and lack of privacy. He obtains little or no intimate information from the patient yet does not hesitate to report the patient as sane and mentally responsible. I realize that the law views this matter differently, but I think that anyone who commits a serious crime, particularly murder, is apt to be suffering from serious mental abnormalities. Before deciding that a patient is mentally responsible, one should be absolutely certain that one has penetrated through the patient's rationalizations and surface defenses and has been able to appraise properly the true mental state of the accused individual. I do not wish to imply that all major criminals are insane. But a major criminal action does, in my opinion, carry a heavy medical, even though not legal, presumption of mental illness; and the examiner must be exceedingly cautious in assuming that the defendant is telling the whole story of his thoughts, feelings, and inner life.

All of us like to believe that our actions are the result of our own free will, and we are reluctant to admit that much of what we do is the result of unconscious compulsions rationalized by *ex post facto* intellectualizations. The paranoid schizophrenic is especially averse to admitting that his actions are due to mental disease and will insist, even in the face of the threat of the death penalty, that his criminal actions were intentional. To conceal his delusions he will confabulate logical reasons for his crime and resist all attempts of the psychiatrist to discover his psychopathology. Such schizophrenics pretend to be mentally healthy because to admit to mental illness would destroy their self-esteem and break down the remnants of their contact with reality. Often, too, their delusions and hallucinations involve highly secretive material of a supernatural or sensual nature that must not be communicated to another person. So they would far rather go to prison or even to the gas chamber than to violate the dictates of their delusional systems.

On death row at San Quentin, there is now a paranoid schizophrenic who is awaiting execution for the murder of the couple who employed him. Evidently the double murder was associated with longstanding messianic delusions. Yet during his trial this man refused to reveal any information about himself or the crime, even to his own defense attorney. As a result, it was not possible to establish his insanity and he was convicted of first-degree murder.

Of even greater importance, as pointed out by Judge John Biggs Jr.,[5] the failure to diagnose properly mental illness in a defendant accused of a minor crime will often result in the defendant's release after a short jail term or prison sentence, with the imminent possibility of his committing a much more serious crime later. For practical as well as humanitarian reasons, it is very much to society's advantage that all who are dangerously mentally ill be so diagnosed and hospitalized until such time as they have recovered and all danger of aggressive acts has passed.

Summary

Since biblical times people have feared that criminals would escape punishment by feigning insanity. Yet in actual fact feigned insanity is very uncommon. Much more prevalent is the simulation of sanity—the concealment of delusional systems and other psychopathology even in the face of the death penalty. The psychiatrist has a heavy responsibility not to overlook hidden mental pathology, and he must make every effort to diagnose properly those cases in which the defense mechanisms and paranoid suspicions prevent the defendant from revealing his true mental state. The principles of humanitarian justice, as well as the protection of society, require that the uncovering of dangerous psychopathology not be left to the discretion of the mentally sick individual. The forensic psychiatrist should put aside the traditional, irrational fear that the defendant is going to "get away" with something and concentrate with all the resources at his command on discovering the psychopathology behind the criminal action.

Notes

[1] I. Samuel 21:10-15.
[2] 33 *Henry* 8, C.xx.
[3] Keen, W. W., Mitchell, S. W., Morehouse, G. R. (1864), On malingering, especially in regard to simulation of diseases of the nervous system. *American J. Medical Sciences*, 48:367-394. Cited in Veith, I. (1955). On malingering. *Bull. Cleveland Med. Library*, 2:67-73.

[4] Allen, J. F. (1955), Tell the truth about trouble. *Modern Hospital*, 85:51-54.

[5] Biggs, J. Jr. (1955), *The Guilty Mind: Psychiatry and the Law of Homicide*. New York: Harcourt, Brace.

Addendum[*]

[1986]

Since the publication of my article on the simulation of sanity 30 years ago, my views on this subject have been reinforced by a substantial number of cases of simulation. I have not kept an exact count, but I would guess that during these 30 years, proven cases of faking sanity that I have personally examined have outnumbered the proven cases of malingering three or four to one. How many unproven cases of each existed, of course, is impossible to estimate.

---

[*] Editor's note: At the request of Dr. Quen, Dr. Diamond provided the following addendum to a column on the history of forensic psychiatry. *Newsletter of the American Academy of Psychiatry and the Law*, December 1986, 11:27-28.

In my paper I mentioned the case of a prisoner on death row, awaiting execution, who had refused all psychiatric examinations and would not allow any insanity defense. This man was later executed. As he entered the gas chamber, he revealed his delusional system to the warden: he had been instructed by God to commit the double murders of which he had been convicted. He did so to obtain funds to start a world-wide movement to rescue and reform delinquent teenage girls. His execution, he believed, was to be only a pretense, staged by the state of California for publicity purposes to further his divine mission. At the last minute, before the gas chamber door was to be closed, then President Eisenhower would suddenly appear, stop the procedure, and take him to Washington to complete his mission. The warden ordered the execution to proceed, and the prisoner went cheerfully and optimistically to his death, still waiting for the president.

Another case involved a man who killed three women for the express purpose of getting himself executed. He refused all examinations, refused an insanity defense, and petitioned the California Supreme Court not to consider an appeal. He consented to a psychiatric examination the day prior to his scheduled execution on the condition that the governor guarantee that his execution would not be postponed. A great deal of relevant psychopathology was revealed at this examination, including the extraordinary fact that his case history had been published in a book on crime and psychopathology before he had committed the murders. I published the details of this case in 1975.[1]

In another case, a man murdered a prominent Bay Area doctor who was his wife's physician. The wife had returned home after an office visit to the doctor in a badly battered condition. Reluctantly, the wife revealed that the doctor had raped her during the medical examination. The husband complained bitterly and persistently to both legal and medical authorities, yet nothing was done despite the doctor's well-known reputation for sexually harassing nurses and patients. The wife, depressed, embarrassed, and ashamed, committed suicide several months later. It is likely that she was more disturbed by the husband's obsessive preoccupation with the rape than by the rape itself. The husband then killed the doctor in front of his office.

At his trial he claimed amnesia for all events of the day of the killing. During the trial, the judge had doubts about the defendant's competency and requested that I examine him. The defendant steadfastly maintained that he had no memory of the shooting but freely admitted his hatred for the doctor and his resentment that no one had taken action against the doctor. I could only report that I suspected the defendant was mentally ill but, that I had been unable to elicit any evidence of such, and that the amnesia did not appear to be genuine. The trial proceeded, and he was convicted of second-degree murder.

A year later, I visited him in prison and he spontaneously admitted to me that he had faked amnesia in order to conceal his acute mental illness. After his wife's death he developed auditory hallucinations; heard her voice calling him. He concluded that she was not really dead and that she was being kept a prisoner in the doctor's office as a sex slave. The morning of the killing he had waited outside the doctor's office and, when the doctor came out, demanded that he set his wife free. He thought he could hear his wife calling for help from the office. When the doctor brushed him aside, saying he was crazy and that his wife was dead, he shot and killed him.

The defendant had informed his attorney of this material. The attorney told him that he should never reveal this to anyone, especially not to a psychiatrist, for they would lock him up in a mental institution for the rest of his life; the attorney told him that he could get the defendant off under the "unwritten law" by proving that the doctor was responsible for his wife's death. The defendant said the attorney had instructed him to claim amnesia.

In the trial of Sirhan Sirhan for the assassination of Robert Kennedy, I was able to elicit a good deal of relevant psychopathology through the use of hypnosis during which Sirhan recalled the shooting. In the waking state, Sirhan admitted none of this and claimed amnesia for the shooting. After listening to the tape recording of the hypnotic interviews, he claimed that his attorney and I had faked the tapes and had hired an actor to impersonate him. After I testified at his trial about his psychopathology, which I thought relevant to a diminished capacity defense, Sirhan took the stand and testified that he had never been hypnotized, that he had only pretended, and he denied the truth of most of what I had said about him to the jury. Conviction of first-degree murder with the recommendation of the death penalty was the consequence.

The motive for the concealment of mental illness seems clear in these cases. When a mentally disturbed person commits a crime of violence in response to paranoid delusions, he believes himself to have been fully justified and driven to the act of violence. To admit that one's actions were motivated by delusions, rather than reality, and that one was and is mentally deranged is a public humiliation destructive to one's self-esteem. Such persons are often totally obsessed with their delusional ideas, and their delusions become their very raison d'etre.

A plea of insanity does not exclude the possibility that the defendant is faking sanity. Insanity pleas are usually instigated by the attorney, rather than by the defendant, and the defendant may be doing his best to defeat the strategy of his own defense lawyer.

Unfortunately, psychiatric and psychological examinations tend to be one-way streets. If a person reveals the signs and symptoms of mental illness, a reasonably accurate diagnosis can be made. If the examination elicits no signs or symptoms of mental illness, the examiner may not, in my opinion, conclude that the person is "normal" or "not mentally ill." Such a person may be very seriously ill and delusional and, for some irrational reason, be hiding or minimizing his psychopathological responses. The most the examiner is entitled to say is that he was unable to elicit evidence of mental illness.

Note

[1]Diamond, B. L. (1975), Murder and the death penalty: A case study. *Amer. J. Orthopsychiat.*, 45:712–722.

Inherent Problems in the Use of
Pretrial Hypnosis on a Prospective Witness[*]

[1980]

Recently, hypnotism of witnesses and victims for purposes of memory enhancement and investigation has become widespread in law enforcement.[1] One source[2] reports that recent recipients of special training in the induction of hypnosis include: (1) police personnel in Los Angeles, Portland, Seattle, Denver, Houston, San Antonio, Washington, D.C., and New York; (2) FBI officers; (3) the Air Force Special Investigations Unit; and (4) the Alcohol, Tobacco and Firearms Bureau of the Treasury Department. Even in small communities police officers and sheriffs have received such training; in others cooperative psychiatrists and psychologists have been retained for hypnotic investigations.

Unfortunately, sensitivity to the limitations and hazards of hypnotism, and especially to the myriad ways of intentionally and unintentionally suggesting responses to the subject, requires much more experience and training.[3] In my opinion, even psychiatric and psychological professionals highly skilled in the use of hypnosis for therapeutic purposes are apt to be naive in recognizing its limitations as a "truth-telling" technique.

Absent judicial intervention, however, the hypnosis "boom" seems likely to continue. The technique of hypnosis induction is easily learned. A police officer can become a reasonably skilled hypnotist with a few hours of practice, with or without formal instruction. Thus, it becomes critical to reexamine the general rule of law that hypnotically induced testimony is admissible but that its credibility may be attacked.

[*]Acknowledgment is made to all of the defense attorneys in the cases in which I participated for their indispensable help. I am particularly indebted to Thomas S. Worthington, Esq., of Salinas California, for the wealth of case law material and arguments he provided me.

169

In many cases, presentation to the jury of all facts, whether legally relevant or not, may be desirable.[4] Indeed, I have often expressed the opinion that traditional rules of evidence restricting the information available to the trier of fact may impede a just decision.[5] This principle does not, however, apply to the testimony of witnesses whose memories have previously been enhanced by hypnosis. I believe that, once a potential witness has been hypnotized for the purpose of enhancing memory, his recollections have been so contaminated that he is rendered effectively incompetent to testify. Hypnotized persons, being extremely suggestible, graft onto their memories fantasies or suggestions deliberately or unwittingly communicated by the hypnotist. After hypnosis, the subject cannot differentiate between a true recollection and a fantasy or a suggested detail. Neither can any expert or the trier of fact. This risk is so great, in my view, that the use of hypnosis by police on a potential witness is tantamount to the destruction or fabrication of evidence. Some courts have shown a healthy suspicion of the veracity of this sort of testimony.[6] Yet even under stringent safeguards, including presentation to the trier of fact of the fullest possible information on the effects of hypnosis, the trier will not be able to sort out reality from witness fantasy and weigh this testimony properly.

It appears that the principal reason for the continuing admission of hypnotically enhanced testimony is an inadequate understanding of the nature of hypnosis and its impact on the process of recall. In most cases, busy judges have simply lacked the benefit of counsel who cogently explained the nature of hypnosis, of scholarly authority that applied scientific research to legal questions, and of expert testimony that dispassionately assessed the high risks of evidentiary distortion or abuse. Once a court has this evidence of the nature of hypnosis before it, however, it need not and will not follow precedents decided by courts that had to reach a decision without a clear idea of the inherent danger to the factfinding process posed by the use of hypnosis on witnesses.

This paper first reviews the nature and history of hypnosis; then discusses the reported cases and surveys the sparse legal literature on the subject; and finally argues that testimony by previously hypnotized witnesses should never be admitted into evidence.[7]

The Nature and History of Hypnosis

There are many descriptions of hypnosis. Webster's Dictionary defines it as a "state that resembles sleep but is induced by a hypnotizer whose suggestions are readily accepted by the subject."[8] Perhaps the best description is found in the characteristics observed by Hilgard in subjects highly susceptible to hypnosis:

1. *Subsidence of the planning function.* The hypnotized subject loses initiative and lacks the desire to make and carry out plans of his own. . . .

2. *Redistribution of attention.* . . . [U]nder hypnosis selective attention and selective inattention go beyond the usual range. . . .

3. *Availability of visual memories from the past and heightened ability for fantasy production.* . . . The memories are not all veridical and the hypnotist can in fact suggest the reality of memories for events that did not happen.

4. *Reduction in reality testing and a tolerance for persistent reality distortion.* . . . Reality distortions of all kinds, including acceptance of falsified memories . . . and all manner of other unrealistic distortions can be accepted without criticism within the hypnotic state.

5. *Increased suggestibility.* The suggestibility theory of hypnosis is so widely accepted that hypnosis and suggestibility come to be equated by some writers on hypnosis.

6. *Role behavior.* The suggestions that a subject in hypnosis will accept are not limited to specific acts or perceptions; he will, indeed, adopt a suggested role and carry on complex activities corresponding to that role.

7. *Amnesia for what transpired within the hypnotic state.* . . . [Amnesia] is not an essential aspect of hypnosis. . . . Yet it is a very common phenomenon, and it can be furthered through suggestion.[9]

These empirical facts about the hypnotic state are generally accepted as verifiable scientific observations.[10] There is, however, much less agreement about the theories proposed to explain these facts. Barber and Calverley have explained hypnosis in behavioristic and situational terms;[11] Hilgard has described it as a particular established state;[12] Sarbin and Andersen, in terms of role enactment;[13] and Pavlov, as a partial sleep state.[14]

The existence of various conflicting theories that attempt to explain the phenomenon of hypnosis does not mean that hypnotism is unscientific.[15] As medical treatment it is indeed legitimate and scientific. This fact, however, has no relevancy whatsoever to its use in a legal context or to the question of the admissibility of testimony of witnesses who have had their recall manipulated by hypnosis. Unfortunately, this kind of uncritical leap, as well as reliance on unscientific claims, has typified legal treatment of hypnosis.[16]

The history of hypnosis undoubtedly begins in ancient times with artificially induced somnambulism, and something like it is practiced in many primitive societies.[17] Accurate information differentiating artificially induced somnambulism from spontaneous and psychotic trance states is not, however, available for the period before the late eighteenth century. That was the era of Franz Anton Mesmer's "animal magnetism" and of the artificial somnambulism (later known as "hypnotism")[18] of his disciple, the Marquis de Puységur. From then to the present time controversy has surrounded hypnosis. It has passed through three or four cycles in which intense interest was followed by condemnation as quackery or by discovery of a better substitute for a specific use. Hypnosis thus periodically fell into disrepute and became the province of nomadic faith healers, spiritualists, and a wide variety of quacks.[19] Late eighteenth-century interest in hypnosis waned when a French Royal Commission denounced Mesmer as a charlatan.[20] In the mid-nineteenth century the discovery of ether anesthesia displaced interest in psychological anesthesia by hypnosis.[21] Then in the late nineteenth century[22] its use in the treatment of nervous and mental disease[23] gave way to the psychoanalytic movement led by Sigmund Freud's[24] new theories of causation and treatment of nervous and emotional illness.

Throughout its history, hypnosis has been the subject of theatrical exhibitions and novels in Europe and America. This treatment reached a peak in the character of Svengali in du Maurier's 1894 novel *Trilby*,[25] which reinforced the popular image of the hypnotist as a mysterious, evil person. Later, the popular mind identified the infamous monk Rasputin with malignant hypnotic influence.[26]

A few researchers in the United States did, however, continue scientific and clinical investigation of hypnosis.[27] World War II, with its many psychological casualties and widespread use of psychiatrists in the armed forces, produced a resurgence of interest in hypnosis for the treatment of the so-called war neuroses.[28] The war years also saw the introduction of sodium amytal, which was injected as a "truth serum." Indeed, "narcoanalysis," requiring less physician skill and experience and less patient cooperation than hypnosis, became the method of choice and convenience.[29]

Since World War II, legitimate hypnotism has been the preserve of a minority of psychiatrists who have used it to treat mental and emotional conditions. Although it has not approached the popularity of other methods of psychotherapy, it has avoided condemnation as fakery, as so often occurred in the past. Particularly in the last 30 years, academic psychologists and clinicians have accepted hypnosis as a proper subject of research. In the mid-1950s, the British and American Medical Associations formally approved its medical use.[30] A 1972 bibliography on hypnosis contains well over 1,000 references to scientific publications of hypnosis research, the great majority of the references being post-World War II.[31]

After two centuries of research and particularly the postwar scientific research, there is simply no doubt that hypnosis has been clinically and experimentally verified *as a phenomenon*. It is quite another question, though, whether it is a phenomenon that has a helpful role to play in criminal factfinding and, particularly, in the "enhancement" of the recall of a prospective witness.

Legal Background of Hypnotically Enhanced Testimony

Case Law

The case law on testimony by witnesses who have previously been hypnotized for the purpose of "enhancing" their recall can be summarized briefly. First, it is admissible. The rationale appears to be that the combination of an opportunity for cross-examination of the witness and the admissibility of expert testimony on the contaminating effect of hypnosis on recall permits the trier of fact to give proper weight to the testimony. Second, audio or video recordings of the hypnotic sessions, while apparently not mandatory, are deemed highly desirable as a record of what actually took place during the sessions.[32] Third, it seems settled that the defense must be given notice that a prosecution witness has been hypnotized for the purpose of memory enhancement.[33]

These cases must be distinguished from those in which a party seeks to introduce statements made during the hypnotic trance for the purpose of establishing the truth or falseness of alleged facts. Such statements are consistently excluded.[34] Moreover, no trial court, to my knowledge, has ever endorsed hypnosis of a witness before the trier of fact.[35] Further distinction must be made from cases that discuss the use of hypnosis on a defendant for the evaluation of his mental state by an expert defense witness.[36]

The first reported decision concerning the use of hypnosis for enhancement of a witness's memory was the 1968 case of *Harding v. State*.[37] A psychologist hypnotized the complainant, the victim of rape and assault with intent to murder, for the purpose of restoring her memory of the events of the crime. She then was able to testify (in the normal waking state), and almost entirely on this evidence[38] the defendant was convicted. Full information about the hypnosis was presented at the trial, and the hypnotist testified in detail as to his procedure with the witness. The admissibility of the testimony of both the complainant and the psychologist was upheld by the appellate court, and the judgment was affirmed. This case apparently set the trend for subsequent rulings that pretrial hypnotism affects credibility but not admissibility of the evidence.[39]

It is to be noted that the psychologist in the *Harding* trial testified that hypnosis does not dispose the subject to suggestion. Similar claims, commonly made by prosecution-oriented hypnotists, directly contradict all scientific evidence, as will be discussed later. Perhaps if the *Harding* trial and appellate courts had been presented a more accurate description of the nature of hypnosis and the extreme vulnerability of the subject to suggestion, they might have been less disposed to admit the evidence, and the subsequent trend of the law might have been different.

If the *Harding* case stated the general rule of admissibility, *United States v. Narciso*[40] showed how far some courts will go to apply it even when the validity of the testimony is extremely suspect. Two nurses were accused of five murders and ten counts of adding poison to the food and medicine of hospital patients. The nurses allegedly injected a curare derivative[41] into the tubing through which patients were receiving medication, causing them to suffer cardiopulmonary arrest. There were 51 such episodes of cardiopulmonary arrest and a number of deaths.

Richard Neely, a patient who survived a respiratory arrest, was questioned by FBI agents on two occasions. Both times he stated that he had no memory of the poisoning. He then voluntarily submitted to two sessions of hypnosis. He vaguely described two persons he believed to have been near his bed the night of his respiratory arrest, but he made no identification. At the end of the second session, he was shown a group of photographs that included one of defendant Perez. He recognized her as one of his nurses but did not identify her as one of the two persons who had been near his bed. He did, however, *incorrectly* identify a person unconnected with the case as one of the nurses who had harmed him. A month later Neely unqualifiedly identified Perez as one of the perpetrators. In a deposition taken nine months after that identification, Neely stated that he had known all along that Perez was one of the persons in his room just before his poisoning but that at first he had deliberately refused to identify her in order to protect her.[42]

The defendants, relying on *Simmons v. United States*,[43] moved to suppress all testimony by Neely. They claimed that the hypnotic interrogation sessions, together with the photographic array, created a "very substantial likelihood of irreparable misidentification," the *Simmons* standard for exclusion.[44] At the hearing, Dennis Walsh, a psychiatrist, testified on behalf of the defense that his psychiatric examination of Neely had revealed a terminally ill patient who had been alcoholic for many years and had a borderline personality organization as well as memory problems. He believed that the witness was a suggestible person whose memory consisted of fragments of actual memory and fantasy blended together in response to his felt need to be helpful to the FBI.[45] Dr. Martin Orne[46] also testified on behalf of the defense and concluded that Neely's testimony was at least in part the product of fantasy formulated in response to subtle cues from the interviewers. Dr. Herbert Spiegel[47] testifying to the contrary on behalf of the government, concluded that there was no danger that Neely's statements and memories were not from his own memory.

The court determined that the defense had failed to fulfill the "heavy burden" required by *Simmons* and admitted Neely's testimony. The court said that it would "exercise its powers to see that the factors raised by the pretrial events discussed herein are presented to the jury in an intelligible fashion."[48] The two nurses were convicted, but their motion for a new trial was granted on other grounds.[49]

On the other hand, particularly outrageous abuses associated with hypnosis may lead to exclusion of the "refreshed" testimony. The 1975 combined cases of *Emmett v. Ricketts* and *Creamer v. Hopper*,[50] which involved habeas corpus writs brought by Georgia prisoners convicted of murder, provide an example. There the United States District Court rebuked the state prosecution and the psychologist who had hypnotized Deborah Kidd, the chief prosecution witness to the alleged homicide.[51]

After a largely unsuccessful investigation of the sensational murder of two Georgia pathologists in 1971, indictments were brought against the two petitioners and seven other alleged coconspirators. At the separate trials of Emmett and Creamer, convictions rested almost entirely on the testimony of Deborah Kidd. No physical evidence was offered to link the petitioners or the coconspirators to the crime. Kidd's testimony was given credence by four separate juries, who were unaware of the numerous discrepancies in her various versions of the crime, discrepancies deliberately concealed from the defense. Moreover, when the petitioners (then defendants) attempted to obtain access to the records and tapes of the psychologist's hypnotic sessions with Kidd, the trial court ruled them to be privileged.[52]

The police had maintained Kidd, an admitted prostitute and amphetamine addict, in isolation for some time prior to the trials. For several weeks she was quartered in the apartment of a detective assigned to the case, had sexual relations with him, and claimed to be in love with him. During this time, the police supplied her with amphetamines, and she continued her heavy drug use. At the suggestion of the county police department superintendent of detectives, Kidd was taken to a psychologist, purportedly to help her "kick" her drug habit. The United States District

Court found, however, that the real purpose was to employ hypnosis to improve her memory and fill in the gaps in her recollections. Although the psychologist denied that he had given her suggestions or information about the crimes, he had instructed her to scan the newspapers and clip relevant articles about the case. As to the psychologist's credibility, the district court commented, "The Court has further observed his demeanor and considered his responses to questions during his many hours of testimony in this case. The Court does not credit his testimony as to the matters here involved."[53]

The *Emmett* and *Creamer* trials were a veritable nightmare of abuse by police, prosecutors, and a cooperative psychologist/hypnotist. For that reason, the granting of the writs of habeas corpus in those cases does not represent a per se rejection of pretrial hypnosis of witnesses. Those cases are important, however, because of their holding and their illustration of the unfortunate tendency of some psychologists to cooperate in abuses of hypnosis.

It may be surprising that in only two reported cases have courts considered imposing any procedural requirements to prevent abuse of the hypnotic refreshment of memory. In the first, *United States v. Miller*,[54] defense counsel requested hypnosis of a principal prosecution witness in the hope of impeaching his previous identification evidence. It then turned out that the witness had been hypnotized before in Texas in connection with the trial of Miller's alleged coperpetrator. The Texas hypnosis had been conducted in part by an independent expert and in part by the attorney who later served as the prosecution interrogator of this same witness in the *Miller* trial. The prosecution had failed to inform the defense of these facts. The appellate court held that withholding the fact of prior hypnosis was reversible error.[55]

The second decision that recognized the need for procedural protections was the consolidated case of *United States v. Adams* and *United States v. Pinkerton*.[56] The two defendants and a third person tried separately were prosecuted for conspiracy, assault with intent to rob, robbery, and murder. Postal inspectors hypnotized an alleged eyewitness during the investigation of these crimes (which had arisen out of a potential robbery). The court commented that no record had been made of the identity of those present during the hypnotic session nor of the questions and responses. The defense, however, did not object to the adequacy of the foundation laid for the receipt of the testimony. Instead, it sought to exclude all testimony of the witness on the grounds that no testimony from witnesses who had been hypnotized can be reliable and that therefore such witnesses are legally incompetent to testify. The United States Court of

Appeals for the Ninth Circuit rejected this argument, stating that previous hypnosis of a witness affects the credibility but not the admissibility of the testimony.

The Ninth Circuit, however, did warn of the dangers of abuse:

> We are concerned, however, that investigatory use of hypnosis on persons who may later be called upon to testify in court carries a dangerous potential for abuse. Great care must be exercised to insure that statements after hypnosis are the product of the subject's own recollections, rather than of recall tainted by suggestions received while under hypnosis.[57]

And in a footnote the court added:

> We think that, at a minimum, complete stenographic records of interviews of hypnotized persons who later testify should be maintained. Only if the judge, jury, and the opponent know who was present, questions that were asked, and the witness's responses can the matter be dealt with effectively. An audio or video recording of the interview would be helpful.[58]

Although well intended, these warnings and cautionary remarks are not sufficient, as will be discussed later.

The Legal Literature

Evidence textbooks[59] and law journals have largely ignored hypnosis of witnesses as a means of enhancing witness recall. If mentioned at all, hypnosis has usually been in the context of a general discussion of the admissibility of "truth serum"-induced statements and polygraph evidence. Furthermore, the emphasis is usually on the use of such procedures on the defendant, either to obtain specific evidence (e.g., a confession or exculpatory facts) or to probe his mental state to aid a psychiatrist's forming an expert opinion.

The earliest comprehensive American article on the subject, *Legal Aspects of Hypnotism*, was published in the *Yale Law Journal* in 1902. The author warned that evidence obtained from the use of hypnosis was unreliable since hypnotic subjects can consciously lie and are extremely susceptible to "illusions and hallucinations." He advocated the use of hypnosis only "for detective purposes."[60]

The next major work was Després's 1947 article, "Legal Aspects of Drug-Induced Statements," which cautioned that hypnotically induced statements are every bit as unreliable as statements made under the influence of drugs. The article is also noteworthy for Després's observation that at about the beginning of the century, the question of using confessions by hypnosis was widely discussed in the United States, and the medical and legal professions apparently agreed that suggestibility played too great a role in the confessions, because "even honest questioning may act as false suggestion."[61]

An extensive 1952 student note emphasized the unreliability of hypnotically induced information: "A person in [a] hypnotic state is prone to hallucinations which frequently originate false ideas which are afterwards believed true by the subject. . . ."[62] The note continued: "[A] witness's opinion may be colored by suggestion or hypnosis so that his account of a factual situation may miss the truth by a wide mark."[63]

In a 1955 article, Levy vehemently demanded legal recognition of hypnosis. He advocated the admissibility of both testimony from witnesses who have been hypnotized and evidence of the hypnotism for purposes of credibility.[64] Because it appeared in a journal widely read by law enforcement personnel, this article was probably an important encouragement to police use of hypnosis.

A 1961 law review article stated that "falsification of testimony can theoretically be obtained by hypnosis since retroactive hallucinations can be firmly cemented in a subject's mind during hypnosis."[65] Its concern was with the legal issue of posthypnotic influence and especially with subornation of perjury (as it termed this use of hypnosis) by the defense. The article did not anticipate the widespread police use of hypnotism with witnesses.

Two law review articles and a number of student notes, some quite naive,[66] followed the unreported 1962 Ohio trial of Arthur Nebb. He was accused of the nonfatal wounding of his estranged wife and their daughter and of the murder of his wife's lover. The defendant had been hypnotized twice by a psychiatrist/hypnotist employed by the state. By agreement of counsel and outside the presence of the jury, the expert hypnotized the defendant in the courtroom, probably the first time in the history of American jurisprudence that a witness was so hypnotized.[67]

Herman, apparently regarding the Nebb trial as a landmark, described the trial in great detail.[68] He repeated the hypnotist's extravagant claims of the reliability and validity of hypnotically induced evidence but recognized that the scientific literature, by and large, did not support such claims. Herman cautioned against a blanket refusal to admit hypnotically enhanced evidence and recommended a case-by-case approach. This article, like the Teitlebaum article, was preoccupied with hypnosis of the defendant and did not concern itself with what is now the major use of hypnosis for legal purposes: pretrial hypnosis of prosecution witnesses.

A 1977 article by Spector and Foster, Admissibility of Hypnotic Statements: Is the Law of Evidence Susceptible?,[69] was the first to discuss fully and extensively the use of hypnosis to spur the recollection of witnesses. Although the article is replete with references to the medical and psychological literature, the authors, in my opinion, failed to distinguish hypnotically induced memories from more normally induced recollections. They cited many references from the scientific literature that demonstrate that all memory is fraught with uncertainty and distortion and is subject to distortion through suggestion.[70] Their conclusions, however, did not follow:

> [A] witness whose memory has been refreshed through hypnosis may be able to recount an observed event more fully and accurately than any other witness. . . . Where the processes of partial regression or hyper-amnesis are the hypnotic stimulants, the testimony of the witness whose recollection has been so revived presents no more potential for inaccuracy due to the disabilities of perception, memory, and articulation than that of any witness.[71]

The authors did agree, however, that hypnosis greatly increases the suggestibility of the witness owing both to the inherent nature of hypnosis and to the bond between hypnotist and witness. They admitted that subsequent cross-examination of the witness at the trial is ineffective in revealing the implantation of false suggestions and that a subject who has accepted a posthypnotic suggestion to forget aspects of the hypnotic procedure will generally remain unaware of the source of statements he makes while testifying. Their solution, however, was very naive: the hypnotist should testify first to lay a foundation for the witness's testimony by describing fully the hypnotic procedures employed and by vouching for the accuracy of the restored memory. Supposedly, cross-examination *of the hypnotist* would reduce the hazards inherent in hypnotic preparation of the witness to "that which is ordinarily tolerated during pretrial witness preparation or interrogation sessions."[72]

Spector and Foster then discussed another inherent problem in hypnotically induced statements—deliberate fabrication. They minimized its importance, however, with the assertion that cross-examination, fear of perjury prosecution, sanctity of the oath, and solemnity of the proceedings are as effective in preventing the fabrications of previously hypnotized witnesses as of ordinary witnesses.[73] The problem, however, is that the fabrications that occur in hypnosis are, in my clinical experience, honest in the sense that the subject is not aware that he is fabricating. Therefore, it can hardly be expected that the usual inducements to honesty in ordinary witnesses are apt to be effective for pretrial hypnotized witnesses.[74]

The third problem of hypnotically induced evidence that Spector and Foster recognized is the undue weight that a jury might accord to such evidence. They agreed that this effect would be pronounced with in-court hypnosis, but they saw no problem with pretrial hypnosis if a proper foundation is laid by the hypnotist's testimony.[75] No mention was made of a fundamental and unresolvable problem with hypnotic enhancement of memory, that is, its impact on the attitude and demeanor of the witness, which will be discussed later.

Dillhoff's 1977 article[76] is of special interest because it was written from the perspective of a Navy judge advocate and presented a number of military cases involving the use of hypnosis. Generally, the military courts have excluded all hypnotic evidence including identifications achieved through the use of hypnotic enhancement of memory.[77] Dillhoff was unusually aware of the limitations and evidentiary dangers inherent in the use of hypnotism, and he provided excellent descriptions of these serious problems. Dillhoff believed, however, that these problems could be countered by expert testimony of the dangers involved in the use of hypnosis on witnesses. Ultimately, Dillhoff concluded, like most writers before him, that, despite the unreliability and the possible invalidity of hypnotism for the enhancement of recall and elicitation of truth, "such testimony should [not] be totally excluded."[78] Hence, he termed "both impractical and unrealistic" the position I take that the entire recollection of the witness is now unreliable due to the taint of hypnosis, rendering the witness incompetent to testify.[79]

A final work that should be recognized is Dr. Orne's affidavit filed in the appeal of *People v. Quaglino*[80] to the United States Supreme Court.[81] A professor of psychiatry at the University of Pennsylvania and a foremost clinical and research expert on hypnosis, Orne has a longstanding interest in its legal aspects. The affidavit contains a thorough, scholarly analysis of the problems associated with the use of hypnosis for memory enhancement. Dr. Orne believes that the subject may later be called as a witness if the safeguards surrounding the use of hypnosis have been sufficiently strict.[82]

Clearly, this review of the law and literature of hypnotically enhanced witness recall offers only mixed support for my view that courts should never admit such testimony. Although some courts and legal scholars have recognized the risks of abuse and injustice that arise from the use of hypnosis to enhance recall, even they have thus far relied on procedural safeguards to minimize the risk.

Evidentiary Problems with Hypnotically Manipulated Recall

Hypnosis may have some value as an investigatory instrument when used to enhance memory.[83] The law should recognize, however, that the use of hypnosis for such a purpose renders the potential witness incompetent[84] destroys the probative value of any evidence that the witness might otherwise have been able to produce. The following set of questions—which might be asked in court of an expert in the field of hypnosis—will illuminate the insurmountable evidentiary problems created by hypnotically refreshed testimony.

1. *Can a hypnotized person be free from heightened suggestibility?*
   The answer is no. Hypnosis is, almost by definition, a state of increased suggestibility. The operator's suggestions control each step of the hypnotism process:[85]

> Hypnosis can be described as an altered state of intense and sensitive interpersonal relatedness between hypnotist and patient, characterized by the patient's nonrational submission and relative abandonment of executive control to a more or less regressive, dissociated state. . . . The patient's dissociated attention is constantly sensitive to and responsive to cues from the hypnotist.[86]

2. *Can a hypnotist, through the exercise of skill and attention, avoid implanting suggestions in the mind of the hypnotized subject?*
   No, such suggestions cannot be avoided. The suggestive instructions and cues provided to the subject need not be, and often are not, verbal. The attitude, demeanor, and expectations of the hypnotist, his tone of voice, and his body language may all communicate suggestive messages to the subject. Especially powerful as an agent of suggestion is the context and purpose of the hypnotic session. Most hypnotic subjects aim to please.

> In order to understand the range of reports about hypnosis and the peculiar diversity of findings, it is necessary to take into account the deeply hypnotized individual's remarkable responsivity not only to explicit suggestions but also to very minute cues, often outside the observer's awareness. . . .
>
> The cues as to what is expected may be unwittingly communicated before or during the hypnotic procedure, either by the hypnotist or by someone else, for example, a previous S[ubject], a story, a movie, a stage show, etc. Further, the nature of these cues may be quite obscure, both to the hypnotist, to the S[ubject], and even to the trained observer.[87]

3. *After awakening, can the hypnotic subject consistently recognize which of his thoughts, feelings, and memories were his own and which were implanted by the hypnotic experience?*
   No. It is very difficult for human beings to recognize that some of their own thoughts might have been implanted and might not be the product of their own volition. It is only with the severely mentally disturbed, as in schizophrenia and in obsessive-compulsive neuroses, that one's thoughts and

resultant behavior are experienced as alien. Normally, mental processes are rationalized and experienced as the product of free will, even when it should be obvious that they are not. I have often demonstrated this to students by hypnotizing a volunteer. I tell him, once he is in the trance state, that some time after awakening, I will take a handkerchief out of my pocket and clean my glasses, at which time he is to walk over to the nearest window and open it. Next, I instruct the subject to have no memory of having received the instruction. The subject is then awakened. After five or ten minutes, I inconspicuously take out my handkerchief to wipe my glasses. Invariably, the subject will begin to show signs of restlessness and start looking at the windows. Some subjects will act as if the room had become excessively warm. Soon the subject will get up, go to the window, and open it. When I ask immediately why he opened the window, the subject will reply, "I felt warm and I wanted to let some air in," or "It's awful stuffy in here," or some similar response. Significantly, the response will show no recognition that the impulse to open the window was implanted; rather, subjects feel it to be their own idea and they come up with a more or less rational reason to justify their belief and action.

This experiment explains why the witness who has undergone pretrial hypnosis can seldom, if ever, recognize that a suggestion implanted intentionally or unintentionally by the hypnotist is not the product of his own mind. Moreover, this misperception will withstand the most vigorous cross-examination.[88]

4. *Is it unusual for a subject to believe that he was not hypnotized when in fact he was?*

No. On the contrary, very often hypnotic subjects refuse to believe they actually went into a trance. Some claim they were wide awake during the whole experience; others, that nothing unusual happened; still others, that they were only pretending to be hypnotized. Sirhan, whom I hypnotized in an effort to restore his memory of the assassination of which he was accused, persisted in his conviction that he had never succumbed to the hypnosis.[89] Actually, he repeatedly went into very deep trances during which he was very susceptible to posthypnotic suggestions. After awakening, he would consistently act out the posthypnotic suggestions but would explain each action with a pseudological rationale. When the audiotapes of the hypnotic sessions were played back to him, he persisted in his denial that he had been hypnotized, claiming that we must have faked the recordings with a professional actor simulating his voice.[90] Finally, it is especially common for lightly hypnotized subjects to deny that the hypnosis has "worked," for they think they remember everything that occurred during the session.

5. Can previously hypnotized persons restrict their memory to actual facts, free from fantasies and confabulation?

No. This question is, of course, central to the decision to admit hypnotically enhanced testimony. Out of a desire to comply with the hypnotist's suggestions, the subject will commonly fill in missing details by fantasy or confabulation. Often these details are portions of other real memories, but ones unrelated to the situation that the hypnosis seeks to probe. Thus, the hypnotically recalled memory is apt to be a mosaic of (1) appropriate actual events, (2) entirely irrelevant actual events, (3) pure fantasy, and (4) fantasized details supplied to make a logical whole. The classical experiment was performed by Stalnaker and Riddle, who asked students to memorize various works of prose and poetry. A year later the students were tested in both the waking and the hypnotic state for their recall. In the hypnotic state, the students tended to recall more of the words of the original, but they consistently made more errors of recall than they did when in the waking state, sometimes confabulating whole verses of a poem. Significantly, the students did not realize that they were making errors of recall.[91] Commenting on this experiment, Hilgard stated, "Confidence of the [hypnotic] subject in the accuracy of recovered memories does not guarantee their accuracy."[92]

6. After the hypnotic subject is awakened, do the distorting effects of the hypnosis disappear?

This too is a critical issue for the admissibility of testimony where there has been pretrial recall enhancement. For courtroom testimony to be admissible, the witness must have emerged from the trance with his powers of recall intact, and presumably enhanced, and must be able to relate from the witness stand his wholly conscious recollections as he now perceives them.[93] The evidence, however, is that the effect of suggestions made during hypnosis endures. Although the more theatrical types of posthypnotic suggestion may last only hours or days, less obvious suggestions may last years or even a lifetime. A highly pertinent example is the "posthypnotic source amnesia." This occurs when something learned under hypnosis is carried into the wakened state but the fact that the memory or thought was learned under hypnosis is forgotten.[94] A sizable proportion of hypnotic subjects spontaneously do forget and the incidence of source amnesia can be increased by suggestions from the hypnotist.[95] A subject who has lost the memory of the source of his learned information will assume that the memory is spontaneous to his own experience. Such a belief can be unshakable, last a lifetime, and be immune to all cross-examination. It is especially prone to "freeze" if it is compatible with the subject's prior prejudices, beliefs, or desires. This type of distorted memory is very apt to appear genuine and spontaneous and is unlikely to disappear.

One can only conclude that hypnosis can induce subtle but highly significant distortions of memory that will persist indefinitely, distorting all subsequent related recall of the subject. My own experience has convinced me that even communications and other cues to the subject made in the normal, waking state, both before and shortly after the hypnotic session, may be similarly influenced by the hypnotic experience. Thus the police may tell a witness something just before hypnosis and then hypnotize him. When he awakes, his "source amnesia" may lead him to believe that the police statement was a product of his own memory. Sometimes communications made to the patient after hypnosis may be retroactively integrated into the hypnotic recall. The subject may recall a fact with no awareness that it was not the product of his own mind. Or he may recall being told the fact but insist that he had prior knowledge of it. This often happens when subjects are shown photographs or line-ups for identification just before or just after hypnotic sessions. In my experience, time, rather than weakening the effects of the hypnotic distortion, tends to fix it into a permanent pattern. Therefore, the pretrial hypnosis of a witness appreciably influences all of his subsequent testimony in ways that are outside the consciousness of the witness and difficult, if not impossible, to detect.

7. *Can an experienced hypnotist or other expert detect the simulation of hypnosis?*

This question is relevant, for some persons do pretend to be hypnotized when they are not. One might suppose that a skilled hypnotist could detect such faked hypnotism. Rigorous scientific experiments, however, have repeatedly demonstrated that even the best experts cannot consistently distinguish between actual and pretended hypnosis.[96] This illustrates one of the most pressing problems of our understanding of hypnosis—no reliable and truly objective criteria of the state of hypnosis have yet been discovered.

8. *During or after hypnosis, can the hypnotist or the subject himself sort out fact from fantasy in the recall?*

Again the answer is no. No one, regardless of experience, can verify the accuracy of the hypnotically enhanced memory. Those who attempt to do so usually rely on such factors as detail, coherence, compatibility with facts gained from other sources, and the like. True, if the recall is incoherent, illogical, and incompatible with the known facts, one can evaluate it as fantasy. Even if it has all the earmarks of accuracy, however, it may still be fantasy. The subject under hypnotic influence is often eager to please by complying with the demand, explicit or tacit, that he produce a correct memory. Thus, unwittingly, the subject may comply by producing a memory out of fantasy and formulating it in as realistic terms as he is capable.[97]

9.   *Is the specificity and richness of the recalled memories an assurance that the hypnotic or posthypnotic subject is recalling fact?*
      In ordinary life experience we tend to judge the validity and accuracy of memories by the amount of detail recalled. If I am very vague about what I had for lunch ten days ago, we doubt my memory. But if I recall every item of the lunch and its environment in all particulars, we tend to have faith in the accuracy of my recall. Subjects under hypnosis often recall events with amazing detail and verisimilitude—age-regression experiments have demonstrated that a person can be hypnotized and instructed to return to and believe he is living in a former period of time, for example, his childhood.[98] He will be able to describe in most minute detail events and surroundings of that period. Whenever I have performed this experiment, my belief in the reality of the acted out recall is unshakable. But the experiment of age *progression* readily proves that detailed recall can be totally confabulated. A subject is hypnotized, instructed to progress in age, say, ten years in the future, and then asked to describe his surroundings. He will relate what he imagines he sees in the greatest detail, producing in the observer the same sense of confidence in his accuracy as does the age-regressed subject. Obviously, what is principally involved in both cases is the remarkable ability of the human mind to confabulate.[99]

10.   *Does the independent corroboration of some of the hypnotically enhanced memories assure that all or most of the witness's memories are reliable?*
      No. In using hypnosis for the therapeutic recall of traumatic psychological events such as in the treatment of combat neuroses, therapists are unconcerned with factual accuracy. Rather, they are after the cathartic recall of the *emotions* surrounding the traumatic event since they assume these to be the cause of the neurotic symptoms. In this process, elicitation of all the embellishments and distortions of the neurotic process is desirable. Hence, even hypnotists experienced in the therapeutic use of hypnosis may be extremely naive in their appraisal of the validity of hypnotic recall.

Particularly, they are apt to assume that because some aspects of the subject's recall are verified by completely independent information, the remainder of the recalled memory is also likely to be authentic. A footnote to *United States v. Narciso* states:

> It is of interest to note that Dr. Orne, one of defendants' experts, relies on the validity of his testing of suggestibility on corroboration by outside facts; thus, if a subject under hypnosis states a fact that is later found to be true by independent investigation, the probability that the statement was not "suggested" is increased. In that respect, at least, the methods of the psychiatrist-hypnotist and the trier of fact are identical.[100]

If this is a correct statement of Dr. Orne's view, I must strongly disagree.[101]

The hypnotist often unconsciously cues the subject into making certain statements. Then, when they prove correct, the hypnotist believes the memories to have been independently recalled by the subject and thus "independently" corroborated. In fact, the subject may have been merely responding to the cues of the hypnotist, who knew all along from other sources what the actual facts were. This is particularly likely to happen when the hypnotist has a prior familiarity with the police record or other facts of the criminal event.

11. Is it possible or practical to make an adequate record of the hypnotic experience?

Obviously, it is better to have an audiotape, or preferably a videotape, recording of the pretrial hypnotic sessions with the witness than no record at all.[102] A mere transcript of the hypnotic sessions can be particularly misleading since the hypnotist often communicates cues and suggestions through tone of voice and body language. In unsophisticated readers the transcript may thus produce a false sense of confidence that no such cues or suggestions were transmitted.

A complete record of the hypnotic experience is, however, never possible for, as described earlier, influences exerted both before and after the hypnotic session become integrated into the hypnotic experience and significantly distort the validity of recall. The only adequate record of the hypnotic experience would be a videotape of everything that transpired before, during, and after the sessions. Yet even that would be a powerful distorting factor, for the knowledge that one is being recorded can alter one's attitudes and behavior. Therefore, the confidence expressed by some courts[103] in the protection offered by stenographic, audio-, or video-recording of a hypnotic session is not justified.

12. *Do a witness's posthypnotic demeanor, attitude or self-confidence, and appearance of integrity and honesty remain unaffected by pretrial hypnosis?*

A remarkable feature of hypnosis is its apparent ability to resolve doubts and uncertainties. Most persons, when aware of the deficiencies of their recall of events, will communicate their awareness by hesitancy, expressions of doubt, and body language indicating lack of self-confidence. The jury relies on these indicators of lack of certainty of recall, and their importance in the determination of the weight of the evidence may be equal to or greater than the bare substance of the testimony. Without adding anything substantive to the witness's memory of events, hypnosis may significantly add to his confidence in his recall. Thus, a witness who honestly reveals that he is unsure of the identification of a defendant from a photograph or a line-up, may, after hypnosis, become quite certain and confident that he has picked the right man. Yet no additional memory has been recalled that would justify the increased confidence. Reviewing the transcripts of hypnotic sessions, I have repeatedly observed how often a hypnotist gives a strong, direct suggestion to the subject to remember, to be sure of his memory, to concentrate on the details, to look inward as if looking at a photograph. As the policeman/hypnotist in *People v. Davis* instructed the witness, "What you'll find at the end of [the hypnotic session], you'll have practically a photographic recall of everything I ask you and everything you answer. . . ."[104] The nature of hypnosis is such that the subject's critical judgment is suspended, and he responds to the demand for exact, photographic recall even when his actual recall is vague and doubtful. It is this suspension of critical judgment which allows the hypnotist to induce illusions and hallucinations into the mind of the subject.[105]

13. *Can an experienced hypnotist or other expert have a reliable and valid opinion that the recall of a particular witness whose memory has been enhanced by hypnotism is reliable and valid?*

The admissibility of testimony of witnesses whose memory has been hypnotically enhanced has been justified by also admitting testimony of the hypnotist and other psychiatric and psychological experts knowledgeable about hypnosis to impeach or support the testimony of the witness. The expert either attacks or vouches for the validity of the testimony insofar as it is related to the hypnotic experience. The jury, however, can experience this only as testimony by the experts as to the truth or falsity of the testimony—hardly a proper function of the expert witness.

It would be wrong to claim that hypnotically enhanced memories are always false or distorted. I contend, rather, that there exist no means to determine with certainty whether or not such falsity or distortion has been introduced by hypnotism. In my view, an expert can testify only to the probabilities of the effect of the hypnosis. This is especially true of the defense expert, who may read the transcript of the hypnotic sessions, listen to the audiotapes, or see the video-recording, but still have absolutely no way of knowing whether the hypnotically recalled memory is true or false. But it is true as well of the hypnotist who performed the memory enhancement and who also qualifies as an expert witness. Yet one often finds testimony by such persons in unequivocal terms that no undue suggestions nave been given to the subject and that his recall was entirely spontaneous and undistorted. Usually the hypnotist also expresses his conviction in the truth of the recall.[106]

An especially serious problem in this context is that courts accept as qualifications for expertise in hypnosis the usual criteria of training and experience. I have found that, with very few exceptions, such so-called experts may be highly skilled in the therapeutic and diagnostic use of hypnosis, yet be totally unaware of its shortcomings in a legal situation. Usually, they are familiar with the literature of hypnotherapy[107] but often lack knowledge of the extensive experimental work of Hilgard, Orne, and the many other researchers who have made important scientific contributions to this field. Law enforcement-oriented author/hypnotists, police staff psychologists, and policemen/hypnotists especially tend to be ignorant of the extensive body of scientific knowledge that has accumulated through research on hypnosis. Many policemen/hypnotists have taken only short courses in hypnotic technique but have read avidly and uncritically articles and books on its use in criminal investigation and have become highly skilled in inducing the hypnotic state and interrogating subjects. They have no difficulty in qualifying as experts. Yet, their lack of scientific background and of familiarity with the research literature causes them to assert palpably false or misleading positions concerning hypnosis. In the cases in which I participated, the hypnotists who had professional training in psychology or medicine were similarly deficient in real knowledge about hypnosis even though they were skilled in its use.[108] The very nature of the hypnotic experience makes it peculiarly difficult for the subject, the hypnotist, and the observer to remain objective and emotionally detached. Here, more than in any other field of expertise, the claim of being an impartial expert is likely to be fallacious (see "The Fallacy of the Impartial Expert," this volume).

14. *Are the uncertainties of ordinary eyewitness testimony and those of hypnotically enhanced recall sufficiently similar that the legal rules of procedures designed for coping with one are sufficient for the other?*

Recent research has conclusively demonstrated that conventional eyewitness testimony is fraught with grave problems of inaccuracy and distortion.[109] People quite commonly fail to see things that happened and claim to have seen things that did not happen. Particularly, the key words used by the interrogator exert a powerful influence on the memory of the subject, and the distortions introduced by such suggestion may last indefinitely, with the subject unaware that his memory has been so altered.[110] Even Bernheim, nearly 100 years ago, knew that the distortions of suggestion were not limited to subjects in a state of hypnosis, and he described cases of unhypnotized witnesses succumbing to suggestion and producing imaginary evidence.[111]

Nevertheless, the hypnotic subject is a great deal more vulnerable to suggestion than is the normal person, and the hypnotic distortions persist into the posthypnotic period with much greater force. The accepted view, that the law cannot exclude the usual eyewitness testimony where there may have been some unreliable distortions, should not justify the admission of testimony that is *known* to have been subject to the inevitable distortions of the hypnotic process. The present legal attitude expressed in most case law on hypnosis is analogous to a claim that we should not even attempt to eliminate the disease of smallpox because chicken pox is so common and cannot be controlled.

I am in complete agreement with the following statement made by a public defender in the brief for a recent unpublished case:

> There is no practice in which false testimony is more "apt to harden" than hypnotic "memory enhancement". . . .[T]he state of hypnosis is one of high suggestibility for the willing subject. The tendency for such a subject to confabulate, or manufacture a memory, even with very strong subjective conviction, is inherent in the hypnotic technique. . . . The real danger is that if the subject confabulates, and the recalled memory is "eminently plausible," then it is virtually impossible for even a skilled therapist to detect such deception; and the process is irreversible.[112]

Pretrial hypnosis of a witness cannot be considered a harmless form of "coaching" or legitimate preparation of the witness for the courtroom experience. In some respects it is worse than ordinary subornation of a witness for it accomplishes the same effect, yet allows the perpetrator, the witness, and the trier of fact to remain unaware that perversion of the evidence has occurred.

Recent Hearings on the Admissibility of Testimony
from Witnesses Whose Memories
Have Been Enhanced by Hypnosis

From July 1978 to July 1979 I testified in three *in limine* hearings challenging the admissibility of testimony by witnesses who had been previously hypnotized. In each case I testified that the hypnotic experience had irrevocably contaminated the proposed testimony and that, were it to be introduced at trial, the trier of fact could not properly weigh its credibility. In each hearing the particular California court involved followed the trend of the case law and ruled that the testimony was admissible, but that the fact and circumstances of the hypnosis, including my expert testimony, were to be considered by the trier of fact. Details of these three cases are presented here because they so clearly illustrate the problems facing attorneys who seek to have hypnotically enhanced testimony excluded.

In the first case,[113] G. Z., age 59, was charged with sexual molestation of a nine-year-old neighbor, M. M., who testified at a preliminary hearing that ten months previously the defendant had asked her if she wanted to come to his house to help clean it. After obtaining permission from her mother, the child entered the defendant's house, where, she testified, the defendant removed his pants and underpants, placed his penis against her leg, and asked her to remove her pants and lie on the bed, which she did, after which he "stuck his finger up [her] rear end."[114]

The defendant strongly denied that he had molested the child, although he conceded that he had asked her to help him clean his house on the day of the alleged molestation in April 1977. However, this otherwise routine child molestation case had some extraordinary features. The defendant had been convicted of a single episode of child molestation 12 years earlier, was placed on probation, and received private psychiatric treatment for about one year. His victim, K., had lived in the same house now occupied by M.'s family, who had rented it from K.'s parents in February 1977. In January 1978, K. returned to her former house and stayed with M.'s family. When M. reported that G. Z. was asking questions about K., K. revealed her molestation of 12 years before and cautioned M.'s mother not to allow G. Z. to molest M. as he had done to her.

The mother immediately concluded that this molestation had already happened, probably on the child's visit to the defendant's house. She vigorously and repeatedly interrogated the child, who denied that anything wrong had happened between her and the defendant. On August 10, 1977, the mother brought her child to the local police department and related her belief that the child had been molested. An officer, W., interviewed the child at length, but again she denied that the defendant had molested her. Officer W. and M.'s mother then took her to a psychologist who had previously lectured to the police department on the use of hypnosis for criminal investigative purposes. The psychologist was informed by the officer that there was a possibility the child had been molested but that she did not want to talk about it. The psychologist immediately hypnotized her.[115] At this first session the child persisted in her denials. On November 17, 1977, the officer took the child again to the psychologist, and this time he remained in the room throughout the hypnotic session. There was a third session on December 7, 1977. Now, finally, the child dictated the description of the alleged molestation into a tape recorder at the police station.[116]

There was no audio- or video-recording made of the hypnotic sessions with the child, nor any record of the questions that had been asked or answers given. The hypnotist had, however, made a very brief note about the sessions in her clinical records.

The technique of hypnosis, as described by the psychologist in her testimony at the *in limine* hearing, was usual—a visual stimulus and suggestions to relax and sleep. The hypnotist then suggested to the child that a bunny would take her on a trip to "wonderland," a place full of toys. The child was next told that she was meeting "Officer Teddy Bear" and that she was to sit on his lap and tell him everything that happened between her and the defendant. At the first hypnotic session the child persisted in stating that nothing had happened. At the second one she showed considerable emotion and was visibly upset when instructed to sit on Officer Teddy Bear's lap, but still related nothing about sexual molestation. At the third session, without hypnosis and in the mother's presence, the child for the first time said that there had been a sexual experience with the defendant. The police officer then arranged for the child to dictate the story into the recorder.

I testified that in my expert opinion the hypnotic sessions could have firmly implanted in the child's mind the belief that the sexual experiences recounted by the 19-year-old friend had actually happened to her. This would be especially likely to occur in view of the suggestive effect of the repeated interrogation of the child by the mother, the police officer, and the psychologist. I emphasized that the psychologist's hypnotic instruction to believe that she was sitting on Officer Teddy Bear's lap and to tell him what happened between her and the defendant was strongly suggestive and encouraged her to confuse sexual fact and sexual fantasy. I concluded that, as a consequence, the child's subsequent testimony was so contaminated by the hypnotic experience that no cross-examination or other means could sort out fact from fantasy. The hypnotist countered in her testimony that the child's later statements were not related to the hypnosis: "During both hypnotic sessions, she said nothing. I don't think it had anything to do with the hypnosis."[117]

The court ruled:

> I don't believe that the evidence has shown any deliberate tampering with the child on the part of the people or the people's agents. My view is that the testimony of the child should be tested in the crucible of the courtroom and the truth ascertained by a trial jury and I rule that her testimony will not be excluded. . . . I do not find it to be the proximate result of a hypnotic trance. Now, the jury might find otherwise but I do not so find.[118]

The defense agreed that the criminal charge should be tried on the record of the preliminary hearing together with the record of the special evidentiary hearing. The defendant was found guilty as charged, despite the total absence of any corroborative evidence.[119] Appeal to the district court was unsuccessful.

The second case, *People v. Diggs*,[120] more closely resembles some of the reported cases. A 26-year-old woman had been the victim of assault and attempted rape in the women's restroom of a bar. The assailant grabbed her from behind, and she struggled. When she screamed that she was pregnant and that he would kill her baby, he fled. She told the police that although she had been unable to get a good look at the man, she knew that he was black and of medium build, and she had seen his eyes briefly. She picked the defendant's photographs out of eight sets that she was shown but was not entirely certain of her identification.[121] Later, at a line-up, she again identified the defendant but was not certain that he was her assailant. The victim was the principal witness at trial, where her testimony revealed the same hesitancy and uncertainty about the identification of the defendant that she had felt during the police investigation. There was a hung jury, and a mistrial was declared.

On the recommendation of the District Attorney, a local psychiatrist hypnotized the victim. Before interviewing her, he reviewed copies of the police reports and of her testimony at the previous trial.[122] At the first of three interviews the psychiatrist took a history and performed a routine psychiatric examination. At the second and third interviews (the next day and a week later), he hypnotized her. Tape recordings and transcripts of these two hypnotic sessions were made, beginning only at the moment of hypnotic induction and ending at the moment of awakening. No recording or transcript was made of the initial interview.

The hypnotic sessions were devoted entirely to efforts by the hypnotist to regress the subject back to the original incident and to sharpen her mental image of her assailant. He stated in his report to the District Attorney that "I have reviewed [the tapes] and feel that I offered no suggestions which would have altered [her] recall of the situation."[123] It was my opinion, however, that the tapes and transcripts of the hypnotic sessions were replete with suggestions by the hypnotist that markedly altered the subject's recall. For example, the hypnotist frequently would first introduce some idea in his question and then receive back the same idea in her response. Thus, although the subject had originally stated that she had only caught a glimpse of her assailant's eyes, general build, and black skin color, and had made no mention of a mirror, in the sessions she quickly responded to the hypnotist's suggestion that there was a mirror on the restroom wall that enabled her to see her assailant. She then described, while hypnotized, more details of the assailant's clothing and appearance as though she were viewing them in the mirror. Toward the end of the last session, the hypnotist gave her a final suggestion: "Q. Susan, as you run through this, do you feel like I have suggested anything to you, or tried to change the memory, that you're running through, in any way? A. No. I see everything."[124] The subject was also encouraged to recall all that she had related in the hypnotic sessions. She was now very certain that she could identify the defendant as her assailant.

At a hearing to determine the admissibility of her testimony, the psychiatrist/hypnotist testified that he had not suggested anything to the witness and that she was in such a light state of hypnosis that he could not have influenced her recall of the assault or her identification of her assailant. I testified to the contrary. The court ruled to admit either her testimony or expert testimony such as the hypnotist's and mine. Bargaining between the prosecution and the defense at the urging of the defendant resulted in a plea of guilty to a lesser offense. The defendant still professed his innocence but feared that another trial might result in a long prison sentence.

The third case concerned the hypnotism of a key witness to a homicide and armed robbery.[125] It was alleged that the two defendants had entered a bar in a rural community early in the evening to "case" it, returned later with their faces, except for their eyes, covered with handkerchiefs, robbed the patrons, and killed the bartender. The prosecution of one of the defendants depended heavily on the ability of a woman, Connie D., to identify him as both one of the "casers" and one of the robbers. As part of the criminal investigation, Connie D. was hypnotized by the local police lieutenant.[126] A complete transcript of the hypnotic session was made available to me.

The policeman/hypnotist testified at the evidentiary hearing that he had not made any suggestions to the subject. Yet, consider this flagrant example:

> Q. Now Connie I'm going to count to three and touch you lightly on the left arm, and when I do, these *two* people who were wearing masks, you'll be looking at them. When I touch you you'll be able to see them perfectly. You'll be standing right where you can get the best possible look at them. One, two, three. That's fine. How many of them are there?
>
> A. *Two.*[127]

During and after the hypnotic session, the witness was still not certain of her identification of the robber, nor did she recognize a photograph of the defendant. Nearly a year later the local newspaper published an account of the crime with a photograph of the suspect. As soon as she saw it, the witness called the police and told them that she was now absolutely certain that the defendant was one of the two robbers and one of the two men who had "cased" the bar.

At the evidentiary hearing, I testified that, despite the long interval between the hypnosis and the identification of the defendant, the hypnosis still might have contaminated the witness's memory and probably affected her subjective certainty of the correctness of her recall. The court admitted both her testimony and my expert testimony[128] on the possible effects of hypnosis on her memory and on the identification. The defendant was acquitted, an outcome defense counsel attributed chiefly to the expert testimony.[129]

Conclusion

Many courts currently admit testimony from previously hypnotized witnesses without an adequate understanding of the nature of hypnosis and its dangers to truly independent recall. Perhaps influenced by often naive legal scholarship and biased expert testimony, these courts apparently believe that cross-examination and expert witness attacks on the credibility of such testimony will reveal any shortcomings in the hypnosis and get to the truth. This hope is misplaced. Even if the hypnotist takes consummate care, the subject may still incorporate into his recollections some fantasies or cues from the hypnotist's manner, or he may be rendered more susceptible to suggestions made before or after the hypnosis. A witness cannot identify his true memories after hypnosis. Nor can any expert separate them out. Worse, previously hypnotized witnesses often develop a certitude about their memories that ordinary witnesses seldom exhibit. Further harm is caused by "expert" witnesses (often self-styled and police-oriented) who, testifying on the state's behalf, make extravagant, scientifically unjustified claims about the reliability of hypnotically enhanced testimony. The plain fact is that such testimony is not and cannot be reliable. The only sensible approach is to exclude testimony from previously hypnotized witnesses as a matter of law, on the ground that the witness has been rendered incompetent to testify.

Notes

[1]Monrose (1978), Justice with glazed eyes: The growing use of hypnotism in law enforcement, *Juris Doctor*, Oct./Nov.:54.

[2]Ibid., p. 55.

[3]The recent popularity of hypnosis among law enforcement personnel may be attributable in large part to three books:

Arons, H. (1967), *Hypnosis in Criminal Investigation*. Springfield, IL: Charles C Thomas; Bryan, W. (1963), *Legal Aspects of Hypnosis.*; and Teitelbaum, M. (1969), *Hypnosis Induction Techniques*. Springfield, IL: Charles C Thomas. These books make extravagant claims of the usefulness and reliability of hypnosis for criminal investigative purposes. Bryan, for example, states, on the basis of personal experience, that "it is extremely difficult for a subject to lie while in a deep hypnotic trance. What happens is this: the questions are directed at the subconscious mind rather than at the conscious mind; hence the true answers come from the subconscious mind. This is especially true if the questions are rapidly fired one after the other. The patient does not have time to 'think' on a conscious level; and because his thinking process is distributed by hypnosis, he can release information only from the subconscious mind. He therefore invariably responds with the correct answer. These conclusions have been verified by polygraph and truth serum examinations" (p. 245).

Arons's incautious approach is demonstrated in his belief that "instruction by physicians would [not] be advantageous" (p. 29). Arons similarly understates the importance of divulging the use of hypnosis to the trier of fact; he views this as "not really pertinent to the matter" (p. 27). For an example of Teitelbaum's approach, see note 7.

Another author of articles and books aimed at law enforcement personnel who strongly advocates the use of hypnotism in criminal investigation is Martin Reiser. Reiser claims that his use of hypnosis in criminal investigation has resulted in "an approximate 60 percent increment of success over traditional interrogation techniques" (Reiser, M. [1976], Hypnosis as a tool in criminal investigation, *The Police Chief*.Nov., p. 36}.

[4]Dieden & Gasparich (1964), Psychiatric evidence and full disclosure in the criminal trial. *Calif. L. Rev.*, 52: 543.

[5]See, e. g., Diamond, B. L. & Louisell, D. W. (1965), The psychiatrist as an expert witness: Some ruminations and speculations, *63 Mich. L. Rev.*, 63:1350–54.

[6]The United States Court of Appeals for the Ninth Circuit, for example, has urged procedural safeguards for the use of such testimony. *United States v. Adams*, 581 F.2d 193 (9th Cir.). *cert. denied*, 439 U.S. IM6 (1978).

[7]The following legal issues concerning the use of hypnosis will not be discussed except insofar as they relate to this topic:

(a) Use of hypnosis as a coercive or suggestive instrument by one person to cause another to commit a criminal act with consequent relevance to the defense of the hypnotized person charged with the crime and to the prosecution of the hypnotist. See, e.g., Reiter, P. (1958), *Antisocial or Criminal Acts and Hypnosis: A Case Study*. Copenhagen: Munksgaard, p. 958; see also Erickson, M. (1939), An experimental investigation of the possible anti-social use of hypnosis. *Psychiat.*, 2:391.

b) Use of hypnosis by law enforcement agents, with or without the consent of the subject, to obtain a confession. This use was vigorously condemned in *Leyra v. Denno*, 347 U.S. 556 (1954). For details of the improper hypnotism used on Leyra see also Levy (1955), Hypnosis and legal immutability. *46 J. Crim. Law, Criminol. & Police Sci.*, 46:333, 342n. Despite the United States Supreme Court's unequivocal prohibition of such use, the suspicion remains that this practice continues. A "how to" book on hypnosis, written by a lawyer/hypnotist and directed at law enforcement personnel, gives fully detailed instructions on what to say and how to behave in order to hypnotize a defendant without his being aware that this is happening. The author prefaces his description by stating: "Without going into the ethics of its use, we will merely present here a technic [sic] for involuntarily hypnotizing a criminal suspect" (Teitelbaum, op. cit., sup. note 3, p. 168).

(c) Defense use of hypnosis on a defendant for the purpose of establishing his innocence or at least eliciting some information helpful to the defense. In *People v. Sirhan*, 7 Cal. 3d 710, 497 P.2d 1121, 102 Cal. Rptr. 385 (1972), for example, I hypnotized the defendant to obtain information that might underpin a diminished capacity defense.

(d) Use of hypnosis by a psychiatric or psychological expert as part of a clinical examination that is to serve as the basis of an expert opinion. Such use has occurred both with and without the consent of the subject and has been employed by experts for the defense, experts for the prosecution (or police), and by court-appointed experts. Although there is still some controversy in other United States jurisdictions, in California it has been settled that information obtained through the use of hypnosis is admissible as part of the foundation for an expert's opinion of a defendant's mental state. *People V. Cornell* 52 Cal. 2d 99, 338 P.2d 447 (1959), is authority for such use by the defense expert when the subject consents.

(e) Use of hypnosis to calm a nervous or distraught witness so that his credibility may be enhanced. See W. Bryan, op.cit., sup. note 3: "An important legitimate use of hypnosis exists with the purpose in mind of relaxing this nervous witness and creating an aura of calm self confidence so that she may present her evidence in a manner which the truthfulness of the evidence has every right to demand" (p. 194).

(f) Its use for the purpose of enhancing the memory of a witness to facilitate the investigation of a crime or tort. An example is the sensational Chowchilla kidnapping case in which the bus driver was able to recall a key license plate number (see Monrose, op. cit., sup. note 1). For an example of its investigatory use in a tort action, see *Wylier v. Fairchild Hiller Corp.*, 503 F.2d 506 (9th Cir. 1974), as modified with respect to the crucial issue of admissibility of hypnotically adduced testimony by *United States v. Awkard*, 597 F.2d 667, 670 (9th Cir. 1979).

[8] *Webster's New Collegiate Dictionary* (1976). Springfield, MA: G. & C. Merriam, p. 563.

[9] Hilgard, F. (1968), *The Experience of Hypnosis*. pp. 6–10.

[10] Hilgard, E. (1972), Evidence for a developmental-interactive theory of hypnotic susceptibility. In: *Hypnosis: Research Developments and Perspectives*, ed. E. Fromm & R. Short. New York: Aldine, p. 3876.

[11] Barber & Calverley (1963), The relative effectiveness of task-motivating instructions and trance-induction procedure in the production of "hypnotic-like" behaviors. *J. Nerv. Ment. Dis.*, 137:107.

[12] Hilgard, E. (1969), Altered states of awareness. *J. Nerv. Ment. Dis.*, 149:68.

[13] Sarbin & Andersen (1967), Role-theoretical analysis of hypnotic behavior. In: *Handbook of Clinical and Experimental Hypnosis*, ed. J. Gordon, p. 319.

[14] Pawlow (1923). The identity of inhibition with sleep and hypnosis. *Sci. Monthly*, 17:603.

[15] But it does mean that the law's quest for certainty is unscientific as well as futile. See Diamond, B. L. (1967), The scientific method and the law. *Hastings L. J.*, 19:179.

[16] Compare Bryan, op. cit., sup. note 3: "It has been my personal experience that it is extremely difficult for a subject to lie while in a deep hypnotic trance" (p. 245) with Redlich, Ravitz, & Dession, (1951), Narcoanalysis and truth. *Amer. J. Psychiat.*, 107:586. See also Herman (1964), The use of hypno-induced statements in criminal cases. *Ohio State L. J.*, 25:1, naively relying on the equivocal testimony of the expert witness in the unreported case of *State v. Nebb*, No. 39540 (Ohio C.P., Franklin County, May 28, 1962), that there was no "probability" (although there was a "possibility") of a subject's lying under hypnosis. The *Nebb case* is described in Teitelbaum (1963), Admissibility of hypnotically adduced evidence and the Arthur Nebb case. *St. Louis L. J.*, 8:205. Compare Sheehan (1972), Hypnosis and the manifestations of "imagination" in Fromm and Shor, op. cit., sup. note 10 (reviewing research on fantasy production, role-playing, imagination, hallucinations, etc., in the

hypnotic state) with the following statement from *Encyclopedia Britannica, Macropaedia* (1979), vol. 9: "Hypnosis has not been found reliable in obtaining truth from a reluctant witness. Even if it were possible to induce hypnosis against one's will, it is well documented that the hypnotized individual still can willfully lie. It is of even greater concern that cooperative hypnotized subjects remember distorted versions of actual events and are themselves deceived. When recalled in hypnosis, such false memories are accompanied by strong subjective conviction and outward signs of conviction that are most compelling to almost any observer. Caution and independent verification are essential in such circumstances."

[17]In ancient and primitive societies trance states frequently were induced through drugs and toxic chemicals and may have been more analogous to modern "truth serums" than to hypnosis (Rogers [1947], Egyptian psychotherapy. *Ciba Symposia*, 9:617, 621.

*[18]Modern interest and research in hypnosis date from 1778, when Mesmer, a Viennese physician, moved to Paris and established his clinic for the practice of "animal magnetism" (Mesmer, F. A. [1779], *Memoire sur la Découverte du Magnétisme Animal*. Geneva). Mesmer's magnetic treatments, however, ordinarily did not include the induction of sleep or trance states, and, strictly speaking, "mesmerism," "animal magnetism," and "hypnotism" are not synonymous, although they are often incorrectly used thus. The first two terms apply to the treatment of illness by the touching of the patient and the supposed transmission of magnetic influences from the therapist's body to the patient's. Mesmer's disciple, the Marquis de Puységur, treated a young peasant for toothache by the usual animal magnetic "passes." To de Puységur's surprise, his patient fell into a trance state in which he appeared to be asleep but was able to talk and answer questions. This is the first fully documented case of the induction of artificial somnambulism (de Puységur, Marquis (1786), *Memoires pour Servir à L'histoire et L'Établissement du Magnétisme Animal*. London, pp. 28–33, 390n).

[19]Bramwell, J. (1906), *Hypnotism: Its History, Practice and Theory.*

[20]Composed of famous scientists and headed up by Benjamin Franklin, in 1784 it investigated Mesmer and the practice of animal magnetism and denounced both. It attributed the benefits of his magnetic treatments to his patients' "imagination" (*Rapport des Commissaires Chargés par le Roi, de l'Éxamen du Magnétisme Animal*, [1784]. Paris, p. 64). Mesmer fled Paris. Soon after, animal magnetism and induced somnambulism fell into disrepute.

[21]A revival of medical and scientific interest in hypnosis occurred in 1837 in England. In that year, Dr. John Elliotson began treating patients in a London hospital with mesmeric methods, and his demonstrations of the efficacy of the treatments aroused great public and professional interest (Rosen, G. [1948], From mesmerism to hypnotism. *Ciba Symposia*, 9:838, 841). Dr. James Esdaile returned to England from a long practice of medicine and surgery in India and informed Elliotson of his observations there on the use of artificially

induced trance states as an anesthetic in major surgical operations. In 1843, after experiments in London, Elliotson published numerous case reports of successful surgical operations performed painlessly on patients in a trance state (Elliotson, J. [1843], *Numerous Cases of Surgical Operations Without Pain in the Mesmeric State*. London). In the same year, James Braid published in London a famous work in which he coined the word "hypnosis" to designate the artificially induced somnambulistic state (Braid, J. [1843], *Neurypnology, or the Rationale of Nervous Sleep*. London: John Churchill). A medical journal also appeared for the purpose of publishing the many medical reports and investigations being done in the field. *The Zoist: A Journal of Cerebral Physiology & Mesmerism, and their Applications to Human Welfare* was published in London from March 1843 to January 1856. Most of the reports emphasized the anesthetic properties of hypnosis, but the therapeutic aspects remained of much interest. Efforts were made to dissociate medical and surgical use of hypnosis from its earlier mystical, supernatural, and quack images. The reports in *The Zoist* were written in an objective, scientific manner. Many were by dentists reporting painless tooth extractions with the use of hypnosis.

Notwithstanding this activity, two factors produced a sharp decline of interest in and medical respectability of the mesmeric movement. First, painless surgery with the patient's inhalation of ether was discovered (Morton, W. T. G. [1847], *Remarks on the Proper Mode of Administering Sulphuric Ether by Inhalation*. Boston). Immediately, chemical anesthesia—ether or chloroform—proved successful throughout the world. Second, the English medical hypnotists were fascinated by phrenology. Phrenology began as a genuine scientific study of the morphology of the brain (Gall, F. & Spurzheim, J. [1810-19], *Anatomie et Physiologie du Systéme Nerveux en Général, at du Cerveau en Particulier*), but enthusiastic followers soon transformed it into a pseudoscience. By the mid-nineteenth century, it was in disrepute in England, and all reputable medical and scientific interest in hypnosis had ceased as well (Rosen, op. cit., sup. note 21, pp. at 843-44).

[22]Hypnosis as a therapeutic method was soon revived, this time in France. A. A. Liébeault had read many of the English writings on hypnosis, and he experimented with its use on many of his patients at his clinic in Nancy. He described his successful treatment of a wide variety of nervous and medical conditions (Liébeault, A. [1866], *Le Sommeil, Provoqué et Les États Analogues*. New York: Aron Press). This book is of great significance in psychotherapy; it was among the first to show an awareness that the treatment techniques were purely psychological and that their effects were not due to magic, religious miracles, or mysterious natural forces such as magnetism. (See also Diamond, B. L. [1961], Ten great books in the history of psychiatry. *Mental Hospitals*, 12:32.) Liébeault was not given appropriate recognition for his pioneer book, for the first edition (1866) sold only two copies and remained almost entirely unknown until a new edition was published in 1889.

The new edition was much abridged, and its title page gave no indication that there had been an earlier edition. By 1889, the concept of psychotherapy as a psychological method of treatment was no longer a novelty.

[23]Hypnosis had rapidly become an accepted treatment for nervous and mental disease throughout France. Jean-Martin Charcot and his disciples, who operated the world's most famous clinic for the research and treatment of nervous and mental diseases at the Salpêtrière in Paris, accepted hypnosis as a legitimate, potent instrument of cure. There, Charcot and his students avidly researched the true nature of hypnosis, its relationship to hysteria, and the mechanisms of its healing effects. Charcot maintained a photographic laboratory, and many photographs were taken of the hysterical patients and the hypnotic experiments performed on patients and staff. A three-volume album of these photographs was published between 1876 and 1880 (Bourneville, D. & Regnard, P. [1886], Iconographie Photographique de la Salpêtrière). Liébeault and his associate, Hippolyte Bernheim, did similar research at Nancy (Bernheim, H. [1886], Suggestive Therapeutics: A Treatise on the Nature and Uses of Hypnotism, trans. from 2d rev.[French ed.]. New York: Aronson, 1973). The intense rivalry between the Nancy and the Salpêtrière groups yielded a flood of scientific publications advocating their conflicting theories of hypnosis (Galdston, I. [1947], Hypnosis and modern psychiatry. Ciba Symposia, 9:845).

[24]As a young physician, Sigmund Freud was the translator of the German editions of a number of the works of both Charcot and Bernheim. For a listing of the works translated by Freud, see Grinstein, A. (1977), Sigmund Freud's Writings: A Comprehensive Bibliography. New York: International Universities Press, pp. 127–28. At this point in his career Freud had yet to develop his theories of psychoanalysis. Freud also studied under Charcot at the Salpêtrière from October 1885 through February 1886 (Jones, E. [1953], The Life and Work of Sigmund Freud, Vol. 1. London: Hogarth Press). Hence, he was thoroughly familiar with the practice of hypnotic therapy and the conflicting theories as to its nature. When he established his own practice in Vienna, he followed the then conventional and respectable use of hypnotic suggestion for the treatment of his nervous patients. By 1893, however, he had established, with Joseph Breuer, the foundations of a new theory of causation and treatment of nervous and emotional illness and soon abandoned his use of hypnosis (Breuer, J. & Freud, S. [1893–95], Studies on Hysteria. Standard Edition, 2. London: Hogarth Press, 1955).

[25]The novel first appeared in serial form in Harper's Magazine from January to August 1894. It was enormously popular, and its publication was quickly followed by stage versions and ultimately motion pictures.

[26]There is no evidence that Rasputin practiced hypnosis, but his influence over the Czarina was popularly believed to be hypnotic. This idea was reinforced by the 1932 movie Rasputin and the Empress, starring Ethel, Lionel, and John Barrymore.

[27]Notably M. Erickson, M. Orne, E. Hilgard, H. Spiegel, T. Sarbin, J. Schneck, M. Gill, and M. Brenman. For bibliographies of their work, see Hilgard, op. cit., sup. note 10, pp. 587–638.

[28]Menninger, W. (1948), *Psychiatry in a Troubled World.* New York: Viking Press, pp. 309–12.

[29]Grinker, R. & Spiegel, J. (1945), *Men Under Stress.* New York: Irvington, 1979. This treatment involved inducing a trance state or partial unconsciousness by the intravenous injection of these powerful sedatives, which could overcome emotional blocking, fear, and inhibitions. Repressed memories would return along with a flood of cathartic emotional outpouring, and spectacular results were often achieved in the treatment of war neuroses and combat fatigue. It was generally recognized that the psychological principles of treatment with narcoanalysis were essentially the same as with hypnosis. Intravenous injection of drugs was, however, far simpler and more reliable than hypnosis, required less skill, and was free from hypnotism's disreputable aura of mysticism and magic.

[30]*Encyclopedia Britannica* (1964), vol. 24.

[31]See Hilgard, op. cit., sup. note 10.

[32]These recording are not, of course, admissible to establish the substance of what the witness related during hypnosis. *United States v. Adams,* 581 F.2d 193, 198–99 (9th Cir.), *cert. denied,* 439 U.S. 1006 (1978).

[33]See *United States v. Miller,* 411 F.2d 825, 832 (2d cir. 1969). This case involved a normal situation in which the police used hypnosis on a potential prosecution witness. Hence, the issue of notice to the defense was squarely presented. The issue could also arise where the defense hypnotized a potential defense witness (e.g., an alibi witness). However, this use has not been common, and there appear to be no reported cases of it. Since cases hold that the defense need not give notice to the prosecution when it uses hypnosis in aid of establishing a mental-state defense, a requirement of notice might not be applied to the defense where it had hypnotized a potential witness. My analysis of the nature of hypnosis and its impact on recall suggests, however, that neither side should be permitted to use hypnosis to enhance recall and thus obviates the notice problem entirely.

[34]For a summary of such cases, see Annot., 92 A.L.R.3d 442, 454 (1979).

[35]But see the descriptions of the Arthur Nebb trial by Teitelbaum and by Herman, op. cit., sup. note 16. Even in the, Nebb trial, the hypnosis took place before the trial judge and not in the presence of the jury.

[36]See *Cornell v. Superior Ct.,* 52 Cal. 2d 99, 338 P.2d 447 (1959) (approving use of hypnosis for such evaluation); *State ex rel. Sheppard v. Koblentz,* 174 Ohio St. 120, 187 N.E.2d 40 (1962) (disapproving use).

[37]5 Md. App. 230, 246 A.2d 302 (1968), *cert. denied,* 395 U.S. 949 (1968). Prior decisions involved attempts to introduce testimony of or about a defendant who had been hypnotized. The first such case was *People v. Ebanks,* 117 Cal. 652 (1897); where expert testimony by a hypnotist was held not admissible

to show that, while under hypnosis, the defendant had made statements that pertained to his knowledge of the homicide. The 1905 decision in *State v. Exum*, 138 N.C. 599, 50 S. E. 283 (1905) concerned the possibility of posthypnotic effects on a witness, but the context differed completely from the concern of this paper. Exum's wife was called to testify on his behalf in his murder trial. The court ruled that the allegation that the defendant had previously hypnotized his wife on numerous occasions was admissible as relevant to her credibility.

[38]The other evidence was that sperm had been recovered from the complainant's vagina.

[39]See, e.g., *Kline v. Ford Motor Co.*, 523 F.2d 1067 (9th Cir. 1975) (consolidated torts cases where the appellate court held erroneous the trial court's exclusion of hypnotically enhanced testimony of one plaintiff); *Wylier v. Fairchild Hiller Corp.*, 503 F.2d 506 (9th Cir. 1974) (plaintiff in suit against helicopter manufacturer underwent hypnotic treatment to restore his memory, which had been impaired by the crash); *Connolly v. Farmer*, 484 F.2d 456 (5th Cir. 1973) (first reported civil case where hypnotically enhanced testimony—by the plaintiff—was admitted); *People v. Smrekar*, 68 IU. App. 3d 379,385 N.E.2d 848 (1979) (a murder case in which, prior to hypnosis, the principal witness had stated that there was only a "50-50" chance that the defendant was the person she had seen commit the murders); *State v. McQueen*, 295 N.C. 96, 244 S.E.2d 414 (1978) (sustaining the admissibility of hypnotically refreshed testimony on the theory that hypnosis is no less acceptable than any other memory-enhancing procedure); *State v. Brom*, 8 Or. App. 598, 494 P.2d 434 (1972) (relying on *Harding*, the court admitted testimony by a witness whose amnesia was cured by hypnosis and sodium amytal); *State v. Jorgensen*, 8 6r. App. 1, 492 P.2d 312 (1971) (same witness as in *Brom*).

[40]446 F. Supp. 252 (E.D. Mich. 1977). 1

[41]Used as a muscle relaxant by surgeons during anesthesia and by psychiatrists to minimize the convulsions of electroshock therapy, it will, in excess dosage. cause a paralysis of all muscles, including those of respiration, with fatal results.

[42]446 F. Supp., pp. 277–78.

[43]390 U.S. 377 (1968).

[44]Ibid., p. 394.

[45]446 F. Supp., pp. 280–81.

[46]Dr. Orne is the author of many scientific publications on hypnosis and is the coauthor of the article on hypnosis in *Encyclopedia Britannica Macropaedia* (1979), vol. 9.

[47]Dr. Herbert Spiegel of Columbia University is a well-known authority on hypnosis. He is coauthor, with David Spiegel, of *Trance and Treatment: Clinical Uses of Hypnosis* (1978, New York: Basic books) and of the section on hypnosis in *Comprehensive Textbook of Psychiatry*, vol. 2 §30.4 (ed. A. Friedman, H. Kaplan & B. Sadock [1975]. Malvern, PA: Williams &

Wilkins). Dr. Spiegel is the discoverer of a reliable, objective test of the hypnotizability of a subject. He hypnotized Neely in December 1975.

[48]446 F. Supp., p. 284.

[49]Motion for new trial, *United States v. Narciso*, 446 F: Supp. 252 (E.D. Mich. 1977). At the second trial, the government failed to obtain conviction.

[50]397 F. Supp. 1025 (N.D. Ga. 1975). See also *Emmett v. State*, 232 Ga. 110, 205 S.E.2d 231 (1974), and *Creamer v. State*, 232 Ga. 136, 205 S.E.2d 240 (1974), which had approved of the admission of the testimony later condemned by the federal district court.

[51]The major abuse consisted in the psychologist's acting as a police agent and literally using the hypnosis sessions (for which he was paid $3,515 by the county) to manufacture evidence against the petitioners.

[52]*Emmett v. Ricketts*, 397 F. Supp. 1025, 1038 (N.D. Ga. 1975). In 1959 Georgia became the first state to adopt a psychotherapist–patient privileged communication statute that was distinguished from and much stricter than the usual physician–patient privileged communication laws. See Group for the Advancement of Psychiatry (1960), Report No. 45, *Confidentiality and Privileged Communication in the Practice of Psychiatry*, p. 96.

[53]397 F. Supp., p. 1038n.

[54]411 F.2d 825 (2d Cir. 1969).

[55]Ibid., p. 830.

[56]581 F.2d 193 (9th Cir.), *cert. denied*, 439 U.S. 1006 (1978).

[57]Ibid., p. 198.

[58]Ibid., p. 199.

[59]McCormick, C. T. et al. (ed.) (1978), *McCormick's Hornbook on Evidence*. St. Paul, MN: West.

[60]Ladd, G. T. (1982), Legal aspects of hypnotism. *Yale L. J.*, 11:187–88. Other early legal articles on hypnosis were published between 1891 and 1902, but these did not discuss enhancement of witnesses' memory. They were concerned much more with hypnosis as a possible cause of crime and the hypnotized state as a criminal defense. For a listing of these articles, see *Neb. L. Rev.* (1952). 31:575n.

It is noteworthy that Bannister (1895), Hypnotic influence in criminal cases. *Alb. L. J.*, 51 cautioned: "When an individual is fully in the hypnotic condition he can be made to say anything, and even honest questioning may act as false suggestion. It is easy to see, moreover, what would be the possibilities of post-hypnotic suggestion in this regard" (pp. 87–88).

[61]Després, (1947), Legal aspects of drug-induced statements. *Univ. Chic. L. Rev.*, 14. He documents that the first use of a drug to induce a statement in a criminal case occurred in the Dallas County Jail on February 13, 1922. A physician injected scopolamine (the original so-called truth serum) into two convicted criminals and "established to his satisfaction that they were not guilty of the crimes charged" (p. 607).

[62]Hypnotism, suggestibility, and the law (1952), *Neb. L. Rev.*, 31:583.

[63.]Ibid., p. 593. The note ultimately concluded that "there seems to be no serious reason why hypnotism should not be employed to aid in crime detection as the lie detector has, and it is in this capacity that hypnotism can be of great service to the administration of justice."

[64]Levy, op. cit., sup. note 7, p. 34.

[65]Swaine, W. P. (1961), Hypnotism and the law. *Vand. L. Rev.*, 14:1515. The author was a recent law graduate at the time of publication. He cited Allen (1934), Hypnotism and its legal important. *Canadian B. Rev.*, 80:88, as authority for this statement. but then he said, "An able and rigorous cross-examination can minimize the danger of falsified testimony by means of hypnosis" (p. 1515n).

[66]Herman, op. cit., sup. note 16. Teitelbaum, op. cit., sup. note 16. Teitelbaum, an attorney–hypnotist, is the author of the "how-to" book on hypnosis referred to in note 7. The Nebb trial also stimulated the publication of an extensive student note, "Hypnosis in court: A memory aid for the witness" (*Ga. L. Rev.* [1967], 1). Although this student apparently had read widely in the psychological and legal literature on hypnosis, he was very naive to accept uncritically the pseudoscientific claims so frequently made in that literature. He urged that hypnosis be used on witnesses while they were on the witness stand in the courtroom whenever a witness needed some sort of prodding or refreshing of memory. An equally naive student comment was "Hypno-Induced Statements: Safeguards for Admissibility" (*L. & Doc. Ord* [1970]). This student also demonstrated wide but uncritical reading in the literature on hypnosis and a lack of comprehension of the legal hazards of hypnosis. For example, he stated: "if the hypno-examination is properly conducted, the resulting testimony has the same attributes of credibility—basic honesty versus personal interest—as any other testimony. Through pretrial discovery, an opponent can ascertain whether the witness's memory was refreshed through hypnosis, or even altered through post-hypnotic suggestion. The fact that a witness has been hypnotized and thereby possibly influenced by the post-hypnotic suggestion seems irrelevant to a determination of the truth of his testimony. Absent any evidence of impropriety, it might be assumed that the witness' memory was simply restored. Because hypnoinduced testimony has the same basic attributes of credibility as any other testimony, to inform the jury of the hypnosis with no evidence of impropriety runs the risk of unnecessarily arousing unfounded prejudices" (pp. 112-13).

[67]Teitlebaum, op. cit., sup. note 16, p. 210.

[68]Herman, op. cit., sup. note 16.

[69]Spector & Foster (1977), Admissibility of hypnotic statements: Is the law of evidence susceptible? *Ohio State L. J.*, 38:567.

[70]An excellent review of the older literature is contained in Redmount, (1959), The psychological basis of evidence practice: Memory. *J. Crim. Law, Criminol. & Police Sci.*, 50:249. For more recent research, see Buckout (1978), Eyewitness testimony. *Sci. Am.*, Dec., p. 23; Fishman & Loftus, E. (1978),

Expert psychological testimony on eyewitness identification. *L. & Psych. Rev.*, 4:87.

[71]Spector & Foster, op. cit., sup. note 69, p. 590.

[72]Ibid., p. 594.

[73]They also assert that proper instruction of the jury regarding the nature and function of hypnosis eliminates the motive for dissembling while in a trance state.

[74]A witness may actually believe quite honestly that he was not hypnotized when he in fact was. Sirhan Sirhan persists in his conviction that I never hypnotized him.

[75]Spector & Foster, op. cit., sup. note 69. They say, however, that "an exception may be made when the witness suffers a lapse of memory on the witness stand. [Hypnotic] induction should be permitted, out of the presence of the jury, to revive his remembrance through induction" (p. 596).

[76]Dillhoff (1977), The admissibility of hypnotically influenced testimony. *Ohio N.U.L. Rev.*, 4:1.

[77]"[T]he conclusions based upon, and the statements of the person interviewed made during, a drug-induced or hypnosis-induced interview are inadmissible in evidence in a trial by court-martial" *Manual for Courts Martial* § 142(e) (rev. ed. 1969).

[78]Dillhoff, op. cit., sup. note 76, p. 22. One might conclude that the acquittal of the defendant in the case I describe in the text accompanying notes 137–141 *infra* substantiates Dillhoff's belief. I think not, however, as the only witness who served as an expert to vouch for the validity of the witness's testimony and for the general reliability of the hypnotic method was the police officer hypnotist, and I doubt that the jury regarded him as impartial and uninvolved. A basic problem of this kind of expert testimony is that the experts who perform the hypnosis for prosecutorial purposes, in many instances, seem only too willing to make strongly definitive statements as to the validity, reliability, and efficacy of the use of hypnosis for enhancing recall. In effect, they vouch for the truthfulness of their hypnotic subjects. An expert such as I, who attacks the credibility of the evidence, has no way of knowing whether the hypnotically influenced testimony is true or false. In all honesty, he can only testify that the hypnosis has contaminated the evidence in such a manner that it is impossible for him or anyone else, including the trier of fact, to make such a determination. Hence, a strong, positive opinion of the state's expert is pitted against the somewhat implausible, but I believe accurate, claim by the defense expert that he does not know the truth and that neither he nor the trier of fact can ever find out.

[79]Ibid., p. 21.

[80]Crim. No. 29766 (Cal. 2d Dist. Ct. App.), *cert. denied*, 439 U.S. 875 (1978). The facts of the unpublished *Quaglino* case can be obtained from an unpublished manuscript, T. Worthington, Hypnotically induced or enhanced testimony (on file with *Calif. L. Rev.*).

[81]*Leave to file granted*, 439 U.S. 875 (1978). 1 am indebted to Dr. Orne for a copy of his affidavit.

[82]Certain of the concepts expressed in this paper are derived in part from personal communications from Dr. Orne and from his affidavit.

[83]For example, in the Chowchilla kidnapping of 26 children riding in a school bus, the bus driver was able to recall under hypnosis a license plate number. This recollection proved instrumental in the apprehension of the kidnappers (Monrose, op. cit., sup. note 1, p. 54).

   In my opinion, however, the value of hypnosis for investigative purposes has been greatly overstated by exaggerated claims in irresponsible books and articles. As Freud discovered long ago, whatever can be done by hypnosis can also be done without hypnosis; it merely takes longer and requires greater skill and patience. My own experience convinces me that safe and effective enhancement of recall, with less hazard of suggestion and contamination of future testimony, can be accomplished without gimmicks such as hypnosis and "truth serum."

[84]A hypothetical case could, of course, be imagined where law enforcement agents have a witness from whom they would like further information about the crime for investigative purposes as well as testimony for trial use. Adoption of this rule forces them to a decision. Arguably, the public interest in effective administration of justice is misserved whichever course the police choose. But at least two responses are possible: (1) the burden will be small since this hypothetical situation will occur only infrequently; and (2) more fundamentally, the law has aims other than the apprehension of criminals, and a defendant's right to be free of a conviction aided by the "transgressions of the constable" is one of its strongest.

[85]Hilgard, op. cit., sup. note 1. See also Orne, M. (1972), On the simulating subject as a quasi-control group in hypnosis research: What, why, and how (1972). In: *Hypnosis: Research Developments and Perspectives*, ed. E. Fromm & R. Short. New York: Aldine, pp. 399, 400.

[86]Spiegel, H. (1978), Hypnosis: An adjunct to therapy. In: *Comprehensive Textbook of Psychiatry*, op. cit., sup. note 47.

[87]Orne, op. cit., sup. note 85, p. 402.

[88]See Allen, op. cit., sup. note 65, p. 8 or 19.

[89]A number of thoroughly reliable observers witnessed the trances.

[90]Sirhan maintained this conviction on the witness stand despite vigorous interrogation and the harm that his denial did to his defense.

[91]Stainaker & Riddle (1932), The effect of hypnosis on long delayed recall. *J. Gen. Psychiat.*, 6:429.

[92]Hilgard, op. cit., sup. note 85, p. 166. See also *Encyclopedia Britannica*, sup. note 16.

[93]See *People v. Blair*, 89 Cal. App. 3d 563, 152 Cal. Rptr- 646 (2d Dist. 1979). In that case the witness emerged from the hypnotic trance with a complete amnesia for what she had recalled during the hypnotic state.

[94]Although everyone has some degree of this source amnesia for information learned in childhood or many years ago, persons in the normal state of consciousness do not ordinarily maintain an amnesia for the source of their information soon after it is acquired.

[95]Cooper Hypnotic amnesia. In: Fromm & Short, op. cit., sup. note 10, pp. 217, 223.

[96]One must not make the error of assuming that, therefore, all hypnosis is simulated.

[97]See Hilgard, op. cit., sup. note 85, pp. 164-75.

[98]Often, he will change his tone of voice and his mannerisms to suit that age and will misidentify persons about him as those appropriate to that time of his life. See Orne, M. (1951), The mechanisms of hypnotic age regression: An experimental study. *J. Abn. & Soc. Psych.*, 46:231.

[99]Rubenstein & Newman (1954), The living out of "future" experiences under hypnosis. *Science*, 119:472.

[100]466 F. Supp. at 282 n.11.

[101]Dr. Orne and I usually agree on most of the legal issues concerned with hypnosis, although he takes a somewhat more benign view of its use for purely investigative purposes. See Orne, op. cit., sup. notes 46 & 87.

[102]Having counsel for both sides present during the hypnotic sessions is also clearly preferable to the common practice of private, unrecorded sessions.

[103]*United States v. Adams*, 581 F.2d 193, 199 n-12 (9th Cir.), *cert. denied*, 439 U.S. 1006 (1978).

[104]No. 52660 (Super. Ct. Placer County, California, July 30, 1979).

[105]See Hilgard, op. cit., sup. note 85, pp. 120-49.

[106]This occurred in each of the three cases in which I participated and that are discussed later.

[107]They will usually know, for example, Erickson, M. & Rossi, E. (1979), *Hypnotherapy: An Exploratory Casebook*. New York: Irvington; Spiegel & Spiegel, op. cit., sup. note 47; or earlier books by these and other therapists.

[108]The technique of hypnotic induction is very easy to learn and requires only confidence and practice. One can be a skilled hypnotist and yet know nothing about the nature and theory of hypnosis.

[109]See Woocher (1977), Did your eyes deceive you? Expert psychological testimony on the unreliability of eyewitness identification. *Stanford L. Rev.*, 29:969.

[110]Fishman & Loftus, op. cit., sup. note 70.

[111]Bernheim, op. cit., sup. note 23, p. 177.

[112]Brief for Appellant at 29, *People v. Jones*, No. 67183 (Super. Ct. Alameda County, California), quoted in Worthington, op. cit., sup. note 80, p. 65.

[113]*People v. Zehner*, No. 68047 (Super. Ct. Santa Clara County, California, July 21, 1978).

[114]Ibid. Clerk's transcript on appeal, p. 8.

[115]The psychologist neither performed any type of clinical examination of M. nor even obtained a history of her mental state.

[116]There is some conflict between the statements of the child and those of the psychologist as to when the child first admitted to the molestation during the hypnotic sessions.

[117]*People v. Zehner*, sup. note 113. Reporter's transcript of proceedings held on Friday, July 21, 1978, p. 102.

[118]Ibid, p. 204.

[119]The defendant was also found not to be a mentally disordered sex offender.

[120]*People v. Diggs*, No. CR 6490 (Super. Ct. Monterey County, California, Apr. 23, 1979).

[121]It is significant that the photographs of other persons shown to the witness included a frontal and a side view, while those of the defendant were two frontal views.

[122]The psychiatrist stated in his report: "Although these materials were totally reviewed, the emphasis was to attempt to determine the areas where Mrs. A. would benefit from enhancement of her memory, and as a result of this the pictures of the defendant were purposely not viewed" (*People v. Diggs*, sup. note 120. Report of Dr. Wilcox, March 14, 1979).

[123]Ibid.

[124]Ibid. Transcript of tape no. 2 of hypnosis session, p. 8.

[125]*People v. Davis*, No. 52660 (super. Ct. Placer County, California, July 30, 1979).

[126]Before inducing hypnosis, the hypnotist/policeman repeatedly emphasized to the subject that human memory is like a photograph: "Now they've pretty well determined that everything that you ever see or hear or touch or taste or smell is all recorded. It's recorded just the way it went in and it doesn't change. It doesn't fade or anything like that" (Ibid. Auburn Police Department transcript of hypnosis of Connie D., p. 2).

Later, the hypnotist said (still before inducing the trance): "People are also kinda concerned that they won't remember what went on during the hypnosis and it may even effect [sic] their memory of the incident that they're trying to remember. What you'll find at the end of it, you'll have practically a photographic recall of everything I ask you and everything you answer. . . ." (ibid., p. 9).

[127]Ibid., p. 17 (italics added).

[128]Due to the defendant's indigence, the county bore the expense of my appearance. To avoid my return for another court appearance, the trial judge permitted me to testify out of sequence. I thus was placed in the unusual situation where my testimony attacked the credibility of a witness yet to testify.

[129]One might conclude that the acquittal of the defendant substantiates Dillhoff's conclusion that "[t]he primary antedote [sic] for possible deception of the trier of fact is expert testimony describing the dangers to the judge or jury so that they may properly evaluate the witness's testimony" (Dillhoff, op. cit., sup. note 76, p. 9). I think not, however. I suspect that the controlling factor was that the police officer/hypnotist was the only expert to vouch for the validity of the witness's testimony and for the general reliability of the hypnotic

method. I doubt that the jury regarded him as impartial and uninvolved. A basic problem of this kind of expert testimony is that the experts who perform the hypnosis for prosecutorial purposes often seem only too willing to make categorical statements as to the validity, reliability, and efficacy of the use of hypnosis for enhancing recall. In effect, they vouch for the truthfulness of their hypnotic subjects. An expert, such as I, who attacks the credibility of the evidence, can in all honesty only testify that the hypnosis has contaminated the evidence in such a manner that it is impossible for him, or anyone else, including the trier of fact, to determine the veracity of the hypnotically influenced testimony. Hence, a strong positive opinion of the state's expert is pitted against the somewhat implausible, but I believe correct, claim by the defense expert that he does not know the truth and that neither he nor the trier of fact can ever find out.

Reasonable Medical Certainty,
Diagnostic Thresholds,
and Definitions of
Mental Illness in the Legal Context

[1985]

Dr Seymour Pollack frequently used the phrase "reasonable medical certainty" in his forensic reports and in his expert testimony. In at least two articles, he discussed at some length what he meant by that phrase and his rationale for its use:

> I also believe that the forensic psychiatrist should be held to a higher level of proof in his psychiatric-legal opinion-making than is customarily required. We need more certainty in determining a mental state or psychopathological condition for legal purposes than we do in identifying it for treatment purposes.[1]

Pollack justified the need for this higher level of proof in forensic psychiatry in the following way:

> The treating psychiatrist can change his initial clinical impression as a result of his ongoing relationship with the patient and his evaluation of response to treatment. Such monitoring is difficult, if not impossible, in the usual practice of forensic psychiatry. Also, the legal consequences of judicial decisions based on psychiatric opinion may be quite serious. If the psychiatric opinion is to be influential in determining the final decision, it should be offered with as high a level of confidence as possible.[2]

Pollack accepted as valid differences between clinical, social, and legal definitions of mental illness:

> To some extent all forensic psychiatrists experience conflict in being required to use legal definitions and concepts of mental illness that differ from those definitions and concepts traditionally used for treatment purposes.[3]

211

Pollock also accepted a differential threshold for the diagnosis of mental illness for treatment purposes and for legal purposes. Recognizing the problem of false positives, he agreed that the risk of overinclusion and overprediction is more desirable than overlooking mental illness. He added, however:

> By contrast, however, the threshold for legal definition of mental illness is considerably higher than that for treatment definition. In other words, fewer people are identified as mentally ill for legal purposes than mentally ill for treatment purposes.[4]

Pollack's position is bolstered by the assertion of some appellate courts that have adopted a similar distinction between clinical and legal definitions of mental illness. For example, the Court of Appeals for the District of Columbia Circuit, in *McDonald v. United States*, stated:

> What psychiatrists may consider a "mental disease or defect" for clinical purposes, where their concern is treatment, may or may not be the same as mental disease or defect for the jury's purpose in determining criminal responsibility. Consequently, for that purpose the jury should be told that a mental disease or defect includes any abnormal condition of the mind which substantially affects mental or emotional processes and substantially impairs behavior controls.[5]

The original Model Penal Code of the American Law Institute test of insanity also includes a legal definition of mental disease in its second paragraph, the caveat, which states, "[T]he terms 'mental disease or defect' do not include an abnormality manifested only by repeated criminal or otherwise anti-social conduct."[6]

In this chapter I discuss the following questions: (1) What is meant by the phrase "reasonable medical certainty," and should there be a higher level of proof for psychiatric diagnoses in the legal context than in the clinical context? (2) Should the threshold for the diagnosis of psychiatric illness be higher and the definition and diagnostic criteria be different in the legal context than they are in the clinical context?

Reasonable Medical Certainty

I believe Pollack's concept of reasonable medical certainty is valuable because, without such an expression of the level of confidence of the psychiatric expert witness, it is difficult, if not impossible, to relate medical testimony to the traditional levels of evidentiary proof.

These traditional levels of proof are (1) probable cause, the lowest level; (2) preponderance of evidence, that is, 51%; (3) clear and convincing evidence, that is, more than preponderance, but less than beyond a reasonable doubt; and (4) proof beyond a reasonable doubt, or at least 90%.

Each legal process that calls for expert psychiatric testimony has its own requirement for level of proof. For example, very short-term commitments usually require only probable cause; longer commitments are required by the United States Supreme Court to be proven by clear and convincing evidence.[7] The California Supreme Court requires proof beyond a reasonable doubt for conservatorship proceedings and long-term commitment.[8] Criminal convictions always require proof beyond a reasonable doubt, yet a criminal defendant in most jurisdictions can be exculpated by proof of insanity by a preponderance of evidence.

Reasonable medical certainty, in my opinion, should express the psychiatrist's highest level of confidence in the validity and reliability of his opinion. This level of confidence must, necessarily, be formulated within the matrix of clinical experience and scientific knowledge. It cannot be directly translated into the legal scale of levels of proof. It is the obligation of the trier of fact, rather than the expert witness, to make that translation in its decision of the ultimate issue, the verdict.

Confidence in the validity of a clinical opinion rests on a dual foundation: the validity of the underlying scientific knowledge about the issue in question and the validity and reliability of the application of that scientific knowledge to the particular case.

To illustrate, for a psychiatrist to express an opinion with reasonable medical certainty that a given individual is suffering from schizophrenia requires that there be a fund of knowledge about the condition known as schizophrenia. This fund of knowledge must not be idiosyncratic to the particular expert but must be knowledge generally shared by the relevant scientific community. There must be generally agreed on definitions of schizophrenia, and the parameters of the condition must be reasonably well defined. There must be minimal conditions (i.e., symptoms and manifestations) present to warrant the diagnosis and also criteria that permit one to distinguish schizophrenia from other conditions.

Without this underlying fund of scientific knowledge, there can be no reasonable medical certainty. But this underlying knowledge is not in itself sufficient. There must be the application of this knowledge to the particular individual. Thus, the psychiatric expert must express his confidence in the existence of a condition known as schizophrenia and the known effects of that condition on human behavior. He must then claim a high probability that the individual in question actually has that condition and that the inferences he has made concerning the effects that condition has had on the behavior of that individual are clinically justified. Only then can he claim reasonable medical certainty for his opinion.

I emphasize that an expert opinion, expressed in such terms is, of necessity, a clinical and scientific judgment, not a legal judgment, and that no concessions should have to be made to legal standards or definitions. Legal standards and definitions come into play when clinical opinion, expressed with its appropriate level of clinical probability, is interpolated into the ultimate issue. Thus, in a criminal trial, the psychiatrist may express his opinion that a defendant is mentally ill, that the defendant is suffering from chronic paranoid schizophrenia, that his illness existed throughout a particular period of time, and that it affected the defendant's thinking, feeling, judgment, control, and behavior in certain ways. By using strictly clinical and scientific criteria, the expert forms his opinion to the highest possible level of probability—to the level, it is hoped, of reasonable medical certainty.

To make legal inferences from this clinical information requires knowledge and the use of appropriate legal definitions and criteria. The type of legal inference permitted to expert witnesses will vary; and, if it reaches the ultimate question, and depending on the legal issue and the particular jurisdiction, it may be prohibited. For example, in a criminal trial on the issue of insanity as defined by the American Law Institute rule, the psychiatrist may properly express his opinion on the existence and nature of the defendant's mental illness, how the mental illness affected the defendant's ability to appreciate the criminality of his conduct or his ability to conform his behavior to the requirements of the law; but the psychiatrist may not, in many jurisdictions, express an opinion that the defendant is either sane or insane. Note that, while the existence and nature of mental illness are determined by clinical psychiatric criteria, concepts such as "appreciate the criminality of his conduct" or "ability to conform his behavior to the requirements of the law" are legal issues, and the expert must accept the legal constraints on their meanings.

Some authorities would contend that all components of an ultimate issue are themselves ultimate issues and thus denied to the expert witness. They say that, because "mental disease or defect" is a component of the ultimate issue of insanity, it is itself an ultimate issue that can be decided only by the jury. In this view, a psychiatrist should not be allowed to state whether the defendant does or does not suffer from a mental illness nor give an opinion about any other component of the legal issue before the jury. He would be permitted, however, to describe the psychopathology demonstrated by the defendant and the jury (or judge) would decide whether a mental disease or defect existed.

I believe this position is incorrect and that it caricatures, rather than expresses, the intent of the law. The ultimate issue, in this example, is expressed in the verdict: guilty, not guilty, or not guilty by reason of insanity. The components of this ultimate issue are issues, but not ultimate issues. To deny an expert his expression of opinion about these component issues is to limit his role so seriously that one may question whether it might not be wiser to eliminate the expert altogether from the legal process.

The assertion has also been made that psychiatrists have no expertise outside of strictly clinical issues and that they should not be permitted to testify on any legal issues, even issues that are not the ultimate ones. A psychiatrist should, therefore, describe in his testimony the mental condition of the subject but leave all inferences and legal issues to others. This may well be so in the case of a psychiatrist practitioner who has had no experience outside of the clinical realm. But the designation "forensic psychiatrist" implies a knowledge, skill, and expertise that includes the kinds of inferences required for making a rational legal decision, and most certainly he should possess an in-depth knowledge of the legal definitions, standards, and procedures relevant to the case.

Many legal terms have specialized meanings that differ from their ordinary meaning. For example, "malice aforethought" does not necessarily denote anything resembling the ordinary meaning of malice or malicious, nor does it necessarily imply premeditation. Many legal terms have been modified by judicial decisions or statutes that apply only to certain jurisdictions. If a psychiatrist is not familiar with the proper meaning of these terms and uses them incorrectly, his expertise as a forensic psychiatrist should certainly be questioned.

An expert witness may not be able at all times, on all issues, to reach the level of confidence implied by reasonable medical certainty. He may testify, for example, that schizophrenia is, with reasonable medical certainty, an illness manifested by delusions and hallucinations, impaired judgment, and distorted affect. But he may also qualify his opinion by stating that it has not been possible to determine with that level of confidence whether the defendant is actually suffering from that condition. If the clinical facts warrant, he can testify that the defendant has many of the symptoms usually associated with schizophrenia, but that certain symptoms are those found in manic–depressive psychosis and that it is not possible to give more than a probability answer (say, two to one odds) that the defendant is schizophrenic. He may also properly state that, regardless of the uncertainties of the diagnosis, he is of the opinion, with reasonable medical certainty, that there existed at the time in question an impairment of judgment and self-control that made it impossible for the defendant to control his behavior as would a normal person. One can conceive of all possible mixtures of varying levels of probability and uncertainty with some difficult, complex cases. Yet, for each significant element of the expert's testimony, he communicates to the trier of fact, his level of confidence.

I do not think that the law requires a higher level of proof from psychiatric experts than they would normally use in clinical practice. Experts can express only the levels of proof that their clinical observations and scientific knowledge allow, but it is exceedingly important that they accurately communicate to the trier of fact the levels that do realistically exist for each component of his testimony.

This is, I believe, what Seymour Pollack was striving for in developing his concept of reasonable medical certainty. I believe, however, that it was an error for him to link this with other issues, such as a legal or social threshold for diagnosis of mental illness that differs from the clinical threshold, or that the definition of mental illness can differ in the legal context from that which has been accepted in the clinical context.

The Threshold and Definition of Mental Illness

I believe it is wrong to concede any threshold definition of mental illness other than that determined by scientific and clinical knowledge. We may agree that the present state of our knowledge does not allow us to define precisely that threshold in many cases. We may even agree that with some forms of emotional and psychologic disorders it is likely that no threshold exists. There is much valid clinical information suggesting that many psychopathologic conditions exist on a spectrum that extends from normalcy, on one hand, to serious disturbance, on the other, with no clear delineation of the normal from the abnormal. But other conditions, and I believe the major psychoses to be such, can be, or ought to be, clearly differentiated from the normal, with a diagnostic threshold established by appropriate clinical experience.

DSM-III represents a good start in this direction, and the diagnostic criteria that are there set forth can represent, *for the time being*, the diagnostic thresholds with reasonable medical certainty. Obviously, they are not the final word, for, as for all scientific knowledge, constant revision and refinement are required.

This clinical threshold is the only threshold for the definition of mental illness that I am prepared to recognize. I do accept, however, that there are other thresholds for social and legal intervention in the lives of mentally ill persons and that those thresholds can be much higher (or conceivably lower) than are customary for clinical interventions. Thus, I insist that the diagnosis of mental illness is strictly a clinical matter to be determined in all instances by clinical criteria and definitions. But the point at which society determines a mentally ill person to be sufficiently disabled to warrant invoking a *parens patriae* intervention is a social and legal decision whose threshold can be much higher than that required to establish a diagnosis of mental illness. Similarly, it is not up to the law to establish the threshold for the existence of mental illness in a criminal defendant. But it is up to the law to determine the particular forms and degree of psychopathology it will recognize as exculpatory.

The three distinguished psychiatrists who participated in the drafting of the American Law Institute rule of insanity in the Model Penal Code emphatically opposed the caveat paragraph. They maintained that it is not the business of the law to decide what is or is not a mental disease.[9] They were quite right; it is no more within the province of the law to define mental illness than it is within the province of medicine to define exculpatory insanity.

It was the intention of the committee that drafted the ALI rule to exclude from the insanity defense persons suffering from sociopathic personality disorders and who were not otherwise mentally ill. This exclusion could have been accomplished without intruding on clinical territory by directly specifying those conditions, mental illness or not, which do not exculpate even if they meet other criteria, such as causing the defendant to lack the ability to appreciate the wrongfulness of his conduct. One may challenge the wisdom of such a restriction, but not the right of the law to so restrict the application of the insanity defense or any other legal intervention it so chooses.

Because the net effect is the same, one might question whether this is only a trivial distinction from the actual draft of the ALI rule. It is precisely this failure to distinguish territories, however, that has led to so much confusion and lack of understanding of the proper role and function of the expert witness. The law has usurped medical functions and psychiatry tends to usurp legal functions, to the disadvantage and mutual recriminations of both disciplines.

Conclusions

The phrase "reasonable medical certainty" is a valid and valuable expression of the level of confidence maintained by the psychiatric expert witness for his opinions. It is a clinical concept with roots in both the relevant fund of scientific knowledge and the specific clinical observations of the psychiatrist. Although consideration by the trier of fact of this clinical level of confidence is relevant to the legal standard of proof, it is not synonymous or contiguous with any of these legal standards. The definitions of mental illness and the criteria for diagnosis should be determined solely by scientific and clinical standards, and the law should not encroach on scientific territory by creating its own definitions of mental illness and its own threshold levels.

The ultimate issue to be decided by the trier of fact contains a variety of component issues. Some of these component issues are strictly matters of science and clinical knowledge; others are purely legal; some are, perhaps, hybrid. Even though a psychiatric expert may be prohibited from expressing an opinion about the ultimate issue, he should not be prevented from expressing opinions about the component issues, provided he does, in truth, possess the requisite expertise.

Addendum

California appellate courts have increasingly indicated that, at least in medical negligence cases, the proper word is "probability" rather than "certainty" (*Barton v. Owen*, 71 Cal. App.3d 484; 139 Cal. Rptr. 494). I favor dropping the phrase "reasonable medical certainty" altogether and have experts testify only as to "reasonable medical probability." This would be more in accordance with scientific reality. The issues discussed in this article would not change, however; they would be equally relevant to reasonable medical probability.

Notes

[1]Pollack, S. (1974), The role of psychiatry in the rule of law. In: *Forensic Psychiatry in the Defense of Diminished Capacity*. Los Angeles: University of Southern California Press.

[2]Pollack, S. (1971), Principles of forensic psychiatry for psychiatric-legal opinion-making. In: *Legal Medicine Annual,* ed. C. Wecht. New York: Appleton-Century-Crofts.

[3]Pollack, op. cit., sup. note 1, p. 195.

[4]Ibid., p. 196.

[5]*McDonald v. United States,* 312 F.2d 847, 851 (D.C. Cir. 1962)

[6]See *Wade v. United States,* 426 F.2d 64, 72 (9th Cir. 1970) for discussion of this caveat and reasons for its rejection.

[7]*Addington v. Texas,* 441 U.S. 418, 99 S.Ct. 1804, 60 L.Ed. 323 (1979).

[8]*Conservatorship of Rotlet,* 23 Cal. 3d 219, 152 Cal. Rptr. 425, 590 P.2d I (1979).

[9]Freedman, L. Z., Guttmacher, M. & Overholser, W. (1961), Mental disease or defect excluding responsibility: A psychiatric view of the American law institute model penal code proposal. *Amer. J. Psychiat.,* 118:32–34.

The Fallacy of the Impartial Expert

[1959]

I t is generally assumed that the battle of the experts—that always disconcerting and often sensational disagreement of psychiatrists in testifying on issues of legal insanity and criminal responsibility—could be eliminated through the device of the neutral or impartial expert.

Such neutral expert witnesses are supposedly entirely outside the traditional adversary system of the courts. Not in the employment of either the defense or the prosecution, but acting in the name of the court, such witnesses presumedly can remain detached and objective. Disagreement between expert witnesses is supposed to be greatly reduced, thereby aiding the court in reaching a higher level of fair, just, and impartial decisions.

Elimination of the battle of the experts would, it is claimed, much improve the public relations of the psychiatric profession. For a considerable segment of the population, the only direct contact with psychiatry and psychiatrists is that obtained through sensational trial reports in the newspapers, radio, and television. It is entirely understandable that this segment of the population regards psychiatry as a most uncertain affair, with violent disagreement, contradictory opinions, and dubious ethics the hallmarks of its practitioners.

I would guess that, today, nine-tenths of the psychiatrists in this country would probably unhesitatingly agree to the desirability of removing psychiatric experts from the legal adversary system. It is the purpose of this paper to challenge this widespread agreement. It is proper that this discussion take the form of an editorial, rather than that of a scientific paper. For opinions pro and con on this matter can hardly be considered as objective facts to be solemnly presented as a scientific advance. Quite properly they are to be considered as personal opinions of the author and nothing more.

It is a fiction of the law that only the immediate parties to a legal action—the defendant and the plaintiff or prosecutor and their counsel—are adversaries. All others—the judge, the jury, and the witnesses—are not to be partisan. All witnesses, both expert and lay witnesses of fact, are sworn to tell the truth, the whole truth, and nothing but the truth. This truth, as revealed in the testimony of the witnesses, may favor one or the other side, but the witnesses may not. That this assumption is a fiction, not a reality, is evidenced by the convention of labeling witnesses as *for* the defendant or *for* the prosection.

I will thus concede at the outset that the expert witness called by either adversary is likely to be biased to some degree, that his opinions are not truly impartial, and that he himself, as a party to the adversary system, becomes to a certain degree an advocate. I concede this with full awareness that both legal and medical codes of ethics alike demand impartiality of the expert witness, irrespective of the side that calls him. The desirability of such an ethical ideal must not blind us to the reality that the ideal is seldom, if ever, achieved.

The crude charge is sometimes asserted that under the adversary system expert witnesses sell their opinions. Because they are paid by one or the other side, they are accused of prostituting their medical knowledge by providing untruthful testimony in return for the money they are paid. This charge is too base to defend by more than just a simple statement: I do not believe that this happens.

Undoubtedly what does happen is that the expert witness, through his close operational identification with one side of the conflict, becomes an advocate. Because his testimony, in fact, supports one side of the legal battle, he, if he is at all human, must necessarily identify himself with his own opinion, and subjectively desire that "his side" win. This identification can vary from deliberate, conscious participation in the planning of the legal strategy with the lawyers who call upon him for expert advice and opinion, to an aloof, detached facsimile of impartiality that masks his secret hope for victory of his own opinion. Such a detached witness may be totally unconscious of the innumerable subtle distortions and biases in his testimony that spring from this wish to triumph.

This is well recognized by our courts of law. It is the duty of the counsel for the opposing side to cross-examine the witness to reveal these distortions and biases and to attempt to impeach his testimony. It is wholly legitimate to impeach the testimony through an attack on the witness himself—that is, by eliciting evidence to show that the witness is not the expert he proclaims himself to be; that the clinical facts on which the expert bases his opinions are not complete or may not even be true; that the skill and knowledge of the expert in his professional field are deficient; and that his expert opinions are faulty and unwarranted. Under such cross-examination or through redirect examination by the counsel who engaged him, the expert is expected to defend his expert status, his clinical facts, and his professional knowledge and to justify his opinions. It is absurd to pretend that the psychiatric expert remains neutral under such a legal procedure. For the sake of his own ego integrity, he must, I repeat, identify himself with his own opinions and become the advocate of those opinions. But to the degree that those opinions favor one side or the other, the witness loses his presumed impartiality.

Certain other factors also contribute to the lack of impartiality of court-appointed experts. Let us place these issues within the framework of a specific case. I deliberately choose a trial in which all elements are greatly exaggerated. I do not mean that the following description of the trial is exaggerated, for the description of what occurred is entirely accurate. But the facts of the case and the circumstances of the expert examinations and testimony are far more extreme than is usual.

A certain California multimillionaire was charged with perverse sexual acts on two adolescent boys. It was a matter of common public knowledge that the defendant had overtly and unashamedly practiced homosexuality for many years, but he had never previously been accused of seducing children. He pleaded not guilty by reason of insanity. The defendant had no insight into his mental illness, nor did he consider himself insane in any sense of the word. He consented to the plea, however, at the insistence of his attorneys and his family. Practically unlimited sums of money were available for his defense. An exceptionally high-powered battery of attorneys, headed by the most outstanding criminal lawyer in the area, represented him. He was quickly convicted of the acts charged in the indictment, for the evidence was conclusive. Then he was tried on the question of his insanity, as is required by the peculiar split-trial system used in California. A jury trial had been waived.

Two court-appointed psychiatrists had examined him and submitted reports to the court stating the he was sane under the M'Naghten rules and that he was a sociopath, manifesting a sexual deviation that made him a menace to society; hence he came under the California sexual psychopathy law permitting indefinite confinement.

Two other psychiatrists, who had been engaged by the defense, testified that they had examined the defendant and found him to be suffering from a major psychosis; that he was insane under the M'Naghten rules; that his long-standing homosexuality, and the specific perverse sexual acts with the children, were symptoms of his psychosis; and that he was not a sociopath or a sexual psychopath.

The court-appointed psychiatrists received the usual fee for their examinations and time spent in court, probably not more than $50 or $100 each; the two defense psychiatrists each were paid several thousand dollars for their examinations and time in court.

Here we have an extreme instance of the battle of the experts. How to explain the disparate testimony of the experts? Would the verdict of the judge have been more just if all four psychiatrists had been neutral? What role did the sharp discrepancy in fees paid to the witnesses play?

The differences in the diagnoses reached by the court-appointed witnesses and the defense witnesses hinged largely on the question of whether certain statements asserted by the defendant were actually delusions or whether they were either true, or possible exaggerations, or perhaps even deliberate lies. The neutral experts had only the usual hour or so of examination time, and no sources of information outside the defendant's statements to formulate their opinion on this very difficult question. The defendant had no intention of admitting even the possibility that he might be suffering from a psychotic thinking disorder. He went to great lengths to rationalize his peculiar thoughts and to justify his conduct, both past and present, as the actions of a sane person who chose voluntarily to lead an eccentric life. He concealed from the court-appointed psychiatrists the details of his past history, which included hospitalization in private sanitariums in England and in France on nine previous occasions.

It was certainly no reflection on the clinical abilities of the two neutral experts that they reached the conclusions they did. Under the limited circumstances of their examination and with the restricted information that they had access to, it is difficult to imagine how they could have reached any other conclusions.

On the other hand, the defense psychiatrists were paid to spend practically unlimited time and to use all possible clinical facilities in their study of the defendant. Batteries of psychological tests were administered. An exhaustive neurological investigation was done, including spinal puncture and an EEG (certain symptoms suggested general paresis). An attorney was dispatched to Europe to obtain copies of the previous hospital records and to take depositions from all the European physicians who had treated him over a period of some 30 years. The aged mother of the defendant was brought to California from her home in Europe and made available for a social history. When the clinical evidence was all in, the conclusion was inescapable that this man was psychotic and not responsible for his actions. The judge agreed and found him not guilty by reason of insanity, and he was committed to a state hospital.

Beyond doubt the verdict was just. The great wealth of the defendant was not used to purchase biased and untruthful testimony from dubious experts. Rather it was used to make certain that every scrap of evidence, every clinical possibility, was exhaustively investigated, and that nothing was overlooked. The injustice inherent in this extreme example is, of course, if this defendant had been a poor man he would have probably been found to be sane and would have been imprisoned.

The assumption is often made that the elimination of adversary expert witnesses will lead to testimony of greater objectivity, thoroughness, and accuracy. Corollary to this assumption is the implication that examinations performed by adversary witnesses are neither objective, thorough, nor accurate. In our case of the millionaire sex offender, just the opposite was true. But how about ordinary cases? It is very difficult to give a definite answer to this question without having some basis of statistical information. I believe, however, that there are logical reasons to infer that, generally, privately funded psychiatric investigations done for the defense are likely to be more thorough than are those done by ordinary court-appointed psychiatrists. The latter are apt to approach the examination situation in a routine manner, as a job to be done, so to speak, and to restrict their time, energy, and thought on a case to a level determined by the fees usually paid for this work. The public funds available to court-appointed psychiatrists are very limited, the courts taking it for granted that the experts should be able to perform an adequate examination and reach a conclusion in one or two hours. Rarely is money available for auxiliary examinations, such as projective techniques. That there are a few notable exceptions to this situation does not alter the general inference. One exception is the City of Baltimore, where, under the dedicated direction of Dr. Manfred Guttmacher, a court clinic has evolved by which any defendant has available to him a type of psychiatric investigation approaching that which was utilized for the millionaire defendant described earlier. Another exception is in Washington, DC, where Dr. Winfred Overholser has followed the great Dr. William Alanson White in developing St. Elizabeths Hospital into an outstanding center for medicolegal psychiatric training and research.

These special instances aside, it is clear that the psychiatrist engaged by defense counsel is in a quite different position from that occupied by the usual court-appointed expert. Whatever money can conceivably be scraped together by the defendant or his family is used freely to reimburse the psychiatrist for whatever time he feels necessary to perform an adequate examination and investigation. Occasionally, a defense counsel, particularly a public defender, may call on a psychiatrist with the express understanding that only a very limited amount is available for examination time. The psychiatrist is under no obligation to accept the case and may decline, or as very often happens (especially when the case is unusual or challenging) the psychiatrist may accept the case, having agreed in advance to spend whatever time is necessary without adequate remuneration.

In short, I think it is possible to make the generalization that court appointments tend to be handled by psychiatrists as a kind of routine job, to which, in the face of totally unreasonable time restrictions, they bring a mediocre level of clinical competence. The psychiatrist called by the defense, on the other hand, is much more apt to regard the examination situation as a highly challenging task, to which he devotes considerable time and effort, with or without adequate remuneration. If for his own personal reasons he cannot enter into the case on this superior level, he is likely to turn it down altogether rather than handle it in a merely routine manner.

Does the fact that a psychiatrist is called as a witness for the court, that he is neither directly involved with the prosecution nor the defense, make it more likely that his opinion is less biased and more truthful and objective than that of the adversary witness? I concede that the defense psychiatrist is apt to be biased in favor of the side that has engaged him. It is my opinion that court-appointed experts are consistently biased in favor of the prosecution. Court-appointed psychiatrists are seldom selected randomly from the universe of the psychiatric population. Certain psychiatrists tend to be appointed over and over again. These are generally men who have an active interest in forensic psychiatry. More often than not they tend to be Kraepelinian and less dynamic in their approach to their cases. They are often drawn from the ranks of administrative psychiatry, an area deficient in psychoanalytically oriented therapists. They are less inclined to probe deeply, more inclined to accept uncritically surface manifestations, and are prone to interpret the legal criteria for insanity in a narrowly restricted way. (Many of my forensic psychiatrist friends will take me to task for making these assertions—I will merely tell them that they are the exceptions who prove the rule.)

A second reason for this biased selection of court-appointed experts is the unfortunate fact that dynamically oriented psychotherapists with liberal, enlightened, and nonmoralistic attitudes toward mental illness and criminal behavior shamefully avoid their social responsibility to participate in the administration of justice. They make it clearly known that they would not accept appointment as expert witness, and, by exhibiting an abysmal ignorance of even the basic principles of forensic psychiatry, they ensure that they will not even be asked.

Third, in many communities, the district attorney has an undue influence over the courts in the selection of the panels from which court-appointed experts are drawn. Psychiatrists who have liberal views, as revealed through their testimony in previous cases, may be systematically excluded from appointment by the court. It is only natural for the district attorney to recommend a panel of psychiatrists who are known to be reliable in expressing extremely conservative opinions and who follow the strictest possible interpretation of the M'Naghten rules. Granted that the defense psychiatrist is chosen by counsel precisely because he is liberal and advanced in his views. And those psychiatrists who do a great deal of defense work are apt to be unconsciously identified with the defendant, overly sympathetic, and motivated to be an advocate for the underdog. But I assert that those psychiatrists who seek out and tend to receive appointment by the court as so-called impartial witnesses have an equal probability of being overly identified with authority, being a sort of watch-dog of the public morals, and motivated towards seeing that no criminal "gets away with anything."

The defense of insanity is nearly always raised in crimes of violence, especially homicide. Such acts of violence arouse strong emotions within everyone, and psychiatrists are no exception. Premature and prejudicial judgments must inevitably occur. Such emotions demand that one identify oneself with either the defendant or the authority of society, usually the latter. The determining factors that will decide the direction of the identification frequently have less to do with the facts and circumstances of the crime and criminal than with the predispositions and temperament of the observing individual. It is far-fetched to suppose that even an experienced psychiatrist remains neutral in his evaluation of acts of violence and murder.

So I claim that there is no such thing as a neutral, impartial witness. No matter whether a psychiatrist is engaged by the defense or by the prosecution or is allowed to remain completely outside the system of adversary conflict, he is bound to be biased and partial and strongly motivated toward advocacy of his particular prejudiced point of view.

This lack of impartiality of expert witnesses need not be a serious obstacle to the administration of justice. It is inherent in our traditional system of adversary procedure that both sides be presented to the jury and the jury is to choose within the conflict of evidence that side which is most credible. Serious injustice may occur, however, when an adversary witness is disguised as a neutral witness. When actual partiality is masked as impartiality, the judge and jury are deceived and misled. The response is less to the credibility of the witness and the logic of his testimony and more to his status as a so-called neutral. In Massachusetts, where the Briggs law has been in operation for a good many years, it is still permissible for the defense to call its own expert witnesses. But advocates of the neutral system of expert testimony use as one of their chief arguments the fact that juries almost invariably accept the opinions of neutral experts. Neutrality advocates consider it progress that under such circumstances it is hardly worthwhile for the defense to call in its own experts. Thus the battle of the experts is eliminated. But does this provide a better brand of justice than does the adversary method? I doubt it. In a legal situation where impartiality is impossible, let us frankly label the witness for what he is, and let the jury choose. To be sure, there will be instances of bad choice, of incorrect, illogical, or unjust verdicts. But to disguise the partisan character of the expert through status labels of neutrality and court appointment will not contribute to a more rational jury decision.

Sending the defendant to a state hospital, supposedly an independent agency for medicolegal evaluation, does not remedy this situation. In fact, it may only further distort the issues. For example, a defendant is committed to a public hospital for observation and is detained there for, let us say, a period of three months. He is assigned to a staff physician, who takes a history and performs a mental examination. Better hospitals will also obtain a social history from the family and write for records of previous medical care. The patient is presented to the staff at least once and usually several times; the case is discussed; a decision is reached; and a report is sent to the court. The staff physician or an administrative official of the hospital will appear in court as a witness. He will testify that the defendant has been under continual observation for the three months, that he has been thoroughly examined, and that the hospital staff has agreed as to the diagnosis and legal responsibility of the defendant.

On the surface, this would seem like a superior solution. Months of observation time are certainly better than a few hours of clinical examination, and the opinion of an entire hospital staff is more reliable than that of a single examiner. It is understandable why a judge or juror would give much greater weight to the testimony of such an institutional report than they would to that of an adversary expert.

A closer scrutiny of the institutional examination procedure, however, casts considerable doubt on whether this greater weight is justified. In the first place, it is not true that the defendant has been under observation for the period of time claimed. More likely the ward physician has spent only from one to a few hours in direct contact with the patient. All public hospitals are extremely busy places, with a heavy overload of patients. Ward physicians invariably have many more patients than they can adequately examine and care for. Time is very precious and must be strictly rationed among the patients. Medicolegal cases in the average mental hospital or psychopathic ward of the large city hospital are not welcomed with enthusiasm. Because there is no treatment contemplated, but merely diagnosis and medicolegal evaluation, there is apt to be much less time and interest devoted to the case. Most physicians are treatment oriented; justifiably, the hospital physician regards the need of those patients who are hospitalized for treatment purposes as taking priority over those who are there merely for diagnostic or custodial purposes. Over and over again I have examined hospital records of forensic cases and found the clinical investigation to be second rate compared with the quality of professional care provided for active treatment cases. I see little to choose between a one- or two-hour examination done in the hospital followed by three months of nonobservational custodial care and the same amount of time spent by an ordinary court-appointed examiner in the county jail setting. Yet the court and jury are misled into believing that the defendant has been subject to an exhaustive scrutiny for a prolonged period of time by the full hospital staff.

It is customary in most public mental hospitals to present the case at a staff conference. Each staff member, having listened to an abstract of the history and examination findings, then expresses his opinion. There may be varying amounts of discussion and then a sort of vote is taken. In some hospitals, the majority vote decides the issue. In others, the superintendent or the physician in charge of the conference has the final say. Many different systems are used. But whatever method is used in reaching a decision, the report that goes to the court almost invariably implies that the decision was unanimous.

Some time ago, a case I had occasion to look into involved a most difficult diagnostic problem. He was a 17-year-old boy, who, while confined as a patient in a state hospital, had strangled another patient. He was regarded as too mentally ill to be subject to trial and was sent by the court to another state hospital for medicolegal observation. The diagnostic choices lay between schizophrenia and a schizoid personality disorder. Which diagnosis was made would naturally have great bearing on his criminal responsibility. When the case was presented to the staff conference, there was great division of opinion among the staff physicians. It was recommended that he be returned to his ward for further observation. In a few months, he was staffed again. And again there was no agreement. After repeated staffing over a period of a year, it was agreed that further observation was futile and that a diagnosis would have to be agreed on. The vote was five to four in favor of psychopathy. A report was then sent the court stating that this diagnosis had been made, following a year's observation, and that the patient was now sane and could stand trial. The wording of the report clearly implied that the diagnosis was definitely established and that there was full agreement. There was no reference to the uncertainty of the actual diagnostic formulation, nor was any information conveyed to the court that the hospital staff were strongly divided, sometimes voting one way and sometimes the other. With such a report, the court erroneously assumed that the matter was settled beyond dispute.

What we have here, of course, is nothing else than the familiar star-chamber proceeding. The hospital staff usurped the function of the jury and settled the whole matter within the hospital star-chamber, and the court was then deprived of the full evidence, the conflict of medical opinion, and the reasonable doubt of the correctness of the diagnosis and the boy's legal responsibility.

Such hospital reports are false and misleading and certainly do not contribute to the proper administration of justice. The only thing they seem to accomplish is to create the illusion that psychiatrists are more consistent, more omniscient, and more unanimous than they actually are.

Furthermore, public mental hospitals are not the independent agencies they claim to be. In a criminal case the adversary to the defendant is the People of the State. The institutional psychiatrist is a full-time employee of the People of the State. It is only logical to suppose that persons who are permanently employed by the state identify themselves with that state and are prejudiced in its favor. Because of the hierarchical system within the hospital, the attitude of the hospital superintendent tends to influence unduly the decisions of the entire staff. The hospital superintendent, as a permanent state employee, with ambitions within the state bureaucratic system, may be totally identified with the authority of the state. He may be an excellent hospital administrator yet be completely out of touch with modern psychiatric attitudes toward criminal behavior or responsibility. Such an administrator may not have actually practiced clinical psychiatry for many years. He may give his staff a free hand in ordinary clinical decisions; but he considers medicolegal evaluation as basically administrative and within his province. He may employ only outmoded, moralistic, or even theological criteria for his evaluation of questions of legal responsibility. As a consequence, what purports to be the impartial decision of a group of doctors may in fact be the expression of only a particular doctor's prejudice or limited clinical knowledge.

Again, I reiterate, there are exceptions. There are hospitals where none of the foregoing criticisms would apply. But the advocates of the impartial-witness system seem to take for granted that hospital observation in all cases will automatically lead to a more accurate psychiatric conclusion and, therefore, to a superior type of justice.

Everyone would concede, I think, that the ideal solution would be to provide every defendant with the type of clinical investigation that was afforded to the millionaire defendant of our earlier example. Unlimited funds would be available for investigational purposes, and only the most competent and experienced witnesses, well skilled in the presentation of technical clinical data to lay audiences, would be employed in the courtroom. Obviously, this is not going to be the case in the foreseeable future. The average defendant will be examined and evaluated in a highly abbreviated procedure by experts with varying degrees of skill, experience, bias, and partiality.

The traditional adversary system of calling witnesses for each side and then examining them by direct and cross-examination has evolved for the purpose of exposing these shortcomings and biases. The court and jury are then free to take them into consideration in attaching appropriate weight to the testimony of each witness. To use a system in which expert witnesses are labeled as "impartial" in no way eliminates its shortcomings; it merely conceals them from the jury and creates the illusion of psychiatric omniscience. Such illusions may be good for the public relations of psychiatry, but they are not good for the administration of justice.

If and when the time comes that the following conditions are met, I would freely abandon the adversary system insofar as it applies to problems of mental illness:

(1) Each defendant, rich or poor, rural or urban, in an enlightened community or in a backward community, can be reasonably guaranteed the type of exhaustive clinical investigation that is now available to only a few fortunate defendants.

(2) All expert witnesses are highly trained and experienced and adept in transmitting their findings to the court.

(3) Observation hospitals are staffed with dynamically oriented psychiatrists who fully appreciate the important specific role they play in the administration of justice.

(4) Such psychiatrists, through their own enlightenment and self-understanding, can be relied on to detach themselves from their own prejudices and refrain from homogenizing their moral judgments with their medical opinions.[1]

(5) Our whole profession of psychiatry is less preoccupied with proving its own omniscience, and sufficiently secure in its public status, that it is

unafraid to expose its deficiencies of knowledge about some of the most fundamental problems of human nature.

(6) Forensic psychiatrists are permitted to operate within a legal framework that allows them to apply their professional judgment to appropriate questions of psychological reality and not to philosophical and theological rules and syllogisms—when they can apply their knowledge to human reality instead of legal fiction.

(7) Society is able to leave behind its archaic need for vengeance and retribution and learn that its own best protection is inextricably woven in with the rehabilitation of individual deviants; that to degrade any member of that society with either the formal vengeance of punishment or the stigmata of legal insanity is to degrade only itself.

Then and only then would I admit the superiority of the impartial expert over the adversary witness. But, then, if such a utopia were to be achieved, perhaps there would be no need for experts.

Note

[1] Rood, R. S. (1959), Comment on California Assembly bill 437: Legal insanity. *Amer. J. Psychiat.*, 115:1038. See also Watson, A. S. (1959). Book review. *Univ. Pennsylvania L. Rev.*, 107:899.

The Psychiatrist as Expert Witness

[1983]

There are two distinct types of legal situations involving participation by psychiatrists.[1] In one situation, the psychiatrist has examined or treated a patient in usual course of clinical practice, a legal process has arisen because of some action—criminal or civil—by the patient, and the psychiatrist is required to testify about clinical findings. This may involve both factual and opinion testimony. For purposes of discussion, I designate this as "clinical testimony."

A very different situation exists when a psychiatrist is asked to perform an examination specifically for legal purposes and testify as an expert witness. I designate this as "forensic expert testimony." I also include under this rubric expert testimony that is based only on theoretical or hypothetical information and for which no psychiatric examination has been performed personally by the expert. The roles appropriate to these different legal functions by the psychiatrist are somewhat different—although overlapping—and will be discussed separately.

Clinical Testimony

The ethical and professional issues involved in clinical testimony are relatively simple: willingness to participate, proper preparation for the court appearance, adequate records, reasonable objectivity, and scrupulous honesty.

Many, if not most, therapists are reluctant to respond to the legal demand to produce their records and testify in legal proceedings in which their evidence may be legally relevant, but in which, from the perspective of the therapist, the legal demand violates therapeutic confidentiality. The view has frequently been expressed that the therapeutic process demands absolute confidentiality and that this need should supersede the requirements of the legal system.[2]

Significant ethical dilemmas arise when a legal demand for records and testimony is made on a therapist who believes that he has, or should have, the right to protect the confidentiality of all information communicated to him by his patients. There may be, in fact, no legal protection for the confidentiality of a patient's communications to his therapist in a criminal proceeding, and in a civil proceeding the patient may have intentionally or automatically waived his right of privileged communication by placing his mental state at issue.[3]

So far there has been no successful attempt to assert the absolute privilege of confidential communications of patients in psychotherapy against the subpoena demands of the law.[4] Some appellate courts, however, respect the problem sufficiently to impose careful restrictions on the exposure of confidential records, thus avoiding the wholesale, indiscriminate disclosure that sometimes occurs when lawyers go on "fishing expeditions" for information.[5] I doubt that the time will ever come when either legislatures or appellate courts will recognize an absolute privilege for confidential communications of patients in psychotherapy. Consequently, therapists must respond to legal demands in a manner that best protects the interests of their patients yet also fulfills the legal requirement for truth. In this way, they at least resolve the ethical conflict to the degree possible.

I believe it is irresponsible and unethical conduct for a psychotherapist deliberately to refuse to comply with a proper legal demand for records or testimony as a matter of principle, knowing at the same time that this refusal jeopardizes the patient's success in the legal action. I can conceive, however, of situations in which a therapist is satisfied that refusal will not harm, and may even benefit, the patient and refuses an order to breach the confidentiality of his patient. Such refusal may well be imprudent on the part of the therapist, who will have to bear the legal consequences of this decision; but it would not be, in my opinion, unethical. I do not necessarily equate ethical conduct with legally correct conduct.

Proper preparation for the court appearance is essential. A psychiatrist who goes to court and testifies in a confused, contradictory, or unconvincing manner because of lack of preparation may do great harm to the patient/litigant. An expert witness is obligated to present clinical information about the patient in clear and understandable language that will be meaningful to the trier of fact. Sometimes psychiatrists may strongly resent being compelled to subordinate their sense of professional duty to their legal obligation and will express their resentment, consciously or unconsciously, by refusing to prepare and by arrogantly testifying in incomprehensible jargon. Such conduct may well serve as a release for the therapist's feelings, but it harms the legal rights of the patient in an unprofessional and unethical manner.

Clinical records must be adequate to the task of substantiating the information to be presented. Usually a subpoena includes a demand for all clinical records. There is no legal distinction between "official" and "unofficial" records, and a psychiatrist who withholds portions of records because he or she labels them as private notes is violating the oath "to tell the whole truth. . . ." Altering records by addition, subtraction, or falsification can result in a charge of perjury against the psychiatrist.

Despite the legal consequences of tampering with records, psychiatrists sometimes do so in the belief that they are acting in the best interests of their patients. They should seriously consider the possibility that such a belief is a rationalization of their hostility and resentment toward the legal system and its compelling authority.

Reasonable objectivity must be sought, even though often not obtained (see "The Fallacy of the Impartial Expert," this volume). Scrupulous honesty is always required and the oath of the witness to tell the truth, the whole truth, and nothing but the truth applies just as much to the expert witness as to the ordinary witness-in-fact.

A psychiatrist who is giving clinical testimony about a patient treated or examined for therapeutic purposes does not depart from his traditional fiduciary relationship to the patient. The role as physician is clear, and ethical obligations to the patient, with the possible exception of confidentiality, are not altered just because the psychiatrist is required to take the witness stand; this is not so for the forensic expert.

Forensic Expert Testimony

Testifying as a forensic expert, a psychiatrist is employed by the legal system solely for legal purposes. There may or may not have been a clinical examination of a litigant; if there was, it was performed specifically for legal purposes, rather than with therapeutic intent. Usually such an examination is done at the behest of an attorney or a court. Payment may be by someone other than the subject; and control over the information elicited by the examination is not retained by either the psychiatrist or the subject of the examination. Instead, control passes to attorneys, to a court, or sometimes to the police or other government agency.

It is immediately apparent that if there is the slightest confusion in the mind of the person being examined concerning the nature of the examination—that is, whether it is therapeutic or forensic—grave ethical problems arise. One would think that the context of the examination alone would be sufficient to establish a clear-cut differentiation. In practice, this is not so. Some persons naively assume that anything a doctor does is necessarily therapeutic. Even when examined in jail by a police psychiatrist, the subject may still assume that the examination is for the purpose of helping or healing and that the traditional rules of confidentiality apply. A defendant may assume that the court-appointed psychiatrist who examines him or her relevant to a plea of insanity is there to help with the defense. Even when a person knows better and intellectually is aware of the nontherapeutic role of the examining psychiatrist, the emotional pressure of guilt, or a need for catharsis, or the absence of anyone else with whom to talk may result in a pouring forth of confidences inappropriate to the situation and against the subject's best interests.

A partial remedy is that the forensic psychiatrist in every case explain carefully to the subject the purpose of the examination, the limits on confidentiality, who will have control over the information elicited, the possibilities of self-incrimination, and the role the psychiatrist will be playing in subsequent legal proceedings.[6] Even these explanations may not be sufficient for some subjects, who, because of great tension or mental illness, cannot control their outpouring of potentially incriminating information.

Many defense lawyers believe that there should be a legal right that they be present at all times during the psychiatric examination of their clients so that they can exercise control over inappropriate revelations. They also want to be able to validate the accuracy of statements attributed to their clients that are later reported by the psychiatrist. Most psychiatrists strenuously object to the presence of what they view as an interfering third party. Accustomed as they are to an intimate, one-to-one relationship with their patients, they believe that the presence of an attorney will inhibit the subject to such a degree that accurate evaluation is impossible. This may well be true. There is no convincing proof, however, that the presence of an attorney is, as claimed, an interference. A controlled study of this issue would be valuable.

Some difficult, essentially unsolvable ethical problems arise when a defendant who is being examined for a limited purpose, such as competency to stand trial, insists on confessing not only the crimes of which he is charged, but other crimes as well. What should the psychiatrist do with such information? Is it ethical to exclude it from the formal forensic report and testimony but confide the information unofficially to the attorney? To the prosecutor or judge? To the police? If the interview is being recorded on audiotape or videotape, as is becoming increasingly prevalent, should the psychiatrist erase that portion of the incriminating tape? These are tricky, difficult ethical issues for which clear-cut prescriptions are not available.

It is my conviction that a defendant who relies on any type of psychiatric defense, such as insanity or diminished capacity, must be willing to expose a full portrayal of his psychologic condition to the judge and jury if the defense is to be credible. Taking refuge in technicalities of the law restricting the introduction of certain evidence can only raise doubts in the minds of the juries as to the validity of the expert testimony. To reveal everything, without reserve, to the jury is a defense strategy known as "total disclosure."[7] But what if the defense attorney does not wish to take the risk of total disclosure yet still desires to use a psychiatric defense? Is the forensic psychiatrist ethically bound to participate even though he may feel his evidence has little credibility without total disclosure? The following case illustrates such a dilemma.

> A male college student killed a female student under bizarre circumstances indicative of much psychopathology. A diminished capacity defense was planned by the defense attorney, and extensive psychiatric investigations were instituted. Two weeks before the homicide there had been another, even more bizarre homicide attempt. The police suspected that the defendant might have also been the perpetrator of the earlier crime. He was exhaustively interrogated by the police and managed to convince them that he was not responsible for the earlier homicide attempt. During his psychiatric examination by me he, however, confessed that he had, indeed, committed the other offense. He further revealed that he had participated in numerous other dangerous and illegal activities over a period of years.

I felt that this information was crucial to my evaluation of the defendant's psychopathology[8] and that it would be dishonest to withhold that information from the jury. I further believed that I could not describe in a credible manner the defendant's mental state concerned with the killing of the woman without including information about the previous dangerous acts. The defense attorney, on the other hand, did not wish the jury to know about the other offenses for fear that if they rejected the psychiatric opinion of diminished capacity, they might be so alarmed by the defendant's dangerousness they would bring in a verdict for the death penalty. The defense attorney wanted me to testify about the mental illness of the defendant and his reduced responsibility, but to omit all reference to previous illegal acts. I refused to testify unless I could tell all. The unsatisfactory solution was a plea of guilty to first-degree murder by the defendant, who thus escaped the death penalty. If a suitable psychiatric defense had been possible, however, he might have been found guilty of only second-degree murder or possibly manslaughter.

Conflicts of ethical values between psychiatrist and lawyer arise in situations such as the foregoing one even though each participant believes he or she is exercising a legitimate ethical judgment. Many examples could be given, however, in which the ethical position of the forensic psychiatrist is questionable, if not clearly unethical. The temptation to play detective can be irresistible for some psychiatrists, who then subordinate their efforts to uncover psychopathology to a police and prosecutorial role. Psychiatrists have deliberately falsified their evidence of insanity because they feared a highly dangerous, mentally ill offender might be prematurely released. Psychiatrists have concealed their specialty from defendants and in the guise of providing medical treatment attempted to elicit a confession.[9] Psychiatrists, acting as agents for the police, have hypnotized and otherwise harassed defendants to obtain incriminating information.[10] Interviews have been tape recorded and the defendant informed that the recording was for the psychiatrist's use only and would be immediately erased. The tape was erased, but only after a transcript was made and used in evidence. The psychiatrist knew that a transcript would be made but deliberately allowed the defendant to believe the erasure of the tape would mean that no record would be made of what had been revealed during the examination.[11]

Deliberate deception and falsification can be dealt with by existing legal regulation if they are discovered. Unfortunately, such unethical and illegal conduct may often occur in situations of low visibility. If a legal remedy is not possible, reliance must be on professional organizations to discipline their own members for ethical violations and unprofessional conduct. Such organizations have not usually, however, had the power or the willingness to take the legal responsibility for such disciplinary action. And some of the worst offenders do not belong to any professional associations and are thus beyond their disciplinary reach.

Role Confusion

Flagrant, intentional violations of ethical conduct can be revealed and dealt with. More difficult are the inadvertent, less obvious deviations from ethical professional conduct that result from the role confusion inherent in forensic psychiatry. The forensic psychiatrist claims to present objective, scientific evidence. Yet, directly or indirectly, he or she is acting as an agent for an attorney or a court and, as such, is a participant in the adversarial legal system. In such a context, it is unreasonable to assume that the psychiatrist can maintain objectivity and impartiality, and the adversarial role should be made clear to all concerned. In his role as an agent of the legal system, the forensic psychiatrist's function, methods, and goals may differ greatly from the traditional role of the healer. Is it ethical to permit oneself to deviate from the physician/healer role at all? The famous psychiatrist and psychoanalyst Karl Menninger stated without equivocation, "What all courts should do, what society should do, is to exclude all psychiatrists from the courtroom!"[12] I would argue to the contrary (see "Psychoanalysis in the Courtroom," this volume). As long as society has a legal system that has the need for opinion evidence by psychiatric and psychologic experts, it would be irresponsible not to respond to that need. When necessary, the required adjustments in role and function should be made and taken into account.

A more difficult question is whether such a need does, in fact, exist. If it does exist, would it be desirable to eliminate it by appropriate changes in legal procedure? This is the arena in which I anticipate the great debate over psychiatry in the courtroom will take place in the coming years.

Should the defense of insanity be abolished? Is so-called expert opinion really expert? Is psychiatric clinical knowledge scientific? Is mental illness, as analogous to physical disease, a myth? Should all persons, regardless of mental state, be held equally responsible for their evil deeds? Do psychiatrists actually possess scientific information about the questions the law asks of them? If civil commitments are based on anticipated dangerous behavior, can psychiatrists predict dangerousness more accurately than lay persons can? Are all forensic psychiatrists unwitting tools of the legal system? Or do forensic psychiatrists usurp and dupe the legal system, departing from the paths of justice?

These questions are beyond the scope of this chapter, but rational answers to such questions must eventually be provided. There already exists a huge literature on these issues, but it is mostly in polemic terms with little empirical information. Particularly on the issue of criminal responsibility there is an incredible mythology that grossly exaggerates the number of offenders who are found to be not guilty by reason of insanity.[13] Public and legal skepticism of the value of forensic psychiatry is emerging in more insistent ways. Such skepticism may, in fact, have little to do with the realities of forensic psychiatry but is probably more related to the growing fear of crime and media exploitation of sensational cases.

In 1981 the California legislature eliminated the defense of diminished capacity and prohibited psychiatric experts from testifying whether a defendant did or did not possess a particular element of criminal intent.

Psychiatrists can still testify about the symptoms and effect of a defendant's mental illness that might be relevant to the jury's verdict on that element of the crime. In 1982, by popular vote, California adopted even more stringent limitations on such expert testimony and replaced a fairly liberal rule of insanity with one that is even harsher than the original M'Naghten rule.[14]

Despite serious questions of constitutionality, the state of Montana abolished the insanity defense in 1979. Idaho and Alabama did so in 1982. Public opinion in the wake of the Hinckley trial is pressuring numerous other state legislatures either to abolish the defense of insanity or to impose stringent limitations on its use. A number of states have followed Michigan's example and adopted the verdict of "guilty but mentally ill" either as a replacement for the verdict of not guilty by reason of insanity or as an alternative verdict. The guilty but mentally ill verdict is a sham, for it neither mitigates the punishment of the offender nor ensures that the offender will be appropriately treated for mental illness.

Similar attacks are being made on commitment proceedings that grant authority to psychiatrists to hospitalize and treat patients involuntarily without going through complicated legal procedures. In the 1960s a number of states adopted greatly liberalized commitment laws intended, for humanitarian reasons, to eliminate legalistic rituals and undue restrictions of patients needing involuntary psychiatric treatment. Only now are the appellate courts scrutinizing these mental health acts and are finding portions of them in violation of basic constitutional rights of the patients.[15] Challenges are often made to the principle of *parens patriae*, and some would eliminate all involuntary confinement and treatment of mental patients. Extensive litigation is now in progress in a number of states over the issue of the involuntary patient's right to refuse treatment.[16]

The Frye Test

The leading appellate court decision on the criteria for the admissibility of scientific evidence is *Frye v. United States*[17] by the United States Court of Appeals for the District of Columbia. In this famous 1923 decision the court stated:

> Just when a scientific principle or discovery crosses the line between the experimental and demonstrable stages is difficult to define. Somewhere in this twilight zone the evidential force of the principle must be recognized, and while courts will go a long way in admitting expert testimony deduced from a well-

recognized scientific principle or discovery, the thing from which the deduction is made must be sufficiently established to have gained general acceptance in the particular field in which it belongs.[18]

The most severe critics of forensic psychiatry assert that just about all clinical knowledge claimed by psychiatrists lacks a sufficient scientific foundation to meet the Frye test.[19] If such an assertion were to be sustained, it would result in the elimination of nearly all testimony of forensic psychiatrists. It can be expected that the Frye test will be used with increasing frequency to challenge the admissibility of all kinds of psychiatric and psychologic evidence. The California Supreme Court ruled in 1981 that a prospective witness who had undergone hypnotic enhancement of memory could not be allowed to give testimony because of the probable contamination of memory by the hypnotic experience. The court relied heavily on the contention that hypnotic enhancement of memory was not accepted as valid by the scientific community and hence, did not meet the Frye test.[20] Not all courts, however, rely on the Frye test of general acceptance by the scientific community; instead they hold that the admission of expert testimony is a matter of "reliability" to be judged by the court on the basis of the expert evidence offered in the particular case.[21]

I doubt that challenges to the validity of psychiatric expertise will succeed very often. Nevertheless, psychiatrists will be called on to defend the scientific basis for their diagnoses and the inferences they draw concerning the mental processes of the subjects of forensic psychiatric evaluation. They certainly can expect sharp limitations on the extent to which they can make legal inferences from their clinical data. Attacks on the credibility of all psychiatric testimony can be expected to continue, and psychiatrists should become familiar with the arguments used by attorneys to undermine and discredit expert psychiatric testimony.[22] The diagnostic criteria (DSM III)[23] adopted by the American Psychiatric Association will assist in achieving more uniformity of diagnosis and will tend to reduce the so-called battle of the experts. But challenges, such as the writings and testimony of Thomas Szasz, will continue and will not be ignored by the courts.[24]

It is paradoxical that, while the use of psychiatric testimony is losing its credibility for the determination of criminal responsibility and for involuntary hospitalization of the mentally ill, increasing use of such testimony is made in other areas of law, such as Workers' Compensation, retirement disability, personal injury suits, and other legal actions concerned with monetary compensation. Attorneys customarily take such cases on a contingent fee basis, and ethical issues of the "hired gun" type can be expected to increase in proportion to the large sums of money at stake. The trend toward no-fault divorce laws has shifted much of the controversy inherent in divorce to issues of child custody, and demand for psychiatric testimony relevant to the welfare of the children has increased.

The future is not dismal for the forensic psychiatrist. The growth of membership in the American Academy of Psychiatry and Law and the establishment of specialty examinations and certification by the American Board of Forensic Psychiatry will raise the general level of forensic practice to a more respectable one. Increasing attention is being paid to the ethical problems that arise in all psychiatric practice, including forensic work, and the literature devoted specifically to psychiatric ethics is increasing rapidly.[25] Greater sophistication on the part of courts by rejecting testimony of experts who persist in dubious tactics will promote the validity of appropriate expertise soundly based on clinical experience. Contrary to the proverbial principle that the bad drives out the good, I think that as large numbers of skilled, well-trained, ethically conscious psychiatrists participate in the legal process, the less qualified, less ethically responsible, "hired guns" will be rejected. But vigilance is necessary, for so far the credibility of psychiatric experts' testimony has been in inverse proportion to the increase in the admissibility of such testimony.

The Public Image of the Psychiatric Expert

In the middle ages and through the sixteenth century, it was easy to determine the public image of all occupational groups from king to peasant. The Dance of Death was a familiar art form that vividly portrayed the meeting of death with all social and occupational ranks of society. At this final meeting with Death, portrayed as a dancing skeleton, the true character of all humans was revealed. Holbein's *Dance of Death*, published in 1538,[26] shows Death meeting the Advocate as the following:

> The rich client is putting a fee into the hands of the dishonest lawyer. Death also contributes but reminds him that his [hour] glass is run out. To this admonition he seems to pay little regard. Behind is the poor suitor, wringing his hands and lamenting that poverty disables him from coping with his wealthy adversary.[27]

The physician meets Death as the following:

> He holds out his hand to receive, for inspection, a urinal which Death presents to him, and which contains the water of a decrepit old man who he introduces, and seems to say to the physician, "Canst thou cure this man who is already in my power?"[28]

These caricatured images of the doctor and the lawyer persist to the present day, the doctor as impotent and helpless to cure—a quack—and the lawyer as dishonest and venal. Unfortunately, the public image of the forensic psychiatrist tends to combine the Dance of Death image of both lawyer and doctor: dishonest, for sale and hire, but also impotent and ineffectual, for the testimony has no credibility.

This state of affairs should be of grave concern to all psychiatrists, not just those few who go to court. Relatively few of the general population have had first-hand contact with psychiatrists, in therapy or otherwise. Most people form their impression of psychiatry from the media, especially from the reports of psychiatric testimony in sensational criminal trials. The Dan White trial in San Francisco, in 1979, and the Hinckley trial in 1982 were hardly the first trials to arouse skepticism of the role of psychiatric experts in criminal law. In 1895 Justice Harlan wrote in the United States Supreme Court decision in *Davis v. United States:*

> It seems to us that undue stress is placed in some of the cases upon the fact that in prosecutions for murder the defense of insanity is frequently resorted to and is sustained by the evidence of ingenious experts whose theories are difficult to be met and overcome. Thus, it is said, crimes of the most atrocious character often go unpunished.[29]

In the nineteenth century, the practice of psychiatry in the United States was concerned mostly with problems of hospital administration, custody, criminal responsibility, and the protection of society against the alleged hazards of the mentally ill. Only a minority of psychiatrists had a direct interest in the treatment of mental patients. The professional role of nineteenth-century psychiatrists was very similar to that of forensic psychiatrists today, and the public image did not correspond to the benign, healing physician. The 1880s and 1890s were a critical transition period, changing the image of the psychiatrist from custodian to therapist. In 1887 Wagner von Jauregg first proposed fever treatment for psychoses (he received the Nobel prize in 1927 for the malaria treatment of central nervous system syphilis). In 1893, the same year in which the great Charcot of Salpêtrière died, Breuer and Freud published their extraordinary article "On the Psychical Mechanism of Hysterical Phenomena," thus laying the foundation for psychoanalysis.[30] Kraepelin[31] was soon to publish his new classification of mental disease, and the beginnings of modern psychiatric diagnosis and treatment were well underway by the early twentieth century.

There were no such spectacular contributions to the earlier problems of custody, commitment, criminal responsibility, and other critical forensic issues. Forensic psychiatry became a low-status occupation, and courtroom testimony of psychiatrists was often greeted with great skepticism. Experts were commonly regarded as corrupt, selling their services to whichever side was willing to pay the price for their prostitution.

Freud had an early interest in forensic problems. In 1906 he had been a guest lecturer at a University of Vienna seminar in jurisprudence, where he discussed the use of psychoanalysis for the obtaining of legal evidence. He strongly emphasized the highly experimental nature of such a method and insisted that it be used only in the spirit of research and that findings, if any, not be made available to the trial court.[32]

The 1924 trial of Leopold and Loeb, in Chicago, was a tremendous media event and aroused great public interest in psychoanalysis and psychiatry. It was not a hearing on the issue of guilt or insanity. Clarence Darrow, then the nation's most famous trial lawyer, pleaded the two youths guilty to murder, and the hearing was solely for the purpose of determining whether they should receive the death penalty or life in prison. Darrow hoped to win sympathy and understanding for their inexplicable crime by a parade of psychiatric and psychoanalytic experts who, for the first time, would reveal the unconscious psychodynamics of a bizarre murder. Among the experts for the defense were such famous psychoanalysts as William A. White, William Healy, and Bernard Glueck.

During the hearing, Freud was offered $25,000 by the Chicago Tribune to come to Chicago, observe the proceeding, and "psychoanalyze" the defendants for the newspaper. Freud, already suffering from cancer of the palate, politely declined, stating that he was ill and could not travel in public. The Hearst papers then offered Freud any sum he would name as well as a chartered ocean liner on which he would be the only passenger. This offer, too, was declined.[33]

Judge Caverly, who had the difficult task of deciding whether the lives of the two youths should be spared, thanked the experts who testified in the Leopold-Loeb hearing, saying, "The Court is willing to recognize that the careful analysis made of the life history of the defendants and of their present mental, emotional and ethical condition has been of extreme interest and is a valuable contribution to criminology."[34] Nevertheless, he made it quite clear that his rejection of the death penalty for the youths was based solely in consideration of their age.

Freud was always most cautious about the "half-baked" application of psychoanalytic concepts in legal proceedings, and most psychoanalysts seem to have followed his example in staying clear of the courtroom after the Leopold-Loeb hearing. A number of psychoanalysts, such as Franz Alexander, Gregory Zilboorg, Karl Menninger, Robert Waelder, and Anna Freud, made significant contributions to the literature and theory of forensic psychiatry, but with few exceptions, psychoanalysts regularly avoided the practice of forensic psychiatry.[35] Consequently, as the prestige and power of psychoanalysts came to dominate American psychiatry, the professional status of forensic psychiatrists seemed to sink lower and lower.

Currently there is much agitation and concern about the role of psychiatrists in the criminal justice system. Both the American Psychiatric Association and the American Bar Association have taken more conservative positions than they have in the past.[36] It is not clear from which professional sources will come the progressive leadership that might produce significant developments in the future. By adopting a conservative stance, both the legal and the psychiatric organizations may well have forfeited their ability to pioneer new roles for forensic psychiatrists and new paths to justice.

Erik Erikson, speaking about the formation of ego identity and the adolescent's finding his niche in society, stated: "In finding it the young adult gains an assured sense of inner continuity and social sameness which will bridge what he *was* as a child and what he is *about to become*, and will reconcile his *conception of himself* and his community's recognition of him."[37]

Clearly, something very similar exists for the role and identity of the forensic psychiatrist. To find his niche in society, he, too, must bridge what he *was*, in terms of the historical background of his profession; what he is *about to become*; in relation to the constantly changing use of psychiatry in the legal process; his *image of himself* as scientist, as clinician, as adversary, as detective, as pseudo-lawyer, as protector of the underdog, or as watchdog of the public morals; and the *community's perception* of him. An adolescent who fails to achieve an appropriate ego identity will suffer from identity diffusion marked by confusion, uncertainty, doubt, anxiety, and chaotic mental processes. I think that much of the trouble with the current use and role of forensic psychiatrists can be understood as an identity crisis in the true Eriksonian sense. Maturity may, though, someday be achieved, and the science and art of psychiatry can make its proper contributions to law and justice.

Notes

[1] With minor exceptions, everything in this article that refers to psychiatrists and their patients would also apply to psychologists, social workers, and other psychotherapists and their clients.

[2] *In re Lifschutz*, 2 Cal.3d 415; 85 Cal. Rptr. 929, 467 P.2nd 557 (1970).

[3]In most states the physician–patient privilege laws provide no protection of confidentiality if the patient is involved in criminal proceedings. A minority of states have additional psychotherapist–patient privilege laws that usually protect patients' confidential communications in psychotherapy even in criminal proceedings unless the patient places his mental state in issue.

[4]In re Lifschutz, note 2, *supra; Caesar v. Mountanos*, 542 F.2nd 1064 (9th Cir. 1976).

[5]In re Lifschutz, note 2, *supra*. "Fishing expeditions" were sometimes done in the hope of uncovering some type of derogatory information against a litigant that could be used to coerce a settlement or withdrawal of the litigation.

[6]In *People v. Bennett*, 58 C.A.· 3d 230; 129 Cal. Rptr. 679 (1976) the appellate court reversed a conviction because the police psychiatrist had not personally given the full *Miranda* warning to the defendant and obtained a waiver of his *Miranda* rights. See also *Estelle v. Smith*, 101 S.Ct 1866 (1981).

[7]See Dieden, L., & Gasparich, C. (1964), Psychiatric evidence and full disclosure in the criminal trial. *Calif. L. Rev.*, 52:543–561. See also Diamond, B. L., & Louisell, D. (1965), The psychiatrist as an expert witness: Some ruminations and speculations. *Mich. L. Rev.*, 63:1335–1354.

[8]I may have been wrong about this for, following a relatively short term in prison, the defendant made an excellent social and personal adjustment.

[9]*People v. Nash*, 52 Cal.2d 36, 41; 336 P.2d 416 (1959).

[10]*Leyra v. Denno*, 347 U.S. 556 (1953).

[11]From documents supplied to me by Dr. Melvin Goldzband.

[12]Menninger, K. (1966), *The Crime of Punishment*. New York: Viking Press, p. 138.

[13]See, for example, Pasewark, R. A. & Pantle M. L. (1979), Insanity plea: Legislators' view. *Amer. J. Psychiat.*, 136:222.

[14]California Penal Code ßß25, 28. In 1972 the California Supreme Court had adopted the fairly liberal Model Penal Code (A.L.I.) rule. The June 1982 initiative, Proposition 8, overturned this court decision and replaced it with new criteria for insanity: The defendant must be "incapable of knowing or understanding the nature and quality of his or her act and of distinguishing right from wrong at the time of the commission of the offense." Note the substitution of the conjunctive "and" for the "or" of the original M'Naghten rule. This makes the California Proposition 8 criteria the most stringent of all definitions of criminal responsibility except those that abolish it altogether.

[15]*O'Connor v. Donaldson*, 422 U.S. 563 (1975); *Suzuki v. Yuen*, 617 F.2d 173 (9th Cir. 1980); *Addington v. Texas*, 441 U.S. 418 (1979); *Doe v. Gallinot*, 486 F.Supp. 983 (C.D. Cal. 1979).

[16]*Rogers v. Okin*, 634 F.2d 650 (1st Cir. 1980); *Rennie v. Klein*, 653 F.2d 836 (3d Cir. 1981).

[17]*Frye v. United States*, 293 F. 1013 (D.C. 1923).

[18]Ibid., p. 1014.

[19]See, for example, Ziskin, J. (1975), *Coping with Psychiatric and Psychological Testimony*. Beverly Hills, CA: Law and Psychology Press.

[20]*State v. Hall*, 297 N.W. 2d 80 (Iowa 1980).

[21]Unfortunately, the source information for this note was inadvertently omitted from the original text.

[22]See Ziskin, op. cit., sup. note 19.

[23]*Diagnostic and Statistical Manual of Mental Disorders* (DSM III) (1980), Washington, DC: Amer. Psychiatric Press.

[24]Szasz, T. (1961), *The Myth of Mental Illness—Foundations of a Theory of Personal Conduct*. New York: Harper & Row, Hoeber Medical Division; (1963), *Law, Liberty, and Psychiatry: An Inquiry Into the Social Uses of Mental Health Practices*. New York: Macmillan; (1963), *Psychiatric Justice*. New York: Macmillan. Dr. Szasz testified for the prosecution in an Alameda County, California, murder trial that the defendant could not have been insane at the time of the offense because there was no such thing as mental illness and that the crime was committed because the defendant was an evil person and that she deserved to be punished. Dr. Szasz admitted that he had not examined the defendant but was testifying on purely theoretical grounds. The psychiatrists for the defense, for the prosecution, and for the court had each examined the defendant and found her to be suffering from schizophrenia and it was their opinion that she was legally insane. The jury found the defendant guilty of first-degree murder, and she was sentenced to life imprisonment without possibility of parole. *(People v. Cronen, Alameda Sup. Court, 1981)*.

[25]See Bloch, S. & Chodoff, P., ed. (1981), *Psychiatric Ethics*. New York: Oxford University Press; Hofling C. K., ed., (1981), *Law and Ethics in the Practice of Psychiatry*. New York: Brunner/Mazel.

[26]For a discussion of the more than 300 editions of Holbein's *Dance of Death* see Warthin, A. S. (1931), *The Physician and the Dance of Death*. New York: Paul B. Hoeber.

[27]Holbein, Plate 19.

[28]Holbein, Plate 26.

[29]*United States v. Davis*, 160 U.S. 469, at 492, 16 S. Ct. 353 (1895).

[30]Breuer, J. & Freud S. (1893), On the psychical mechanism of hysterical phenomena: Preliminary communication. *Standard Edition*, 2:1–17. London: Hogarth Press, 1955.

[31]Kraepelin's classification of diseases began with his textbook's 1883 edition and continued throughout his life. His sixth edition (1899) was the first to include *both* dementia praecox and manic-depressive psychoses. [See Kraepelin, E. (1883), *Textbook for Students and Physicians*, ed. J. M. Quen (trans. H. Metoni, Vol. 1; S. Ayed, Vol. 2). Canton, MA: Watson, 1990.]

[32]Freud, S. (1906), Psychoanalysis and the establishment of the facts in legal proceedings. *Standard Edition* 9: London: Hogarth Press, 1959.

[33]Jones, E. (1957), *The Life and Work of Sigmund Freud*, Vol 3. New York: Basic Books, p. 103.

[34]Higdon, H. (1975), *The Crime of the Century: The Leopold and Loeb Case*, New York: G. P. Putnam's Sons, p. 265.

[35]It is significant that a substantial majority of the psychiatrists who have received the highest award for law and psychiatry—the Isaac Ray Award of the American Psychiatric Association—have been Freudian psychoanalysts.

[36]In December 1982 the American Psychiatric Association issued an official position statement on the insanity defense. In February 1983 the American Bar Association House of Delegates voted acceptance of a position statement of its Committee on Standards for Criminal Justice. Both organizations repudiated their previous approval of the Model Penal Code (A.L.I.) rule in favor of the so-called Bonnie Rule, which accepts only cognitive impairment and not volitional impairment as the basis of all insanity defense.

[37]Erikson, E. (1959), The problem of ego identity. In: *Identity and the Life Cycle,* ed. G. S. Klein. *Psychological Issues,* Monog. 1. New York: International Universities Press, p. 111.

From *M'Naghten* to *Currens*,
and Beyond

[1962]

The decision in *United States v. Currens*,[1] setting forth a new rule of the criminal responsibility of the mentally ill, provided new fuel to the fire of controversy over *M'Naghten*.[2] When the *Durham*[3] rule replaced the ancient *M'Naghten* rule in the District of Columbia, there were high hopes that reform would spread throughout the nation.[4] But only the Virgin Islands and, with serious restrictions, Maine[5] have been willing to adopt *Durham*. All other jurisdictions have remained impervious to the onslaughts of its reform implications.

Here, I shall not debate the desirability of replacing the *M'Naghten* rule. I shall start with the assumption (which many readers will question) that *M'Naghten* is dead—that the "knowledge of right and wrong" test of criminal responsibility remains only to be buried and that the real question is how long must the funeral services go on and how many decades must pass before the law ceases to mourn at its grave. For the truth is that the principle behind *M'Naghten*, namely, that defect of cognition as a consequence of mental disease is the primary exculpating factor in the determination of legal insanity, has probably never been other than a legal fiction. I assert, without attempting to prove it here, that all psychiatrists of high caliber and experience invariably use, as the basis of formulating their own expert opinion about the mental responsibility of a given defendant, criteria other than defects of cognition. They may or may not give lip service to *M'Naghten* and may or may not advocate its change. But in their own reasoning about the defendant's mental condition, in their own appraisal of the mentally ill defendant's criminal responsibility, they give cognitive defects small measure compared with other psychopathological manifestations. If it were otherwise, extremely few defendants would ever be found legally insane (see "Criminal Responsibility of the Mentally Ill," this volume).

The difficulty is that these "other criteria" of criminal responsibility are, in most instances, unformulated, unexpressed, idiosyncratic to the particular expert, perhaps even to the particular defendant, and most certainly not endorsed by appropriate judicial decision or legislative enactment. That expert testimony in criminal trials appears chaotic, inconsistent, and sometimes absurd is no reflection on the state of knowledge of psychiatry. Rather, it reflects upon the obstinacy of the law, which demands an impossible adherence to a fiction of little relevancy to the issue being decided (see "The Fallacy of the Impartial Expert," this volume). Since M'Naghten there have been various modified and substitute rules of criminal responsibility, all of which were attempts to bring the issue of the criminal responsibility of mentally abnormal defendants into harmony with the realities of human abnormal psychology. None of these new rules has ever achieved widespread acceptance. They include the irresistible impulse rule,[6] the New Hampshire rule,[7] the *Durham* rule,[8] and, in 1961, the *Currens* rule.[9] Innumerable rules have been proposed, but never accepted by any jurisdiction. The only one that has received serious consideration is the American Law Institute formula.[10]

Judge John Biggs, Jr., in the *Currens* decision, provided the following new rule: "The jury must be satisfied that at the time of committing the prohibited act the defendant, as a result of mental disease or defect, lacked substantial capacity to conform his conduct to the requirements of the law which he is alleged to have violated."[11]

The decision discusses in a most scholarly manner the beneficial implications of this new rule over *M'Naghten* and *Durham*, as well as its relationship to the American Law Institute formula from which it is derived. It is a temptation here to quote much of Judge Biggs's decision, to compare the implications of *Currens* phrase by phrase with *Durham*, and to assert the superiority of those decisions over both *M'Naghten* and the irresistible impulse test.[12] This would require an extensive treatise beyond the scope of this paper. Hence, I must presume that readers will also familiarize themselves with these decisions and the basic issues involved in determining the criminal responsibility of the mentally ill.[13]

In short, the present situation can be summed up by stating that despite the esteem psychiatrists have for *Durham* and despite their high hopes for its adoption throughout the nation, the legal opposition to its further adoption is enormous. Moreover, I think it will be only a short time before it is abandoned in the District of Columbia.[14]

Currens is superior to *Durham* if for no other reason than that it omits the troublesome "product" clause of both the *Durham* and the New Hampshire rules. Criminal behavior is not the "product" of mental disease in the strict cause-and-effect relationship that the law would like to believe. The vast majority of mental illnesses result in no criminal behavior of any kind. But certain psychological abnormalities in certain individuals so affect the motivational, ideational, and volitional psychology of those individuals that, under special environmental circumstances, aggressive, destructive, or immoral antisocial behavior occurs. In most of these instances the psychiatrists can say with probability, but never with certainty, that if it were not for the mental illness, the overt act would not have occurred.

The essential phrase of *Currens*, "lacked substantial capacity to conform," should, I think, be much simpler for both the psychiatric expert and the lay juror to ponder. Further, it provides opportunity for the expert to describe any aspect of the defendant's psychology that he thinks may have some relevancy to the defendant's capacity to conform, whether it is a lack of knowledge of the wrongfulness of his act, or of its nature and quality, as required under *M'Naghten*, or whether it is the defect of volitional control specified by the irresistible impulse test, or the "product" relationship of *Durham*.

Currens is thus more inclusive than any previous rule of responsibility. This will make *Currens* more appealing to those who believe that the existence of mental illness of any kind should be given the fullest possible consideration in a criminal trial. But for all those who believe that mental illness and what they regard as the fantasies of psychiatrists and humanist reformers already receive more attention than they deserve in our courts of law, *Currens* will be a threat, and vigorous opposition is to be expected.

As much as I admire Judge Biggs's enlightened understanding of psychiatry, his scholarly historical knowledge, and his impeccable legal reasoning, and as much as the *Currens* rule appeals to me as a psychiatrist who must examine particular defendants, appraise their mental condition, and communicate my opinions to the trier of fact, I still do not think that *Currens* will achieve significant acceptance. The reasons are simple: the public will not like *Currens* or its consequences; judges will not approve for much the same argument as Judge Burger uses to assault *Durham*;[15] and what is worse, psychiatrists will not like its consequences as soon as they feel their full impact on their mental hospitals.

The problems of reforming the rules for determining the criminal responsibility of the mentally ill become greatly intensified with two categories of defendants: (1) those who are suffering from a borderline or latent schizophrenia; and (2) those suffering from a character disorder variously described by such nebulous words as psychopathic personality, sociopathic personality, sexual psychopath, psychopathic deviant, and the like. The vast majority of troublesome, difficult, and debatable verdicts and appeals result from the trials of defendants who suffer from one or the other of these two conditions. No one knows for sure what proportion of our prison population consists of such individuals, but it must be very high.

Are borderline schizophrenia and character disorders mental diseases? Much ridicule has been heaped on the staff of St. Elizabeths Hospital in Washington, DC, for committing themselves, in 1957, to the view that sociopathic personality was henceforth to be considered a mental disease.[16] Between 1954 and 1957, St. Elizabeths Hospital psychiatrists generally had testified that sociopathic personality was not a mental disease, and hence a defendant suffering from such a condition was not insane under *Durham*. The immediate consequence of their shift in position in 1957 was a 10-fold increase in acquittals on the ground of insanity in the District of Columbia.[17] Yet this change of attitude by the Washington psychiatrists was imperative, for their earlier position was untenable and inconsistent with all the standard diagnostic classifications.[18]

It is true that many voices in psychiatry protest that no type of deviant psychological behavior is a mental disease, that there is no analogy between disease of the body and disease of the mind or emotions, and that the terms *disease* and *illness* should not be applied even to the conceptualization of psychological abnormality.[19] Although the adherents of this view have much logic on their side, it is unlikely that many psychiatrists agree. Most of us still regard psychiatry as a specialty of medicine, and we look upon the various categories of mental abnormality as divisible into entities properly called *diseases*. Such abnormalities, be they manifested by disorder of mind, emotion, character, or behavior, are correctly considered to be illnesses in a sense analogous to the use of the term in describing pathology of the body.

Nevertheless, this poses a serious dilemma for the law. For if conditions of borderline schizophrenia and sociopathic personality are not mental diseases, then neither are conditions of active schizophrenia or any other psychoses that the law regards as producing mental abnormalities exculpating under *M'Naghten*. On the other hand, if active schizophrenia and other psychoses are accepted by psychiatry and the law as *diseases*, then the borderline conditions and most, if not all, of the character disorders must also be acknowledged as *mental diseases*. The reasons for this are discussed later, but for the moment, let us assume its correctness. Then what are the consequences for the law and for penology?

Consider the consequences if *Currens* becomes the law of the land. Very large numbers of defendants accused of crimes both great and small, who are now regarded by the public and by the law as not sick but as bad people, will be acquitted on the ground of insanity. Presumably, they will be sent to mental hospitals for indeterminate stays rather than to prisons for defined periods of time. In the nonjudgmental view of psychiatrists, such mentally diseased defendants will almost invariably be considered as lacking "substantial capacity to conform" their conduct to the requirements of the law.[20] A considerable proportion of our potential prison population will then be sent to hospitals staffed and administered by psychiatrists ill-equipped by temperament or training either to treat these borderline and character disorders or to maintain the necessary security precautions that society demands. Modern trends in public and private mental hospitals are definitely toward the open-door hospital with voluntary admission of patients. It would not be easy, and certainly not at all acceptable to the psychiatric profession and to the public, to reverse this trend and return to the maximum security state hospital of the past in order to accommodate the new patients to be committed under Currens.

Then why not do what the American Law Institute recommends, and what the Maine statutory version of Durham specifies, and exclude the sociopath and his ilk from the benefits of the relaxed rule of responsibility?[21] The answer is that such restrictive clauses aimed at excluding certain specified categories of individuals from exculpation simply do not make any psychiatric sense. They are as arbitrary and capricious as excluding defendants with red hair or blue eyes or Negro blood from the benefits of the law of criminal responsibility. They define by legislative fiat what is and what is not a psychiatric condition. Further, they grossly discriminate against defendants who are poor. In practically any case where the crime itself, or alcoholism or drug addiction, is supposedly the only evidence of mental disease, a skilled, competent, and interested psychiatrist who spends sufficient time could discover other manifestations of mental abnormality sufficient to exculpate under the American Law Institute or Maine rules. But routine cases, superficially examined by court-appointed psychiatrists devoting inadequate time to the study of the defendant, would seldom end in acquittal. It costs a good deal of money for a defendant to engage psychiatric experts to make a full study of his case. Defendants who have such money would have no difficulty demonstrating to the trier of fact that their criminal behavior was not the only thing that troubled them. In all likelihood, defendants without such funds would be passed by routinely as "sane." Thus a type of economic discrimination, which is bad enough under our present rule of M'Naghten, would become much worse.

Until shortly after 1900, psychiatry was generally a subspecialty of neurology. Intensely medically oriented, psychiatry reached its peak with the diagnostic and classification system devised by Kraepelin.[22] Emphasis was placed on the overt, demonstrable evidence of mental disease (such as delusions and hallucinations), and it was hoped that exact descriptions of such overt disease manifestations would eventually result in an ability to catalogue mental disease with the precision customary to the science of neurology. It was already possible by that time for neurologists to locate exactly the lesion in the brain, spinal cord, or peripheral nerves that caused a particular paralysis or sensory disorder. This was done by obtaining a careful history of the onset and progression of symptoms and then meticulously mapping out the areas of the body demonstrating the paralysis, reflex disturbances, or sensory loss. If one possessed sufficient knowledge of the anatomy and function of the nervous system, deducing the size and position of the lesion was easily possible. Then, knowing the location of the lesion, one could often deduce the etiological agent and sometimes prescribe a remedial treatment. Neurologists were able, through these methods, to demonstrate the existence of hundreds of discrete neurological diseases with particular, well-defined, and uniformly located lesions, disclosed by reasonably constant subjective and objective symptoms and pathological manifestations of body function. It was anticipated that the same would be accomplished in the area of mental disease.

The anticipations of the neurologists were thoroughly shattered by the publication of two books: Sigmund Freud's *The Interpretation of Dreams*, published in 1900; and Eugen Bleuler's *Dementia Praecox, or the Group of Schizophrenias*, published in 1911.[23] It would take many volumes to describe adequately the revolutionary changes in psychiatry that are directly attributable to the work of Freud and of Bleuler. And we are still in the midst of the revolution. Suffice it to say that Freud's discoveries led to the development of psychoanalysis and psychodynamic psychiatry, which is the dominant psychiatry of the present day in every situation *except the court-room*. Bleuler completely altered the concept of schizophrenia. Although he did not discover the cause and cure of the disease (nor has anyone else yet done so), he did demonstrate that schizophrenia was a completely different type of disease, or group of diseases, than the Kraepelinians had thought. He showed that the overt manifestations of the illness, such as delusions and hallucinations, were only secondary symptoms—the end products of ego disintegration—rather than clues to the illness itself. The basic disorder in schizophrenia was a very serious, though subtle, disturbance in the integration of thought and feeling,[24] together with certain difficult to demonstrate, but nevertheless malignant, alterations in the nature of the patient's ability to conceptualize and to experience appropriate emotion.

Modern psychotherapeutic psychiatry as practiced today by well-trained physicians conceptualizes mental illness as a complex interplay of forces: instinctual as well as acquired and environmental social forces interacting with the defenses and adaptive functions of the ego. As a result of this interplay of forces, abnormalities of thought, feeling, volition, motivation, and behavior arise and are manifested by various symptoms. In fact, it is no longer possible to speak of specific abnormalities of single mental functions, such as volition. Rather, every disorder of this fluid balance of forces results in disturbances describable only in terms of the total person and his environment.

Obviously, such a dynamic conceptualization of mental illness sacrifices much of the precision and discreteness so eagerly sought by the early neurologists. But what has been gained has been a marvelously useful, psychologically broad concept of all human behavior, not just of gross mental abnormality. Medical psychology has expanded far beyond its old borders and has contributed significant insights into almost every field of human activity—the arts as well as the sciences.

During this modern psychodynamic revolution, however, organically oriented psychiatry, with its heritage from Kraepelin, has not been dormant. Shock therapy, initiated by Manfred Sakel[25] in 1934, with the use of insulin coma, was later supplanted by electroshock therapy, discovered by Cerletti and Bini.[26] Electroshock therapy has, in turn, has been nearly superseded by tranquilizers and the antidepressant drugs, which have kept very actively alive a system of psychiatric treatment based on nonpsychological approaches.

At times there have been serious schisms—almost ideological conflicts—between psychodynamic psychiatrists with their psychotherapeutic treatment, and organically oriented neuropsychiatrists with their physical and chemical remedies. It is difficult for a psychoanalyst such as I, who was professionally born and raised, so to speak, in the psychology of Freud, to admit that there might be something to the organic, physical, and chemical approach toward mental disease. Yet the evidence is accumulating rapidly; the therapeutic efficacy of the recently developed phenothiazine tranquilizers and the antidepressant drugs such as imipramine and tranylcypromine is very impressive.[27]

It would be a mistake to assume that the recent resurgence of interest in the physical and chemical causes and treatment of mental disease means that psychiatry will soon return to the precise, specific symptom-lesion concept of nineteenth-century neurology. These biochemical approaches toward mental disease have, like the earlier psychological approaches, further blurred the distinctions among what little remains of our psychiatric disease entities. For example, antidepressant drugs are effective to some degree against emotional depression no matter what the cause of the depression. Schizophrenia, manic–depressive psychosis, psychoneurosis, character disorders, and normal grief are all conditions that may result in serious emotional depression. An antidepressant drug, if it works at all, tends to discriminate little between diagnostic classifications. The same is true of the tranquilizers. The most that can happen is that one can learn empirically that a particular drug possibly may work better or worse in a particular disease entity. But the differences are very crude and uncertain.

Furthermore, the neurophysiological postulates on which the use of these drugs is predicated involve exceedingly complex neurohormonal mechanisms that are little, if at all, related to conventional diagnostic entities. One can only predict that if and when the theory and practice of biochemical psychiatry is well developed, it too will turn out to be dynamic, in the sense of the complex interaction of metabolites, enzymes, genetic defects, and biophysical electrical activities. It will be far from a static, specific, lesion-oriented neurology.

So the law cannot look hopefully toward either modern psychodynamic psychiatry or biochemical psychiatry for a solution to its needs for categorical, all-or-none, sane-or-insane dichotomies. All we psychiatrists can tell the law is that if you think you have trouble with our inconsistencies now, just wait and see what the future holds.

All of this leads us back to the discussion of the borderline or latent schizophrenic, that is, the schizophrenic person without obvious, overt signs of psychosis, such as hallucinations and delusions, yet seriously mentally ill, and the person with a character disorder, including those with sociopathic personality. These are chiefly the conditions producing mental states that will preclude criminal responsibility under *Currens*, but not under *M'Naghten*, and that may well include a majority of criminal offenders. They must be acknowledged as mental diseases, if one acknowledges anything as a mental disease.

First, let me say that what follows must not be regarded as scientifically demonstrated psychiatric truth. Nor is it even the accepted opinion of a majority of psychiatrists. These are matters about which there is little agreement. Opinions from one extreme to the opposite can easily be found in the current psychiatric literature, and one would have no difficulty obtaining suitable citations to articles by reputable authorities that would "prove" or "disprove" any given point. Further, much of what I am saying is in the nature of a prediction of what will be discovered rather than what has already been demonstrated. Nevertheless, I believe it is impossible to discuss the inherent difficulties of any rule of criminal responsibility of the mentally ill without considering the possible future progress of our psychiatric knowledge about these troublesome cases.

Two areas of intensive research now going on are relevant to this issue. First, there is intensive research, rapidly progressing, whose goal is to demonstrate specific biochemical or neurophysiological factors (or both) as the cause of schizophrenia.[28] If this goal is fulfilled, it will be a relatively simple matter to prove conclusively the presence or absence of schizophrenia. Then all those borderline and latent cases that now cause so much dispute among the experts[29] will turn out to be unequivocally as sick as, or sicker than, the cases with hallucinations and delusions now excused by M'Naghten. Second, the widespread electroencephalographic testing of habitual criminal offenders, sociopaths, and those with character disorders has revealed what many of us had long suspected: that many of these unfortunate persons are suffering from an organic, neurophysiological disease of the brain, that completely dominates their behavior. Their appearance of normalcy, their apparent ability to exercise free will, choice, and decision (and somehow invariably choose the wrong instead of the right) is purely a façade, an artifact that conceals the extent to which they are victims of their own brain pathology.[30]

So, at the risk of future mortification, I make the following predictions:

1. Within ten years, biochemical and physiological tests will be developed that will demonstrate beyond a reasonable doubt that a substantial number of our worst and most vicious criminal offenders are actually the sickest of all. And that if the concept of mental disease and exculpation from responsibility applies at all, it will apply most appropriately to them. And further, that it will apply equally to the vast horde of minor, habitual, aggressive offenders who form the great bulk of the recidivists. The law and the public, whether they like it or not, will be forced by the stark proof of scientific demonstration to accept the fact that large numbers of persons who now receive the full, untempered blow of social indignation, ostracism, vengeance, and ritualized judicial murder are sick and helpless victims of psychological and physical disease of the mind and brain.[31]

2. That it will be ten times ten years, or even much longer, before the discovery of any consistently effective, thoroughly reliable method of psychiatric treatment for those sick persons who now plague society with their behavioral disorders. Long before that day arrives, the treatment of noncriminal psychiatric patients will be conducted in hospitals entirely free from the taint of the bars, the locked doors, and the prison atmosphere of the old state hospital. Much of the psychiatric treatment of ordinary civilians will be done in out-patient clinics and in private offices. Few, if

any, of the physical facilities that would ensure maximum security will persist in the mental hospital of the future. Even now, with each passing year, mental hospitals are becoming less and less suitable for the care of mentally ill patients who are criminal offenders and whose danger to society demands that social protection take priority over the welfare of the individual patient.

3. Finally, my third prediction: that for many, many years to come, and certainly long after the ten years specified by my first prediction, all criminal offenders—sick or well, schizophrenic or sociopathic, or just plain normal, if such there be—will require various combinations of institutional control, probation, and parole supervision providing a range of facilities from the strongest possible maximum security to nearly total social freedom. Although psychiatric and psychological treatment techniques will be in evidence throughout the system, the main burden of rehabilitation of individual offenders will still rest on essentially nonmedical methods. These will still include the old standbys (as inadequate as they may be) of restriction of freedom, humanely tempered discipline, educational and vocational training, together with some kind of moral indoctrination, which will probably continue to be administered, as it is now, through a system of rewards and punishments. Certainly there will be increased use of psychiatric diagnostic techniques, together with a wide use of easily applied treatment methods such as group psychotherapy, psychopharmacological remedies, and whatever new methods come forth from our clinics and laboratories. But it is to be hoped that there will also be a substantial increase in the use of social and economic methods of behavioral control, such as job placement after release, preservation of family relationships, realistic acceptance back into the social community, and so forth.

The interesting thing is that these nonmedical social rehabilitation techniques are just as desirable for mentally ill offenders as they are for offenders who show no evidence of mental disease. And, paradoxically, specific psychiatric techniques, such as group therapy, are just as useful for normal offenders as they are for mentally ill offenders. By and large, it has already been demonstrated by prison hospitals, such as the California Medical Facility at Vacaville, that just about any type of psychiatric treatment that can be given at a mental hospital can also be given in a prison, provided properly trained psychiatric personnel are available.

There are encouraging signs that many of the detrimental, destructive, inhumane, and just plain wasteful aspects of the prison system are slowly diminishing, at least in California. Overcrowding is still an urgent liability everywhere, but at least in some areas of the California prison system (such as Vacaville and the various minimum security camps) the old-time atmosphere of fear, distrust, suspicion, and explosive aggressiveness on the part of both inmates and personnel is giving way to a more hopeful climate of enthusiastic rehabilitation.

In the days of Daniel M'Naghten and before, the defense of not guilty by reason of insanity had much more intrinsic logic than it has now. In the eighteenth and early nineteenth centuries in England, there were only three possible verdicts for most major felony cases: acquittal, conviction and execution by hanging (with chance of reprieve by the King), and acquittal on the ground of insanity. Those defendants who escaped capital punishment by reprieve or legal technicality were usually punished by transportation to the colonies; benefit of clergy had largely disappeared. A successful defense of insanity meant lifetime incarceration in a hospital that was not greatly different from a prison. The typical English prison and workhouse was filled with prisoners of a variety that corresponds to our present county jail population. Thus, with any crime of serious proportion, be the offender sane or insane, there was no thought of rehabilitation and eventual restoration to society. The verdict of insanity meant only that the defendant would not be executed; it did not mean that he would be set free. This dichotomous disposition by means of the death penalty for the sane or the equivalent of true life imprisonment for the insane lent itself well to the development of an all-or-none, sane or insane, rule of criminal responsibility. There was no thought of any concept of responsibility that would provide diminished or intermediate grades of responsibility, because there were few, if any, possibilities for any type of intermediate form of punishment. This English pattern was carried over to the United States by our general adoption of the English common law. But it was not long after the Revolutionary War that both England and the United States began to alter the harshness of their penal laws. Fewer and fewer felonies were subject to capital punishment, and prison confinement for a specified number of years became the fate of the average felon. Much later, and more gradually, the eventual release of some of the criminal insane from their prison-like hospitals became possible.

Only in comparatively recent times have we reached the state of affairs where only a tiny minority of felons are actually executed, where a very small number actually serve out life sentences, and where very few of the criminal insane spend the rest of their lives in hospitals. It is now anticipated at the time of sentencing or commitment that rehabilitation and restoration to society will occur with both the sane and the insane. The only question now is how long it will take.

California, being a state with a phenomenal population boom, requires a continual expansion of both its prison and its mental health facilities. The expansion cannot keep up with the population increase; hospitals and prisons are always badly overcrowded. But this very pressure of population growth forces the development of a much wider variety of prison and hospital institutions than one sees in other areas of the country. Most of all, it makes it imperative that there be no "warehousing of human beings,"[32] no locking up either prisoners or patients and throwing the keys away.

Inevitably, this will mean that future expansion of both mental health and correctional services will place an emphasis on decentralized, community facilities. The California Department of Mental Hygiene is making impressive plans for the establishment of local clinics and day-care centers, and for many other significant experiments in the utilization of treatment methods in the patients' home communities. They do not contemplate any increase in the old-style, isolated, large state hospital type of installation. Economic, if not humanitarian, reasons will, it is hoped, force a similar development on the State Department of Corrections. It can be anticipated that the day of the large, centralized, isolated prison will soon be over. Large numbers of criminal offenders who are not immediately dangerous to society must be dealt with in some way on the local level and by means other than physical confinement.

There is an urgent need for some sort of correctional system analogous to the medical model of hospitals, clinics, and home care. In medicine, a patient is not irrevocably committed to receive his treatment in just a hospital or just a clinic. When he is sick enough to require it, he is put in a hospital. The minute he recovers to the point at which he can be effectively treated as an out-patient, he is discharged from the hospital. If he relapses, he goes back into the institution. This switch from in-patient to out-patient takes place often during the course of any single, chronic ailment.

A correctional system could be organized around the same philosophy. Prisons of the conventional type would be used mainly for short-term diagnostic and treatment programs. Release on parole with close supervision at the community level would occur as quickly as it could be determined that it was reasonably safe to do so. If there was a relapse of deviant behavior, the offender could then be immediately returned to an institution, to be released again as soon as it appeared that there was a reasonable chance of adjustment. Only a few highly dangerous prisoners would be kept inside a prison for the long periods of time that are now customary. A realistic view of human nature would accept the fact that many offenders would have to shuttle back and forth between institutional and parole facilities many times before their ultimate rehabilitation was accomplished.

Such a system would, of course, do offense to the traditional view of imprisonment as part of a system of punishment and retribution. There will be much objection to the calculated risks inherent in early release from confinement. Nevertheless, the population explosion will soon teach the public the stern lesson that locking up criminal offenders for five, ten, and twenty years is an economic luxury they cannot afford.

California is progressing rapidly in the direction of this type of penal reform. If further reform is accompanied by appropriate public and legislative education, I think that the full development of this infinitely more flexible, more effective, and more humane correctional system is certain to occur. It is to be hoped that other states may soon follow the lead of California.

There is a danger that liberalization of the rules of criminal responsibility, as is achieved by *Durham* and *Currens*, may inadvertently subvert the basic principles of humanitarian penal reform. Large numbers of offenders can, under these laws, be labeled as insane, then confined for indeterminate periods up to life in institutions called mental hospitals, which are really prisons in disguise, with only a pretense of treatment and with gross disregard of civil liberties and due process.

This is particularly likely to happen under the circumstances of my predictions, where the majority of criminals are recognized as sick, yet no definitive medical treatment is available. The institutions in which these insane offenders are kept may be worse than a prison. The social stigma of the label "criminally insane" may be more degrading than the label "convict." The custodial officers, although called "doctors," may be more punitive and antitherapeutic in their attitudes than are true correctional officials. Such a state of affairs would permit an elaborate hoax to be perpetrated whereby society creates a smug illusion of reform, yet basically changes nothing. In the name of psychiatric enlightenment, penal reform can be obstructed. One can surround the criminal law with all sorts of admirable protections of due process and civil liberties, then cancel it all out by using so-called welfare laws, purportedly of a noncriminal type, to inflict punishment and social sanctions on the very class of persons who least deserve them. This is no idle threat, for precisely this has already happened in the usual hospitals for the criminally insane, psychopathic delinquents, and sexual psychopaths. The tragedy is that this punishment can be inflicted in the name of mental health, with the expedient rationalization that it is necessary for the protection of society.

Hence, I am very concerned that efforts to obtain reform of our archaic methods of administering criminal justice through liberalization of the rule of criminal responsibility of the mentally ill, while still retaining the irrational all-or-none principle of sane or insane, may backfire in ways that the authors of these reforms did not intend. The new classes of the mentally ill offenders established by these decisions will still be punished and degraded, but now they will lack many of the traditional safeguards of the criminal law. At the same time, sane offenders, the supposedly normal persons who violate the law, can be relegated (with the implied approval of the psychiatrists who have certified their normalcy) to a prison system without even the pretense of a rehabilitative atmosphere.

It is for these reasons that I believe it is more desirable to emphasize general reform of the whole body of criminal law and the entire correctional system rather than attempt to solve this problem by dividing the population of criminal offenders into two categories of responsible and not responsible. The M'Naghten rule draws the line between the two categories far off to one extreme. Currens rectifies this by drawing the line close to the middle or even beyond. But it is just possible that the line should not be drawn at all. Rather, efforts should be directed toward the elimination of capital punishment, toward the reduction of public and governmental attitudes of punishment and vengeance, and toward the evolution of a correctional system that will truly rehabilitate the offender and restore him to a normal life in his community as quickly as possible. If psychiatric and medical techniques can be used in this process of rehabilitation, so much the better. If other, nonmedical means are effective, let them be used. But let all useful means be applied to all offenders, be they mentally ill or not.

It seems to me that, at least currently in California, the legal doctrine of limited or diminished responsibility may accomplish more than would the adoption of Durham or Currens, or any other rule that reinforces the sane-insane dichotomy.[33]

All of this adds up to the bare thesis that the arbitrary division of criminal offenders into the two classes of the sane and the insane no longer makes any sense. Shifting the line of demarcation between the sane and the insane, as is accomplished by Durham and Currens, is at best only a transitional remedy that may be expedient for an incompletely developed correctional system.

The ever-growing body of scientific, psychiatric, and sociological knowledge about deviant behavior no longer permits a division of the responsible from the not responsible. This is so because modern science has accumulated a vast amount of information indicating that a very large proportion of criminal offenders are very sick people. Much of the evidence for this is not convincing to those preoccupied with moral judgment and vengeful retribution, but very soon the evidence may become so convincing that even the most conservative thinker will have to accept its validity. Yet it does not follow that, just because a criminal is recognized as mentally sick, medicine will be able, by itself, to cure or control this sickness.[34] Nor will hospitals of the conventional type, or of the type projected in future developments, be of a sort where mentally sick criminals can be adequately cared for with due regard to the protection of society.

Responsibility as a concept is losing its usefulness as a moral judgment and is acquiring a new, and much more valuable, therapeutic meaning. Thus, one may speak of the "extended responsibility" of many mentally ill persons.[35] Extended responsibility means that mentally ill persons are to be treated as if they were more responsible for their actions than they really may be, simply because it is therapeutically and socially desirable to do so.[36] At the same time, it may be therapeutically and socially useful to diminish the responsibility of those whom society and the law have previously held to be fully accountable.

Such far-reaching changes in ancient concepts of absolute morality and supposed natural law are not going to be eagerly received by many in our society. There will be wailing and outcries by those who habitually long for the real or imagined virtues of the past. Yet even the most cursory historical analysis of the behavioral sciences,[37] and of the trend of philosophy, theology, economics, social welfare, and politics makes it inescapably clear that these changes are already occurring.

It is evident that there are constitutional, historical, moral, and religious reasons why the total defense of insanity will not soon be completely abandoned. Actually, there is no need for psychiatry to urge its full abandonment. If constitutional due process requires that the defense of insanity retain a token place in our system of criminal justice and if this results in a limited number of mentally ill offenders receiving total exculpation by the law, no harm is done. Harm is done, however, if psychiatry and the law divert our attention and limited energies from the urgent problem of the great mass of criminal offenders toward the peripheral issue of insanity.

It makes more sense to focus reform efforts directly on the total system of administration of criminal justice and thus attempt to cope with the bulk of antisocial deviation in constructive, humane, and effective ways. From such a viewpoint, the solution is not to make new laws that will displace large portions of the prison population into mental hospitals, which then become prisons in disguise. Rather, it would be better to transform correctional systems and prison institutions into fit places to which mentally ill persons may be sent for treatment, rehabilitation, and eventual restoration to a normal life in their families and communities.

It will not be just a coincidence if, in the final analysis, the same humane psychological, medical, and sociological methods that are conducive to the rehabilitation of mentally ill and emotionally disordered criminals turn out to be identical with those required for supposedly normal and fully responsible offenders.

Notes

[1]*United States v. Currens*, 290 F.2d 751 (3d Cir. 1961).

[2]*M'Naghten's Case*, 10 Clark & F. 200, 8 Eng. Rep. 718 (1843).

[3]*Durham v. United States*, 214 F.2d 862 (D.C. Cir. 1954).

[4]Sobeloff (1955), Insanity and the criminal law: From McNaghten to Durham, and beyond. *Amer. Bar Assn. J.*, 41:793.

[5]*Maine Rev. Statutes Ann.* (suppl. 1961). Ch. 149, SS 38-A.

[6]*Parsons v. State*, 81 Ala. 577, 2 So. 854 (1887) ; see Perkins (1957), *Criminal Law*, p. 762.

[7]*State v. Jones*, 50 N.H. 369 (1871); *State v. Pike*, 49 N.H. 399 (1869).

[8]*Durham v. United States*, 214 F.2d 682, 874 (D.C. Cir. 1954).

[9]*United States v. Currens*, 290 F.2d 751, 774 (3d Cir. 1961).

[10]Model Penal Code SS 4.01 (1) (Tent. Draft No. 4, 1955). The text of this rule is given in full in *United States v. Currens*, sup. note 9, p. 774.

[11]Ibid.

[12]For the directly opposite view see Mueller, G. (1961), M'Naghten remains irreplaceable: Recent events in the law of incapacity. *Ga. L. J.*, 50:105.

[13]See Donnelly, R. C., Goldstein, J. & Schwartz, R. D. (1962), *Criminal Law*. New York: Free Press. Although it is too old to include the modern decisions, an excellent reference is Glueck, S. (1925), *Mental Disorder and the Criminal Law: A Study in Medico-Legal Jurisprudence*. Boston: Little, Brown.

[14]See *Blocker v. United States*, 288 F.2d 8S3, 860 (D.C. Cir. 1961) (Burger, J., concurring).

[15]Ibid.

[16]See Mueller, op. cit., sup. note 12, p. 116. See also *Blocker v. United States*, 288 F.2d 853, 874 (D.C. Cir. 1961) (Miller and Bastian, JJ., dissenting).

[17]Statistics obtained by the staff of the California Special Commissions on Insanity and Criminal Offenders established by executive order of the Governor, May 4, 1960.

[18]American Psychiatric Assn. (1952), *Diagnostic and Statistical Manual–II*. Washington, DC: American Psychiatric Press.

[19]See Szasz, T. (1961), *The Myth of Mental Illness*. New York: Hoeber-Harper. See also *Blocker v. United States*, sup. note 16.

[20]The opposite view is asserted by a Dr. Cushard, quoted in *Blocker v. United States*, sup. note 19, p. 961 n.12. I think Dr. Cushard's view, as quoted, is nonsense and reflects a judgmental and moralistic attitude inappropriate to a psychiatrist. He is quoted as stating: "I think these people are able to control their acts if they make the necessary effort."

[21]*Model Penal Code* 14.01(i) American Law Institute (Tent. Draft No. 4, 1955) excludes "an abnormality manifested only by repeated criminal or otherwise anti-social conduct." All the psychiatrists who participated in drafting the ALI formula repudiated it because of the inclusion of this restrictive clause. Observe that Judge Biggs does not include it in *Currens*. The Maine statute,

although modeled after Durham, has a similar exclusion of criminality, and also of drug addiction and alcoholism (*Maine Rev. Stat. Ann.*, [supp. 1961], Ch. 149, 1 38–A.

[22]Kraepelin, E. (1905), *Einführing in Die Psychatrische Klinik.* Leipsig: Barth. [See Kraepelin, E. (1883), *Textbook for Students and Physicians*, ed. S. M. Quen (trans. H. Metoni, Vol. 1; S. Ayed, Vol. 2). Canton, MA: Watson, 1990].

[23]Freud, S. (1900), *The Interpretation of Dreams. Standard Edition*, 4 & 5. London: Hogarth Press, 1953; Bleuler, E. (1911), *Dementia Praecox, or the Group of Schizophrenias.* New York: International Universities Press, 1950.

[24]The term schizophrenia, coined by Bleuler, literally means "split mind." Bleuler, however, did not mean this in the sense of split or double personality. The split personality is an hysterical phenomenon and is not a type of schizophrenia. The splitting in schizophrenia refers to a fragmentation of the ego, particularly to a dissociation between the intellectual and the emotional functions of the personality.

[25]Sakel, M. (1934), Schizophreniebehandlung mittels Insulin-Hypoglykamischer Shocks. *Wiener Medizintscher Wochenschrift*, 84:1211.

[26]Cerletti, U. & Bini, L. (1938), L'elettroshock. *Arch. di Psicologia, Neurolgia e Psichiatria*, 19:226.

[27]These drugs are usually referred to by their trade names: i.e., Tofranil (imipramine), Parnate (tranylcypromine), and Thorazine, Compazine, and Stelazine, which are varieties of the phenothiazine tranquilizers. Closely related drugs of similar purpose are manufactured by various companies under a variety of other trade names.

[28]See Tulane Dept. of Psychiatry and Neurology, School of Medicine, Tulane University (1954), *Studies in Schizophrenia, A Multidisciplnary Approach to Mind-Brain Relationships.*

[29]See *People v. Nash*, 52 Cal. 2d 36, 338 P.2d 416 (1959), as an example of a so-called borderline schizophrenic defendant executed as a horrifying vicious murderer but who was very mentally ill, indeed.

[30]Thompson (1961), Psychopathy. *Arch. Crim. Psychodynamics*, 4:736 expresses the view that this is already a demonstrated, scientific fact. This is an extreme position.

[31]The reader must not assume that I believe that all criminal behavior is a consequence of disease of the mind or brain. Sociological and situational causes play the dominant role in large numbers of crimes. Further, the emphasis in this paper on organic and physiological disorders does not reflect an abandonment of interest in the psychological, such as discussed in Diamond, B. (1961), Identification and the sociopathic personality. *Arch. Crim. Psychodynamics*, 4:456. It is just that the imminent research discoveries in biochemical and neurophysiological psychiatry are best suited to illustrate the thesis of the present paper. The cause of crime is not now, and probably never will be, reducible to a single factor. Each individual offender must be

analyzed in terms of his social environment, his unique life situation, the psychodynamic forces within his personality, as well as the effects of functional or organic mental and brain disease. Each of these factors must be allotted its due significance. In addition, the law chooses to place its emphasis upon the moral element of the crime, a factor about which the psychiatrist, being no expert on that subject, has little to say.

[32]I attribute this descriptive phrase to Richard A. McGee, Administrator of the Youth and Adult Corrections Agency, State of California.

[33]See "With Malice Aforethought" and "The Fallacy of the Impartial Expert," this volume. See also Weihofen, H. & Overholser, W. (1947), Mental disorder affecting the degree of a crime. *Yale L. J.*, 56:959.

[34]The considerable lag between the recognition of a condition as an illness and the discovery of an effective treatment is not a problem restricted to mental diseases. Remember that physical diseases such as cancer and tuberculosis were recognized as specific diseases for thousands of years before cures were discovered that would be effective in even a few cases. There is apt to be a much shorter time lag between the discovery of the essential etiological agent of a disease and the discovery of an effective cure.

[35]This phrase comes from the Menninger Foundation, Topeka, Kansas, where I first heard it used in this sense by Dr. Joseph Satten. Freud did not use the phrase, but he certainly originated the idea of extending personal responsibility to the patient for the patient's own psychopathology and the consequences of his unconscious mind. See Freud, S. (1925), Moral responsibility for the content of dreams. *Standard Edition*, 19:131–134. London: Hogarth Press, 1961.

[36]This idea is more fully developed by Szasz, T. (1961), in *Legal and Criminal Psychology*, ed. H. Toch. New York: Holt, Rinehart & Winston.

[37]See Dain, N. & Carlson, E. T. (1962), Moral insanity in the United States 1835–1866. *Amer. Psychiat.*, 118:795 for a description of how a change in the opposite direction took place in the attitudes of psychiatrists within a very brief span of time. It is astonishing to me that Professor Gerhard O. W. Mueller, a distinguished authority on criminal jurisprudence, can in this day and age make the statement that "Since the definition of what constitutes a crime has not changed and cannot possibly change as long as humanity exists, how can the concept of what does not constitute a crime change? Crime remains crime and no crime remains no crime. This remains constant." (Mueller, G. [1961], M'Naghten remains irreplaceable: Recent events in the law of incapacity. *Ga. L. J.*, 50:105, III).

Index